STORIES THEY NEVER TOLD US

BY JANETTE SILVERMAN

RelativaTree

ISBN 979-8-9906744-0-0 (softcover)
ISBN 979-8-9906744-1-7 (epub)

Printed in the United States of America

Table of Contents

*This book is dedicated l'dor v'dor—
from generation to generation.*

*To my grandparents, who connected me to the past:
Harry and Blima Raitza (Grass) Silberman and Barnett
and Sylvia (Miller) Moldofsky*

*To my parents, who are the bridge from the past to the
present: Milton and Rhoda
(Moldofsky) Silverman*

*To my life partner, who keeps me focused on the present:
Robert Clinton*

*To my children, who are the bridge from the present to the
future: Arielle Silver and
Efrem Weiss*

Preface

Gravestone from cemetery in Zhytomyr

A fundamental value of Judaism is to remember and to communicate that memory. Yosef Hayim Yerushalmi's book *Zakhor: Jewish History and Jewish Memory*, written in the mid-1980s, was an important part of the revolution in thinking about the writing of history that occurred during the last quarter of the twentieth century. He wrote:

> In its totality modern Jewish historiography presents both a general and a Jewish aspect, each of which can be a subject for extended discussion. The first concerns its contribution as pure scholarship to the sum of man's historical knowledge and understanding; the second, its place as a cultural and spiritual phenomenon within Jewry itself.[1]

Rabbi Lord Jonathan Sacks[2] commented about the importance of both history and memory in Judaism. Referring to Yerushalmi's book, he said that a reader of the book would:

> Understand that the distinction between memory and history is crucial to Judaism. Three-quarters of the Hebrew Bible is historical. Jews were, in Baruch Halpern's phrase, "the first historians." They were, as J.H. Plum says in The Death of the Past, the first people to see meaning in history, history as a narrative. Yet it's very interesting to ask what the biblical word for history is and [to find that] there isn't one. When Hebrew was revived for the modern state of Israel and they wanted a word for history, they came up with historic; they chose the Greek word. Instead, the Bible uses a quite different word which appears 169 times: zachor, or remember. There is a difference between history and memory; to be very crude, history is his story—it happened sometime else to someone else. Memory is my story.[3]

Bereishit:[4]
The Beginning of Jewish Genealogy

While genealogical research is not new, the advent of the internet and the availability of personal computers opened a world of genealogical research, in general, and for the Jewish community specifically. The story of the transition from analog to digital in genealogy is as revolutionary as the disintermediation of print news media by internet news sources and blogging.

According to the *Encyclopaedia Judaica*, "[i]t is not known when the tradition of recording genealogies became established in Israel, but it is undoubtedly an ancient one, as only by proving connection with some family or clan could an individual claim the privileges of citizen status."[5] The first Jewish genealogies appear in the Bible, linking one generation to another. Bereishit 4:17-22 describes the descendants of Adam and Ḥava through their son Kayin:[6]

> [Kayin] knew his wife, and she conceived and bore Enoch.
> And he then founded a city and named the city after his son
> Enoch. To Enoch was born Irad, and Irad begot Mehujael, and
> Mehujael begot Methusael, and Methusael begot Lamech.
> Lamech took to himself two wives: the name of the one was
> Adah, and the name of the other was Zillah. Adah bore Jabal;
> he was the ancestor of those who dwell in tents and amidst
> herds. And the name of his brother was Jubal; he was the
> ancestor of all who play the lyre and the pipe. As for Zillah, she
> bore Tubal-cain, who forged all implements of copper and iron.
> And the sister of Tubal-cain was Naamah.[7]

The story of creation links the first people, Adam and Ḥava, to creation. The lists of their descendants through Kayin, and from Noaḥ[8] to Kayin and ultimately to Abraham, binds the progenitor of the Jewish people of today to the creation of the world. Census lists in the book of Numbers, chapters 1 and 26[9], are only of the men of military age and do not give us insight into family composition. Although censuses in modernity enumerate entire households, the type of census described in the biblical account resemble conscription lists, which can be found in many

cultures and countries. Lists of descendants and ancestors continue throughout
the Hebrew Bible and their occurrences are too numerous to mention here. The
point of mentioning them is only to comment that, however modern the pursuit of
genealogy may seem, it has ancient roots.

Scholars compiled and researched the first "modern" Jewish genealogies to
document rabbinic dynasties. Logically, rabbinic dynastic documentation makes
a great deal of sense. The rabbis of the Middle Ages kept track of their forebears.
For the most part, these rabbis had an interest in proving their ancestry through
generations of rabbis and scholars. According to Joseph Dan, the forerunners
of today's autobiographies were medieval chronicles and family genealogies.[10]
Byron Sherwin insightfully commented that, during this period, "one's genealogy
was considered predictive of one's personal destiny."[11] Since these ancestral rabbis
were exclusively male, the genealogies they maintained primarily traced their
forefathers. On occasion, a scholar or rabbi from a lesser-known family would
marry the daughter of a well-known rabbi, and in those instances, the scholar,
wanting to be associated with that family, put his wife and her ancestors on his
tree. Sometimes, the lesser-known scholar and his new family took the surname of
the wife's family.

Jewish Genealogical Research Challenges

For most Jewish genealogical researchers, a big gap exists between tracing the movement of an Eastern European family from Europe to the United States and tracing that family back to its rabbinic lineage, or for that matter, to its history in Europe, in general. Between the early days of serious Jewish genealogical research in the mid-twentieth century and the advent of personal computers and access to the internet, genealogists accomplished much. Due to the efforts of several remarkable researchers, Jewish genealogy as a field developed very quickly.

Malcolm Stern could best be called the parent of Jewish genealogy. His groundbreaking doctoral dissertation, "Americans of Jewish Descent," was published in 1960. His goal in that work was to document the origins of Jewish families living in the United States prior to 1840. He wrote, in the preface to the third edition, that:

> ...[m]y goal over more than forty years has been to try to compile the genealogies of Jewish families established in the United States and Canada prior to 1840, tracing their descendants wherever possible to the present. The year 1840 was chosen because an estimated 10,000 Jews had settled in America by then. Within the succeeding twenty years, more than 200,000 additional Jews were to immigrate, creating an insurmountable task for one genealogist working alone.[12]

Stern died in January 1994 but left an everlasting mark on the field of Jewish genealogy. His legacy was followed by monumental work accomplished by people who have become luminaries in the world of Jewish genealogy. Two of these pioneers were Arthur Kurzweil, author of *From Generation to Generation: How to Trace Your Jewish Genealogy and Personal History*,[13] and Daniel Rottenberg, who wrote *Finding Our Fathers: A Guidebook to Jewish Genealogy*.[14] *Avotaynu: The International Review of Jewish Genealogy*,[15] is a journal specific to Jewish genealogy and contains information pertinent to methodology as well as source information. This journal was published quarterly from 1985 until 2022 and included new resources, tips of research, travel experiences, book reviews, summaries of articles in other course, and more.

Finally, a major resource for Jewish genealogists, providing information from tens of millions of records from repositories all over the world, is *JewishGen*.[16] The late Susan E. King founded *JewishGen* in 1985 as a message area on Fidonet bulletin boards. Later, enhanced on the internet as a mailing list and newsgroup, it became an award-winning website. Today, *JewishGen* provides resources for discussion groups and special interest groups and hosts data from many affiliated groups. It has remained, since its inception, an organization primarily staffed by volunteers except for a few paid professionals. Among the groups whose data is hosted by *JewishGen is JRI-Poland*,[17] founded in 1995. Today, it provides indices of data from more than 550 Polish towns. *Litvak SIG*[18] is another independent organization hosted by *JewishGen*. It provides data from archives all over Lithuania, and from some archives in Belarus and Poland that hold records pertaining to Lithuanian Jewish communities. *Gesher Galicia*[19] provides indices to documents from a former province of Austria-Hungary called Galicia, the territory of which is today in southeastern Poland and western Ukraine.

No serious discussion of the research tools available for genealogists, Jewish or otherwise, could fail to mention Steve Morse and his contributions to the field. A visit to his website, http://stevemorse.org/, is enough to astonish any researcher because of the wealth of tools providing research access to countless resources. Morse was one of the architects of the original 8086 microprocessor used in all DOS and Windows-based personal computers. He described the development of his work with the One-Step website system:

> *...as an aid for finding passengers in the Ellis Island database. Shortly afterwards it was expanded to help with searching in the 1930 census. Over the years it has continued to evolve and today includes about 200 web-based tools divided into 16 separate categories ranging from genealogical searches to astronomical calculations to last-minute bidding on eBay.*[20]

Use of the One-Step tools helps to eliminate guesswork and extra steps by a researcher attempting to locate documents. Frequently, multiple databases provide access to the same document using different search parameters, indices, and record transcriptions, and perhaps even different digital copies of the documents.[21]

Gary Mokotoff, co-founder of *Avotaynu*, co-authored the Daitch-Mokotoff Soundex. The Soundex system assigned numbers to consonants and thereby provided a tool for researchers to look for names without knowing the exact spelling. Similar-sounding consonants had the same numerical value, so a search for "Loewenthal" or "Leventhal" would yield the same results. Vowels had no numerical value. Jewish genealogical research involves searching for many names that have been transliterated into Western European languages with Latin-based letters from other alphabets. There was no spelling standard for such transliterated sounds.[22] Initially, a person would substitute numbers for the letters in a name, but today it is done automatically when doing a "sounds like" search. It is important to know about Soundex to understand why searches for particular names yield results that appear to have no relationship to the original search. If search results that don't look like the original search terms are sounded out loud, the similarity is often apparent.

A common belief is that records pertaining to Jews, particularly in the places touched by Nazis during World War II, were all destroyed. Many records were destroyed during the war or through the ages by natural or manmade disasters. However, many records still exist, and due to advances in technology, accessing records outside of the archives in which the originals are held is becoming more common.

The world of genealogical research has changed with the availability of digital records from archives all over the world. Not too long ago, the only way to search records was to visit the archives of interest in person. A major issue in research is identifying records pertaining to the people being researched. Most of the records needed for Jewish research have either not been digitized or, if digitized, have not been indexed. That means often researching through hundreds or thousands of pages of handwritten documents in almost every imaginable language. Although great strides are being made, OCR[23] technology for non-Latin alphabets has not been thoroughly developed. This means that there is no simple way to search records written in Cyrillic or Hebrew, the alphabets in which many records pertaining to Jewish families were written.

Ancestry.com®, the largest digital repository of genealogical records, has partnered with *JewishGen* for many years. In addition to the partnership with JewishGen, Ancestry.com more recently expanded its Jewish resources through partnerships with many resources important to Jewish communities and Holocaust study, including the American Jewish Joint Distribution Committee (JDC), the American Jewish Historical Society, The Miriam Weiner Routes to Roots Foundation, Inc., the United States Holocaust Memorial Museum (USHMM), and the Arolsen Archives, to name a few, to create the world's largest online collection of Jewish historical records.[24]

DNA and Genealogy

For a genealogist, DNA has many uses. It provides some insight into a person's ethnicity and may reveal family tendencies to diseases. But what I think is best of all, on a purely genealogical level, is its ability to reveal cousin matches. For Ashkenazi Jews, that, in itself, poses a major challenge. Because the Jews of Eastern Europe married first and second cousins, and because we didn't just stay in one small village but often moved around through time for hundreds or perhaps thousands of years, the Jewish residents of Eastern Europe all wound up related to each other. An autosomal DNA test of an Ashkenazi Jew will reveal perhaps 10,000 or more 4th-cousin or closer matches and hundreds of thousands of more distant matches. Fourth-cousin matches will share 3x-great-grandparents. This is within modern times, and since many of us are able to discover who our 3x-great-grandparents were, figuring out a connection to a 4th-cousin match sounds easy. But wait—our great-grandparents and perhaps grandparents often had 10 or more children. The challenge will be to find out, through documentation, how the matches are related to those 3x-great-grandparents.

The Genesis of This Work

For many years, my father, Milton Silverman, has said "you ought to write a book" about our families' journeys but also about many other subjects. He and my mother, Rhoda Silverman, had big dreams for themselves and raised their daughters to dream big, too. Many people encouraged me along the way, and without their support, the work that follows would not have materialized. Greg Kratz, the head of the *AncestryProGenealogists*® publications team, made the actualization of my dream of publishing a revisioning of my 2013 dissertation, "In Living Memory," a reality. Lina Kuzminskaite's eagle eye ensured that citations and footnotes were all done properly. Marek Koblanski answered my numerous pleas to translate "just one more record." My partner, Robert Clinton, tirelessly helped me deal with passive voice, and if any instances still remain, it is entirely due to my inability to follow through on all his suggestions.

My sisters, Shari Levy and Randi Smith, shared so many stories and memories with me. My children, Arielle Silver and Efrem Weiss, asked pointed questions that made me remember stories I had long forgotten. When the stories stayed outside the edges of my memory, my aunts Iris Reisberg and Phyllis Lipsky, and my parents helped fill in the gaps.

Endnotes

1.   Yosef Hayim Yerushalmi, Zakhor: *Jewish History and Jewish Memory* (Seattle, Washington: University of Washington Press, 1999), p. 87; researcher's copy.

2.   Rabbi Sacks served as the chief rabbi of the United Hebrew Congregations of the Commonwealth from 1991 to 2013.

3   Rabbi Jonathan Sacks, "Power and Responsibility: Science, Humanity and Religion in the 21st Century," lecture at Cockcroft Lecture Theatre, University of Cambridge, Cambridge, England, 25 November 2003.

4.   This is the Hebrew name of the first book of Hebrew Scriptures, commonly referred to as "Genesis." The word *bereishit* itself is most commonly translated in English as "in the beginning."

5.   Jacob Liver, "Genealogy," in *Encyclopaedia Judaica, Second Edition* (Detroit, Michigan: Thomson Gale, 2007), vol. 7, p. 428; researcher's copy.

6.   "Kayin" is a transliteration from the Hebrew of the Biblical name commonly known as "Cain."

7.   The translation is taken from the *JPS Hebrew English TANAKH*, the traditional Hebrew Text and the New JPS Translation, electronic version of the Second Edition. *JPS Hebrew English TANAKH* (Skokie, Illinois: Varda Books, 2001); researcher's copy.

8.   The ḥ is used here to indicate the guttural sound of the Hebrew letter "ḥet" sometimes spelled in Latin letters as "chet." There is no letter in English that compares in pronunciation with it.

9.   Numbers 1: 2-3 "Take ye the sum of all the congregation of the children of Israel, by their families, by their fathers' houses, according to the number of names, every male, by their polls; from twenty years old and upward, all that are able to go forth to war in Israel..."

     Numbers 25:19 – 26: 2 "And it came to pass after the plague, that the Lord spoke unto Moses and unto Eleazar the son of Aaron the priest, saying: 'Take the sum of all the congregation of the children of Israel from twenty years old and upward, by their fathers' houses, all that are able to go forth to war in Israel.'"

10. Joseph Dan, *Jewish Intellectual History in the Middle Ages* (Westport, Connecticut: Praeger Publishing Co., 1994), p. 80; researcher's copy.

11. Byron Sherwin, *Sparks Amidst the Ashes: The Spiritual Legacy of Polish Jewry* (New York: Oxford University Press, 1997), p. 28; researcher's copy.

12. Malcolm H. Stern, *First American Jewish Families* (Baltimore, Maryland: Ottenheimer Publishers, Inc., 1991); digital image, "First American Jewish Families," Publications, *American Jewish Archives* (https://www.americanjewisharchives.org), accessed June 2017.

13. Arthur Kurzweil, *From Generation to Generation: How to Trace Your Jewish Genealogy and Personal History* (San Francisco, California: Jossey-Bass, 2004); researcher's copy.

14. Dan Rottenberg, *Finding our Fathers: A Guidebook to Jewish Genealogy* (Maryland: Genealogical Publishing Co., Inc., 1995); researcher's copy.

15. "Journal," *Avotaynu* (https://www.avotaynu.com), accessed June 2017.

16. "Databases," *JewishGen* (https://www.jewishgen.org), accessed June 2017.

17. "Search," *JRI Poland* (https://jri-poland.org), accessed June 2017.

18. "Research," *LitvakSIG* (https://www.litvaksig.org), accessed June 2017.

19 The name means Bridge to Galicia. "Home," *Gesher Galicia* (https://www.geshergalicia.org), accessed June 2017.

20. Stephen P. Morse, "Abstracts of Talks," *One-Step Webpages: A Potpourri of Genealogical Search Tools* (https://stevemorse.org), accessed February 2012.

21. Stephen P. Morse, "A Hodgepodge of Lesser-Known Gems," *One-Step Webpages* (https://stevemorse.org), accessed June 2017.

22. "Databases," *JewishGen* (https://www.jewishgen.org), accessed June 2017.

23. Optical character recognition is a system of converting scanned printed/handwritten image files into machine readable text format. OCR software analyzes a document and compares it with fonts stored in its database, noting features typical to characters.

24. "Jewish Family History Collection," Search, *Ancestry* (http://www.ancestry.com), accessed January 2018.

Introduction

Passover Seder, Brooklyn, Kings County, New York

Introduction: The Beginning of the Stories and the Questions

Stories of our ancestors, their departure from the place they inhabited for generations, and their arrival in a new home all have similar components. Yet, each family's stories are significantly different from every other. My ancestors began arriving in the United States in the 1890s. Perl Buchbinder, my great-grandmother and my last direct ancestor to leave Europe, arrived in the 1920s. With the exception of Perl, who traveled 2nd class, they all arrived from Europe in steerage. These are my stories, and theirs.

Barnett Moldofsky, one of my grandfathers, used to sing a song:

"Goodbye, Ma! Goodbye, Pa! Goodbye, mule with a hi-hee-ha!

I may not know what this war's about, but I bet you by golly I'll soon find out.

Oh, my sweetheart, never fear, I'll bring you a king for a souvenir.

I'll bring you a Turk and a Kaiser, too, and that's about all one feller can do." [1]

I'm pretty sure that I never asked him what this song meant, but I'm also certain that if I had, he wouldn't have answered me. Now I know what I didn't know as a young child—this song dates back to World War I, and I understand the meanings of the words "Turk" and "Kaiser." I don't know what my grandfather,

Fig. 1. Cover of sheet music for "Good-Bye Ma!"

born in 1906 in Russia and a 1910 immigrant to the United States, made of the song. As an adult, I wonder about all the other songs, stories, and conversations we never had. That isn't to say I didn't know my grandfather, but rather that he was a man of very few words. That song, however, sung in his voice, is part of the family's memory. He sang it to his three daughters, his nine grandchildren, and Arielle, the first-born of his eighteen great-grandchildren. He died in 1980, shortly after the birth of his next two great-grandchildren, Efrem and Joshua.

Barnett was too young to fight in World War I and too old to fight in World War II. All my grandparents arrived in the United States before 1921. Some of my great-grandparents and great-great-grandparents immigrated to the United States in the 1890s. Most of the parents and grandparents of my Jewish friends were immigrants, arriving just before or after World War II. Since my family arrived so much earlier, I was an oddity.

When my children, Arielle and Efrem, were young, I gave my grandparents and my parents books to fill out in which they could tell their stories. I don't think I realized at the time that those books could be significant for the whole family, if the recipients had ever used them. They never did. I have a lot of blank books. My friends had similar experiences. I'm fortunate my parents, Milton Silverman and Rhoda (Moldofsky) Silverman, lived to see my children and their other grandchildren reach adulthood and to experience the births of great-grandchildren. It is wonderful to watch them play with their great-grandchildren and listen to them telling their stories and sharing memories of earlier generations.

Some of those stories, dating back a half century or more, cannot be connected yet to our ancestral family. In 2020, my mother and her youngest sister, Iris, told me of two cousins, Sura Zisha Kornberg and Annie King. They did not know these women's relationships to the family; all they knew were their addresses. It is through such tiny clues that connections are built. In the pages that follow, I will discuss documenting and proving previously unknown relationships.

I grew up curious about the people who remained in Europe, those about whom my grandparents never spoke. Perhaps a lack of information—the absence of stories from "the old country"—guided my adult passion (often referred to as obsession) for genealogical research. Genealogy is the intersection of history and memory. It integrates memories of a person or family into the historical context in which the family lived. In the pages that follow, using documentation such as vital records, censuses, military registrations, newspaper accounts, and other historical records, I incorporate family stories and memories to bring back those long gone. I do wish, though, that I had heard more of their own stories.

Growing up in New York in the 1950s and 1960s, I understood that, as a Jew whose family came from Eastern Europe, I would never know about the families left behind by the emigrants. I also knew there were no records and no towns remaining in Eastern Europe where Jews lived before the war. These thoughts and this knowledge were not unique to me—I speak with people all the time who are positive, even in the twenty-first century, that there are no records of Jews in Eastern Europe and there is no way to find out about our ancestral past.

As a professional genealogist, I know differently. It has been proven repeatedly that those assumptions of the total destruction of towns and records is incorrect. Of course, many towns and records were destroyed in World Wars I and II and during the many conflicts across Europe over the years. Further degradation of records occurred in archival repositories when records were stored with no climate control, often subject to flooding and fire. There are, however, many records from many places, and as I found out, it is possible, with time and perseverance, to identify our families in those that remain. For me, it is of prime importance to discover the names of our ancestors, especially those who were murdered during the Shoah—the Holocaust. We cannot resurrect them, but we can bring them to life by restoring them and their names to our living memory.

A (Very) Brief View of the History and Geopolitical Boundaries

Although the ancestral history of three of my four grandparents has been traced to what is now Ukraine and Belarus, none of them was born or lived in countries by those names. My maternal families, documentation shows, were from the western part of the Russian Empire, in and around the Pale of Settlement. My paternal families were from Galicia in the eastern part of the Austrian Empire.

In the late eighteenth century, the vast territory known as the Polish-Lithuanian Commonwealth was eliminated. Through wars and treaties, from 1772 to 1795, it was partitioned three times and portioned out by Prussia, the Russian Empire, and the Hapsburg monarchy. Poland did not become an independent country again until after World War I. Although Lithuania declared its independence after World War I, it was quickly divided, and the area that includes its capital, Vilnius, became part of Poland along with a substantial part of what is now Belarus. What follows is an oversimplification of the very complex geopolitical changes that affected millions of people in Eastern Europe in the eighteenth to twentieth centuries.

The Polish-Lithuanian Commonwealth had the largest Jewish population in the world. After the partitions, the areas ceded to the Austrian and Russian Empires became the home of most of them. A smaller number found themselves living in Prussia, in areas now primarily Poland and Germany.

After the first partition, Austria named the area in their territory where most of the Jewish population lived the Kingdom of Galicia and Lodomeria. The status of this kingdom changed slightly between the first partition and 1804. There were other political changes over time. It was commonly known as Galicia or Austrian Poland. Galicia and Lodomeria are Latin versions of Halich and Volodymyr-Volynskyi. The former was a principality in Ruthenia and the latter an area founded centuries earlier by Vladimir the Great. Ruthenians are an East Slavic people. Among the principal cities of Galicia were Krakow and Przemysl, located in Poland today, and L'viv, Ivano-Frankivsk (formerly Stanislawow), and Ternopil, located in Ukraine. About one million Jews called Galicia home before World War I.

The area with a large population that wound up in the Russian Empire became known as the Pale of Settlement. That area today is primarily in Poland, Ukraine, Belarus, Moldova, Russia, and Lithuania. By the end of the nineteenth century, it held more than 95% of the Jewish population of the Russian Empire, or about five million Jews. The Pale ultimately included not only territory ceded from the disintegration of the Polish-Lithuanian Commonwealth but also acquisitions from the Ottoman Empire and some areas previously ruled by the Cossacks. The intent behind establishing the Pale was to keep the majority of the Jewish population within a defined area. Russia had excluded Jewish settlement since the fifteenth century, and these boundaries kept the newly acquired Jewish population within the area in which they were already residing. As the Russian Empire acquired territory along the Black Sea from the Ottoman Empire and looked to expand its colonization, Jews also were permitted to settle there. The term Pale is probably from a Latin word meaning boundary. In Russian, it is called **Черта оседлости** (Cherta Osedlosti), a permanent Jewish area. Not only Jews lived in the Pale; Roman Catholics and Eastern Catholics lived there, too.

As I said previously, this oversimplifies a complex situation. The borders during this period were never stable, and insurrections and uprisings followed by increasingly repressive laws fed into more rebellious actions. Some might argue that events after World War I and into the twenty-first century continue that tradition of instability and ever-changing boundaries in that area.

Endnotes

1. Garr Williams, "Long Boy," sheet music cover, 1917; digital image, "Long boy Goodbye, Ma! Goodbye, Pa! Goodbye, Mule, with Yer Old Hee-Haw," *Wikimedia Commons* (https://commons.wikimedia.org), accessed March 2022.

Cover Art: Provided by researcher.

What's in a Spelling, Anyway? The Moldofsky/Moldawsky and Farber Families

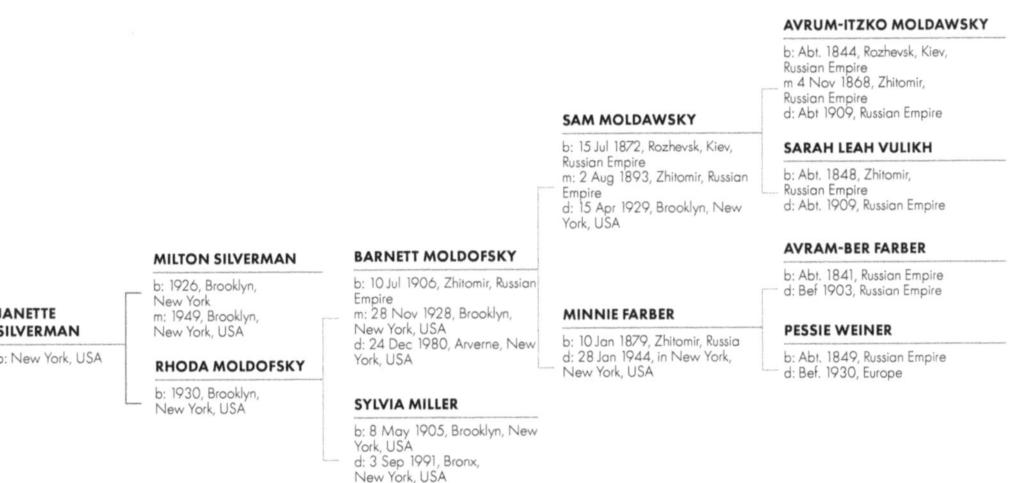

What's in a Spelling, Anyway? Moldofsky/ Moldawsky/Moldovsky/ Молдавский/ מלדאווסקי

O nce upon a time, in a land far, far away, there lived a family with lots of children. That, of course, is not how the story of my family begins, but as I reflect on their stories and history, I often feel that I have stepped into the pages of a fairy tale, or maybe *Alice in Wonderland*. Things are not always what they seem, and facts take strange twists. What people think they remember clearly turns out to be family myths repeated so often that fact is indistinguishable from fiction.

Surprising information may be discovered in unlikely sources. We have a family photo[1] dating from April 1924. For many years, it hung on the wall in the home of Ethel (Moldofsky) Needleman, my great-aunt. It portrays a man wearing a *kitl*[2] sitting at a *seder*[3] table. Seventeen people of varying ages are seated around the table. Ethel identified her parents, siblings, and their spouses. She identified the circumstances of when and why the photo was taken, and to our surprise, said it was the original of a picture printed in the Yiddish newspaper, *The Forward*. She gave me the original, which had faded, and I took it to a print studio in 2010. There, they made high-quality copies and were able to bring out aspects from the original that had faded beyond recognition. Careful examination of the newly enhanced picture showed details missed in the faded copy, including the pattern of the carpet. A portrait of Ethel's grandmother hangs on the wall. Unfortunately, we are unsure of her identity—we only know she is the mother of one of my two great-grandparents, Shaina Mintza Farber and Simche Moldofsky. I wish I had thought of asking Ethel to name that grandmother. As with so many other stories, by the time we think of questions that would lead to clarification, it is too late. Ethel did point out that two of the women in the photograph wore identical dresses made by Ethel's mother. Ethel identified the surnames of some of the others in the photo, whom she referred to as "family friends." Further discussion suggested the possibility that those "family friends" might be her mother's sister, Sura; her

Fig. 1: Family seder in 1924, as it appeared in *The Forward* newspaper

brother-in-law, Elie; and her nephews. It has still not been proven that the people in the photo are more than family friends, but because I thought they were, I went searching. Those searches ultimately led to the documentation of many members of my extended family.

My maternal grandfather and Ethel's youngest brother, Barnett Moldofsky, could best be described as a very quiet person. He rarely had much to contribute to conversations, and a running commentary about a television show is the most I remember him saying at any one time. He always recounted the action on the screen while watching a program. Mitchell, one of my cousins and the son of Barnett's youngest daughter, Iris, remembered a conversation about a city that sounded like Jeetomeer where Barnett and his siblings were born and which is mentioned in the Leon Uris novel, *Exodus*. When we became serious about finding out more about the family, I skimmed through the book, noting the names of places mentioned, and phoned my cousin to see if he recalled which of those places was

Barnett's hometown. It turned out to be Zhytomyr,[4] a city not too far from Kyyiv. Given his reluctance to engage in casual conversations, it was not too surprising that Barnett only gave short answers to my questions about where the family came from in Europe. Typically, he and Ethel would just say "Keef," which we later understood to be Kyyiv.

Research into Jewish genealogy is different from that of many other religious and ethnic groups. Governmental regulations and persecution from

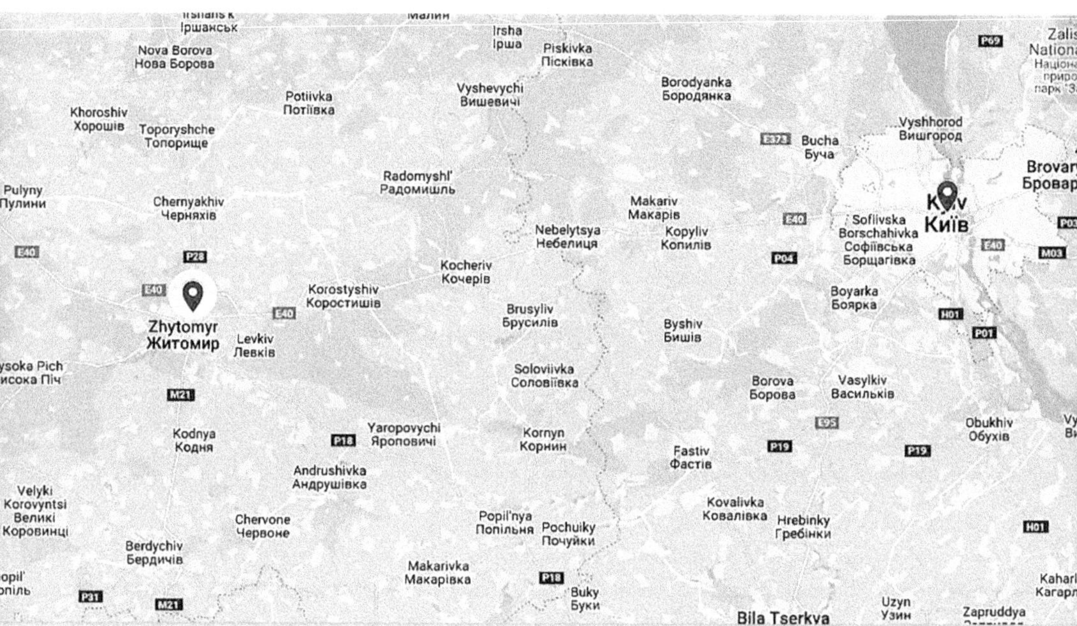

Fig. 2: Kyyiv to Zhytomyr[5]

the majority religious and ethnic groups among whom Jews lived often imposed financial hardships and physical danger. In defiance of the former, Jews looked for ways to avoid complying with the laws. The community often maintained records internally rather than submitting them to a government-mandated repository. Adding another layer of complexity, Eastern European Jewish vital records included names transcribed into the local language from Yiddish, often rendering them incomprehensible. Depending on laws at the time of the event, names might be required to conform to local naming requirements or conventions. On vital records, particularly in the Russian Empire, part of the record might be written in Hebrew in addition to information recorded in Russian, written in Cyrillic. To adequately decrypt the name, sometimes the reader must look at both the Hebrew and Cyrillic.

All records are handwritten and very few indices exist that are contemporaneous with the original documents. Over the last several decades, transcription projects have attempted to index millions of pages of records. For the most part, the indices created from transcriptions are wonderful, but they are replete with errors. These errors are primarily caused by four challenges: 1) transcribing information from one alphabet into another, 2) an inability to accurately read handwritten documents, 3) typographical errors, and 4) lack of standardization of transliteration of letters from one language into another. Still another kind of error, often found in the original document, involves accents—a Yiddish speaker might say a name that is unfamiliar to a civil recordkeeper. Just like in English, accents in Yiddish vary greatly from region to region. Pronunciation of the primary language of the country or region heavily influenced European Yiddish. In 1993, Harry Boodin, in an article in *Avotaynu*, gave some examples of these regional differences. He wrote:

> ...[result in] pronunciation differences between northeastern Yiddish and southeastern Yiddish. In Lithuania and Byelorussia, Jews said kugel (pudding), kush (kiss), and chuppah (wedding canopy); in southeastern Ukraine, the same words were kigel, kish, and chippah. All of these facts and theories may be extremely useful in tracing an individual family.[6]

Jewish birth, marriage, and death records were not always maintained in an official repository or according to local laws. This is in sharp contrast with European church protocol, which resulted in meticulously maintained baptismal, marriage, and death records. In the Jewish community, birth, marriage, and death details were often provided to officials many years after they occurred, resulting in the recording of erroneous dates. During periods before the establishment of civil records, churches held the official repositories, and Jewish records may be found appended to church record books—sometimes sewn in at the end or middle of a book or incorporated in other ways into the church records.

A 1998 *Avotaynu* article described Zhytomyr[7] as follows:

> [O]nce home to almost 40,000 Jews and 68 synagogues, Zhitomir today has no more than 5,000 Jews and a single shul (synagogue), reestablished

a few years ago…Only 250 of the city's Jews have any involvement with the shul. The rest have assimilated, have chosen not to be Jews, have not been found, or simply have not come forward. Many, it is assumed, are waiting to follow their relatives to Israel, the United States, or elsewhere.[8]

Zhytomyr, an ancient city dating back to at least the thirteenth century, had a reputation as a center of culture and Jewish life. Jews did not settle there until the eighteenth century. However, the community grew quickly; there were fewer than 350 Jews in Zhytomyr in 1751, and within 40 years, the Jewish population exceeded 1,200. As with so much else, these figures are refuted by other records. Some records dating to 1795 indicate only about 900 Jews living there.[9] From the earliest time, bloodshed and violence marked Jewish history in Zhytomyr. In 1753, the Jewish community was accused of blood libel, resulting in the ultimate execution of 13 of the 33 accused. The other 20 were forced to convert to Christianity to save their lives.[10]

Accusations of blood libel haunted many Jewish communities in Europe from the thirteenth century until modernity. These superstitious accusations were levied against Jews when children of a community disappeared or died. Blood libel accusations, which were never proven, claimed Jews killed Christians, especially children, to use their blood for medicinal and ritual purposes. Around Passover time in the spring, claims arose that blood was used in baking *matzah* and in wine consumed during the *seder.*

In the early 1800s, Zhytomyr became the capital of the Volhynia Province of the Russian Empire. By the mid-1800s, a Hebrew printing press and rabbinical seminary opened, and the Jewish population experienced rapid growth. In 1845, all but two Hebrew printing presses in the entire Russian Empire were shut down—one in Zhytomyr and one in Vilna (now Vilnius), Lithuania. The Jewish population continued to grow, and by the twentieth century, it was approximately 50% of the total population.[11] Jewish educational facilities, such as schools for children, trade schools, and schools for girls attested to the significance and vibrancy of the Jewish population. However, pogroms in 1905 and 1910 drove Jews away from the city. Many of them, like my great-grandparents, left for the United States. The *New York Times* reported a large, violent pogrom in 1905.[12] During two days of violence, 20 Jews were killed and more than 100 injured.[13] Shirley Gage Hodges commented that "historians

Fig. 3: Gravestone in the Zhytomyr Jewish Cemetery[17]

agree that three social forces were the chief motivators for the mass migration
to America: religious persecution, political oppression, and economic hardship.
It is, however, almost impossible to relate such a combination of overwhelming
circumstances to the experience of one immigrant, or even one family."[14] It
is the opinion of this author that either Gage underestimated the full effect of
those forces or the communities she was researching did not have the Eastern
European Jewish history of persecution, oppression, and hardship.

In addition to the synagogue mentioned above, there is a cemetery still in use
with almost 4,000 surviving *matzevot*, or gravestones.[15] Although there is no way to
tell how many gravestones in that cemetery may have been destroyed over time, the
surviving stones mark both new and old graves. With the help of a native Ukrainian,

Myroslav Sirko, we photographed about 85% of the stones in the Zhytomyr Jewish Cemetery in 2009, and with Milton Silverman, Ella Mintsys, and other volunteers, transliterated and transcribed names and other information from the stones. These transliterations and the photographs were donated to a growing collection of worldwide cemetery records maintained by *JewishGen*. "The *JewishGen Online Worldwide Burial Registry* (JOWBR) is a database of names and other identifying information from Jewish cemeteries and burial records worldwide, from the earliest records to the present. It is a compilation of two linked databases: a database of burial records and a database of information about each particular cemetery."[16]

The Search Begins

Early in the 1990s, Ethel told me that she, her sister May, her brother Jack, her brother (and my grandfather) Barnett, and their mother, Minnie,[18] came to the United States on the SS *President Lincoln* in December 1910. In 1997, I began my foray into archival research. At the time, travel overseas was not an option due to cost, work, and family commitments. However, I knew I needed to access archival records to find details about the family. I hoped to find European records in a collection available to the public. Along with my father, Milton Silverman, I went to the FamilySearch Center (FSC) in Orlando, Florida. This was one of many research centers maintained by The Church of Jesus Christ of Latter-day Saints, all of which were branches of the FamilySearch Library (FSL) in Salt Lake City, Utah. I was looking for a specific record and, in my naiveté, thought that documents would be easy to locate since I knew the name of the ship on which Ethel and Barnett Moldofsky, their two siblings, and their mother traveled from Europe to the United States and the year of their immigration. The librarian at the FSC told me no ship by that name sailed in 1910 and that there was no ship called the *"President Lincoln."* She said there was one ship with a similar name, *Abraham Lincoln,* but it only sailed in 1919 and 1920. This did not sound right, since I knew without a doubt that Ethel and her siblings arrived in the United States when they were all young, and if they sailed in 1919, most of them would have been adults. Research proved Ethel to be correct. The family arrived in December 1910 on the SS *President Lincoln.*

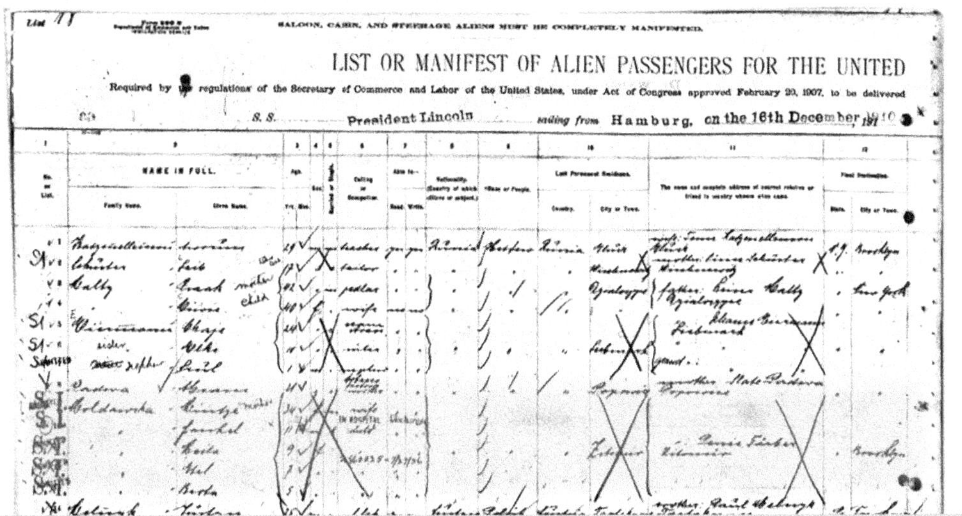

Fig. 4: Excerpt of manifest page of the SS *President Lincoln*[19]

The Church of Jesus Christ of Latter-day Saints (LDS) has a "commitment to helping people connect with their ancestors rooted in our beliefs."[20] Due to that belief, the LDS committed many resources to accumulating vital records over a long period. The largest collection of genealogical records in the world is housed at the FSL. The collection includes names of more than four billion deceased people. FSC branches can be found worldwide, and locating a center is now fairly easy. In 1997, there were very few FSCs. Today, research can be conducted on the FSL website, *FamilySearch.org*, using online databases and indices. In 1997, it was necessary to physically visit the FSL or one of the branches to do any research in their extensive holdings.

In 1990, I became active in the genealogy newsgroup community and avidly read many threads of genealogical discussions on the internet. These threads included research techniques; information on naming patterns, immigration, and geography; and guides about how to read and understand records. I looked at general genealogy newsgroups as well as a Jewish genealogy newsgroup.[21] I found the discussions fascinating and often whiled away time searching through cultural newsgroups as well as genealogy newsgroups. So, in 1997, when I decided to start using the LDS research facilities, I thought I was ready to take this next step. The only thing I discovered in initial searches was how little I knew about my ancestors or how to do genealogical research.

How Do We Know Our Ancestors' Names?

Part of my research success is because an immigrant from Europe was alive well into the twentieth century for each branch of my family. In three of the four branches, multiple generations arrived in the United States, and people who lived in the early decades of the twenty-first century remembered many of them well. My father, for example, knew his grandmother, who emigrated from Europe in the 1920s. My mother knew several of her grandparents who arrived in the United States between 1890 and 1910.

The Moldofsky family constantly argued about the spelling of their last name. My grandparents, my mother, and her siblings spelled it "Moldofsky." Some of my grandfather's siblings and their children spelled it "Moldawsky." This name originated in Europe and would have been written in Cyrillic or the Hebrew alphabet, never in Latin letters. Although Hebrew and Cyrillic both have letters that sound like the Latin "v" and "f," neither of them has a "w" sound, although in Yiddish the sound can be indicated by doubling the Hebrew letter "vav" (וו). As far as I know, the first time that surname was written in Latin letters was on my great-grandfather Sam Moldofsky's ship manifest.[22]

Sam, of course, was not always known as "Sam." From that first name, the assumption could be made that his name in Yiddish was Shmuel or Shmiel, as some Yiddish dialects render it. "Sam" was the name he adopted in the United States. His ship manifest clearly lists his name in Latin letters as "Simche Moldawsky." We do not have a copy of the original documents from which this was transcribed to see what spelling was used for them. We do know that his surname spelled in Cyrillic has a "v," not an "f." This fact indicates that the Yiddish spelling might have used a double "vav." The reason we know how his name was spelled in Cyrillic is that several archival records show the births of the children of Symkha Abraham-Izkhakovich Maldavskiy and Sheina-Mintza Abraham-Berova. On Ethel's 1903 birth record, her surname was spelled Молдавский.

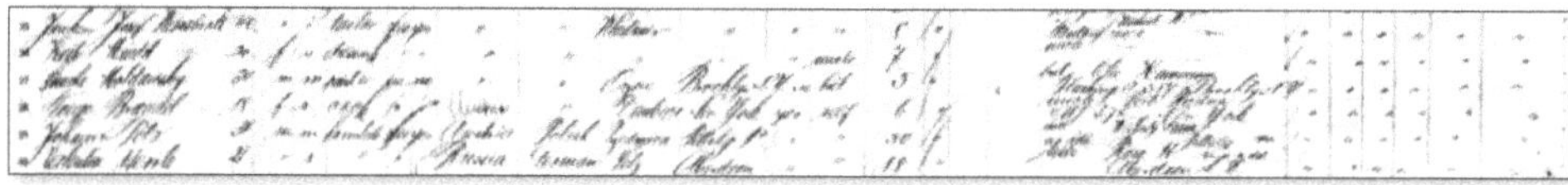

Fig. 5: Excerpt of Simche "Sam" Moldawsky's 1906 manifest[23]

The difference in spelling within the family probably constituted personal preference more than a question of historical accuracy. It may have been due to the accents of the immigrants pronouncing "v" as "f." Ethel, for example, pronounced the city Kyyiv as "Keef," a common pronunciation of the city's name, and close to the modern pronunciation of the city's name in Ukrainian. We do know that the way Simche's name appeared on the United States arrival manifest was identical to the way his name was written on the European manifest. This may not always be the case, generally due to transcription errors from the handwriting of one person to another. Departure and arrival manifests were prepared before the ship left Europe, and two different people wrote them—the outbound manifest was prepared by the shipping company and the inbound manifest by a United States government official.

Alex Bieder wrote:

A change of alphabet necessarily produces a new graphic form. As a result, surnames of individuals who migrated from Russia to Northern America, where Roman-alphabet names were substituted for names originally written in Cyrillic letters, are new in comparison to their old European names, even if they are pronounced in the same way. Similarly, modern Israeli names written in official documents only in Hebrew necessarily are different from names used by the same families before emigration, originally written in Latin, Cyrillic, or Arabic letters.[244]

On the manifest, in addition to Simche's original name, we found his destination in the United States. He listed a person of whom we had no previous knowledge—a brother-in-law, Elie Kaminer. Unfortunately, this manifest, unlike manifests prepared just a few years later, did not require the name of a relative or neighbor in Europe. However, a comment Ethel made many years earlier fell into place after I saw this name. When she spoke of her grandmother's sister, her aunt Sarah, and her family, all she remembered was a name that included "k, m, r." She couldn't remember the exact name but said it was perhaps "Kamer."

Ethel's birth record clearly spelled out the family's surname in Cyrillic, the Russian alphabet: Молдавский. In Latin letters, the exact transcription would be Moldavskii. If the "v" was pronounced like an "f," as Ethel said it, then the Moldofsky spelling my family adopted is close to the original pronunciation. If, on

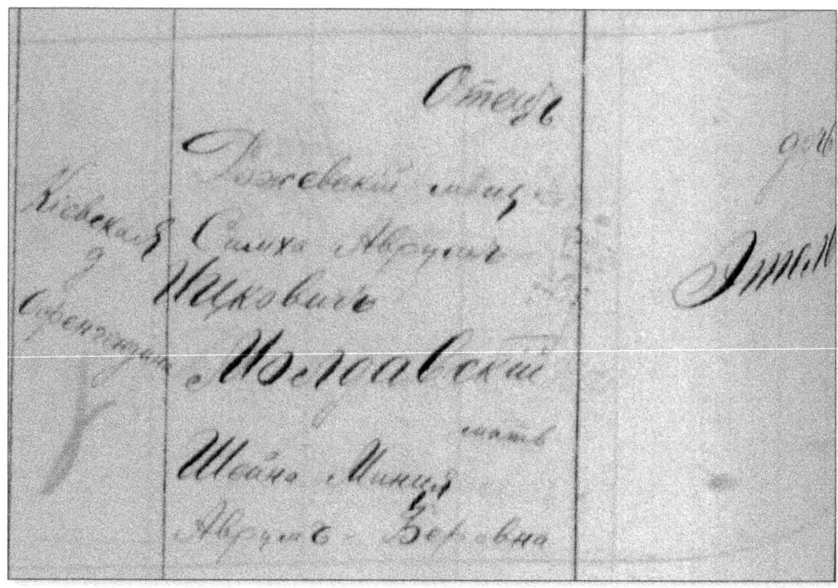

Fig. 6: Excerpt of the record of Ethel's birth in 1903[25]

the other hand, the Yiddish spelling in the Hebrew alphabet was something like מולדאווסקי, written with a double letter "vov" to reflect a "w" sound for which there is no Hebrew letter, then the others in the family were correct. To date, no document has been found with the surname in Hebrew.

We knew Minnie's birth name. In Yiddish, her name was Shaina Mintza. Simche and Shaina Mintza were my great-grandparents. The ship manifest (Fig. 4 above) listed Minnie's first name as Mintza. Simche's and Shaina Mintza's fathers' names are shown on Ethel's birth record (see Fig. 6). Shaina Mintza knew her maiden name was Farber and her mother's first name was Pessie. Pessie's maiden name was Weiner. Pessie was known as Bessie by her American descendants, even though she was never known by that name in Europe and never left Europe. This was not uncommon. Immigrants often "gifted" their relatives back in Europe with American-sounding names.

Following the Eastern European Jewish tradition of naming children after deceased relatives, I am named after Shaina Mintza. Her daughter, Ethel, was named after Shaina Mintza's grandmother Ettel. Shaina Mintza's granddaughter Phyllis was named after Shaina Mintza's mother, Pessie. Although Pessie's date of death has not yet been found, we know that

Pessie died before Phyllis's birth in May 1930. Shaina Mintza was the daughter of Avraham Ber Farber and Pessie Weiner, and Pessie was the daughter of Ettel; we have not yet identified Pessie's father. To determine that, we would need to find a marriage record for Pessie and Avraham Ber, or Pessie's birth or death records, and so far those have proven elusive. The surname Wiener, or Weiner, is very common. There is an indexed record on *JRI-Poland* that appears to be of Ettel Wiener's death and the death of her mother, Eidel Winer. However, there is no way to tell at this point whether these records are for the correct family.

WIENER	Ettel	1884	D	3	F	64 y.		Markus	WIENER		Eidel	WIENER
WINER	Eidel	1852	D		72		388	F	70 y			

Fig. 7: Indices from *JRI-Poland*[26]

One of the challenges with these records is connecting my ancestral family to the place where these deaths occurred, Kamionka Strumilowa. Before World War I, Kamionka Strumilowa was in a district by the same name in Galicia. During the interwar period, it was in the Tarnopol Voivodeship, which was part of Poland at the time. Today, it is Kamianka-Buzka, Ukraine, located at 50°06′ N 24°21′ E. That is 220 miles west of Zhytomyr, where Shaina Mintza's children were all

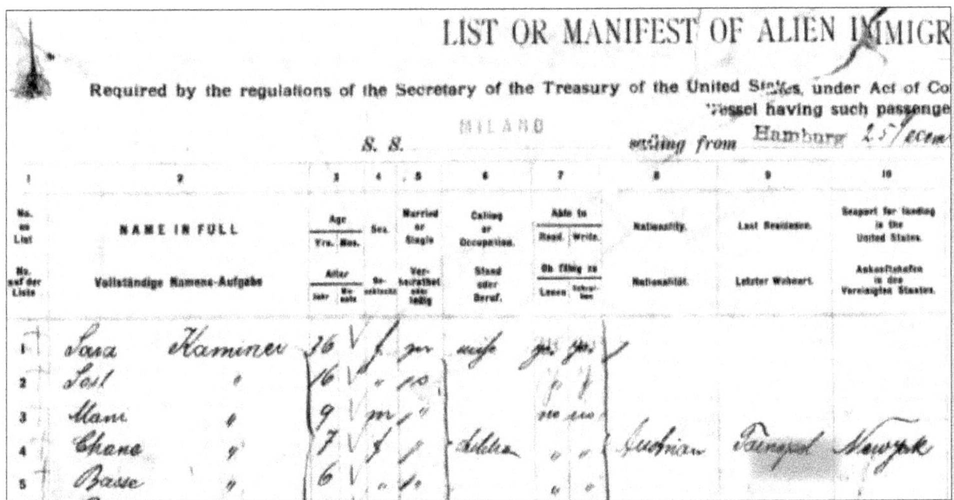

Fig. 8: Sara Farber Kaminer's entry on an excerpt of a 1902 manifest[27]

born. Zhytomyr was in the Volhynia Province of the Russian Empire, which borders Tarnopil District, Galicia Province, Austrian Empire,. In addition to being in different empires, the two towns are more than 230 miles apart. Sarah, Shaina Mintza's sister and the wife of Elie Kaminer, according to the ship manifest, last resided in Tarnopol.

On Simche's ship manifest, his last place of residence was noted as Oszew. A place with that name near Zhytomyr where he and Shaina Mintza lived and their children were born has not yet been identified. It is tempting to say that Oszew is in Tarnopil District, Galicia Province, Austrian Empire, not Volhynia Province, Russian Empire. There is a town named Ordow in the Kamionka Strumilowa District. However, both the inbound and outbound manifests—one prepared by the Hamburg shipping line, the other by United States officials—say the place is Oszew, or Ozzew, Russia. It is quite possible that this should have been Rozhev, which is in Radomysl' District, Kiev Province, Russian Empire, which was the location of Simche's birth in 1869.

Fig. 9: Simche Moldawsky's pre-immigration residence as shown on the manifest[28]

The only thing that can conclusively be discovered about Ettel Wiener[29] and Markus and Eidel Wiener[30] from the Tarnopol records is that they all died in the same house, number 12. It is clear from this that Eidel, who died in 1852, and Markus, who died in 1848, were the parents of Ettel. There is no proof that this Wiener family is the same as that of Shaina Mintza.

An Aside: Samification

Meron Lavie of Israel wrote in a 2012 message to the *JewishGen* discussion group of a phenomenon she called "retroactive Samification," which she later amended to include a related phenomenon, "proactive Samification." She explained the former as "some ancestor who never stepped foot out of his native *shtetl* had his name listed as 'Sam' by his immigrant descendants on documents in the U.S. (name of deceased's father on a death certificate, etc.)." The latter was defined as someone who, in advance of immigrating, began calling himself (or herself) by "Sam" or some other name that, to the potential immigrant, had an "American" sound to it. Sam may have been considered to be the ultimate American name because it was linked to "Uncle Sam," the ideal symbol of America.[31] Although there is no evidence that Simche/Sam ever called himself "Sam" before he came to the United States or that anyone in the United States referred to him as Sam before he immigrated, it is probable that this is how Pessie became known as Bessie. Years ago, before I understood this concept, I wrote a message to the *JewishGen* discussion group and included Bessie's name in it. I remember being taken aback when someone replied asking me how someone in Europe had spelled the name "Bessie." Up until that point, I had just accepted that this was her name and didn't question it.

A Journey to the Zhytomyr Archives

In 2009, I traveled to Ukraine for the first time. After landing in Kyyiv, I headed to Zhytomyr to search in archives. Although I opted not to join a formal tour group or engage a professional guide with archival research experience, I did not travel alone. My cousin, Ella Mintsys, is an English professor at a Ukrainian university. One of her former students, Myroslav Sirko, arranged to help me navigate the complexities of Ukrainian red tape and the language barrier. Myroslav had never been in an archive before but had a valid driver's license and a willingness to embark on an adventure.

Navigating the archives in Ukraine can be challenging. To understand where records are held, at least a cursory understanding of the geopolitical history and nomenclature is required. In a 1996 article, Kahlile Mehr, a genealogist in Utah, wrote that:

A researcher also must be aware of jurisdictional changes. In imperial Russia, an u[y]ezd (county) was the subdivision of a guberniya (province or state). In Soviet Russia and today, a raion (region) is the subdivision of an oblast (district). Modern Russia has more oblasts than there were guberniyas in imperial Russia. For instance, portions of the Volhynian guberniya are found today in the oblasts of Volhynia, Rivne, Zhtyomyr,

*Ternopil, and Khmel'nyts'ka. Often, the records of several modern
oblasts are found in the archive of a single oblast whose capital
happens to be the capital of an imperial guberniya. This is true, for
example, of the records from the 1895 all-Empire census. Thus, the
archive of Zhytomyr, capitol of the Volhynanian guberniya, has
records for neighboring oblasts.[32]*

Searching further, I found additional information:

*...[t]he State Archives of Zhitomir Oblast (Ukraine), one of the 26
Ukrainian regional archives, is a major repository of documentary
sources for the history of the Jews of what was once called
"Volhynia province" (Volynskaia guberniya). Volhynia guberniya
was one of the most densely populated centers of Jewry within the
Pale of Settlement and, indeed, it had the largest numbers of shtetls
(mestechki)—133—of any guberniya in the Pale. On average,
about half the population of the shtetls was Jewish; the proportion
was slightly larger in the cities of this province.[33]*

Zhytomyr and Kyyiv refer to the modern cities, both in Ukraine, and formerly
in the Russian Empire. References to Zhitomir and Kiev in the discussion below
are not due to poor editing or typographical errors, but rather to distinguish the
places as they were formerly known - contemporaneous with the events and
documents discussed. These spellings are of course only transliterations of the
spellings in Russian or Ukrainian Cyrillic.

The approximately 75-mile route from Kyyiv to Zhytomyr provided an
education. The trip took several hours. Although the straight road seemed
fairly clear, travel progressed slowly due to horse-drawn carts traveling
down the middle of the roads and the preponderance of potholes. Myroslav,
driving the car and navigating around the obstructions, found the drive
much less picturesque than I did. My amusement did not last very long when
I realized that we were traveling at a speed typical of a school zone or
residential area in the United States.

When we finally arrived in Zhytomyr, neither of us thought the
archives would be difficult to locate, but despite the insistent voice of our

Fig. 10: Zhytomyr Archives, 2009[34]

handy GPS, it took another hour before we found the correct road. We both expected it to be in an area with other government buildings, but the building was on a side street in a sparsely populated area. Once we arrived, we found red tape, Ukrainian style. Myroslav had not made an advance application and appointment at this archive, although he did at others. First, we waited for the director to return from lunch and then we waited until he could see us. Meanwhile, Myroslav filled out paper after paper. Since all the paperwork was in Ukrainian, this would have been impossible for me to accomplish on my own. Finally, we were ushered into an office and asked many questions about our purpose for the visit. The conversation, like the paperwork, was all in Ukrainian. Since we were granted access to the archives, I guess we passed muster. I've since learned that we could have just as easily been told to return at some point in the future—days, weeks, or even months later. I learned during that trip and subsequent trips to Ukraine and elsewhere in Eastern Europe that many people, even in government positions, only know a few words in English. That surprised me, since many billboards and signs outside shops were in English, or at least in Latin letters. Even in Kyyiv, in restaurants and other places where there might be tourists, people spoke very little English.

Once inside a large reading room, we gave an archivist a list of people and dates that she requested before bringing out records. I'm not sure why she asked for the names of the people for whom we were searching since she brought us stacks of record books and each one covered several years. She explained that the Jewish records were kept separate from other records and that not all the volumes were in their holdings—some had disintegrated over time or been damaged by fire or flood. When we finished reviewing the books, she invited us to look at other books with handmade paper. The paper was beautiful, thick, and quite old. One thing that still strikes me is that, in all the archives I've been to in Eastern Europe, I've looked at books directly—not microfilms or microfiche, but the actual books. With few exceptions, I was not asked to wear gloves, and at some archives, people questioned why I was wearing them.

With the benefit of hindsight, I wondered how she knew we were looking for Jewish records. I asked Myroslav via email in January 2012 why she only pulled out Jewish record books for us. Did we tell her we were looking for information about the Jewish community? He replied:

We gave her the list of surnames (all of which of course were Jewish) and that's how she understood we were looking for Jewish Community data. I do not remember the archivist asking directly if we were interested in some particular nation. The one thing I can be sure about is that she definitely told us that information about Jewish [communities] was stored separately in some special [place] and that is because [the] Jewish community had their own books where the names of the newborn together with the names of his or her parents, dates of birth, [and] place of birth were written down.

Before this experience, I never thought too much about whether the family names were "Jewish names." Hearing from a Ukrainian that the names Moldofsky, Kaminer, Weiner, and Farber were all distinctly Jewish surprised me. They always seemed to me as though they might be found in the general population. I also thought that very few names might be considered distinctly Jewish—in other words, not found in the general population. Moldofsky, because of its ending, seems to be connected to a geographical site while Kaminer, Weiner, and Farber appear, by the word endings, to have something to do with a person's work or place of origin. We often see the ending "er" in names like Englander, referring to a person from England, or Schechter, meaning a butcher or a person who *"schechts."* Why would these names only be found in the Jewish community?

An Aside: What's in a Name?

Names sometimes provide other clues. If, in German, the word *"Kaminfeger"* means chimney sweep,[35] then it stands to reason that *"Kaminer"* might have something to do with a *"kamin,"* or chimney. Likewise, a *"Farber"* is a painter. There were many people on the Farber side of the family who were painters, so the name made sense. Since *"Wein"* could refer to something involving wine and *"Wien"* referred to Vienna, it potentially meant this family might have had to do with either winemaking or that they were originally from Vienna. We have no proof for either assumption, but the former is more likely than the latter. Was there anything particularly Jewish about these occupations or locales?

Although Jews predominated in certain industries, no industry can categorically be said to be exclusively "Jewish" unless, of course, that industry produced something used exclusively by Jews. For example, in nineteenth-century Lithuania,

> *...the distilling industry was almost exclusively in the hands of the Jews. The kretchmers[36] served as wayside inns for the Jewish carriers of agricultural produce who plied their import/export trade between Russia and Germany at that time. Kretchmers were also the main centers of distilling liquor, and the manufacturers were assisted by the carriers in exporting the liquor manufactured in the distilleries. The profitability of the distilleries was so great that kretchmers began to spring up on all of the magnate estates, encouraged by the landowners.[37]*

Jules Levin commented on the tavern and distillery industries in Poland and Russia, writing in January 2012 that:

> *...[i]t is clear that there was never a church prohibition on producing alcohol. In some cases the church was eager to get in on the profits. In Moscow the distilleries were a government monopoly. In Poland the*

*nobility monopolized the production, but gradually they brought in Jews
to manage the trade, and the taverns, because the profits for the nobility
were better and steadier with Jews running the enterprises. There was a
prejudice against middle-man economic activity in Russian culture, but I
doubt there was a single general economic activity that Jews engaged
in where there were no Russian competitors. Is it really conceivable that
over the vast stretches of Eastern Europe and the Russian Empire in places
where there were few or no Jews that a Russian landowner, soldier, or
peasant, could not buy vodka?[38]*

Ann Rabinowitz expanded on this, commenting that the role of
[t]avern-keeping was not only a way of life in the Russian Empire, but there were
many Jews who carried on this occupation in America, the United Kingdom,
and other places, and one can find them listed as such in the census data of the
time. They formed the commercial backbone of many existing and emerging
communities.[39]

There were also distilleries in places where there were no Jews, of course.
The profitability of the industry in the hands of the Jews attracted non-Jews to the
industry. The industry was exclusively Jewish only for a relatively short period of
time. Although the surname "Krechmer" in a variety of renderings could, in some
places, be associated primarily with a Jewish industry, neither the name nor the
occupation was exclusively Jewish. In fact, Bill Yoffee wrote that:

*...[w]hether or not tavern keeping was primarily a Jewish occupation,
a fairly common surname among Jews is KRETCHMER, which means
tavern. This indicates that somewhere in the family's past, possibly even
before the adoption of family surnames, someone in the family was a
tavern keeper.[40]*

Except for industries forbidden to Christians, such as usury, and industries of
low social status, such as tanning, relatively few occupations exclusively employed
Jews. The industries inferred by the surnames for which I was looking should not
have been considered exclusively Jewish.

If the surnames did not lead the archivist to the assumption that we were
interested in Jewish records, it must have been "given names." We gave the

archivist first and last names along with dates for the births, marriages, and deaths in which we were interested. The first names, of course, were Yiddish names—the names by which my ancestors were known in Europe. Myroslav had difficulty reading names in the archival records in which we were searching. One side of the page was in Russian and the other side in Hebrew. Yiddish uses Hebrew letters, but only names were Yiddish, not other words in the text. I did not expect him to be able to read the Yiddish, but I did expect that he would read the Russian without any problem. He wanted to change the names he was reading into names that would be found in the Russian or Ukrainian population—non-Jewish names. Myroslav was a big help when it came to figuring out the handwritten Cyrillic. I figured out a rough sound, knowing what the Yiddish name was likely to be, and Myroslav sounded the name out from the Russian. In this way, working slowly, we managed to decipher the names. On that day in 2009, I discovered the difficulties between reading printed Cyrillic versus handwritten records that were more than 100 years old. It wasn't until Myroslav and I were sitting in the archives that I realized how difficult it was to even decipher names from records.

Ukrainians and Russians do not typically give their children names found in Hebrew scriptures. Primarily, their names are taken from Russian or Ukrainian Orthodox saints and sometimes from pre-Christian heroes. Children are often given the name of the saint on whose day they were born or the name of a saint whose qualities a parent wanted their child to exhibit. Many children had multiple given names. Each day of the year is dedicated to a different saint, and an annual celebration of the saint after whom a person is named is part of the tradition.[41]

A 1987 *Avotaynu* article helped explain some of the similarities and differences which caused Myroslav difficulties in reading the given names:

> *A great number of Hebrew personal names were taken over by the Greek Church and so passed on to the Slavs, for whom they became baptismal names...Numerous Biblical names, however, did not enter the Christian tradition. ... A number of the names that were adopted by the Christian Church still survive in the Jewish tradition in a different form.*[42]

Boris Feldblyum wrote that, in the period following the 1881 assassination of Alexander II, a Commission on Organizing Everyday Jewish Life was formed. Among other things, it mandated that Jews were required to only use names that had been recorded in vital records. In other words, the only name a person could use was the name that appeared in his birth record. The publication of an official list of "correct" Jewish names prevented Jews from using what were termed "distorted names." An amendment in 1893 allowed derogatory nicknames on the list to be replaced in official records by petition and required the government agency maintaining records to inform the head of each household of the family's official names.[43]

I was relieved to figure out that the list of first names we provided the archivist was the likely reason our search was restricted to Jewish records. In a place where anti-Semitism remains part of the landscape, and in the wake of twentieth-century history, it is easy to become paranoid.

Zhytomyr Archives: Discoveries and Questions

In that 2009 day-long research trip and a return trip Myroslav took back to the Zhytomyr archives a couple of weeks later, we found some interesting information. This was the first archive I visited in Europe. My previous experience had been in archives in the United States and Israel. In both places most of the documents in archives at the time were on microfilm and microfiche or completely digitized and generally available through a computer onsite. I was used to finding indices that served as aids for locating specific information. The Zhytomyr archives provided a real treat. That is not a cynical comment. As frustrating as research without an index might be, handling the pages of archival documents and searching through those pages directly without transcriptions to aid or confuse was indeed a treat. I say "confuse" because, as wonderful as transcriptions may be, there are often errors inherent in them either through misreading names or due to typographical errors. The paper in some of these books was gorgeous—thick, beautiful, well-preserved old paper. The downside, of course, was that without gloves or other preservation requirements for researchers handling old documents, the material must be deteriorating quickly. No such precautions were taken in this archive or any of the others we visited on that trip or subsequent trips, not only to archives in Ukraine, but throughout Eastern Europe.

We found many records for people whose surnames were Kaminer, Farber, and Weiner in our searches. We even found several records of name changes in

Kaminer families that primarily affected the spelling or pronunciation of the name. These changes did not render the name unrecognizable. The list of each year's birth records for the Jewish community ended with a tally of births, which provided information regarding Zhytomyr demographics. For example, "there were 347 male Jews and 185 female Jews born in Zhytomyr in 1872 for a total of 532," and, "in 1891, there were 481 males and 656 female Jews born in Zhytomyr for a total of 1137."[44] Although the Jewish births more than doubled in those intervening 19 years, I do not know if there was a similar increase in births in the general population during this period or if this comparison simply exposed a random anomaly in birth rates, or if perhaps something occurred which resulted in more Jewish births being registered than in previous years. An analysis of the number of annual births in Zhytomyr and surrounding towns is a project for another day.

I found it surprising that we only found two records with the surname "Moldofsky" or a similar-sounding name. We did not ask to examine records from towns or villages outside Zhytomyr because, at the time, we did not know of other places where my ancestors lived. The archivist in Zhytomyr told us records for each village are kept separately. To examine records for each of the towns would require a separate trip lasting a week or more to look more through all the Jewish records of towns near Zhytomyr. Feldblyum and Shedevich wrote in 1993 that

>...[i]ncreasingly, it is becoming clear that one must take many factors into account when trying to locate the records of your ancestors. There was mobility in portions of the 19th-century Jewish population. Perhaps the town your ancestor left from was not the town of birth. When primary source (given to us by a genealogist) documents, such as a ship arrival record, passport, or naturalization document, are available, information such as birthplace is likely to be accurate. Most valuable are documents that originated in Russia, written in Russian, Polish, German, etc., before the information was translated and possibly changed. They usually show the correct spelling of the town name and will show the name of the immigrant before it was changed in his/her country of destination.[45]

The ship manifest for Simche Moldawsky noted Oszew as the last place he lived. The birth record for Beryl, who became Barnett Moldofsky, provided no indication that his parents were from any place but Zhytomyr. The record showed

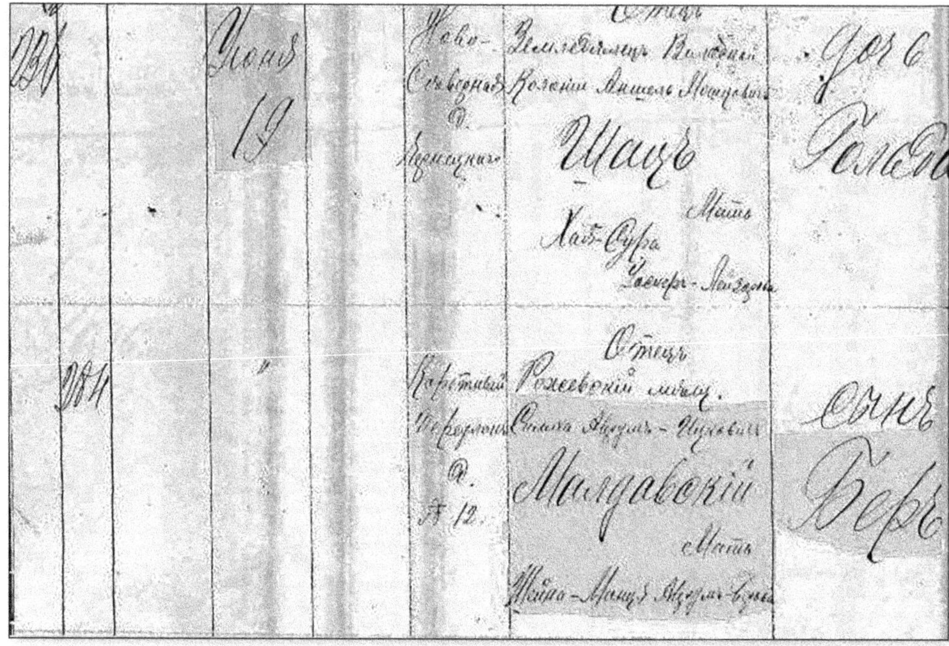

Fig. 11: Excerpt from page containing birth record of Ber Maldavsky (Barnett Moldofsky)[46]

that "Symkha Abraham-Izkhakovich Moldavskiy and Sheina-Mintza Abraham-Berova [had a son] Ber born on June the 19th 1906." These birth records are not birth certificates; they are registrations in a book. Often there are at least four and as many as 10 registrations on a single-page or double-page spread. Birth certificates such as we are used to seeing did not exist.

Beryl is a form of the name "Ber." The birthdate on the record surprised me because we celebrated my grandfather's birthday on July 10. It did confirm the year of his birth, something which had been a matter of contention since his wife, Sylvia Miller, was born in 1905 and women of that era did not like to admit they were older than their husbands. Why were the dates on his birth record and the date his family celebrated in New York different? When Barnett was born in 1906, Russia used the Julian calendar. The United States tracked dates according to the Gregorian calendar.

The Gregorian calendar, which is the calendar used today, was first introduced by Pope Gregory XIII via a papal bull in February 1582 to correct an error in the old Julian calendar. This error had been accumulating over hundreds of years so that every 128 years, the

24

calendar was out of sync with the equinoxes and solstices by one additional day. As the centuries passed, the Julian calendar became more inaccurate. Because the calendar was incorrectly determining the date of Easter, Pope Gregory XIII reformed the calendar to match the solar year so that Easter would once again "fall upon the first Sunday after the first full moon on or after the Vernal Equinox." Ten days were omitted from the calendar to bring the calendar back in line with the solstices, and Pope Gregory XIII decreed that the day following Thursday, October 4, 1582 would be Friday, October 15, 1582 and from then on the reformed Gregorian calendar would be used. The Catholic countries of Italy, Poland, Portugal, and Spain immediately observed the calendar change, but for almost two hundred years Protestant countries refused to change to the new calendar because it had been reformed by a Catholic Pope. The Greek Orthodox countries didn't make the change until the start of the 20th century.[47]

Russia adopted the Gregorian calendar after World War I, on January 31, 1918. The next day was February 14, 1918! When Barnett was born in 1906, there was a thirteen- or fourteen-day difference between the Julian and Gregorian calendars. By that reckoning, 19 June 1906, the recorded date of Ber Maldavsky's birth in Zhytomyr, was equal to July 2 or 3 in the United States.

That left us with a discrepancy of seven or eight days. We puzzled over that for a little while and then realized this was the date of his *bris*,[48] not the day of his birth. Aside from circumcision eight days after the birth of a boy, there was little reason to note a date of birth. Often, birthdates were linked to holidays or other specific noteworthy events. Jewish family records and stories often relate that so-and-so gave birth on the "second day of Passover," or "at Purim." As long as the family remembered the year of the birth, it was easy to ascertain the secular calendar date. More often, a family was vague on that detail. Sometimes, the recollection of the date of birth was general, like "right after so-and-so died" or "the year of the poor wheat harvest." Today, the Jewish community pays attention to the exact date and year of a child's birth to assign a date for a *bar or bat mitzvah*,[49] ceremonies which have become more elaborate and formalized than they were in Eastern Europe.

In 2017, Anna Royzner, a Ukrainian researcher, visited archives in Zhytomyr and Kyyiv looking for evidence of my ancestral family. I hoped her experience in archives there would find what I could not eight years earlier. Anna found a treasure trove of documents. I already knew, from my grandfather's birth record, what his parents' names in records from Zhytomyr should be: Symkha Abraham-Izkhakovich Moldavskiy and Sheina-Mintza Abraham-Berova. These names included patronymics—the names of my grandfather's grandfathers. Symkha was the son of Abraham-Izkhak and Sheina Mintza was the daughter of Abraham-Ber. Having these three generations of names, including the names of Symkha and Sheina-Mintza's other children, helped Anna zero in on the family. She first found the 1893 marriage of Symkha and Sheina-Mintza, which included the bride's maiden surname—Farber. This was a name I already knew from documentation in the United States, but I had no documentation contemporaneous with events prior to her emigration. That record provided an important piece of information—that Symkha was from the town of Rozhev in the Radomyshl *uyezd*.[50] In 1900, Rozhev was in the Kiev *guberniya*.[51] Today, it is known as Rozhiv, Ukraine, and is located at 50°23′ N 29°39′ E, 38 miles west of Kyyiv.[52] Zhitomir, as previously mentioned, was the capital of the Volhynia *guberniya*. Although the cities Zhitomir and Rozhev, both located in the Russian Empire, were not far from each other, they were in different provinces. Depending on rules and restrictions, travel between provinces was often difficult or impossible for Jews. Nevertheless, for my family at least, travel between the two areas occurred. The marriage record identified Sura-Leya's place of origin as Zhitomir. Interestingly, part of the Zhitomir *oblast*[53] was in the Kiev *guberniya* at least for a short time. This, of course, complicated research for the families since records can be found in archives in both Zhytomyr and Kyyiv.

From documents Anna found, I learned who Symkha's parents were. Avrum Itsko Yosifovich Moldavsky married Sura-Leya Moshe-Itskova Vulikh in 1868.[54] Their fathers were identified from the patronymics—Avrum Itsko's father was Yosif and Sura-Leya's was Moshe-Itsko. As mentioned earlier, a challenge in Jewish genealogy is matching up variations of names. On Ber's birth record, his paternal grandfather was noted as Abraham Itzhakovich, yet on his marriage record his name was Avrum Itsko. Itsko is a form of Itzhak, which in turn is the biblical name Yitzkhak. Both Avrum and Abraham (Avraham) are found in the Bible and are two forms of the same name.[55] Itzhakovich is the patronymic, meaning "son of Itzhak."

In addition to learning that Avrum Itsko (Abraham-Itzak) was from Rozhev, birth and death records of the children of Avrum Itsko and Sura-Leya, including those

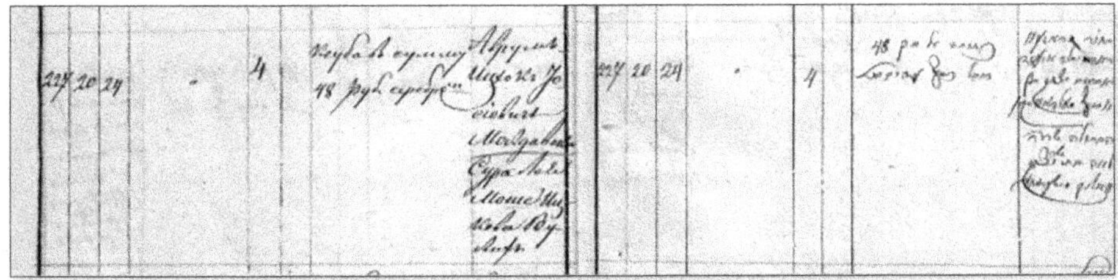

Fig. 12: Excerpt from an 1868 marriage record from Zhytomyr

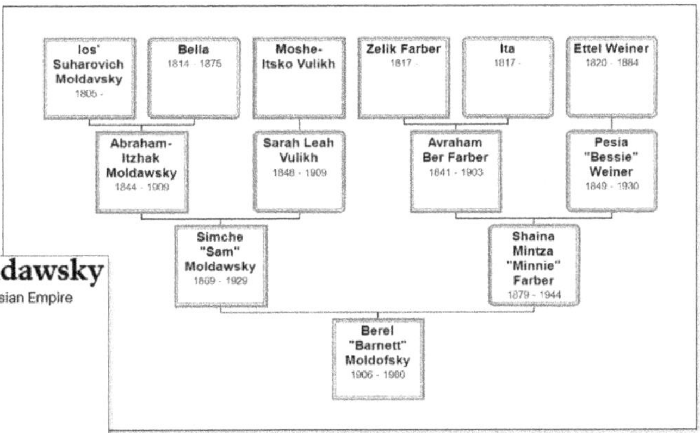

Fig. 13: Simche's siblings, parents, and paternal grandparents

for Symkha in 1869, Beyla in 1875, and Moshe in 1884, along with the record of Enta's death at age 1 in 1883, all indicated their father was from Rozhev. According to Symkha's marriage record he, too, was from Rozhev, although birth records for all the children were from Zhitomir and none of them indicated that the family lived anywhere else. It is possible that, if the father was registered in Rozhev, so were the children. These records, with their links to Rozhev, do not mean that the family actually lived in Rozhev for all these generations, only that this was where they were registered—their legal place of residence. Perhaps that Oszew place of residence on Simche's manifest was a misspelling of Rozhev? The "v" and "w" would sound the same, and the "sz" and "zh" and the "o" in both sound the same. It is easy to miss the initial "r." Records from Rozhev will need to be investigated further to determine whether the family can be found still there in the early twentieth century.

An interesting bit of information is often included in Jewish birth records in the Austrian Empire, and does not appear in Russian Empire records. For a girl, we can find the date when she was named—shortly after birth and generally on the next day when a reading from the scrolls of the *Torah* is mandated—a Monday, Thursday, Saturday, or holiday. The 31 December 1875 birth record of Borukh Gersh notes he was circumcized on 3 January 1876.[56] It is common on these birth records to include the circumcision date and birth date for boys as well as the birth and naming dates for girls. Unless there are special circumstances, such as illness, a boy's circumcision date should be eight days after birth, but the date of a girl's naming will vary.

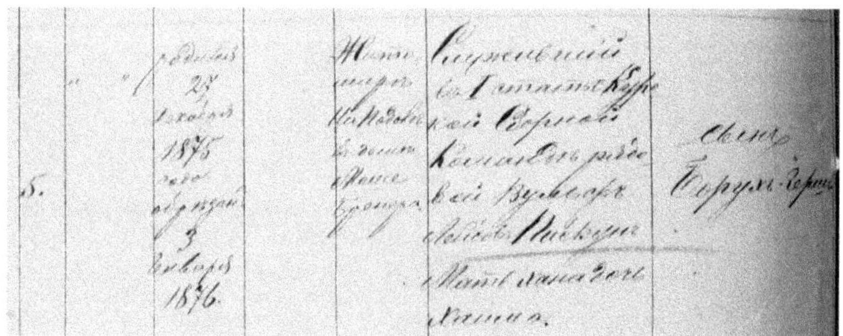

Fig. 14: Excerpt from 1876 birth record containing dates of birth and circumcision

In the Kyyiv archive, we found Revision Lists for the Rozhev Jewish community. Revision Lists, called *Reviskaya Skazka*[57] in Russian, are interesting documents; they are similar to a census but with an important variation. Unlike censuses, these lists are updated and revised until the next census is taken. These censuses, taken in the Russian Empire during the eighteenth and nineteenth centuries, began in 1719. The earliest ones would not have included lists of Jewish families because it was not until the partitions of the Polish-Lithuanian Commonwealth beginning in the 1770s that Jews were permitted to live in the Russian Empire. The third and final of these partitions, in 1795, ceded to Russia areas that included large Jewish populations. The 5th Revision list of 1795 and its subsequent supplement became the first one that recorded Jewish families in the area where the Moldofsky family lived.

The family was first found in the 1850 list enumerated on 25 October 1850. It recorded Avrum-Itsko, age 6, living with his parents, Ios Suharovich Moldavsky, age 45, and Beyla, age 36. Details of the composition of the family included the note that Ios and Beyla had a son Leysor who was born in 1832 and died in 1835. He must have been their firstborn child. In addition to Avrum Itsko, they had a son Yankel, age 3, and daughters Sura Pesia, age 15, and Ruhlia Ita, age 12. Revision Lists enumerated male members of the household first, followed by female members. The list specified the relationship of each person to the head of the household.

With the information from the 1850 Revision List, we were able to go back to the previous list in 1834, in which Ios Soharovich, age 29, was enumerated with his wife, Beyla, age 20. In their household was their son Leysor, age 2, and daughter Malia, age 5. There was a note about Ios's brother Notka, who died in 1823, and who was 7 years old in 1815. Ios and Beyla were in household 19. Since relationships between members of the household are noted, it is not complicated to determine who was the spouse of whom.

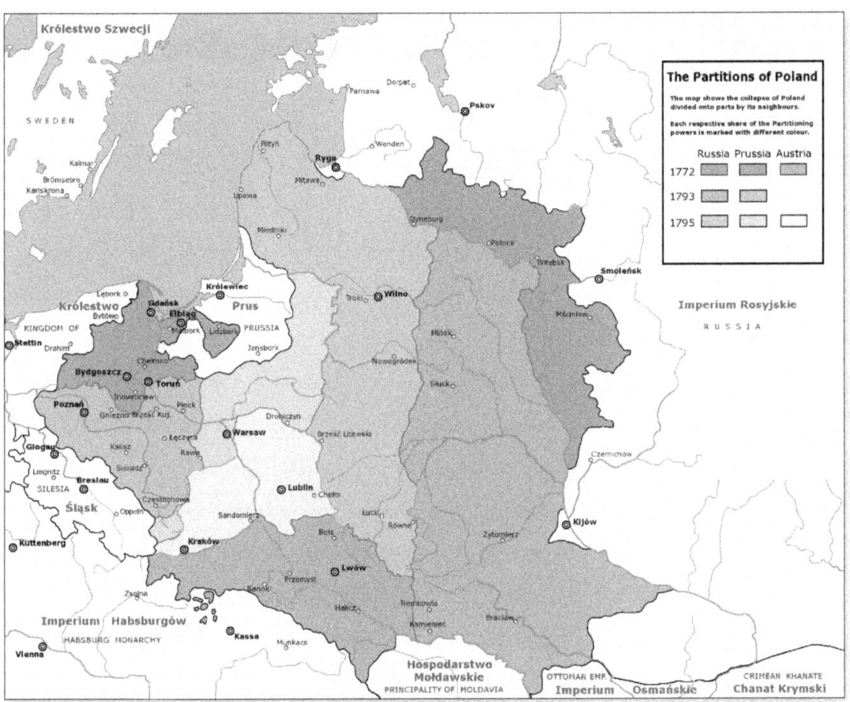

Fig. 15: Partitions of Polish-Lithuanian Commonwealth[58]

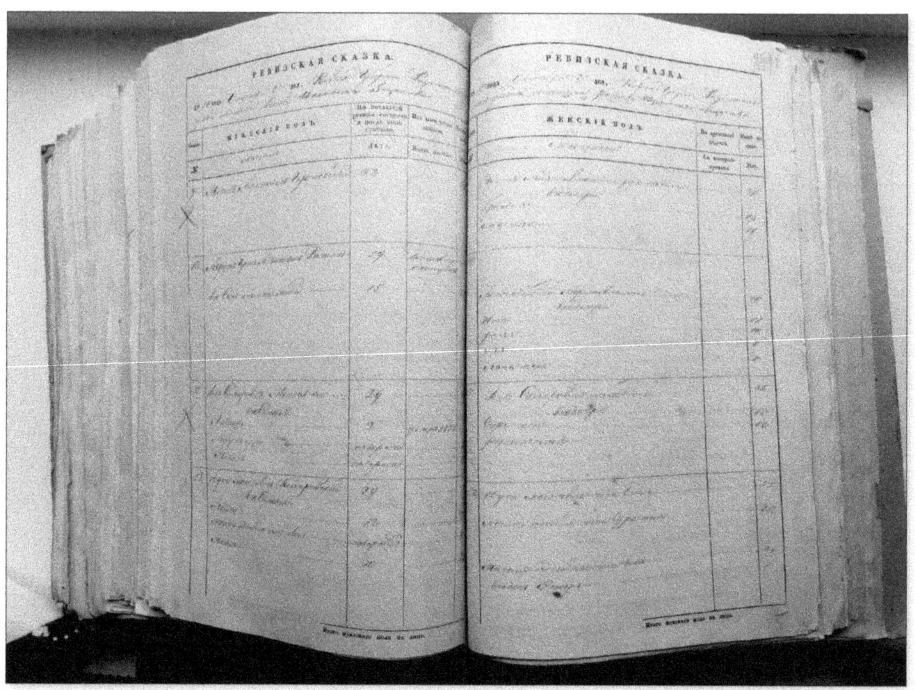

Fig. 16: 1850 Revision List #11[59]

Household 20 was a surprise, as the Revision List enumerated Yudko, a previously unidentified sibling of Ios's, and his household there. Yudko's name was recorded as Yudka Sohar Notkovich Moldavsky.[60] The recording of names was not always consistent; sometimes, the father's name appeared as a middle name with the paternal grandfather (father's father) as the patronymic, as was the case here. Yudko was 39 years old in 1815 and had a son named Avrum, who was born in 1813. More shocking than discovering this family was the note that, in 1834, Yudko converted to Christianity and moved to a Christian community! We had no idea that these types of details of a family's life would be included on Revision Lists.

As we know from other research, families can be traced beginning with the most recent to more distant records. That same Yudko was found enumerated on 29 February 1816 as having moved to Rozhev in 1811 at the age of 34 with his wife, Khana. They had a son, Volko, who died in 1812. Although it didn't give his age, that same record noted that he was 8 years old in 1811. There was a large gap between Yudko's birth, probably about 1776, and Ios's birth in 1805. Often, families had 12 or more children over a 25-year period. This period could be greater if the mother of the oldest children died and their father remarried and had

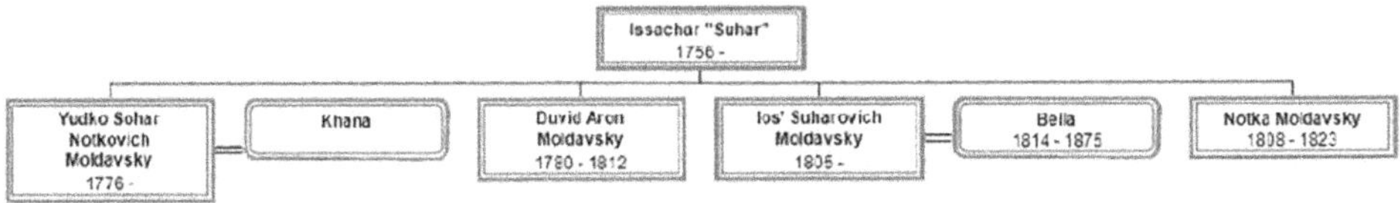

Fig. 17: Issachar "Suhar" and his children

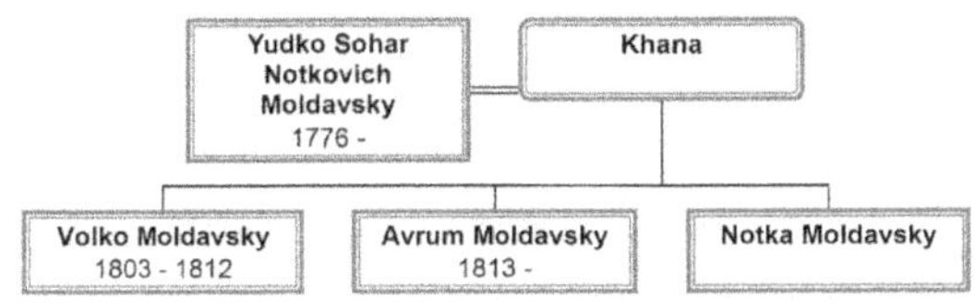

Fig. 18: Yudko and his wife and children

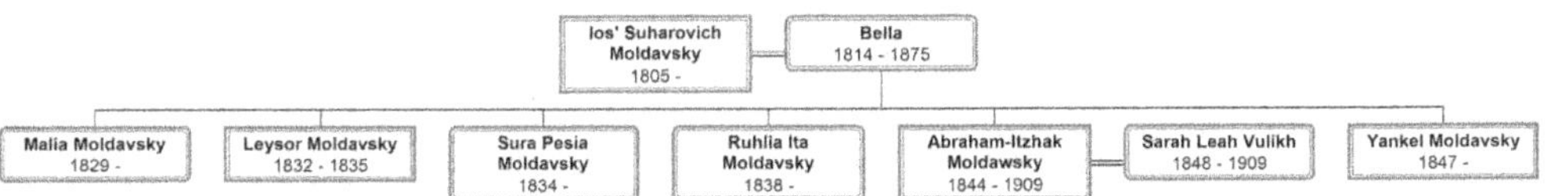

Fig. 19: Ios and his wife and children

additional children. More needs to be discovered about the family to determine whether there were more children or whether Suhar had more than one wife.

We identified Duvid Aron, a brother of Suhar's who was 31 years old in 1811 and died in 1812. Because of the number of children in a family and the spread of their ages, it was not uncommon to have the children and grandchildren of a person be the same age! These Revision Lists gave me a tool to make connections and learn about the places where the Moldofsky family lived. They also provided insight into Farber family members, who were consistently enumerated back as far as 1834 in Zhitomir. More research will be needed to find out whether they moved to Zhitomir from elsewhere and to find the earliest records for them in Zhitomir.

Leaving Europe

Ethel said she came to the United States in December 1910 with her mother and three siblings aboard a Hamburg-American steamship, the SS *President Lincoln*. The *President Lincoln* left Hamburg on 17 December 1910 and docked in

New York Harbor on 29 December 1910. I was surprised at the relatively short voyage—12 days—since, for some reason, I thought it would be longer.

The ship manifest, which I originally located on the Ellis Island website,[61] showed that Mintza Moldawska and her children Jankel, Maita, Etel, and Berta traveled together from Hamburg to New York. They took new names after their arrival and became known as Minnie, Jack, May, Ethel, and Barnett, respectively, in the United States. The manifest provided important information. It recorded their last residence as "Zhitomir," and their relative there was Pessie Farber, Minnie's mother. Minnie's destination in the United States, according to the manifest, was the residence of Simche Moldawski, her husband, on Cook Street in Brooklyn, New York. Column 16 of the manifest seems to indicate that Minnie, in line 11, only had $1. The column heading asks how much money the immigrants brought with them if it was less than $50. In 1910, $50 would have been a fortune. In 1909, a short-lived requirement that immigrants have at least $25 and a train ticket to their final destination was imposed by then-Federal Commissioner of Immigration, William Williams.[62] This policy was very controversial, and Williams left his position in 1913. Was the $50 only an arbitrary amount rather than a requirement? Based on the responses of other passengers on that manifest and on others, it did not seem to be a requirement for admission.

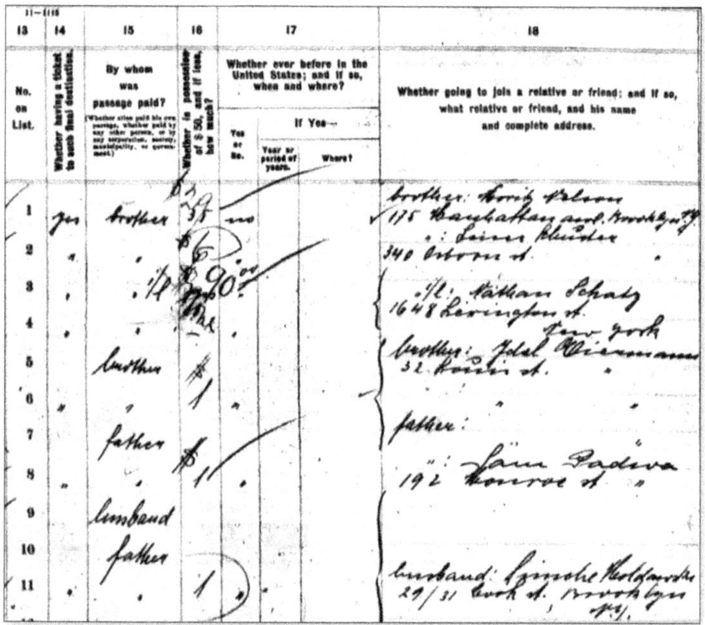

Fig. 20: Page 2 of the SS *President Lincoln* manifest, noting Minnie's destination and cash on hand[63]

Fig. 21: Rivington Street, New York, between 1900 and 1915[65]

Prior to identifying the birth records for Minnie's children in Zhitomir, the manifest provided circumstantial evidence that Minnie's son's birth was in Zhitomir and that Minnie and her children may have lived with her mother after Sam traveled to the United States. A photo of lower Manhattan from between 1900 and 1915 provides a glimpse of what the Moldofsky family may have seen upon their arrival.[64]

In 1910, the Dillingham Commission published a report on immigration that included a section on the steerage experience for passengers leaving from the ports of Bremen and Hamburg, Germany.[66] This description may not reflect the same experience Minnie and her children had on their 1910 journey, but it is probably close.

Individuals traveled from their home in Galicia or Russia to a port city by train, if they had the means. If they could not afford a train ticket, they might travel by foot or by farm wagon. Sometimes, transportation was included in the price of the ticket. For those traveling by train, there might be a transit point along the way for a border crossing. The train journey might take as long as 24 hours. At the border checkpoint, travelers were divided into those going to Bremen and those going to Hamburg.[67] Minnie and her children left Europe from the port at Hamburg. Immigrants to America were separated from the rest of the travelers. Additionally, travelers were segregated into groups of Jews and non-Jews and put in separate cars. Separating immigrants to America from the rest might make sense, as there were different immigration requirements or standards that needed to be verified. There were also quarantine requirements imposed by American immigration to assure newly arriving immigrants did not bring diseases with them that would result in an epidemic. A rational explanation of the separation of Jewish passengers from non-Jewish passengers is not readily apparent.

During the long trip, trains taking emigrants to the harbor stopped briefly several times, allowing passengers to exit and purchase water and food. At the train's final destination, passengers were subjected to physical examinations and interviews, and some were detained. One person reported that, after the examination, the names of steerage passengers were read off. They were told that boarding for steerage passengers had ended hours earlier and the choices remaining were to pay more for third-class passage or wait 10 days for the next ship's departure. Since boarding for other classes on those same ships was still underway, it is probable that the purpose of the announcements was to coerce travelers to purchase higher-priced passage or to enrich the pockets of the proprietors of the rooming houses near the docks. Both options posed financial hardships, as neither one would leave many people with money when they arrived in America. Worse still, the possibility existed that, without sufficient funds, they would be turned away and not permitted entry. The person describing his experience in the Senate report said third-class passage included food, separate toilet facilities, and separate sleeping areas for men and women. This differed significantly from steerage, where there was no privacy and no facilities for toilets or bathing. Passage also included barely-edible food, and ship stewards had their own lucrative businesses selling food. In steerage, passengers were required to clean the spaces in which they lived, but cleaning supplies and receptacles in which to put garbage or other waste was non-existent.

The difference in cost between steerage and third-class passage in the first decade of the twentieth century was only $7.50.[68] In today's terms, that difference sounds minimal, but in 1910, the starting annual salary for a college graduate in New York City was $750, and "[a] loaf of bread cost three cents...In 1909, a

17-year-old earning 20 cents an hour was able to live a comfortable life..."[69] At that time, fresh beef cost 13 cents a pound and soap was 5 cents a bar.[70] My dad, Milton Silverman, told me that, at his first paying job—working for his uncle David in the late 1930s—the hourly wage was 40 cents. In the twenty-first century, that sounds like an impossibly small wage, but it is the equivalent of $20—a higher hourly rate than is found in most of the United States in 2023.

Arrival, Detention, and Deportation

The first official port of disembarkation for the earliest immigrants arriving in New York was on the Hudson River at the old Bowling Green, on the southern tip of Manhattan Island. Castle Clinton, originally a post-Revolution defense against British attack in what is now Battery Park, was converted in the mid-1800s to serve as an immigration station and was renamed Castle Garden.[71] Prior to the creation of Castle Garden as an immigration processing station, immigrants landing in New York underwent no formal processing. The boat left them on shore, and they went wherever they were intending to go.

In 1890, Congress created the Bureau of Immigration, later known as the Immigration and Naturalization Service (INS), now called the United States Citizenship and Immigration Service (USCIS). For two years after the 1890 closure of Castle Garden, before Ellis Island opened in 1892, immigrant processing took place in Battery Park.[72]

From 1892 to 1954, over twelve million immigrants entered the United States through the portal of Ellis Island, a small island in New York Harbor. Ellis Island is located in the upper bay just off the New Jersey coast, within the shadow of the Statue of Liberty.[73] It is 1.5 miles west of Castle Garden. In 1808, New York State bought Ellis Island from Sam Ellis to use as an ammunition dump. In 1892, it became an immigration facility. An 1897 fire destroyed the Ellis Island facility and Castle Garden re-opened until it could be rebuilt.[74]

The Immigration Act of 1891 excluded from entry into the United States those suffering from a contagious illness, among other things.[76] According to Vincent J. Cannato, during the period from 1892 to 1924, approximately 80% of the more

Fig. 22: Arriving at Ellis Island, 1907[75]

than 12 million immigrants who landed at Ellis Island successfully passed through in just a few hours.[77] Family lore held that Jack (Jankel) had a head injury, and when he arrived at Ellis Island, he was detained and sent back to Europe alone. From examining the ship's manifest, we learned something of the circumstances and can verify the family story. Jankel was held in the hospital facility at Ellis Island and the family was detained at Ellis Island. The detention page of the *President Lincoln* manifest indicates Jankel's deportation on the SS *Bavaria* on 20 January 1911, although the rest of the family was released from detention on 31 December 1910, two days after their arrival, and were permitted to remain in New York.

Both Coan and Cannato described immigrants' experiences during their arrival and the procedure at Ellis Island. All immigrants were not treated equally. First- and second-class passengers were processed on board the ship and, except in extreme cases, permitted to disembark at Manhattan without

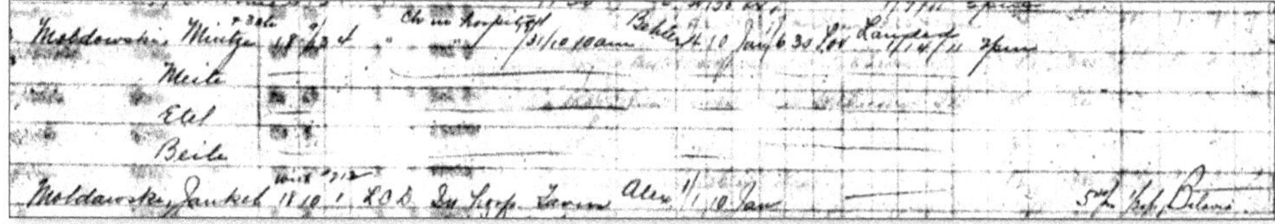

Fig. 23: Record showing details of the Moldowski family detention at Ellis Island[78]

going through processing at Ellis Island. Steerage passengers, a category that included most Eastern European Jewish immigrants as well as immigrants from other backgrounds, went to Ellis Island. Each steerage passenger was given a nametag that included the name of the ship on which they traveled, the page of the manifest and the line on that page on which their name was recorded. Officials would check the information on the name tag against the manifest and send the passenger on for processing. The nametags became an important part of the processing of steerage passengers and help prove the false nature of the myth of names being changed at Ellis Island by immigration officials.

A ferry or barge brought new arrivals from the pier on the west side of Manhattan to Ellis Island, where men and women were separated. Children went with the women. Officials from the United States Public Health Service inspected everyone for cataracts, trachoma, and conjunctivitis. Anyone found to have one of these ailments was immediately excluded and deported back to his or her country of origin on the next ship traveling there. A second set of doctors conducted a general physical and looked for signs of mental illness, deformity, pregnancy, goiter, or favus, a scalp disease.[79]

Jankel was diagnosed with favus, a fungal disease of the scalp. Anyone not considered in good health had a code marked on his/her shirt to identify the diagnosis and was held in detention to await a more thorough examination. Examination by three doctors confirmed or denied the initial diagnosis.[80] Every potential immigrant was subjected to a series of 32 questions. An inspector, accompanied by an interpreter, asked the questions and a clerk recorded the responses. Depending on the answers, the inspectors might decide to ask additional questions before determining whether a person would be free to disembark or would be held over in detention.

It is difficult to dispel myths, even in the face of the details of events. One persistent myth is that of the deliberate changing of names of immigrants upon their arrival at Ellis Island. No matter how many discussions there are in genealogy forums, conferences, journals, and books, the issue arises periodically.

The tags (Fig. 24 and Fig. 25) were attached to the clothing of the potential immigrant. Immigration officials had the manifest in front of them; all they had to do was look at the page and line where the immigrant's name appeared. These manifests were filled out prior to embarkation. The only thing the officials in the United States would have done would have been to check off a person's name or

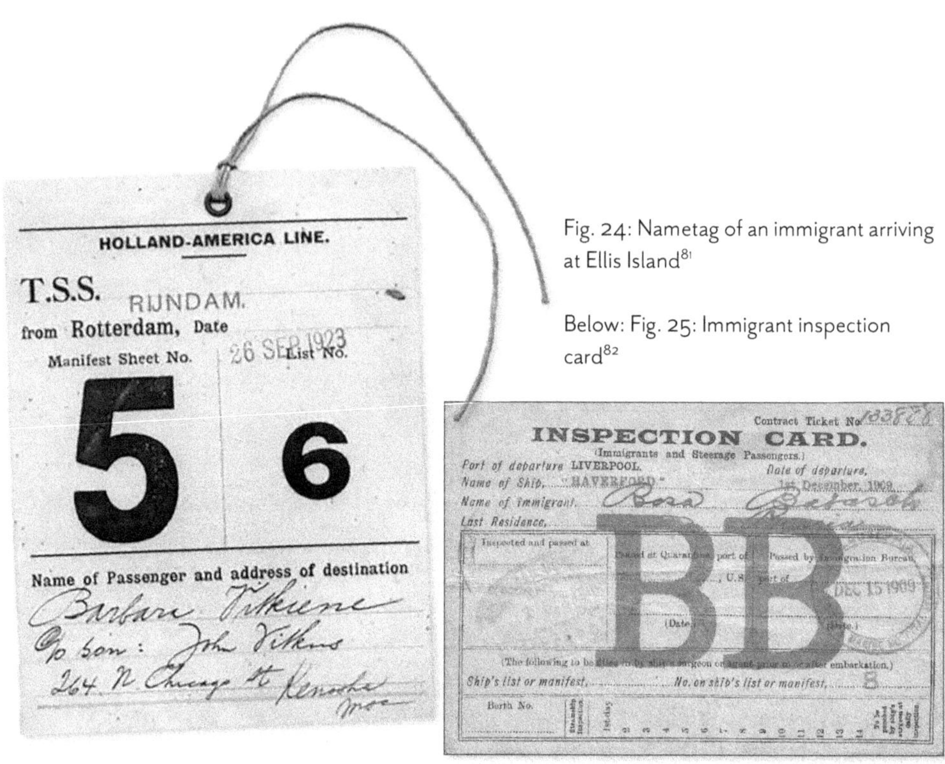

Fig. 24: Nametag of an immigrant arriving at Ellis Island[81]

Below: Fig. 25: Immigrant inspection card[82]

fill out a detention form if the immigrant was held for health reasons or because they needed someone to meet them. Other markings on the manifest that were added after arrival may be references to naturalization petitions; these were added when the manifest was checked against a petitioner's claim of having sailed on a particular ship.

There are at least several reasons why a person would not be traveling under his or her own name. In my research, I encountered situations in which a person traveled from Europe using a ticket purchased by a sibling. In one case, the issue was discovered on the naturalization record when this individual, Shaina, provided the name under which she arrived, Malka, in the United States. Her sister, Malka, arrived a few years after Shaina. Disentangling the records led to a lot of confusion. Another reason a person might travel under an assumed name or with someone else's name might be that they purchased a ticket from someone who couldn't travel. There is nothing, however, that would prevent a person from assuming their own name once they arrived at their destination. If there is no record of the difference between a person's name on the ship manifest and the name they used after immigration, it might appear as if there is no manifest for that person. In the case of Shaina and Malka, that naturalization record was the only clue.

Two brothers I was researching used the names Sam and Samuel, respectively, after they arrived. One was Shimshon and the other was Shmuel. Shimshon is the Hebrew name most often translated as Samson, and Shmuel is Samuel. If it wasn't for Shimshon's marriage record, on which he was identified as Samson, this family's mystery might not have been resolved.

Cannato referred to Ellis Island as a "gate" into New York. Ellis Island functioned as a "sieve"[83]—a way to distinguish acceptable immigrants from unacceptable immigrants. Women and children could not be released without a male relative vouching for them.[84] This was intended to avoid a large population of mendicants and prostitutes from among the immigrants. As Coan noted, detention could be very frightening. Although the "Moldawski" family landed in December 1910, Jankel was held in detention awaiting deportation for several weeks after the release of the rest of his family. Fourteen-year-old Jankel returned alone to Europe in January 1911. Jankel's information on the detention form was filled out at the time of detention. There was no way to know in advance who would be held and refused permission to land once a ship arrived in New York or what the resolution of detention would be.

Jankel, later known as Jack, returned to the United States in September 1912, according to his 1928 naturalization record. He married Sarah Ortman in 1923 in New York. Sarah and Jack had three children, all born in New York. They named the youngest of their three daughters, born in October 1929, after the recently deceased Simche. Sadly, Jack died very young in 1933 at the age of 37. Sarah and their extended family in Brooklyn raised his daughters. May married Eddie Klein and they had a daughter who married and moved to Maryland, where she and her husband raised their family. Barnett married Sylvia Miller and they had three daughters, whom they raised in Brooklyn, New York. Ethel married Ben Nudelman in 1928; they had no children.

Name Changes, Just Because

Ethel told me that Ben's original name was Nudleman. "But," she said, "what kind of name was Nudleman? Now, Needleman, that's a good name. I told Ben it had to be changed." So, Ethel continued to tell me, <u>she</u> changed the name from Nudleman to Needleman. From the way she related this change, I thought she accomplished it early in their marriage. However, it did not happen before they got married or even in the following several years. Their marriage certificate clearly shows the "Nudleman" spelling. The Nudleman-Moldofsky marriage certificate makes it apparent that Ethel herself changed the "u" in Nudleman to "ee" to make Needleman! On an envelope addressed to Ben, after their marriage, his surname is written "Nudleman." In the 1930 census, their name was written as Nudleman. In a 1931 *YIVO Minsk Landsmenschaften* list, Ben, living at 269 Floyd Street, Brooklyn, New York, is recorded as "Needleman,"[85] and on Ethel's 1938 United States naturalization record, she was "Ethel Needleman." The naturalization form does not indicate, as so many other naturalization documents do, that a formal name change occurred. Documents from the 1930s list the name as "Needleman" while others indicate that the Nudleman name was used long after that, at least by Ben.

In a box of old photos and newspaper clippings, Milton found a record that indicated that Ben, if not Ethel, was still known by Nudleman into the 1940s. Milton, in identifying the photograph, wrote:

This was torn out of the section of the Forward newspaper and shows
a group of men and women connected with the 40th Anniversary

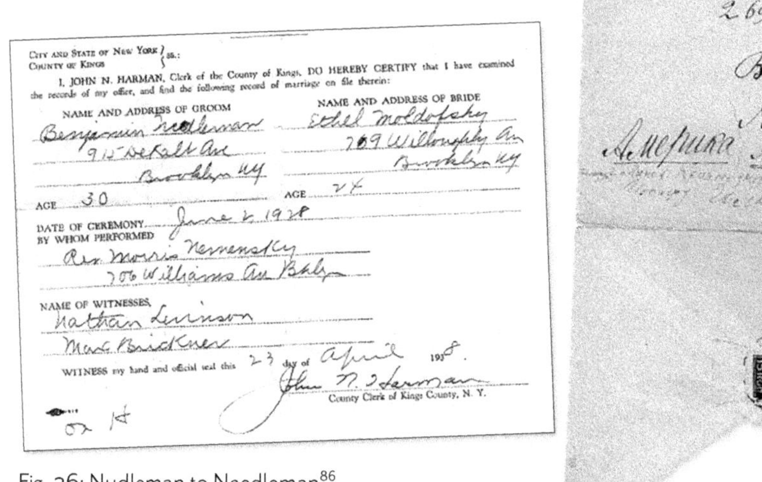

Fig. 26: Nudleman to Needleman[86]

Fig. 27: Envelope addressed to B. Nudleman[87]

Fig. 28: Ben Nudelman, 40th-anniversary celebration of the Workmen's Circle[88]

celebration of the Workmen's Circle. Among those pictured "Marking a milestone in the history of the Workmen's Circle—the Fortieth Anniversary Arrangements Committee—of Branch 4, Workmen's Circle, one of the first units of the famous Jewish fraternal order, in New York City" is Uncle Ben standing in the rear (third row). In Yiddish, his name is spelled "nun-vov (oo)-daled-ayin-lamed-mem-alef-nun." I verbalize that name as "Noodelman." For comparison, "recording," as in "recording secretary," is spelled "resh-ayin-kof-alef-resh-daled-yod-nun-ghimmel" [and] has the "ee" sound in the "yod." So, sometime in the 1940s, he was called Noodelman. This fortieth anniversary has to be in the 1940s, since the organization was founded in 1900.

Ethel nursed her mother and her own husband through their final illnesses. Minnie died in 1944, Ben in 1956. Ethel never remarried and lived by herself until 2001 when, at age 98, she moved into a nursing home. She resided there until her death in 2004 at age 101. Ethel remained sharp as a tack until the end, with almost all her faculties intact. Her diminished hearing posed difficulties in communicating with her on the phone, and because I lived far from New York at that time, I rarely spoke with her during the period when she lived in the nursing home. Although she did not offer her stories freely, she always answered when asked specific questions. The only question she refused to answer dealt with her mother and a second marriage that Ethel claimed occurred. Strangely, none of Minnie's grandchildren remember her living with another man after Simche died.

The Tale of the Two Minnies

During the last decades of Ethel's life, before she moved to the nursing home, she and I spent a lot of time talking. Often, I asked her questions about her family and she would tell me the same stories, with slight variations, as her memory was jogged. There was never a time when I found her recollections to be incorrect, but sometimes it took many years to find information to which she had alluded. One of those instances had to do with Minnie's siblings. Ethel told me that Minnie's sister, Sarah, married Elke. That was proven when we found the record of Simche's arrival in the United States with his destination listed as the home of his brother-in-law Elie Kaminer. Elke was probably the way Ethel remembered the name. One of the challenges in research is identifying people when their names are different than names in family stories. His name appears in various documents in the U.S. as Eli and Elie. Ethel also told us that Minnie had a sister, Meniche, and a brother, Moshe, whose wife's name she didn't know.

All Ethel remembered about Meniche was that she married, moved to Chicago, and had a daughter who perhaps became a doctor. Or maybe, she added, Meniche became the doctor. She didn't remember. Maybe the daughter's name was Khaya or maybe Ida. For many years, whenever I traveled to Chicago to study at Spertus Institute, I searched for an Ida whose mother was Meniche Farber. I never found any records. Through the years, I did meet descendants of Elie Kaminer and Sarah Farber. In today's interconnected world in which the internet and social media reign supreme, I finally found Meniche and her family.

It started in July 2017, with a series of emails between a few of the Kaminers. At the time, I was busy with a project and didn't pay too much attention. By the time I read the correspondence a couple of weeks later, things had gotten extremely complicated. A DNA match had come up with an Abramowitz name that was now being considered as the putative maiden name of Sarah Kaminer, rather than Farber. Further, speculation was circulating that Minnie Moldawsky was not the sister of Sarah Kaminer because Sarah unquestionably had a sister, Minnie, who married Ben Weissbrod, whose surname changed to Weiss. Someone speculated that perhaps Minnie's second husband was Ben Weiss, while others pointed out the impossibility of that given what they knew of the family.

This discussion led to me asking some questions about the Weissbrod/Weiss family, whom I found out had two daughters, one of whom was named Ida. The family lived in Chicago. Ida's husband was a doctor. The puzzle pieces began to fall into place. Meniche was the Minnie in Chicago. Shaina Mintza was the Minnie in New York. How could this be—two sisters named Minnie? Their "real" names were the women's Yiddish names, Meniche and Shaina Mintza. The fact that their descendants knew them by the same name, Minnie, didn't mean that when they were alive either of the sisters considered that to be anything but a pet name or nickname. A close examination of two photographs, one the previously mentioned 1923 *seder* photo and another held by the descendants of Meniche, led to the identification of Meniche with her oldest child, Ber, and Sheina Mintza with her oldest child, Yakov.

Fifteen years after her death, Ethel's memories proved true. Once again, the woman who had given me the name of the ship on which her family sailed and the date of its arrival when she was 7 years old solved a family mystery, which in turn led to connecting with more living descendants and expanding my family. I do not know if Barnett knew he had cousins in Chicago. No one I questioned in my family remembers anyone speaking about a Chicago connection. For whatever reason, "my" Minnie's children and their descendants did not keep in touch with either the Kaminer family or the Chicago family, although these branches stayed in touch with each other. It is understandable how families, separated by an ocean over a generation, lost touch. It is less clear to me how this happened so quickly in the United States. Three sisters settled with their families in New Jersey, New York, and Chicago. Three generations later, the families in New Jersey and Chicago are still connected, and neither of them has any memory of the family in New York. If I had not found that ship manifest, with Elie Kaminer as my great-grandfather's destination, and if Ethel had not shared her stories, we never would have found each other. In 2021, following the long COVID-19 sequester, I connected virtually with one of Meniche's great-granddaughters and met another one—not in New

York, New Jersey, or Chicago, but in New Mexico. Our family, arriving in the early twentieth century in New York, spread out all over the U.S. and Canada over the next 100 years.

One of Many Mysteries Remaining: Resolved

Ethel was the informant for the biographical information on Minnie's death certificate. Ethel gave Minnie's surname as "Fromer." When we questioned Ethel, she was quite emphatic, saying Minnie remarried after her first husband, Sam Moldawsky, died. I checked every New York record I could find—birth, marriage, divorce, death, and census—looking to identify a potential candidate for that second husband. Sam Moldawsky died in 1929, before Barnett's daughters were born, and they all have vivid memories of their grandmother, who died in 1944. My mother, Rhoda, and her twin sister, Phyllis, said they did not remember their grandmother being married. The twins were born in 1930, a year after Sam died. The 1930 census, taken after Sam died, indicated that Minnie lived with one of her married children, Jack; his wife, Sarah; and their children Selma, Florence, and Leona[89] at 438 Kosciuszko Street, Brooklyn. Minnie's daughter, May, and May's daughter, Shirley, also lived at that address. The address on Minnie's death certificate—269 Floyd Street, Brooklyn, New York—is Ethel's address. Ethel claimed not to know the man's first name; she only said she didn't like him. The death record indicated that her husband's first name was Samuel, but since Simche went by Sam or Samuel, it wasn't clear whether Mr. Fromer's first name was also Samuel.

When I mentioned to my mother that her father's family lived on Kosciuszko Street, she said she never realized that her grandmother Minnie lived across the street from the house her mother, Sylvia Miller, lived in! When Barnett Moldofsky and Sylvia Miller married in 1928, Barnett lived at 769 Willoughby Street and Sylvia lived at 467 Kosciuszko Street. Multiple generations of Sylvia's family lived in that house for many years and still owned it in the 1950s.

I found one potential Samuel Fromer and thought I had hit pay dirt, but an email exchange with the grandson of that Samuel Fromer gave me enough details about his grandparents to lay to rest that line of inquiry. Ethel, not known for having flights of fancy resulting in false information, probably did not disclose all she knew. I could verify everything else she told me, so I suspect I missed something, perhaps a small detail. My mother's youngest sister, Iris, who I regard as the keeper of the stories for her generation, confirmed that Minnie was married to someone else before she died. Iris said that she remembered visiting Minnie and a husband whose surname was Frommer or Fromer, and that it was not at Ethel's Floyd Street address. Iris knew that her grandmother, whom she said was called "Bobba," died at Ethel's house, but she was certain that she had a memory of her living somewhere else with a husband. A record of Minnie's second marriage and the identity of her husband had not yet been discovered.

It turns out that Samuel Fromer's identification was likely a red herring. I don't know why Ethel identified her mother's second husband as someone with this name. It's the only piece of any of the stories she told us that does not seem to be true. Sarah Farber Kaminer, mentioned above, died in 1931, leaving her widowed husband, Elie Kaminer. Recently, I was looking at records of Elie and Sarah and a discrepancy in Elie's father's name came up. Some of the extended Kaminer family recorded his father's name as Joseph, but in passing, I saw something that I discounted at first that said his father was Rubin. Elie's 1932 death record further confused me. It said that he was married, and his wife's name was Minnie!

Following a hunch, I went searching for a marriage record for him in the years after Sarah's death, and what I found truly surprised me. Elie did indeed marry a second time after Sarah died; he married Sarah's sister, my great-grandmother Minnie! Their April 1932 marriage did not last long. Just a few months later, in August 1932, Elie died, leaving Minnie twice widowed. No evidence has surfaced indicating she married a third time. That Fromer name, though, is still confusing. Not only was it on Minnie's death record, but we also have Iris' memory of a man with that name living with her grandmother. Speculating about the disconnection between the Kaminer and Weiss/Weissbrod families and the Moldofsky family makes me wonder whether Shaina Mintza's marriage to her deceased sister's widow was the root of the problem. It's one of those many questions that will likely remain unanswered.

A challenge when dealing with vital records, even in the United States, is whether the person who provided the details knew the correct information. For example, a child providing information for the death certificate of a parent might know some of the information by hearsay. Death certificates ask for the name of spouse and parents, when applicable. A child or spouse might not know the names of the decedent's parents or the correct birthdate or birthplace. Sometimes a problem

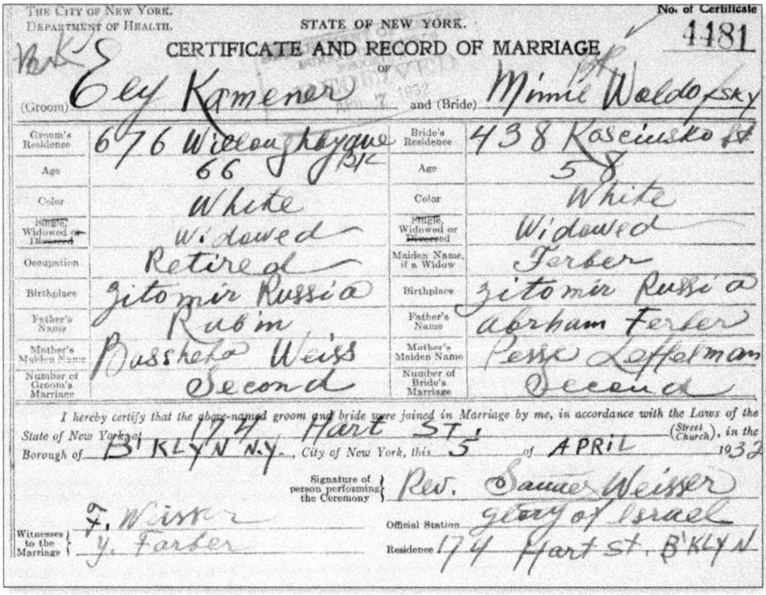
THE CITY OF NEW YORK.
DEPARTMENT OF HEALTH.
STATE OF NEW YORK.
No. of Certificate 4181
CERTIFICATE AND RECORD OF MARRIAGE
OF
(Groom) Ely Kamener and (Bride) Minnie Woldofsky

Groom's Residence	676 Willoughby Ave Bk	Bride's Residence	438 Kosciusko St
Age	66	Age	58
Color	White	Color	White
Single, Widowed or Divorced	Widowed	Single, Widowed or Divorced	Widowed
Occupation	Retired	Maiden Name, if a Widow	Ferber
Birthplace	Zitomir Russia	Birthplace	Zitomir Russia
Father's Name	Rubin	Father's Name	Abraham Ferber
Mother's Maiden Name	Bassheba Weiss	Mother's Maiden Name	Pesse Leffelman
Number of Groom's Marriage	Second	Number of Bride's Marriage	Second

I hereby certify that the above-named groom and bride were joined in Marriage by me, in accordance with the Laws of the State of New York, at 174 Hart St. *(Street, Church), in the Borough of* B'KLYN N.Y. *, City of New York, this* 5 *of* APRIL *193*2

Signature of person performing the Ceremony: Rev. Samuel Weisser
Witnesses to the Marriage: F. Wisser; Y. Farber
Official Station: Glory of Israel
Residence: 174 Hart St. B'KLYN

Fig. 29: Record of the 1932 marriage of Elie (Ely) Kaminer and Minnie Moldofsky[90]

arises with transcription of information from the handwritten form, especially if the person doing the transcription is unfamiliar with a place or a specific spelling of a name. The most accurate information on vital records originates with a parent or the person himself. Obviously, a person is incapable of supplying information for his own birth or death certificates. However, when information that appears on a birth certificate originates with a person other than a parent, it is likely to be suspect.

In the United States in the twenty-first century, it is inconceivable that a birth would go unrecorded and that a birth certificate would not be held by an authorized agency. This was common in the past when home births attended by midwives were the norm. Births frequently went unrecorded or had erroneous information. A birth might be recorded by an attendant days or weeks after it occurred and the person submitting information might have relied on hastily-scribbled notes or memory. To obtain proof of birth where no formal birth certificate existed, it might be possible to receive a document with one or two witnesses attesting to the veracity of the information. These were not witnesses of the event itself, but rather people who testified that the information was correct. These "witnesses" often had no other knowledge of the event than what they had been told. This contrasts with current requirements in the United States for all births to be formally recorded within a short time after a child's birth.[91]

In addition to the record of a birth date and birth name on a birth certificate, a Social Security card in the United States has a person's legal name. Information on birth certificates is usually supplied by a biological parent or guardian, but in cases of adoption, that original birth record may be amended to reflect a new identity. People can apply for Social Security cards for their children soon after birth, in which case the information is filled out by a parent or guardian, or the application can be filed when it is needed, by the person for whom the card is intended. Although a Social Security card is not considered identification, a Social Security number is legally necessary for obtaining a job, receiving certain government benefits, including Social Security benefits. The Social Security Administration is required to verify a birth record for all applicants born in the United States. The only exception is when a parent applies for a baby's Social Security number at the hospital at the time of the baby's birth. To verify a birth record, the office that issued it is contacted.[92] In response to tightened homeland security requirements, some states now require a Social Security number to receive a driver's license or photo identification card.

Often, a Social Security number application (SS-5) is the best way to ascertain a decedent's identity and prove that the person is the ancestor being researched. When an application was filled out by an adult, the person was generally employed and needed to comply with regulations about acquiring a Social Security number. The application, in addition to providing the address of the applicant, included the name and address of the employer, the applicant's date of birth, and frequently included a specific birthplace and the names of the parents. An unemployed woman might apply for a Social Security card to be able to obtain spousal benefits or other benefits that might be available. These changed over time with the passage of new legislation. If a decedent's birth took place fewer than 100 years ago, proof of death needs to be provided with the request to receive a copy of a Social Security application. If it is not, the parents' names and other information are often redacted.

Donald Wayne Cummings wrote that, in earlier centuries, "readers had a definite aural bias."[93] How words, including a name, sounded was the way they were written. That meant that a person's name could theoretically have unlimited spellings. The way Ethel wrote her mother's surname on the death form or the information she supplied might have been spelled incorrectly, either inadvertently or deliberately. If the original handwritten information still existed, it would be possible to compare that original with the formal death certificate on which the information was rewritten. Although we hoped that the 1940 United States Federal Census, released in April 2012,[94] would provide additional information, none was forthcoming. First, I looked in the index for her name. The only Minnie Fromer/ Frommer was the one I had found earlier. Then I searched through the many pages of the enumeration districts in which it might be assumed that Minnie lived in 1940. Since Minnie lived with at least one of her children in the years immediately following her husband's death, I first looked for each of her children, whom I found quickly. She was not listed as living with any of them. I reviewed the census pages looking at the names of the residents of the buildings and streets near her children and still turned up empty-handed.

At the time of the public release of the 1940 census, the entire database had already been digitized—that is, made electronically available for viewing. However, it had not yet been indexed. Lacking a surname index, a page-by-page search was the only way to locate a particular person. The census is organized within each state by city and then by smaller enumeration districts. If an address is known, the first step is to identify its enumeration district and then to examine the pages within that district. The pages containing the addresses within the enumeration districts in which her family lived were the first places I looked for Minnie. Since she was not living with any of them, I looked next at the residents of other buildings on those streets. Because I did not locate her at any of those addresses, I found it necessary to examine the census pages for every street in the enumeration district where her children lived and then branch out to neighboring enumeration districts. Maps of enumeration districts for New York, with its high population density, are complex. In this manner, we initially searched the 1930 census upon its release in 2002 and earlier censuses prior to the availability of surname indices. The index for New York was one of the first indices completed in the 1940 census project—it was ready just two months after the census was released. Since neither Minnie nor her alleged husband, Sam Fromer/Frommer, could be found in either the 1940 census raw data or the index, perhaps Ethel deliberately provided an incorrect name.

Before the 1940 census became available online, many steps were taken to digitize the data and create a searchable index. In the months leading up to the release of the 1950 census in April 2022, similar processes were put in place. First, the originals, or microfilmed images of the originals, were digitized.

Then, trained transcribers type the names and other information recorded on the census. For the 1950 census, a combination of machine-generated transcriptions of the handwritten census combined with human proof-reading were done. This is common in large projects, but prior to the 1950 census, transcriptions were done twice by different people and the duplicate copies were compared electronically to try to avoid errors. Those entries that matched were assumed to have been correctly transcribed. If transcribed entries didn't match, a third transcriber would take a closer look to determine what the original entry was. Frequently, people tell me that a record I found has an error that needs to be corrected. I ask whether the error is on the record or the transcription. If it's on the transcription, there are processes in place on many data collection sites to make the correction. If the error is on the record, that can't be corrected.

All online databases, not only the United States census database, are dependent on indexed information to facilitate computerized searches. The creation of many of the indices relies on volunteer groups. For example, the Italian Genealogy Group in New York, whose main purpose is to provide resources for people researching Italian genealogy, undertook an indexing project years ago. They began to index New York City vital records and naturalization information. The transcription and indexing of the records, which include birth, marriage, and death records, was accomplished by thousands of volunteers scattered all over the United States. As a volunteer with the project, I spent hundreds of hours each year keying in information from records to spreadsheets.

Even with indexed records, navigating between websites, pages, and records is sometimes complex and time-consuming. Steve Morse, the designer of the architecture for Intel's pioneering 8086 processor, which fueled the microcomputer revolution, created a research system that he called "one-step" to permit researchers to navigate through websites more easily. He began this project in 2001 with the Ellis Island database, which had just come online. His system permits researchers to search many databases using one form. His website, http://stevemorse.org, provides a portal for ease of access to many kinds of databases including vital records, immigration records, and censuses for several countries. Now his one-step tool includes translation between languages and between cursive script and block printing, conversion of addresses to and from latitude and longitude, and more.

The search for records is ongoing. The questions that arise while conducting research seem endless. Sometimes, the questions and the resulting answers have little to do with the original subject. Tangents are always lurking, practically begging to be investigated. I imagine that one day, I will discover—or, more accurately, confirm—the real story about why Simche Moldawsky left his pregnant wife and three children in Europe while he went in search of his fortune in the United States. Part of that story will include what he did once he arrived in America and how he was able to send for his wife and children almost five years after he made the journey. It is less probable that I will be able to satisfy my curiosity about what Shaina Mintza and the children did in Europe during the period between Simche's 1906 departure and their own in 1910.

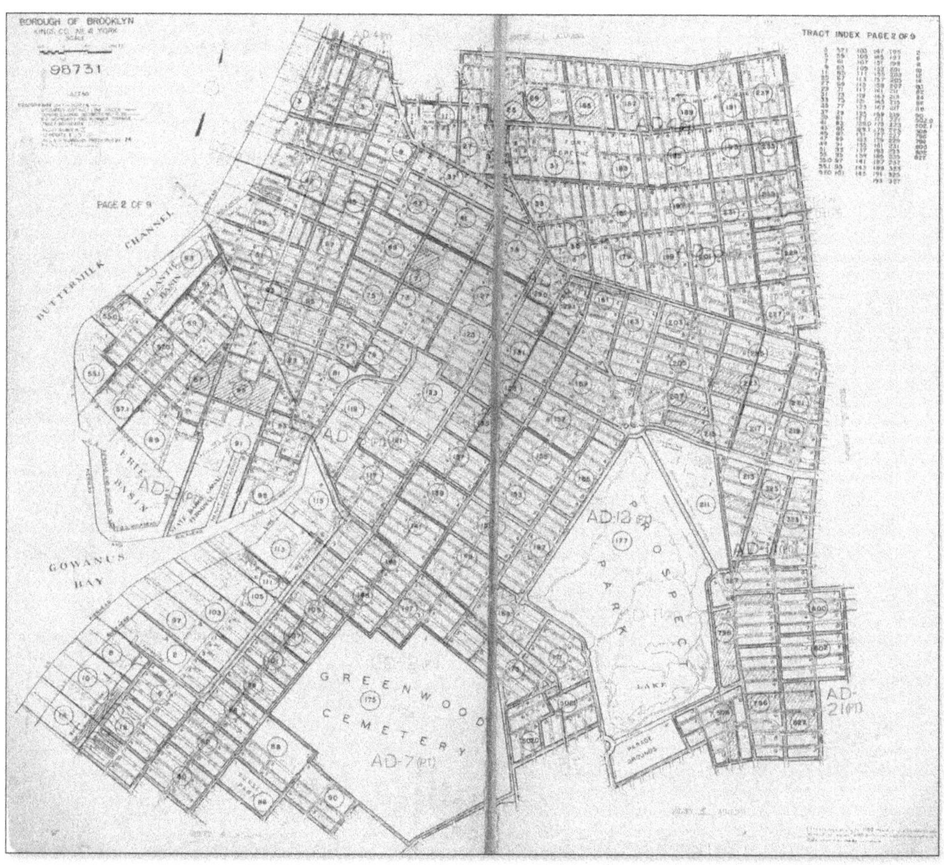

Fig. 30: 1950 enumeration district map[95]

Endnotes

1. This photo is of the Moldofsky family and appeared on the cover of the Yiddish newspaper *The Forward* on April 24, 1924. The photo was taken by an unidentified photographer.
2. Kitl is a Yiddish word: קיטל—a white robe traditionally worn by adult Ashkenazic Jewish men at their wedding and on other holidays and festive occasions. At their death, it is their shroud.
3. The Hebrew word *seder*, meaning order, refers to the ceremonial celebration commemorating the escape of Israelites from slavery in Egypt more than 3,000 years ago. The "order" refers to the 15 steps, including an elaborate meal, symbolic foods, and the re-telling of the exodus through a book called a *Haggadah*.
4. Zhytomyr is located at 50° 15'N 28° 40'E.
5. Harry D. Boodin, "Theories, Assumptions and Implications of Dictionary of Jewish Surnames from the Russian Empire," *Avotaynu: The International Review of Jewish Genealogy* IX (Fall 1993) pp 10-11; researcher's copy.
6. Although place names can be transliterated the way they sound and there are "official" spellings for places with non-Latin alphabets, during my 2009 trip to Ukraine I found signs with the city's name spelled in many different ways. In Ukrainian/Russian, it is written **Житомир**. In Yiddish, it is written זישטאמיר. In Hebrew, it is זיטומיר.
7. Gordon Cohn, "Traces of a Vanished World," *Avotaynu: The International Review of Jewish Genealogy* XIV, no. 4 (Winter 1998) pp 61-63; researcher's copy.
8. Boris Feldblyum, "Some Information About Jewish Zhitomir," *Avotaynu: The International Review of Jewish Genealogy* XII, no. 16 (Spring 1996) pp 16-18; researcher's copy.
9. Seymour Spector, editor, *The Encyclopedia of Jewish Life Before and During the Holocaust* (New York: New York University Press, 2001), p. 1505; researcher's copy.
10. Ibid, p. 1506.
11. Boris Feldblyum, "Some Information About Jewish Zhitomir," *Avotaynu: The International Review of Jewish Genealogy* XII, no. 16 (Spring 1996) p 16-18; researcher's copy.
12. Seymour Spector, editor, *The Encyclopedia of Jewish Life Before and During the Holocaust* (New York: New York University Press, 2001), p. 1506; researcher's copy.
13. Shirley Gage Hodges, "Immigration: The Journey to America," presentation at the Arizona Family History Expo, Mesa, Arizona, 20 January 2012.
14. *Matzevah* is the Hebrew word for a gravestone; *matzevot* is the plural.
15. "*JewishGen Online Worldwide Burial Registry*," Databases, *JewishGen* (https://www.jewishgen.org), accessed February 2021.
16. On the ship manifest, Minnie, Jack, May, Ethel, and Barnett were recorded by their Yiddish names as Mintze, Jankel, Maita, Etel, and Berta, respectively. Minnie's actual Yiddish name was Shayna Mintza and Barnett's was Beryl.
17. "About," *FamilySearch* (https://www.familysearch.org), accessed February 2021.
18. Before the advent of web browsers and email, a lot of communication was done through electronic bulletin boards such as soc.genealogy.jewish, established in 1994 by Susan King.
19. Ship manifests are, simply put, the passenger lists from a ship. Rottenberg mentioned that passenger lists from almost every ship that landed at American ports on the Atlantic Ocean or the Gulf of Mexico after 1820 are held at the National Archives. Dan Rottenberg, *Finding our Fathers: A Guidebook to Jewish Genealogy* (Maryland: Genealogical Publishing Co., Inc.: 1995), p. 33; researcher's copy. Warren Blatt in FAQ #10 "Passenger Lists" on JewishGen.Org wrote: "Lists of passengers arriving at U.S. ports have been maintained by the federal government since 1820. U.S. Passenger Arrival Lists generally provide the name, age, and country of origin for each arriving

person. Relatively few U.S. lists prior to 1890 show the town or city of origin; later lists provide the specific place of last residence and/or birthplace, and much more. Passenger lists are arranged by port, and then chronologically by date of arrival. The National Archives in Washington has custody of these lists, which have been microfilmed. Indices to most ports were prepared by the WPA, but they are incomplete." Found at "JewishGen FAQ – Frequently Asked Questions," Get Started, *JewishGen* (https://www.jewishgen.org), accessed February 2021.

20. Alexander Beider, "A Scientific Approach to the Etymologies of Jewish Surnames," *Avotaynu: The International Review of Jewish Genealogy* XXI (Spring 2005); researcher's copy.

21. Jewish Community of Kamionka Strumiłowa (Lwów District, Galicia Province, Austrian Empire), Death Records 1880-1884, pp. 303-304, Number 3, Ettel Wiener, died 12 January 1884, in Kamionka; digital image, "Księgi metrykalne gmin wyznania mojżeszowego z terenów tzw, Zabużańskich *Archiwum Główne Akt Dawnych.*" (http://www.agad.gov.pl), accessed December 2020.

22. Jewish Community of Kamionka Strumiłowa (Lwów District, Galicia Province, Austrian Empire), Death Records 1789-1876, p. 72, Eidel Winer, died 13 June 1852, in Kamionka; digital image, "Księgi metrykalne gmin wyznania mojżeszowego z terenów tzw. "zabużańskich," Archiwum Główne Akt Dawnych (http://www.agad.gov.pl), accessed December 2020.

23. Meron Lavie, "First Came "Retroactive Samification" and Now Comes...," 16 July 2012, Discussion Group, *JewishGen* (https://groups.jewishgen.org/g/main/topic/70457915), accessed March 2022.

24. Kahlile Mehr, "Russian Archival and Historical Terminology," *Avotaynu: The International Review of Jewish Genealogy* XII, no. 35 (Fall 1996) p35; researcher's copy.

25. Efim Melamed, "Information for Jewish Genealogists in the State Archive of Zhitomir Oblast," *Avotaynu: The International Review of Jewish Genealogy* XII, no. 14 (Spring 1996) pp 14-15; researcher's copy.

26. Nolan Altman, Edward Mitelsbach, and Kurt Friedlaender, compilers, "German Occupation Definitions - English Translations," InfoFiles, *JewishGen* (https://www.jewishgen.org), accessed January 2012.

27. "This German and Polish surname of KRETCHMER is of two-fold origin. It was a locational name meaning 'the dweller at the stream in the marsh or wasteland.' It was also a German occupational name for an innkeeper, derived originally from the Old German word KRETSCHAM (inn). The word is of Slavic origin and rendered in Poland in the form KARCZMA." Definition found at "Kretchmer Coat of Arms / Kretchmer Family Crest," Name Index, *Coat of Arms Store* (https://www.4crests.com), accessed February 2021.

28. Len Yodaiken, "A Synopsis of 18th-Century Lithuanian-Jewish History," *Avotaynu: The International Review of Jewish Genealogy* XVIII (Spring 2002); researcher's copy.

29. Jules Levin (ameliede@earthlink.net), "Tavern keepers," email to *JewishGen* discussion group, sent 5 January 2012.

30. Jules Levin (ameliede@earthlink.net), "Re: Tavern keepers," email to *JewishGen* discussion group, sent 6 January 2012.

31. Bill Yoffee (kidsbks@verizon.net), "Re: Tavern keepers," email to *LitvakSIG* discussion group, sent 6 January 2012. *LitvakSIG* is another of the Special Interest Groups involving Jewish genealogy. This SIG specializes in the Kovno and Vilna guberniyas of the Russian Empire, which includes most of present-day Lithuania.

32. Found at the website of St. Vladimir Orthodox Church in Dexter, MI: "Home," *St. Vladimir Orthodox Church* (http://www.stvladimiraami.org), accessed January 2021. St. Vladimir is a Russian Orthodox Church Outside of Russia (ROCOR).

33. B. O. Unbegaun, "Origin of Russian-Jewish Surnames," *Avotaynu: The International Review of Jewish Genealogy* III (Spring 1987): pp 3-10; researcher's copy.

34. Boris Feldblyum, "Understanding Russian-Jewish Given Names," *Avotaynu: The International Review*

of Jewish Genealogy XIII, no. 7 (Summer 1997) pp3-10; researcher's copy.

35. From Jewish birth records in Zhytomyr for the years 1872 and 1891, respectively.

36. Boris Feldblyum and Yakov Shadevich, "Some Problems in Researching Eastern European Records," *Avotaynu: The International Review of Jewish Genealogy* IX (Fall 1993) p 12; researcher's copy.

37. "Julian to Gregorian Calendar," Tools, *Ancestor Search* (http://www.searchforancestors.com), accessed December 2020.

38. *Bris* is the Yiddish word by which *Brit Milah* is commonly known. It is the circumcision ceremony by which a male enters the covenantal relationship Jews have with God and is observed on the eighth day after birth. Observance of this transcends rules of all Jewish holidays, so the *brit milah* is performed even on days like the Sabbath and Yom Kippur, the two holiest days of the year. The word *brit* in Hebrew means covenant.

39. *Bar* and *Bat Mitzvah* refer to the rituals by which 12- and 13-year-olds are welcomed into the adult Jewish community. At that time, they become obligated to perform certain rituals. Unlike achieving majority in the United States, there are no privileges, such as being able to vote or legally able to drink, attached to this coming-of-age acknowledgement.

40. An *uyezd* is a district.

41. A *guberniya* is a province.

42. Kyyiv is the modern transliteration of the place often written as Kiev.

43. An *oblast* is a region within a *guberniya*.

44. Jewish Community of Zhitomir (Zhitomir District, Volhynia Province, Russian Empire), Marriage Records 1868, Number 227, Avrum Itsko Yosifovich Moldavsky and Sura-Leya Moshe Itskova Vulih, married 4 November 1868; Fond 67, Inventory 3, File 43, State Archives of Zhytomyr Oblast, Zhytomyr, Ukraine.

45. The story of Abraham and his son Isaac begin in the biblical book of Genesis (in Hebrew, *Bereishit*), chapter 12.

46. Jewish Community of Zhitomir (Zhitomir District, Volhynia Province, Russian Empire), Births Records 1876, Number 5 (female), Bayla Moldavsky, born 31 December 1875; Fond 67, Inventory 3, File 3, State Archives of Zhytomyr Oblast, Zhytomyr, Ukraine.

47. The plural is Revizskie Skazki.

48. 1834 Russian Empire Revision List, Rozhev Jewish Community, Radomysl District, Kiev Province, p. 547, Number 20, Yudka Sohar Notkovich Moldavsky household; Fond 280, Inventory 2, File 641, Central State Historical Archive of Ukraine, Kyyiv, Ukraine.

49. The Ellis Island website is now The Statue of Liberty—Ellis Island Foundation, Inc (https://www.statueofliberty.org).

50. "William Williams papers 1902-1943," *The New York Public Library Archives and Manuscripts* (http://archives.nypl.org/mss/3346), accessed February 2021.

51. Detroit Publishing Company, "The Ghetto, New York, New York," photograph, 1900-1915; digital image, "The Ghetto, New York, N.Y.," Digital Collections, *Library of Congress* (https://www.loc.gov), accessed January 2021.

52. Senator William P. Dillingham, Chairman of the Immigrant Commission, *Reports of the Immigration Commission: Steerage Conditions; Importation and Harboring of Women for Illegal Purposes; Immigrant Homes and Aid Societies; Immigrant Banks* (Washington, D.C.: Government Printing Office, 1911): pp. 28-32; researcher's copy.

53. The report may have addressed the experiences of passengers traveling through Rotterdam, Le Havre, or other European ports, but I was only interested in information pertaining to travel from German ports.

54. Dillingham: pp. 32-37.

55. Vanessa Leonardo, "Five Cents a Ride: The Cost of College in 1910," Pace Press, the Weekly Student Newspaper of Pace University NYC Campus, New York, New York, 4 October 2006;

researcher's copy.

56. Frank Eugene Smitha, "The Roosevelt Presidency to 1908," Macrohistory and World Report 1902-WWII, *MACROHISTORY: WORLDHISTORY* (http://www.fsmitha.com), accessed March 2021.

57. Peter Morton Coan, Ellis Island Interviews: *Immigrants Tell Their Stories in their Own Words* p. xxi; researcher's copy.

58. Coan: p. xxii.

59. "Overview and History," Ellis Island, *Statue of Liberty-Ellis Island Foundation, Inc.* accessed March 2021.

60. Coan: p. xxxiii.

61. Coan: p. xiii.

62. Vincent J. Cannato, *American Passage: The History of Ellis Island* (New York, New York: Harper Perennial, 2010), p. 5; researcher's copy.

63. Coan: p. xv.

64. Coan: p. xv.

65. Cannato: p. 6.

66. Coan: p. xvi.

67. Jerry Seligsohn. "1931 Minsk Landsmanshaften organization," *JewishGen* (http://www.jewishgen.org/belarus/1931_minsk_landsmanshaften.htm), accessed January 2021.

68. Selma, Florence, and Leona have always been known by their Yiddish names: Simmy, Faigle, and Layla.

69. "Birth Data," National Vital Statistics System, *Center for Disease Control and Prevention* (http://www.cdc.gov/nchs/births.htm), accessed January 2021.

70. Information was found at the Social Security Administration website: "Social Security Number and Card," *Social Security* (http://www.ssa.gov/ssnumber), accessed January 2018.

71. Donald Wayne Cummings, *American English Spelling: An Informal Description* (Baltimore, Maryland: Johns Hopkins University Press, 1988), p. 21; researcher's copy.

72. The 72-year privacy rule that has kept the 1940 census results from being released previously. *"Home," 1940 Census (http://www.1940census.net), accessed January 2012.*

73. *"Google Maps," Google* (https://maps.google.com), accessed December 2020.

74. Janette Silverman, grave marker of Riva Frishman (14 October 1873–24 October 1960), Zhytomyr Jewish Cemetery, Zhytomyr, Ukraine, photograph, dated 2009; researcher's copy.

75. United States, Department of Justice, Immigration and Naturalization Service, Passenger and Crew Lists of Vessels Arriving at New York, New York, 1897-1957, SS President Lincoln, arrived 28 December 1910, p. 64, Lines 9-13, Mintze, Jankel, Meita, Etel, and Berta Moldawska; digital image, "New York, U.S., Arriving Passenger and Crew Lists (including Castle Garden and Ellis Island), 1820-1957," Ancestry (*http://www.ancestry.com), accessed March 2022.*

76. United States, Department of Justice, Immigration and Naturalization Service, Passenger and Crew Lists of Vessels Arriving at New York, New York, 1897-1957, SS *Amerika*, arrived 1 July 1906, p. 67, Line 27, Simche Moldawsky; digital image, "New York, U.S., Arriving Passenger and Crew Lists (including Castle Garden and Ellis Island), 1820-1957," *Ancestry* (http://www.ancestry.com), accessed March 2022.

77. Jewish Community of Zhytomyr (Zhytomyr District, Volhynia Province, Russian Empire), Births 1903, Number 240, Etel Moldavsky, born 26 April 1903; State Archives of Zhytomyr Oblast, Zhytomyr, Ukraine.

78. "Kamionka Strumilowa PSA AGAD Births 1859-84,90-1903 Marriages 1866-76,80,82-1909 Deaths 1789-1902," Search, *JRI Poland* (https://jri-poland.org), accessed March 202

79. United States, Department of Justice, Immigration and Naturalization Service, Passenger and Crew Lists of Vessels Arriving at New York, New York, 1897-1957, SS *Milano*, arrived 13 January 1902, p. 227, Lines 1-6, Sara, Sosl, Mani, Chane, Basse, and Ruchel Kaminer; digital image, "New York, U.S., Arriving Passenger and Crew Lists (including Castle Garden and Ellis Island), 1820-1957,"

Ancestry (http://www.ancestry.com), accessed March 2022.

80. United States, Department of Justice, Immigration and Naturalization Service, Passenger and Crew Lists of Vessels Arriving at New York, New York, 1897-1957, SS *Amerika*, arrived 1 July 1906, p. 67, Line 27, Simche Moldawsky; digital image, "New York, U.S., Arriving Passenger and Crew Lists (including Castle Garden and Ellis Island), 1820-1957," *Ancestry* (http://www.ancestry.com), accessed March 2022.

81. Janette Silverman, "Zhytomyr Archives," photograph, 2009; researcher's copy.

82. Jewish Community of Zhitomir (Zhitomir District, Volhynia Province, Russian Empire), Births Records 1906, Number 284 (male), Ber Moldavsky, born 19 June 1906; Fond 67, Inventory 3, File 574, State Archives of Zhytomyr Oblast, Zhytomyr, Ukraine.

83. Halibutt, "Partitions of Poland," map, 2005; digital image, "File:Rzeczpospolita Rozbiory 3.png," *Wikimedia Commons* (https://commons.wikimedia.org), accessed March 2022.

84. 1850 Russian Empire Revision List, Rozhev Jewish Community, Radomysl District, Kiev Province, p. 751, Number 11, Yos Suharovich Moldavsky household; Fond 280, Inventory 2, File 1000, Central State Historical Archive of Ukraine, Kyyiv, Ukraine.

85. United States, Department of Justice, Immigration and Naturalization Service, Passenger and Crew Lists of Vessels Arriving at New York, New York, 1897-1957, SS *President Lincoln*, arrived 28 December 1910, p. 64, Lines 9-13, Mintze, Jankel, Meita, Etel, and Berta Moldawska; digital image, "New York, U.S., Arriving Passenger and Crew Lists (including Castle Garden and Ellis Island), 1820-1957," Ancestry (http://www.ancestry.com), accessed March 2022.

86. "The Ghetto, Lower East Side," published 1909, Detroit Publishing Company; accessed at Library of Congress, (https://www.loc.gov) January 2021.

87. "Arriving at Ellis Island," photograph, published 1907; digital image, "Arriving at Ellis Island," Digital Collections, *Library of Congress* (https://www.loc.gov), accessed January 2021.

88. United States, Department of Justice, Immigration and Naturalization Service, Passenger and Crew Lists of Vessels Arriving at New York, New York, 1897-1957, Record of Aliens Held for Special Inquiry, SS *President Lincoln*, arrived 29 December 1910, p. 142, Number 212, Mintze, Meite, Etel, and Beile Moldowski; digital image, "New York, U.S., Arriving Passenger and Crew Lists (including Castle Garden and Ellis Island), 1820-1957," *Ancestry* (http://www.ancestry.com), accessed April 2022.

89. Holland-America Line, Immigration Identification Tag and Inspection Card, SS *Rijndam*, arrived in New York on 6 October 1923, Barbara Vilkiene; digital image, "Ellis Island Immigrant Document Collection," Immigration, *Gjenvick-Gjonvik* (https://www.gjenvick.com), accessed April 2021.

90. American Line, Immigration Inspection Card, SS *Haverford*, arrived in Philadelphia on 15 December 1909, Rosa Barasch; researcher's copy.

91. Kings County (New York) County Clerk, Marriage License, Number 8107, Benjamin Needleman and Ethel Moldofsky, married 2 June 1928; researcher's copy.

92. To B. Nudleman, of Brooklyn, New York, envelope; researcher's copy.

93. "In Charge of Arrangements," The Forward, New York, New York, 1940s; researcher's copy.

94. City of New York (New York(Department of Healthy, Certificate and Record of Marriage, Certificate 4481, Ely Kaminer and Minnie Woldofsky, married 5 April 1932 in Brooklyn; digital image, "Historical Vital Records," NYC Department of Records & Information Services (https://a860-historicalvitalrecords.nyc.gov), accessed December 2022.

95. "Borough of Brooklyn, Kings Co., New York," map, 1950; digital image, "1950 Census Enumeration District Maps," National Archives Catalog (*https://catalog.archives.gov*), accessed January 2021.

Mil-What? Miller/Mellon/ Milontzik and Forman Families

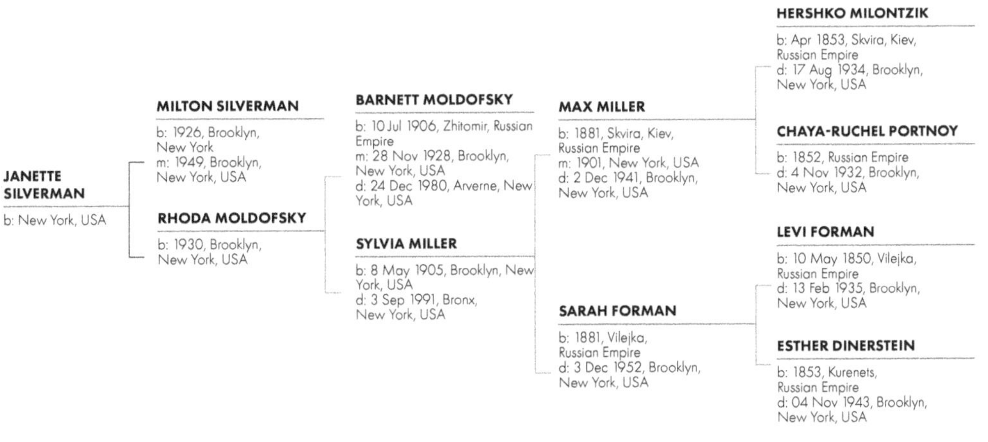

Mil-What? Milyonchik/Милянчік/Miller/ Mellon/Millen/ Melin and More...

My grandmother Sylvia Miller Moldofsky, who died in 1991, was the grandparent I knew the longest. Before writing this book, I would have said I knew her the best of all my grandparents. What I discovered, through my research, was that I barely knew any of my grandparents at all. I did feel a particular closeness to her, but in retrospect, I think she fostered a similar relationship with each of her nine grandchildren. Born in the United States,[1] Sylvia grew up speaking English, but Yiddish may have been her first language since it was spoken at home. Her three siblings and one of her aunts also were native-born Americans.

In a Donna Reed/June Cleaver[2] world where moms stayed at home, cooked, and cleaned all day, my grandmother did not fit the mold. She worked during her entire adult life while also raising three children, including a pair of twins. I never questioned the fact that she worked, although my own mother stayed at home until my youngest sister started school. My grandmother went to work every morning, dressed professionally with a neatly styled wig, a fashion statement, not a religious statement. She worked for more than 25 years as executive secretary and office manager for Louis S. Weiner, Engineering, a zipper manufacturer in Long Island City, New York. Before that, she held a variety of other jobs, all clerical or secretarial. She regarded secretarial work, nursing, or teaching as the ultimate career goal for girls growing up in the 1950s and 1960s.

As opportunities presented themselves and the world opened up for women, she understood before any of us the significance of choices. She clearly understood that women were often taken advantage of financially in the marketplace and urged her seven granddaughters to be prepared and educated. I do not believe she viewed marriage as the ultimate goal for a woman, as so many of her contemporaries did. When she was dying in mid-1991, at the same time I moved with my children to Florida, she urged me to be careful about the employment contract I was about to sign. She pointed out several significant paragraphs in that contract, the contents of which concerned her. She also urged me to examine whether or not I really wanted to relocate because my husband's job required him to move. This reaction from an 85-year-old woman for whom her husband, children, and grandchildren were always at the center of her own life surprised me.

Can You Spell That, or at Least Say It Slowly?

Sylvia was the only one of my grandparents whom I did not think would know anything of her family's background in Europe, since she never lived there. Therefore, I never asked her any questions. I assumed that her maiden name, Miller, should be taken at face value, and that the family may have been "millers" or something similar in Europe. Little did I know.

During the last half-year of her life, as she was undergoing chemotherapy and radiation in the hopes of doing to her colon cancer what surgery had not, I began to ask her questions. Those six months saw her in a weakened state, but she remained determined to stay active and connected. She stubbornly refused to answer when I asked if she knew the town from which her family had come in Europe or if Miller was their original last name. The way her responses were framed told me that she knew both the town and the family name but had decided that I had no reason to know the information! This response, of course, made me even more resolute to know the answers. One day, during a heavily medicated period, she insisted on speaking to me when I phoned. That, in itself, was unusual. Although I called her every day, I usually only spoke to her caregiver or a visiting relative. On that day, I heard her voice loudly asking whoever had answered the phone if I was the caller. She did not have much to say, and I hated having to ask her to repeat what she said, but her words were slurred and difficult to understand. She said: "Milyonchik." I asked her what that meant, thinking I was hearing nonsense syllables. "You wanted to know our name in Europe," she said. "That was it."

To my surprise, after telling me the family name, Sylvia added "and the town we came from was between Minsk and Pinsk." I said that this sounded like the lead-in to a joke and asked if she knew the name of the town. Her response was: "Of course, I do—it is Vil-yay-ka, and it isn't really between Minsk and Pinsk, it's nearer Minsk." Then she abruptly put down the phone. Although I spoke to her many more times before she died, she never spoke again about the family and its European past. I was glad that she gave me the clue about the city being near Minsk, because otherwise, I doubt I would ever have found it in my trusty atlas. I located Vilejka[3] at 54°30'N 26°55'E, which is 100 kilometers, or 62 miles, from Minsk. This is now Vilyeyka, Belarus. Although the current official transliterated name is Vilyeyka, it can be found in various sources as Vilejka (the old Russian transliteration), Vileika (the Lithuanian name), Wilejka (the Polish name), Vileyka (the Yiddish name) and possibly other variations.

Sylvia had never lived in Europe, and there is no telling what she had heard about the lives of her parents and grandparents before immigration. *The Encyclopedia of Jewish Life Before and During the Holocaust* does not include a listing for the town. However, I found many internet sources referring to Vilyeyka, Belarus, and it was to these internet sources that I turned to understand where her maternal Forman or paternal Milyontzik families originated. Did she mean to indicate that the Formans or the Milyontziks came from there? At the time, I understood the surname and the place of origin to refer to the same family; now, I recognize the error of my earlier assumption and realize that the Formans came from Vilejka, not the Milyontziks.

Vilejka was a city and the capital of Vilejka Uyezd. In 1897, Vilejka uyezd[4] had a population of 200,000, 10% of whom were Jews! The city of Vilejka had 3,500 people, 1,300 of whom were Jewish.[5] Farber and Se'evi wrote the following about Vilejka's history:

...the area it is built on was nothing but a stretch of forest until the beginnings of the 18th century. The beginnings of the town were sometime around the year 1766, when it became, officially, a village, the center of a rural district which formed part of the district of Ushimany. In 1793 the town was annexed to Russia. At that time only 257 Jews were living there. After the third partition of Poland, when the province of Minsk came into being, Queen Catherine II of Russia promoted Vileika to the rank of a district town in the newly formed province of Minsk. The inhabitants of the village were granted urban rights. The houses of the village, the estate of the local landlord, and the inn formed the nucleus of the old town. In 1797 the first session of the first district of the old town took place... The first settlers in Vileika were mainly Jews who lived in nearby villages and farms. When the Russian government deported the Jews from the nearby rural

villages, they settled in the town, which thus grew slowly. At the same time, more
villages were added to the district of Vileika, which in 1842 was transferred to
the province of Vilna. But simultaneously with the influx of Jews from rural villages,
there began around 1885, when the population of the town reached a total of
1250, a counter movement: immigration of Jews to the United States of America
and to inner Russia.[6]

The Forman-Milyontzik Clan

As far back as I remember, my grandmother told us little snippets about "Levi S. Forman," her grandfather who had bright red hair. She said he was a learned man in Europe and was treated with a lot of respect in their town. Of course, she only knew of his reputation based on stories she heard from her own grandparents. But nevertheless, we all knew "Levi S.," as we grew to call him. When a cousin was born with red hair, Sylvia was quick to point out that she must have inherited it from "Levi S.," ignoring that cousin's red-headed relatives on the other side of her family!

Levi S. came to the United States in May 1890 or perhaps 1891. I have not located his ship manifest. His U.S. Declaration of Intent to Naturalize, filed in April 1895, does not have the date his ship docked, the name of the ship, nor the port it sailed from, but it does indicate that he arrived in New York. Neither his Declaration nor his Petition for Naturalization, granted in 1901, have much historical information on them. Before 1906, each court and state used different forms for naturalization. In many places, like New York, an applicant's name, address, and prior nation of former allegiance were required. Once the Immigration and Naturalization Service was created in 1906, the standard form all the courts were then required to use was established.

Since Levi S. filed the forms in 1895 and 1901, his naturalization documentation lacks information such as his date of arrival in the United States and his date and place of birth. Levi's documents also do not list the names of other family members or their dates and places of birth. His Petition for Naturalization lists his address as 44 Moore Street, Brooklyn, New York,[7] and his occupation as "grocer." I know wishing cannot change the past, but I really wish he had

Fig. 1: Forman family photo, circa 1902; Front row, seated left to right: Max Miller holding Fannie Miller (baby—my grandmother's older sister); Sarah Forman, Levi Selig Forman, and Esther Dinerstein (Sarah's parents, my great-grandparents) Rear row: Isidor, Harry, Louis, and Ida Forman (Sarah's siblings)[8]

applied for naturalization a few years later, when more information would have been included. The documents are signed in Yiddish: ליב זאלג פארמאן. In English, his name was transcribed as Levi Selig Forman. At this point, one can only assume that the choice of the "o" in Forman was because of the way he pronounced it. Otherwise, from the Yiddish spelling, it could have just as easily been transliterated as Furman, Ferman, Farman, or Firman, especially since the first and last vowel letters in Yiddish are the same for each of those names and yet can be transliterated differently. Esther Dinerstein, his wife, probably came from Europe at the same time he did, along with their four children—Izzie, Louie, Sarah, and Harry—all born in Russia. The reason I say Esther and the children probably came at the same time Levi did is because no family lore suggests otherwise and a fifth child, Ida, was born in 1892 in New York. There is no way to figure out at this point on which ship the family traveled. According to the Castle Garden, New York, records of ship arrivals, 537 ships docked there between April and June 1890, 186 of which docked in May 1890. A similar number docked in the same months in 1891.

An online search for Castle Garden and Ellis Island immigrant ship records can be most efficiently conducted using the Steve Morse One-Step website.[9] Using the tools provided, it is possible to search for a list of ships or passenger manifests, which will include many different websites that offer passenger manifests for New York arrivals. The website search for passengers landing in New York:

> ...[c]overs the years from 1820 to 1957 and includes the following: 1820 to 1855: pre Castle Garden[;] 1855 to 1890: Castle Garden[;] 1890 to 1891: Barge Office[;] 1892 to 1897: Ellis Island[;] 1897 to 1900: Barge Office[;] 1900 to 1957: Ellis Island."[10]

In other words, using the One-Step tool, I currently find links to all ship arrivals in New York Harbor publicly searchable. The Castle Garden lists of passengers contain more than 70,000 names of people who arrived in May 1890. Since persistence is the only way to do effective research, the large number of ship arrivals didn't deter me, and I tried a variety of methods using *Ancestry.com*® to search immigration records. I looked for Lev Forman and had no results. In a surname-only "sounds like" search, there are only 53 passengers, but none of them appears to be the correct person. Given the large numbers of arriving passengers, it is just not feasible to search individually through the actual manifests of every ship that docked in New York for Levi, Esther, and their children. I tried looking for every name that shows up on the index after using the search parameters of a May 1890 arrival and surname of F*r*m*n. Wild cards like "*" that can be substituted for missing vowels or consonants are often good search tools.

This search turned up more than 13,000 people. Although the criteria for the search is wider, I searched for adults whose birthdates were between 1850 and 1860 or children born between 1880 and 1890 to avoid mistakenly eliminating potential candidates. Levi reported his birthdate on naturalization documents as 10 May 1850, but there is no way to ascertain the veracity of this information or know exactly when Esther was born, although her birth year was ostensibly 1853. If that is correct, then her oldest child was born when she was 27, at least according to the information we possess. Based on other research, that would seem a little late for a first child to be born, unless, of course, there were other children who died in infancy, a sad but frequent occurrence. The travelers for whom I was searching could either be adults traveling together or single adults traveling alone. There could be an adult with some or all of the four children born to Levi and Esther in Europe, including a baby born in 1890. The children, given their ages, would not be traveling alone, but could have been accompanied by relatives other than their parents. To cover this possibility, I attempted to look in the manifest for any adult traveling with children whose names and birth years might fit in with the group for which I was searching. Although the search criteria for the ship manifest allowed gender to be specified, I did not specify gender in my search, since gender is often recorded incorrectly and the results for which I was looking should include both males and females. There was no way for me to know what their port of departure was, so I did not include that in the search. Other unknowns were the names under which they traveled or how those names potentially were rendered in a transcription. After an initial search for Levi or Esther did not produce any viable results, I did not search for first names.[11] Ship manifests during the years in which I searched for arrival records of the Forman family would not, as later manifests do, provide me with valuable information such as the name of a person in Europe, the passengers' place of birth and last residence, and their destination in the United States. Unless a future search turns up a family group traveling together with recognizable names, it is likely that this manifest will continue to elude me.

Another possibility is that the Formans did not come into Castle Garden but landed in Philadelphia or somewhere else on the East Coast, or that the manifest from their ship has not yet been digitized. Except for travelers leaving Europe,[12] [13,] most manifests are not digitized or publicly available. Although manifests for the ports of entry into the United States have been digitized, there may be missing manifests. Canadian manifests also need to be considered, since many immigrants came through Canada and then traveled overland to New York State, Michigan, and elsewhere. The dates of arrival on Levi's Petition for Naturalization may be incorrect. Levi's witness, whose statement and signature appear on the document, provided May 1891 as Levi's immigration date and year. The statement made by Levi cites the same month but in 1890. The different information may be due to

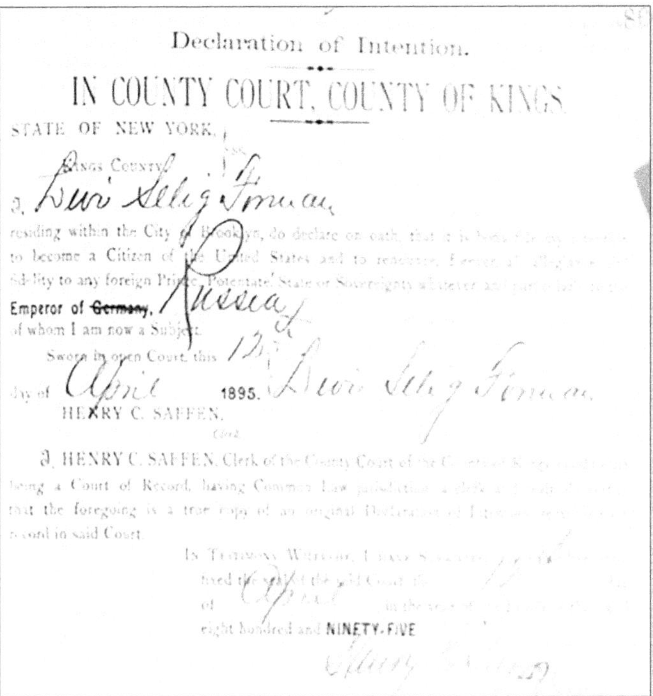

Fig. 2: Levi S. Forman's 1895 Declaration of Intention for naturalization[14]

an error by the clerk, or perhaps Benny Wecht, the witness, testified that he only knew Levi a year after his arrival. It is also possible that Levi (or Benny) gave the incorrect year. As has been previously mentioned, incorrect information is unfortunately common, especially when the information is provided years after the event occurred.

The 1900 census indicated that Esther had given birth to six children, five of whom were still living: Sarah, Harry, Louis, Isidor, and Ida. According to the 1910 census, Esther gave birth to five children, four of whom were still living. Harry died in 1909 in New York. One of her children, Ida, was born in New York in 1892. This presumably meant that there might have been four or five children traveling with Esther or with Esther and Levi. The 1910 census included birthplaces. Three of the four surviving Forman children's births took place in "Russia Yiddish," the fourth in "New York." This means the child who did not survive was born in Europe. Sarah, an adult, was not part of Levi and Esther's household on the 1910 census. Although in 1910 she lived at the same address as her parents, she and her husband, Max Miller, and their children lived in a different apartment. The building in which the

District Court of the United States

FOR THE EASTERN DISTRICT OF NEW YORK.

IN THE MATTER OF THE APPLICATION OF

Levi Selig Forman

By occupation *Grocer*

TO BE ADMITTED A CITIZEN OF THE UNITED STATES OF AMERICA.

PETITION

Filed *August 5* 190 *1*

The above named applicant, being over twenty-one years of age, hereby petitions to be admitted to become a Citizen of the United States of America, and avers that two years or more have elapsed since he declared his intention to become such Citizen, and that a certified copy of said declaration is hereunto annexed.

Subscribed and sworn to before me
this *5* day of *August* 190*1*

Percy G. B. Gilkes

Commissioner.

Applicant.

United States District Court, Eastern District of New York.

IN THE MATTER
of the application of the above named applicant to be admitted a Citizen of the United States.

REPORT. Filed *August 5* 190 *1*

To the Honorable the Judge of the District Court of the United States for the Eastern District of New York.

IN PURSUANCE of a rule of this Court adopted March 1st, 1898, I, the undersigned special Commissioner, do respectfully report:

That I have been attended on such reference by the applicant and his witness, who have been by me orally examined, and have taken the proofs offered by him which are hereto annexed.

And I find and report thereon that the said applicant has complied with the requirements of the Statute in regard to admission to become a Citizen. I further find that said applicant can speak *but not read or* write the English language intelligently.

Dated *August 5* 190 *1*

Commissioner.

IN THE MATTER
of the application of the above named applicant to be admitted a Citizen of the United States.

TESTIMONY ON REFERENCE.

Beny Hecht ______ being duly sworn, deposes and says, that he resides at *361 Moore*, Street, Borough of Brooklyn, ~~Manhattan~~, City of New York ______ and is by occupation *Milk dealer* that he is a Citizen of the United States of America, and personally acquainted with the above named applicant, and has known him for the past *10* years; that the applicant is by occupation *Grocer* and resides at No *44 Moore* Street, Borough of Brooklyn, ~~Manhattan~~ City of New York; that he personally knows that the said applicant has resided continuously within the limits and under the jurisdiction of the United States, since *May* 18*91*, and continuously in the State of New York, since *May* 18*91* and that during the said time of his residence within the United States and within the State he has behaved as a man of good moral character, attached to the principles of the Constitution of the United States, and well disposed to the good order and happiness of the same.

Sworn to before me, this *5* day of *August* 190*1*

Percy G. B. Gilkes

Commissioner.

Beny Hecht

Witness.

Levi Selig Forman

being duly sworn, deposes and says, that he is the above named applicant for admission as a Citizen of the United States of America; that he was born in *Russia* on the *10* day of *May* in the year one thousand eight hundred and *sixty-six* and emigrated to the United States, landing at the Port of *New York* in the State of *New York* on or about the ____ day of *May* A. D. 18*90* and that he now resides at No. *44 Moore* Street, in the Borough of Brooklyn, ~~Manhattan~~ City of New York; that he has resided continuously in the United States since *May* 18*90*, in *Brooklyn, N.Y. City* and continuously within the State of New York since *May* 18*90*

Sworn to before me this *5* day of *August* 190*1*

Applicant.

Fig. 3: Levi S. Forman's 1901 petition for naturalization[15]

226	Fireman	Lazarus	Head	M	W	50	M1	30			Russ Yiddish	Russ Yiddish	Russ Yiddish	1880	Na
		Esther	Wife	F	W	53	M1	30	5	4	Russ Yiddish	Russ Yiddish	Russ Yiddish		
		Louis	Son	M	W	26	S				Russ Yiddish	Russ Yiddish	Russ Yiddish	1890	Na
		Isidore	Son	M	W	22	S				Russ Yiddish	Russ Yiddish	Russ Yiddish	1891	Na
		Ida	Daughter	F	W	19	S				New York	Russ Yiddish	Russ Yiddish		
227	Miller	Max	Head	M	W	29	M1	9			Russ Yiddish	Russ Yiddish	Russ Yiddish	1903	Al
		Sarah	Wife	F	W	29	M1	9	3	3	Russ Yiddish	Russ Yiddish	Russ Yiddish	1890	
		Fannie	Daughter	F	W	7	S				New York	Russ Yiddish	Russ Yiddish		
		Silvie	Daughter	F	W	4	S				New York	Russ Yiddish	Russ Yiddish		
		Sam	Son	M	W	2	S				New York	Russ Yiddish	Russ Yiddish		

Fig. 4: Levi S. Forman and Miller' families on the 1910 federal census[16]

families lived had 10 apartments. The Forman and Miller families lived next door to each other. More extensive searching for the manifest is certainly warranted. Although searches may not be fruitful, they need to be repeated over time as more material is digitized and indices and transcriptions are refined.

Brooklyn and the Formans & Millers

Although Brooklyn, New York, is part of New York City and has been since 1898, it was an independent city located in Kings County, New York State, when Levi S. Forman arrived in 1890 or 1891. At the time, New York City was comprised of Manhattan Borough and part of the Borough of the Bronx. Before the arrival of Europeans, Brooklyn had long been populated by a variety of Native American tribes, including the Lenape and bands of the Nayack and Canarsie.[17] The Lenape, or Lene-Lenape, were also known as the Delaware. The first European settlers in the area were the Dutch, who arrived in the 1620s and established a permanent settlement in the area by 1636.[18] The Dutch West India Company created the Dutch village of Breuckelen in 1646. The original settlement was comprised of six villages: Gravesend, Breuckelen, New Amersfoort (present-day Flatlands), Midwout (present-day Flatbush), New Utrecht, and Boswijck (present-day Bushwick).[19] Many of the communities that, in the twenty-first century, are neighborhoods with a large Jewish presence, such as Williamsburg, were independent villages until the mid-1800s, when they united with Brooklyn to form a larger city. There is no documentation of when the first Jews settled in Brooklyn. However, by 1839, the Brooklyn directory attested to a Jewish presence, listing two Benjamin Levys and a Daniel Levy who were an auctioneer, owner of a variety store, and cartman, respectively. By 1854, a congregation was formed in Brooklyn—Congregation Baith

Fig 5: Brooklyn and surrounding villages[21]

Israel Anshei Emes.[20] A Jewish community was well established in Brooklyn decades before the Forman family made it their home.

Hasia Diner pointed out that, upon their arrival from Europe, Jews, like other immigrants, tended to settle in areas near their place of entry. Jews arriving at Castle Clinton before 1892 or at Ellis Island after that year tended to settle on the Lower East Side of Manhattan.[22] Since the 1840s, Jews had been settling there, and by 1880, about 60,000 Jews lived in lower Manhattan. Of the more than 22 million immigrants who entered the United States through the Port of New York between 1820 and 1920, more than half remained in New York City.[23] Diner described the pattern of immigration and relocation which, for Jews, must have been similar to other immigrant groups.

Immigrant Jews lived as a population in tremendous flux. Neighborhoods operated like sieves, with people leaving and other people coming in to take their places almost simultaneously, at least into the second decade of the twentieth century. An almost universal pattern developed, discernable in almost every city. Newcomers arrived, found places to live near their work, and when they could afford to, they moved to better neighborhoods, turning their apartments over to those who had just landed. In addition, by the early twentieth century the freshest immigrants had many more choices than did those who had come before them. By as early as 1905, the Lower East Side had lost two-thirds of its Jewish population, as newer arrivals headed immediately for neighborhoods that had been unavailable a decade earlier, particularly Williamsburg and Brownsville, across the East River in Brooklyn, and to Harlem in the city's upper reaches.[24]

Williamsburg and Brownsville both had thriving Jewish communities by the 1890s. Howe commented that a common route out of the East Side was to Brooklyn, especially the Brownsville, New Lots, and East New York sections.[25] Although the Jewish population in Brooklyn grew and thrived in the late nineteenth and early twentieth centuries, Jewish residents often found themselves subjected to overt anti-Semitic actions, which ultimately led to the formation of the Jewish Protective Association.[26] Other similar societies were formed during this period in Milwaukee, Wisconsin;[27] Cincinnati and Cleveland, Ohio; and Detroit, Michigan.[28]

Although the Formans may have lived in Manhattan after they arrived, the family was firmly established in Brooklyn by 1895. Their daughter, Ida, was born in New York in 1892. Her birth certificate has not yet been identified, so it is not clear whether they lived in Brooklyn or Manhattan. Her birth like many of her generation and the following one, was at home and probably attended by a midwife. Often births were records days or weeks after they occurred, and errors in spellings of surnames, or indecipherable handwriting, may make some records difficult or impossible to find. There is no basis to suspect that the pattern of residency and migration followed by the Forman family differed from that of other immigrants. If other relatives arrived in the United States earlier and had already moved out of Manhattan, the Formans might have either stayed in Manhattan for a shorter time or perhaps not at all. The movement of the family after they arrived in New York is still being investigated. Locating their ship manifest might clear up some of the missing details. Another often rewarding way to establish where people lived and when is to identify later arrivals who list as their destination an earlier arrival by name and address. A connection such as this has also not yet been found.

Another reason why immigrants might not have remained in an area near their point of entry is that some people emigrated as part of a resettlement project. Agencies like the Industrial Removal Office (IRO), created in New York City in 1901 by American Jewish leaders, intended to relocate Jewish immigrants who needed work from New York City to smaller Jewish communities throughout the United States where they could find jobs. These programs had the added benefit of reducing the number of Jewish immigrants from areas where there was already a sizable population. Some of the thinking was that, with fewer Jewish immigrants in any area, outbreaks of anti-Semitism might be avoided. Between 1901 and its 1922 closure, the IRO relocated more than 75,000 new Jewish immigrants to 1,500 communities in every state.

Both Esther and Levi lived long lives—he died at 85 and she at 90. A 1930 census record enumerated Levi and Esther at 467 Kosciuszko Street with their daughter, Sarah; son-in-law, Max Miller; grandchildren Fanny, Sam, and Abraham; and Fanny's husband, Charles Dorfman. Levi and Esther's great-granddaughter—my mother, Rhoda—said in an interview in December 2011 that the house was not crowded. It had three stories with plenty of room for each family to have their own apartment. The larger apartment downstairs had what my mother described as a huge kitchen table. Family lore says that most of the children in the family before my mother's generation were born on that table in the kitchen. Iris, my mother's youngest sister, said to me during a 2018 conversation that, when Esther died, her body rested on that same table. My mother was quick to interject that the table was always thoroughly washed after a birth or death.

A first-floor bedroom that my mother sometimes shared with her grandmother, Sarah (whom we all called Bubbie), had two iron beds. I have several very distinct early memories of that room. I remember talking to Bubbie there and getting some sort of a large metal ring with skeleton keys from her. I also remember seeing her in that bed right after she died in 1953. My memories include pushing a doll in a carriage on the sidewalk outside that brownstone. Years ago, I realized that the images I had in my mind of that street and brownstone might be actual memories, not dreams or something I read in a book. I asked Sylvia about these images and she verified what I described as having taken place on Kosciuszko Street. When preserving memories and family stories, it is often difficult to distinguish between memories of the event itself, experienced firsthand, and memories of an event formed after seeing photographs of and hearing family discussions about the event. Bubbie and Bobba are basically the same word – each meaning "grandma." In my family, my great-grandmother, Minnie Farber Moldofsky, was referred to as Bobba, and my great-grandmother Sarah Forman Miller was called Bubbie.

Ida and Max Roth also lived in that house on Kosciuszko Street. Ida Forman, born in 1892 in Brooklyn, was the youngest of Levi and Esther's children and the first of the family to be born in the United States. Ida lived until 1981. She and Max never had children of their own.

The grocery store referred to in Levi's naturalization papers was not, it turns out, unique in the family. The Formans owned property that included small markets and apartment houses, including two tenements on Amboy Street in Brooklyn. The Millers, like the Formans, also were involved in the retail food business. Sylvia's youngest brother, Abraham, who died of Hodgkin's disease in 1962, wanted to be an artist. His parents did not approve of this career path, so, according to family lore, he became an artist in food. He owned a small appetizing shop in which he decorated trays and platters to the delight of his customers.

Although rare by the late twentieth century, appetizing shops were once common scenery, especially in New York Jewish communities.

"Appetizing," as a noun, is a Jewish food tradition that is most typical among American Jews, and it is particularly local to New York and New Yorkers. The word "appetizer" is derived from the Latin "appete," meaning "to desire, covet, or long for." Used as a noun, "appetizing" is most easily understood as "the foods one eats with bagels." Its primary components are a variety of smoked and cured salmon, homemade salads, and cream cheeses.

Eastern European Jews started meals with cold appetizers, known in Yiddish as the "forshpayz." In New York, the popularity of forshpayzn among Eastern European Jewish immigrants led to the creation of the institution known as the appetizing store.

Appetizing also originated from Jewish dietary laws, which dictate that meat and dairy products cannot be eaten or sold together. As a result, two different types of stores sprang up in order to cater to the Jewish population. Stores selling cured and pickled meats became known as delicatessens, while shops that sold fish and dairy products became appetizing stores.

In New York City, until the 1960s, there were appetizing stores in every borough and in almost every neighborhood. On the Lower East Side alone there were, at one point, 30 appetizing shops.[30]

Rhoda related that, as children, she and her twin sister, Phyllis, used to deliver platters of blintzes[34] and gefilte fish[35] that their mother made to Abraham's store. A carp lived in the bathtub in their home until it grew large enough to be used for the gefilte fish! Everyone called Abraham "Maihnyu," except for his wife, Charlotte, who called him Herb. It turned out that his full name was Abraham Herbert and his mother used to affectionately call him "Avrumahnyu," based on his Yiddish name "Avraham."[30]

Fig 6: The former family home on Kosciuszko Street in 2012[31]

72

Fig 7: Ida Roth, circa 1965[32]

Fig. 8: Sarah Forman, Milton Silverman, and Rhoda Moldofsky, June 1949[33]

Fig. 9: Sylvia and her youngest sibling, Abraham Herbert, circa 1958[36]

So, what's in a surname, anyway?
Czidovetsky meets Milontzik

Max Miller and Sarah Forman had four children: my grandmother Sylvia and her siblings Fanny, Abraham, and Sam. Sarah was the daughter of Levi S. Forman and Esther Dickstein. Max was the son of Tzvi Herschel Milontzik and Chaya Ruchel Portnoy. Tzvi Herschel and Chaya Ruchel adopted the more American-sounding names of Harris and Rose when they arrived in America. Tzvi Herschel is also referred to as Tzvi Hersch, since Herschel and Hersch are variations of the same word. Tzvi and Hersch have the same meaning—Tzvi is Hebrew and Hersch is Yiddish, and both mean "stag." Double names formed of Hebrew and Yiddish names with the same meaning are common.

Perhaps Marian Smith's explanation of name changes by European immigrants puts Harris's and Rose's decisions about changing their first names and the change from Milontzik to Miller into perspective. They were obviously not the only new Americans to change their names. Marion wrote:

...some name changes are not so easy to trace. Rather than a different spelling of the same-sounding name, an entirely new name was adopted. These are the most American stories of all.

"Who is this new man, this American?" asked de Tocqueville. He was Adam in the Garden, man beginning again, leaving all the history and heartbreak of the Old World behind. The idea that what made America unique was the opportunity for man to live in a state of nature, a society of farmers whose perception of Truth is unfettered by ancient social and political conventions lies at the base of Jeffersonian democratic theory. The New World became a place for mankind to begin again, a place where every man can be reborn and recreate himself. In such circumstances, the adoption of a new name is not surprising. Nor is it surprising in the cases of immigrants who came to America to abandon a wife and family or to escape conscription in a European army. There were all kinds of reasons, political and practical, to take a new name.

A newspaper in California recently ran the story of a Vietnamese immigrant with a long, Vietnamese name so strange-looking to Anglo eyes. *The young man came to this country and began to work and study. He began every day by stopping at a convenience store to buy a "bonus pak" of chewing gum. Chewing all those sticks of gum got him through long days of working several jobs and studying English at night. When he finally naturalized as a U.S. citizen, he requested his name be changed to Don Bonus—the surname taken from the "Bonus Pak" and chosen to signify all his work and effort to become an American. He was a new man.*

If not for the newspaper story, we would not understand this name change. Mr. Bonus' naturalization papers would simply record the name change but not the reasons behind it. If he had not naturalized, his Bonus family descendants, generations from now would be at quite a loss to explain the origin of their name.

The documentation of name changes during U.S. naturalization procedures has only been required since 1906. Prior to that time, only those immigrants who went to court and had their name[s] officially changed and recorded leave us any record. Congress wrote the requirement in 1906 because of the well-known fact that immigrants DID change their names and tended to do so within the first five years after arrival. Without any record, immigrants and their descendants are left to construct their own explanations of a name change. Often, when asked by grandchildren why they changed their name, old immigrants would say "it was changed at Ellis Island."

People take this literally, as if the clerk at Ellis Island actually wrote down another name. But one should consider another interpretation of "Ellis Island." That immigrant is remembering his initial confrontation with American culture. Ellis Island was not only immigrant processing, it was finding one's way around the city, learning to speak English, getting one's first job or apartment, going to school, and adjusting one's name to a new spelling or pronunciation. All these experiences, for the first few years, were the "Ellis Island experience." When recalling their immigration decades before, many immigrants referred to the entire experience as "Ellis Island."[37]

My mother and her sisters, Phyllis and Iris, knew many relatives with the surnames Millen and Melon and knew these names were all somehow connected to their own Miller family. However, they never actually questioned which, if any, of them was the original name, or even how they were related to each other. It was only after we began taking this journey into our family's history that the relationships were clarified.

JewishGen developed many important resources; among them, the Family Tree of the Jewish People (FTJP) and *JewishGen* Family Finder (JGFF). FTJP offers a central collection of Jewish family trees providing connections for individuals researching the same Jewish family branches. JGFF is a compilation of surnames and towns being researched by more than 110,000 Jewish genealogists with more than 585,000 entries. The database contains more than 140,000 ancestral surnames and 18,000 town names. JGFF is indexed and cross-referenced by both surname and town name. These two databases are only two of the component databases that can be found in the *JewishGen* collections. JGFF and FTJP played an important role in my own research. I consulted them often, and several times a year get emails from other researchers with mutual familial connections who located my family through one of these collections.

In September 2005, my dad contacted a researcher, Marvin Goldberg, whose FTJP entry indicated a family connection to Tzvi Hirsch Millenchik. In an attempt to ascertain whether Marvin's Tzvi Hirsch and ours were the same person, my dad asked in an email if Marvin knew whether Tzvi Hirsch was known as "Harris." Marvin responded via email on 5 September 2005, writing:

Re your inquiry. Herschel "Tsvi Hirsch" Millenchick was my Great Grandfather, He died in Brooklyn, NY unknown date. Don't know if name was shortened to Harris. His wife was Rose "Chaya Rouchel" Millen (maiden name—Jitovsky). Children family names changed to Millen, Mellon and Miller. Most buried in Beth David Cemetery, Elmont, NY.

It was very clear, even though Marvin had never heard his great-grandfather referred to as Harris, that this was our family. On Chaya Rouchel's death certificate, her husband was listed as "Harry Mellon" and her name was Rose Mellon. However, her *matzevah*[38] clearly shows her name as Rose Millonchick. In the Yiddish on that stone, her name is *Chaya Ruchel bas*[39] *Yehuda.* Likewise, Tzvi Hersch is inscribed as Harris Millonchick on his *matzevah* and his Hebrew name is *Tzvi ben Avraham Yakov.*

Fig. 10: Grave marker of Tzvi (Harris Millonchick), son of Avraham Ya'akov[40]

Fig. 11: Grave marker of Chaya Ruchel (Rose Millonchick), daughter of Yehuda[41]

Czidovetsky to Goldberg?

arvin told me about his long search for my mother's branch of the family. He shared that he had gathered details from stories passed down in his families, none of it documented. As I integrated his records of names with ours, I sought to validate information. I attempted to verify that the names beyond the few we discussed were, in fact, from the same family. Marvin added confusion to the mix with some of his information, but he also gave us a huge amount of information that he claimed to have acquired from many sources, none of which he remembered. One of the challenges in record acquisition and integration involves documenting the sources and sorting verified and verifiable information from unverified anecdotes.

Over the years, I discovered that I could have been better organized in the way I documented new entries in the family tree database. Occasionally, I would add a note attributing the resource for a particular person, but I was inconsistent, and rarely did I do that for an entire family branch. Now, years later, when I try to locate additional information and verify my data, it sometimes takes hours to locate the precise family member on whose record the verification note appears. I am attempting to rectify this deficiency now, but it is, of course, more time-consuming than if I had understood the necessity of documentation from the start. One of the most important lessons I learned involves meticulously sourcing *all* the data, and information that is speculative needs to be labeled as such.

The confusion stemming from initial conversations with Marvin had to do with understanding how Marvin's Goldberg surname evolved from the name *Czidovetsky*. I felt more than just slightly curious about Chaya Ruchel's maiden name, Jitovsky.[42] Although it did not <u>look</u> like Czidovetsky, it sounded remarkably similar when verbalized. I hoped to find that the two names were the same and discover the relationship between the two families. Marvin did not have many details of how Czidovetsky became Goldberg, but from his stories I understood that Marvin had two theories. One of his family stories held that Marvin's great-grandfather Chaim Yitzchok Czidovetsky married twice. Chaim had several children with his first wife. She died, and he subsequently married a widow whose first husband left her with at least one child and whose last name was Goldberg. According to the story, some of Chaim's children adopted the surname of Goldberg, while others did not. Marvin said that the family arrived in the United States under the surname Goldberg. Subsequent research found that, in fact, Esther Leah; her husband, whose name appeared as Menashe; and one child, Shaic, arrived in the United States in November 1898 under the surname Zidovetsky.[43] Shaic was less than a year old at the time of immigration. He probably became known as Julius, who was born in 1897. Menashe became Samuel. Interestingly, although Samuel's name is listed as Menasche on the ship's manifest, his Hebrew name was Moshe, at least as far as the family knew, although he was sometimes called "Sonda Moshe." Perhaps Sonda was a nickname for Menashe and his name was Menashe Moshe. Until birth or marriage records for him are found in Europe, this will not be proven. Although Esther and Samuel's daughter, Dora, born two years earlier, is not listed on the page of the ship manifest with them, the family story is that she traveled with them. It is possible that she is listed on another page, or even that she was not entered on the manifest. Although not a frequent occurrence, this did sometimes happen with young children. However, since Shaic is listed, it would be surprising if she was not.

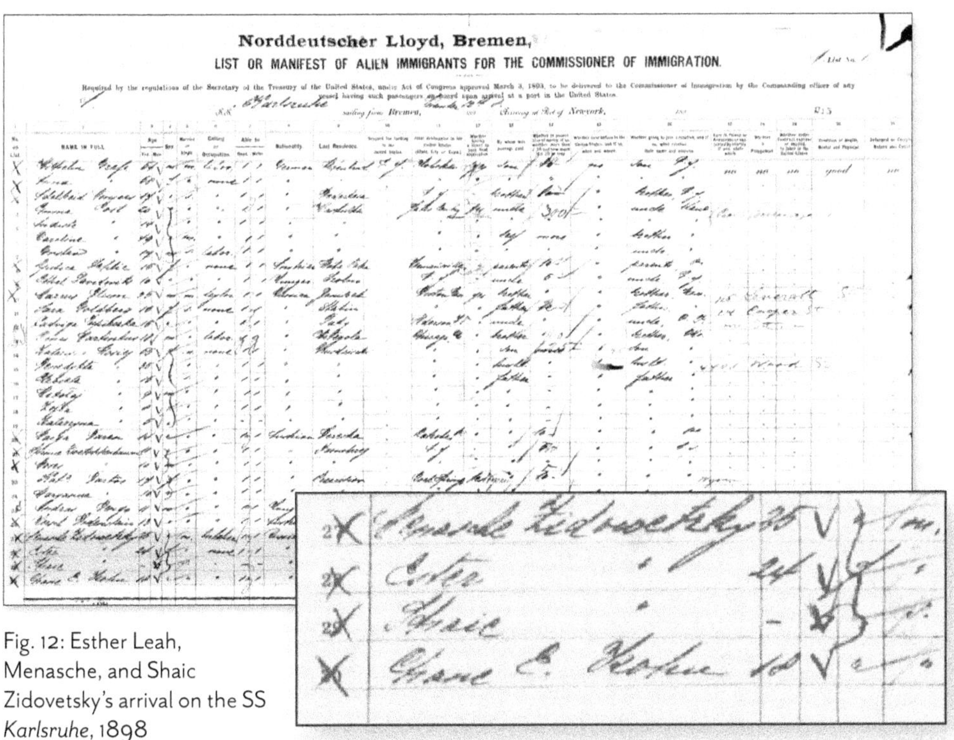

Fig. 12: Esther Leah, Menasche, and Shaic Zidovetsky's arrival on the SS *Karlsruhe*, 1898

The other theory Marvin thought might explain the name was that the surname was the mother's maiden name. This type of inherited name from the mother is not the same as what is known as a metronymic or matronymic surname. A matronymic surname is one derived from the mother's first name or names passed down in a family that originated with a female first name. Thus, matronymic surnames follow the same concept as patronymic names—names derived from a father's first name or from another male ancestor and passed down. Abramovitch and Yakovovna are examples of patronymics. Rakelovitch is an example of a matronymic surname. There is also a tradition of inheriting a surname through the mother's family, rather than the father's. One reason might be if the woman's family was more prestigious than the man's or if a man married into a family with no sons and was given a guarantee of an inheritance if he adopted the wife's family name. There are other possibilities. Chaim Freedman, in his extensive research into rabbinic dynasties, found other reasons for surname confusion. He wrote:

Siblings born to a mutual father often used different surnames from each other and from that borne by their parents. This practice was prevalent in the Tsarist Empire, and was a ploy used to confuse the military authorities. The notoriously anti-Semitic practices of the Tsarist army resulted in male Jews using this surname change as a means of evading conscription. Variation of surnames within the one family leads to confusion in genealogical research.[44]

It was not clear whether Hannah's maiden name was Goldberg or whether that predisposed her husband, Chaim Yitzchak Czidovetsky, and some of her children to choose the name. Maybe, as Marvin thought, the family just liked the name Goldberg. When Samuel Czidovetsky, one of Chaim's sons, came to the United States, he became Goldberg, as did many of his children. Samuel married Esther Leah Milonchik, one of Tzvi Hersch and Chaya Ruchel's children, in Europe. According to Marvin's records, Esther Leah was born in Skvira,[45] Russia, while Samuel was born in nearby Kiev. Their marriage and the births of four of their eight children took place in Skvira. The rest of their children were born in Brooklyn.

Tzvi Hersch himself, along with two of his sons, Charles and Max, arrived in New York at Ellis Island in 1896.[46] Tzvi Hersch's name appears on the manifest as Hershko. Charles, whose Yiddish name was Shmuel, and Max, whose Yiddish name was Mordecai, appeared on that manifest as Schmul and Mordke, respectively. Their surname was Molontzik on the manifest. Until Marvin mentioned Skvira, I had never heard of it, nor had my mother, Rhoda. She does not remember her grandfather Max Miller or any of the aunts and uncles who emigrated from Europe speaking of their childhood in Europe.

Kiev and its Environs

Skvira—in Yiddish, סקווירא—is in the Kiev oblast.[47] In his 2007 book, *Zhid: A Russian Odyssey*, Marvin Goldberg described twenty-first-century Skvira as "a nondescript, drab place with a cluster of small buildings including fences, barns, a tavern, a butcher shop, a bakery, a concrete plant, a general store, and a meeting hall." As he pointed out, the bustling early-twentieth-century Jewish community that once made Skvira its home is a shadow of its former self.[48] The prosperous Polish and later Tatar castle and surrounding villages that became Skvira were founded in the fifteenth century. Following the sixteenth-century destruction of the ancient city, it remained a wasteland for centuries. Skvira does not appear in records again until the early part of the eighteenth century, when it is recorded as a village held by a Jewish lessee![49] During the eighteenth and nineteenth centuries, most of the Jewish population was Ḥasidic. Their primary source of income came from the twice-weekly markets and sixteen annual fairs. The principal commodity sold at these markets and fairs was grain.[50]

Marvin Goldberg's ancestors Chaim Yitzchok Czidovetsky and his wife, Hannah, left Skvira sometime after 1850 and resettled in Romanovka in southeastern Ukraine[51] in the wake of a large migration of Jews moving to the Skvira area from Kiev.[52] Tsar Nicholas I established punitive laws regarding the conscription of Jewish boys as part of his attempt to eliminate Jewish life, and ultimately, the Jewish people. However, an exemption provided a way to escape forced military service. The government encouraged Jews to leave cities by exempting from conscription those who settled in agricultural villages.[53] As Jews left the major cities, like Kiev, small, sleepy villages turned into relatively large towns. According to Marvin, Hannah and Chaim Yitzchok did not want to live in a city with a large Jewish population, so they left! The reality may have been that once they left, they were not permitted to return.

The May Laws of 1882 were clear that, once a Jew left his village, he was not permitted to return to it but had to settle in a town.[54] Alexander III's adoption of the harsh May Laws of 1882 and its later refinements established many restrictions; however, they also permitted some privileges. Artisans were among those accorded privileges, as were honorably discharged soldiers and Russian university graduates. They were permitted to reside anywhere in Russia, not restricted to the Pale of Settlement. However, these privileges could also easily be revoked. "Artisans were not permitted to give a night's lodging to any non-privileged person, even a near relative. If an artisan died and his widow was not able to continue the trade, she and her children had to return to the Pale."[55] Perhaps some of the Czidovetsky family qualified under one of the privileged classifications to choose their place of residence.

By 1897, shortly after my great-great-grandparents left Skvira for America, the Jewish population numbered several thousand.[56] Marvin's ancestor Menashe Moishe, later known as Sam, was the son of Chaim Yitzchok Czidovetsky and his wife, Hannah. Sam married Esther Leah Milyontzik, the daughter of Tzvi Hersch and Chaya Ruchel, in 1890. Chaya Ruchel, later called Rose, was the daughter of Yetta Cohen and Joseph Portnoy. Marvin Goldberg's family notes indicate that she also went by the surname "Jitovsky." Jitovsky was likely Yetta's mother's surname and probably a corruption of Czidovetsky. Marvin's narrative clearly states that Chaya Ruchel arranged the marriage of her daughter, Esther Leah, to Sam Czidovetsky, the son of her first cousin, Chaim Yitzchok.[57] Marriage between first cousins was not uncommon in Jewish families. A British 1875 population study indicated that 7.5% of all English Jewish marriages were between first cousins, a figure that was three times greater than among the non-Jewish population.[58] In England, which had a much smaller Jewish population overall, first-cousin marriages may have occurred because there were not a lot of choices. In Eastern Europe, it is possible that these marriages were driven by a sense of familiarity, trust, and comfort—knowledge of the family of a child's spouse. Marvin referred to Esther Leah as Tzvi Hersch's youngest daughter,[59] but since records reveal that she had, in fact, been born in 1873, she was their oldest child. Her six siblings were all born between 1875 and 1888.

We know almost nothing of the earlier history of the Milyontzik family in Europe. We know that Abraham Jacob Milyontzik married a woman named Kraina Dora and they had at least five children. The name of the place where their children were born became garbled over time and we understood it as

Beletzerkoff, which turned out to be Bila Tserkva, a town located about 20 miles from Skvira. Just to keep things confusing, there is now a similarly pronounced location, Bila Cirkev, located in the Carpathian region of Ukraine. Bila Cirkev is located at 47º57'N, 23º55'E. The place of their birth almost certainly was near Skvira and Kyyiv. The Bila Cirkev in Carpathia is almost 350 miles from Kyyiv! In Russian, the city is pronounced "Bilaya Tserkov" and in Ukrainian, "Bila Tserkva." Like so many other cities in Ukraine, Bila Tserkva[60] is ancient. Founded in the eleventh century on the Ros River, it took several hundred years before the Jewish population grew large enough to attract notice. By the early seventeenth century, it was heavily populated by Jews. In the mid-1600s, six hundred Jewish families were murdered there in the Chmielnick, riots.[61]

Bogdan Chmielnicki was a Cossack leader of anti-Jewish Ukrainian groups in the mid-seventeenth century. He led a rebellion to establish an independent Ukraine that began in 1648.[62] He convinced the serfs that independence would bring relief from Polish overlords and their tax collectors, overseers, recruiting officers, the Jews, and the Jesuits, who also evoked religious hostility among Christian Orthodox Ukrainians.[63] Directed against the Polish rulers and those allied with them, such as the Jewish estate managers, the uprising destroyed hundreds of Jewish communities, and tens of thousands of Jews were murdered.[64] Jewish perseverance and insistence of survival in the face of all odds are at work here. Isaac Bashevis Singer described a town rebuilding itself after the massacre in his story *Satan in Goray*. Meyer Levin, in his review of that book, described the beginning of the restoration: "The isolated village of Goray[65] had been gutted. But after some years, the ancient rabbi returned from Lublin, and remnants of the population crept back, shops opened, and there was a quorum for the synagogue."[66] After the rabbi's return, a hierarchy and sense of order were reestablished. To accomplish that,

"[t]he [rabbi] began to supervise the observance of the laws of ritual diet, saw to it that the women went to the ritual bathhouse at the proper time, and that young men studied the Torah."[67] As unimaginable as the level of devastation must have been, the Jews of Eastern Europe did what Jews had been doing for millennia and would continue to do: recreate a community and attempt to feel safe. If my ancestors did not live in Singer's town of Goray, they certainly resided where the effects of Chmielnicki's Cossack mobs were felt. Somehow, Jews persevered and survived. Just as they did after the horrific devastation of the twentieth century, that remnant recreated itself and rebuilt the Jewish people.

Reconciling Conflicting Information

Since there were two demonstrable errors in the information supplied by Marvin—he indicated that Sam and Esther Leah had a child, Yetta, born in 1885 and that Abraham Jacob and Tzvi Hersch were brothers—we needed to consider that some of the other unconfirmed data from his family's stories might be suspect. If, as Marvin indicated, Sam was born in 1872 and Esther in 1873, they could not have had a child born in 1885.

Marvin had a very well-developed tree branch for many of the children of Sam and Esther Leah, but besides the birth date of 1885, it did not have any information about Yetta. I believe, but cannot prove, that Dora Etta, born in 1895, was identified as Yetta and a typo in her birthdate led Marvin to believe that she was born in 1885. In the 1910 census,[68] Esther Leah reported that she had given birth to eight children, six of whom were still living. These children were all still living at home in 1910: Etta D., age 14; Julius, age 11; Clara, age 8; Aron W., age 6; Rebecca, age 4, and Hannah, age 2. Hannah, born in 1907, grew up to marry David Katz. She and my grandmother (the granddaughter of Harris Millontzik), who was born a year earlier, became close friends and remained such throughout their lives.

Marvin thought that Tzvi Hersch and Abraham Jacob were siblings, not parent and child, and, as is easy to do, confused siblings and children by the same

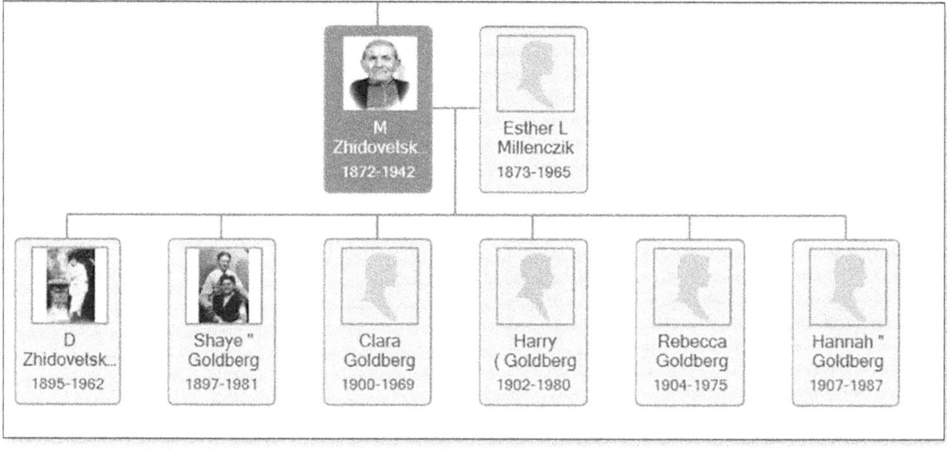

Fig. 13: Dora Etta, born 1895; Shaye, born 1897; Clara, born 1900; Harry, born 1902; Rebecca, born 1904; Hannah, born 1907

names. Tzvi Hersch had siblings named Esther, Anna, Samuel, and Nathan. His children were Esther Leah, Nathan, and Samuel.

It was obvious that the information needed to be verified. Initially, I believed that it would require significant research, possibly in European archives, to resolve the discrepancies. I reviewed the data, thinking that, since Anna and Esther had turned out to be Harris's sisters, perhaps Samuel and Nathan were his brothers. Abraham Jacob, who we thought was Harris's brother and the father of Samuel and Nathan, was Harris's father. The birthdates of Samuel and Nathan of 1874 and 1878, respectively, have now been verified through census and draft records. Abraham Jacob ostensibly was born about 1835, which meant he was about 40 years old at the time of Samuel's and Nathan's births. If Samuel and Nathan were Harris's brothers, an age difference of more than 20 years existed between Harris and them.

Typically, in large families that often had 12 or more children, births were spread out over a period of 20 or more years. Infant mortality rates were high, and it was a lucky family that saw more than half of their children survive into adulthood. It is probable that there are unidentified children born to Harris's

Fig. 14: Tzvi Hersch, his siblings, and their parents

Fig. 15: Tzvi Hersch, Chaya Rochel and their children

parents, since that would be the most logical explanation of the spread of ages between Harris's birth in 1853, his sister Anna's in 1856, and the births of their younger brothers in the 1870s.

Harris's father's birth did not occur before 1820, as we originally speculated. We had guessed that year based on the birth date of the person we thought to be Harris's older brother, Abraham Jacob, born about 1835. We now know that Abraham Jacob was Harris's father, not his brother. In Marvin's records, Abraham Jacob's wife was reported to be Katie Cohen. Our family knew Harris's mother as Dora. Could Dora and Katie Cohen be the same person? This is a possibility. Her name in Yiddish, according to some family records, was Kraina. It could conceivably have been Dvora Kraina or Kraina Dvora, or something similar. Some of the family could have referred to her as Dora and others as Katie. According to our records, neither Dora nor Katie left Europe, so the names we know were the names by which their American descendants referred to them. Harris's birth year was 1853, and it is conceivable that his father was born in 1835. This line of questioning Tznd research is ongoing. Based on this reasoning and speculation, I adjusted my records to include Samuel and Nathan as Harris's brothers. I noticed in other research that the first and middle names, which in American twenty-first-century culture are fixed as either first or middle, were often flexible and frequently interchanged in our ancestors' time. Harris's gravestone clearly showed that his father's name was Avraham Yakov. The gravestone's well-preserved lettering has the names spaced out oddly. At first glance, it might appear that Tzvi was the son of Avraham. It is only upon looking more closely and carefully that Avraham's second name, Ya'akov, becomes apparent.

Fig. 16: Grave marker of Tzvi Hersch (Harris Millonchick), son of Avraham Ya'akov[69]

The Family Saga: Tzvi Hersch in Europe

According to the 1910 United States Federal Census, 232 Hopkins Street in Brooklyn, New York, was a building with three apartments. The occupants of the three apartments are listed as Harris Mellon; his wife, Rosy; and their sons Nathan and Charles; Harry Mellon and his wife, Minnie, with their children Lottie, Abraham and Nettie; and Joe Mellon with his wife, Birdie, and son Leo. Harris's occupation was a "presser of pants," while Harry was an "operator" in the pants industry, as was Joe. Nathan was a "foreman in a pants shop," and Charles was an "inspector" of something called "bell lamps."[70] However, according to Marvin's book, 14 years earlier in 1896, Tzvi Hersch led a very different life in Europe. There, he was a butcher.

Marvin Goldberg remembered and told many stories of his grandparents and great-grandparents. Such stories were not handed down in my branch of the family, so I was glad to tap his memory. In *Zhid,* Marvin described Tzvi Hersch in 1896 Skvira. His tales took place that spring, a few months before Tzvi Hersch left Europe in July 1896 as Herschko Molontzik and a few years before the rest of the family emigrated.

When I asked Marvin what his sources were for his recreation of the life and activities of the family in Europe, Marvin told me he relied primarily on family stories. The stories and descriptions he related were fascinating—I had not heard any of them, nor had my mother or my aunts. Unfortunately, there is no one of that generation still alive who remembers life in Europe or who heard the stories from those who experienced the events who can confirm what Marvin remembered. Regretfully, there is no way of checking the information Marvin wrote, since it was unsourced. The descriptions that follow of the family's life in Europe are based on Marvin's writing.

Just like the butcher, Lazer Wolf, in *Fiddler on the Roof,* Tzvi Hersch was a man of substance, a very wealthy man who was well-known in his community and had contacts in Kiev outside the Jewish community because of his business. Mondays were his day to go to Kiev from his home in Skvira to inspect the cattle in the market and arrange to purchase the best he could find to stock his butcher shop. After he made his livestock purchases, he purchased other equipment and provisions and ended the day with a long drink of potato vodka, which he carried with him in a jug hidden under the buckboard.[71] According to Werner Wagon Works:

...[t]he Buckboard is a distinctively American-made vehicle, brought from the homesteads of Adirondack farmers and other eastern mountain regions. The Buckboard moved west with the pioneers to become a pleasure carriage in many parts of the U.S. The original vehicles were described as merely a seat attached to a springboard.[72]

It is possible that Wagon Works has their history wrong, but more likely, whoever told the story to Marvin used the word "buckboard," with which he might have been familiar, to describe a Russian wagon that looked like the American wagon.

Marvin's description of Tzvi Hersch's day included nailing the Yiddish newspaper he purchased in Kiev earlier that day to a pole on his return to Skvira. Tzvi Hersch purchased three copies—one to remain on the pole, one for himself, and one for the rebbe.[73] Tzvi Hersch, then, was literate. The picture Marvin drew is similar to that shown in the movie *Fiddler on the Roof* with the townspeople gathered around the rebbe, who would read them the latest news, which provided food for discussion and argument. After bringing the latest news to Skvira, Tzvi Hersch would stop at the tavern to deliver bottles of slivovitz,[74] kosher wine, schnapps, beer, and other distilled beverages. The assistant to the manager of that tavern was named Czidovetsky; this was Tzvi Hersch's daughter Esther Leah's husband, Sam. At one point, Sam's father had held the position of manager.[75]

Why was this particular spring of 1896 so important? Why did the memory of events that transpired remain so vivid that, three generations and an ocean later, the story was still being repeated? Because, according to Marvin's grandfather Sam, that was the last spring Tzvi Hersch spent in Skvira. Life changed very dramatically and very rapidly. He may have told and retold the story of his regularly scheduled activities to his children and grandchildren over the years. Perhaps they all heard the stories and only some of his children repeated them. Perhaps only some of his children heard or remembered the stories. Perhaps the reason that the story was handed down only in Marvin's family was that Tzvi Hersch made arrangements with his son-in-law to travel with Esther Leah and their children, and the rest of the family was not involved. If this story really had been handed down in the family, then Marvin heard it from someone other than Sam, who died when Marvin was 3, or Tzvi Hersch, who died before Marvin's birth. He may have heard it from his grandmother Esther Leah or from his father, Julius. The story may also have been greatly exaggerated in the telling. In Marvin's family, the story became important.

For me, the story takes on great significance because it is the only story that specifically suggests why part of the family left Europe. In all the other branches of my family, the memories are vague. There are stories of what happened in America and there are physical remnants of furniture, photos, and decorative objects obtained by the family after arrival. But I have no stories or objects that survived the crossing with the immigrants. Tzvi Hersch and his sons did arrive in the United States in 1896, but Esther Leah and her husband and children did not arrive until 1898.

Marvin related that, in the late spring of 1896, an order from the local constabulary to the *kahal*[76] demanded that one male representative of each family be ordered to report for active military duty.[77] Tzvi Hersch, as a local butcher, was singled out by name to report to army headquarters in Kiev for duty for an indefinite period. In this tale, Marvin speaks of a late spring snowstorm coinciding with the arrival of these orders and he also references subsequent events, including a family Passover gathering. That year, Passover began on April 20, according to the Gregorian calendar, which could have been as early as April 6 on the Julian calendar.[78]

According to the story,[79] Tzvi Hersch met with some influential people in Kiev during one of his regular weekly treks and made arrangements to obtain false papers so that he could leave the country and travel overseas. He also arranged for diamonds to be sewn into the lining of their clothing so they would have funds when they arrived at their destination.[80] Interestingly, emigration from Russia had become regulated just a few years earlier.

> *Emigration was not legally regulated in Russia until 1892, but everyone who wished to travel abroad was required to obtain permission from his hometown government and to obtain a travel passport from the local governor's office. Jews, most leaving illegally, migrated from the western provinces of the Russian Empire chiefly by railway to the German seaports of Bremen and Hamburg to board ships for America.*[81]

Marvin's story related that Tzvi Hersch was already engaged in international trade with some Christian partners. The rest of the story sounds like it came from a

James Bond or *Mission Impossible* movie. In the finest style of political intrigue and espionage, Marvin wrote:

You will not take with you or wear anything that will betray you as Jews. Not even a yarmulke, Bible, or prayer shawl. You will stay in your cabin as much as possible. Try to go on deck only at night and not together. When you reach your destination, two Gentile trading partners I have worked with for the last ten years will meet you. They will be wearing red carnations in their lapels, and I will arrange a secret word for them to say to you in German. They will take you directly to the customs house. Be careful not to talk to anyone else because the tsar's secret agents are everywhere, looking for Russian army deserters. Arrangements will be made with certain immigration agents, and you will be escorted directly from the customs house to the ship. I will not tell you the name of the ship or its final destination.[82]

Aubrey Newman, a former president of the Jewish Historical Society of England, asked whether the immigrants made a decision to leave and what routes were available to them. He asked whether the availability of transportation affected decisions and what information the emigrants had about their destination in advance—did they even know where the ship would leave them?[83]

In this case, at least, Sam was kept completely in the dark—all the decisions were taken out of his hands and, ultimately, Sam did not follow his father-in-law's plan. He and Esther Leah did not leave Europe until two years later. Sam apparently had many issues with his father-in-law, and perhaps at the heart of them was Sam's lifestyle, as evidenced by his modern dress and hairstyle in contrast to Tzvi Hersch's traditional clothing and style, by which he was easily identified as a Jew. A 1902 photograph of the Milyontzik family shows Sam and Esther Leah; he is the seated man in the front row on the right and Esther Leah stands next to him with her hand on his shoulder. I cannot tell whether the stories Marvin related are true or not. Marvin claimed to write his stories the way he remembered them. So, for Marvin, they were true. My assumption is that they had a kernel of truth at their heart. I do not believe that Marvin invented the stories, but like any good game of telephone or the construction of *midrash*, those kernels of truth were exaggerated and adapted to fill in gaps and perhaps even to impress the children.

Fig. 17: Milyontzik family photo, circa 1902; Seated in the front row (second and third adults from the left) are Tzvi Hersch and Chaya Ruchel, my great-grandparents. They are the parents of Max Miller,[84] who is in the Forman 1902 photo.

What we do know is that, if Tzvi Hersch had been a butcher in Europe, he very quickly became something else in the United States. On his ship manifest in 1896, his occupation was listed as "laborer."[85] In the various censuses in which he appeared in New York—1910,[86] 1920,[87] 1925,[88] and 1930[89]—his occupation is given as a "presser," sometimes in a "shop," sometimes of "pants," but clearly an occupation that had to do with the manufacturing of clothing.

A Family of Immigrants—From Europe to the United States

Because of transcription errors listing his first name as Herschdo, and the spelling of his surname on the manifests, finding the ship manifest documenting Tzvi Hersch's arrival in the United States was not easy. The search seemed like that proverbial needle in a haystack. There were few clues to follow. The 1910 census reported an immigration year of 1896. Although the census is not always a reliable source,[90] at least this provided a starting point. The 1910 census recorded that Chaya Ruchel immigrated in the same year, but I have been unable to find a ship manifest for her in any year. Perhaps the manifest did not survive, but more likely the name was transcribed incorrectly, and without looking through thousands of pages of ship manifests it may be impossible to identify her. I have also been unable to find any record of the family on the 1900 census. Besides the ship manifest on which Harris and his two sons appear, the earliest record I found of the family in New York is the 1910 census. Although many ship manifests indicated the last address or city of the emigrant, a contact in the country from which they traveled, and the name and address of and relationship to a person who was at their final destination, the manifest from the 25 July 1896 SS *Palatia* did not. Manifests after 1906 are required to include answers to the questions about destination and closest relative or friend in the country from which an immigrant came, but the information is lacking on earlier manifests.

The research into and searches for the ship manifests and census forms and other potential sources of information are continuous rather than one-time investigations. Ongoing digitization and transcription projects mean that unsuccessful searches must be repeated over time. It isn't only the ongoing digitization and transcriptions that require repeated searches. As new information is added to the family's history, previous searches have to be repeated to determine whether newly found clues identify previously overlooked documents. Sometimes this triggers someone's memory and a long-forgotten snippet of a story is remembered. Everything becomes a clue. Esther Leah; her husband, Moshe (or Menasche Moishe), who became Sam in New York; and their son Julius, who in Europe was known as Shaic, appear on a ship manifest. It records their names as Ester, Menasche, and Shaic Zidowetzky.[91] The transcription of Menasche's name had an error and appeared as "Henasche" and their city of origin was transcribed as "Kisa" rather than Kiev. Menasche gave his occupation as "butcher." Perhaps Marvin, in his retelling of the family story, confused the men about whom the stories were told. Although Marvin Goldberg said repeatedly that his father and grandparents came to the United States as "Goldberg," the ship's manifest clearly indicated the error of Marvin's claimed "fact."

Marvin had wonderful stories to share, and I learned important lessons through those stories. First, I learned the importance of speaking with people from all branches of the family to see what might be known in one branch but not passed down in another. Second, I learned the necessity of checking facts whenever possible. Although the documentation does not support many of the conclusions Marvin reached nor many of his stories, I do not discount the value of the oral tradition within the family. Oral traditions are often based on a kernel of documented proof and, although what grew up around that kernel may be far from the original event, it may provide clues to finding the event and also tell us something about the family or at least their surroundings. Comparing Marvin's story about Tzvi Hersch and his cattle-shopping to Sholom Aleichem's stories may bring us close to the truth about the family. Sadly, Marvin died in 2011, before I had a chance to go over my findings with him or discuss the inconsistencies between the documentation and his stories. I feel certain that we would have found more stories if we were able to work through the inconsistencies. After Marvin's death, I hoped his widow would share some of the photos he had or permit me to look through boxes of material. She agreed but moved shortly after his death, and then became ill and died a few years later.

Many of Sholom Aleichem's[92] stories were based in the area around Kiev, where the Milyontzik and Czitovetsky families lived. Sholom Aleichem's stories are considered to provide valuable insight into the lives of Jews in the late 1800s in Russia and the Pale of Settlement. Maybe the stories Marvin heard were not the exact family stories. Maybe some of them were modeled on the famous Yiddish stories written by Sholom Aleichem, or maybe the family experienced some of the same events and daily challenges Sholom Aleichem saw in the Jews who inhabited his world. So, I discount or, at the very least, amend those stories for which I find contradictory documentation. I accept the other stories until I find proof that these, too, should be discounted. Marvin, I believe, was less concerned with the absolute incontrovertible veracity of the stories than he was of relating the tales that his family passed down over three generations.

Finding Some Missing Links

Since the initial 2005 communication from Marvin Goldberg, many previously unknown descendants of the Milyontziks have been identified and I have been in communication with them. As we experienced with Marvin, part of the initial communication with a potential relative is discovering information about our common ancestor. In Marvin's case, we shared several ancestors. Max, who used the surname Miller in the United States, had six brothers and sisters who came to

Fig. 18: Avraham Yacov, Kraina, and their children

the United States. We do not know if there were additional siblings who remained in Europe. The 1910 census reported that Chaya-Rochel, Max and Esther's mother, had given birth to 12 children, six of whom were still living. My research found 7 of her children living in the United States! Esther Leah was Max's oldest sister. She was born in 1873 and Max in 1881, and there was at least one sibling born between the two. My mother, Rhoda, knew of Esther Leah. Esther Leah and Sam Goldberg's youngest child, Hannah, born in New York in 1907 and known as Chansel, was one of my grandmother Sylvia's favorite cousins. My mother knew Chansel and her husband, Dave Katz, as did I, and my mother also knew at least one of Chansel and Dave's four children, Nancy.

Marvin made the first connection with the descendants of another Esther Millonchick, whom we originally thought was a descendant of Tzvi Hersch's brother, Abraham. As discussed earlier, Tzvi Hersch did not have a brother named Abraham, and we realized that Abraham and his wife, Katie Cohen, from Bila Tserkva were Tzvi Hersch's parents, and the people identified as their children were Tzvi Hersch's siblings, not his cousins. Tzvi Hersch's sister Esther, identified in Tzvi Hersch's will, remained in Bila Tserkva. She married Joseph Bass and they had six children, about whom we know almost nothing, except for one daughter, Bertha, born in 1901.

Bertha's 1913 arrival in the U.S. eluded me. No matter how many ship manifests I looked at I could not locate her. Then, when I had just about given up, I found her 1941 Declaration of Intention. In it, she reported that she arrived on 23 August 1913, on the SS *Cedric* from Liverpool under the name Broche Boss! On the manifest, she identified her father as Jossel Boss and her destination was her uncle Sam Millon at 498 Marcy Avenue, Brooklyn. Sam was Bertha's uncle—her mother was his sister. Sam had lived at that address on Marcy Avenue since at least 1910 when he was enumerated there with his wife Sarah and their four oldest children. In 1920, Bertha married Harry Omansky in New York and they moved to Baltimore, where they lived out their lives and raised their two children. Harry Omansky, born in 1892, arrived in the United States with his parents, Joseph and Sophia Omansky. By 1910, they were living in Baltimore, Maryland. Harry and Bertha's daughter, Selma, married Morton Braiterman and they, in turn, had four children. Stuart, the second of those four children, and Marvin discovered each other. I was in contact with Stuart, thanks to Marvin's connection with him. In 1991, Stuart sent Marvin a printed family tree that Marvin shared with me in 2007. The confusion identifying Abraham, Tzvi Hersch's father, as his brother originated with that tree. On it, Stuart had marked an unidentified brother whom Marvin named "Abraham." Stuart had listed, correctly, the names of all of Abraham's children, with the exception of Tzvi Hersch, who was, as I said, listed as Abraham's brother. Until 2012, we accepted this information as correct. A discussion of what occurred that led us to untangle these relationships is shared below.

Fig. 19: The Bertha Bass and Harry Omansky family

Harris's children took the surnames of Miller, Mellin, and Millen. His sisters kept the surname of Millonchik until they married, but his brothers both took the name Melin. Although we may think of surnames as fixed, Harris and his siblings did not – their first names and their surnames changed over time. Occasionally it was only a spelling that changed, but sometimes the name was not recognizable from one document to another. I am sure that there are many documents I have not yet found because of this.

The internet and the means it offers for people to connect have proven to be an invaluable resource facilitating the ability to exchange information. The information Marvin sent me paved the way for connections with the descendants of Harris's other siblings. His sister Anna married Max Uliss in Europe and, according to the 1910 United States Federal Census, emigrated from Europe with their seven children in 1906. Their daughter, Shaindel—called Jenny in America—married Samuel Carpiloff. Jenny and Samuel's granddaughter Ellen Smithberg and I discovered our connection through an online resource. She and I spoke via phone, email, and social media, and first met in-person in New York in 2011.

Early in 2011, I submitted a message to the *JewishGen* discussion group, looking for information about Samuel Mellin's naturalization. One of Tzvi

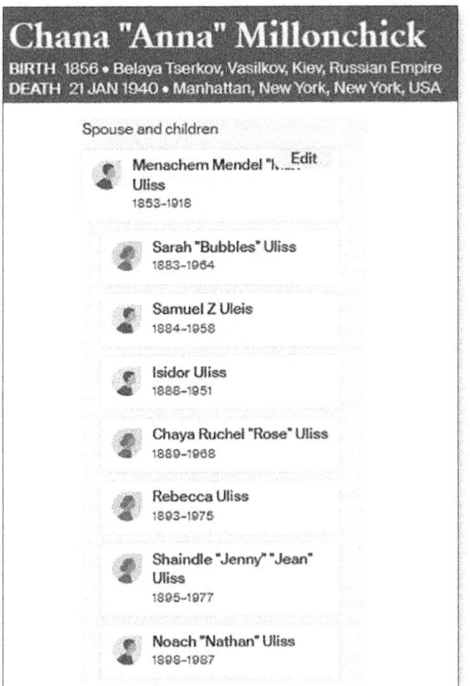

Fig. 20: The Anna Millonchick and Max Uliss family

Hersch and Rose's children was named Samuel, but I was pretty sure he had chosen the surname of Miller, not Mellin. Tzvi Hersch also had a brother named Samuel. I was pretty sure that he took the surname of Mellin. About six months after my initial inquiry, I got an email from someone named Sam Melin! The person whose naturalization I was asking questions about turned out to be his grandfather, Samuel Melin. This was the same Sam Mellin that Bertha Bass named as her destination when she arrived in New York in 1913. Samuel Melin married Sarah Borofsky and they had five children, all born in New York. Their son, Arthur, married Miriam, and it was Arthur and Miriam's son Sam who got in touch with me. Sam was the grandson of Samuel Melin. He and Ellen, the great-granddaughter of Samuel's sister, Anna, did not know of each other. They have since been in touch with each other. Sam told me that his aunt Annie Mellin Wilder Castrol, born in 1916, lived in Connecticut. I knew of Annie because Stuart included notes about her on the family tree he sent to Marvin. Some of those notes included quoted conversations with Annie as anecdotal documentation for some family facts. Sam put me in touch with Annie's daughter Gail. I was fortunate to have exchanged emails with both Gail and Annie. Annie died in 2014.

Due to the accessibility of online family trees through *Ancestry.com*, I also had the opportunity in 2011 to "meet" Forman relatives and reconnect with members of

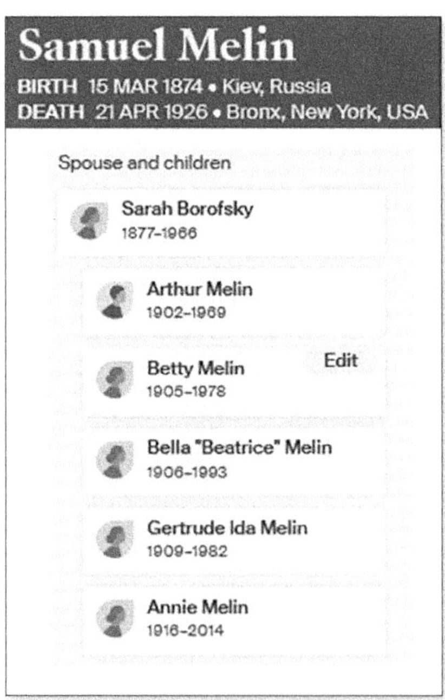

Fig. 21: The Samuel Melin and Sarah Borofsky family

the Forman family whom I had not seen in decades. Levi Selig and Esther, as I said, had five children. One of them was Louis. One day, I found Louis's branch of the family on an *Ancestry.com* public member tree.

The person to whom the tree belonged did not have a familiar name, and I did not know anyone on Louis's branch personally. I had their names and some vital statistics, and I remembered stories my grandmother Sylvia used to tell about her cousin Sylvia, Louis's daughter. I contacted the person to whom the tree belonged via email and quickly received an answer. In the email, I asked how she connected to the tree, and she replied that it was by marriage only but told me where she intersected the tree. She also shared the email message with the people to whom her husband was related. I heard back from one of them, Samuela—Sylvia's daughter—who said she did not know me but perhaps her cousin Leonard did. Leonard's grandfather Isador was another of Levi S. and Esther's children! Although I had not seen Leonard since childhood, we grew up down the street from one another, and I often saw his parents at family celebrations. I met Leonard and his wife, Barbara, in New York in July 2011. When I related the email conversation with Samuela to my mother, she commented that she remembered when Samuela was born.

The intricacies of family relationships are fascinating. In Europe, when families maintained close contact with each other, even as they moved to other towns and cities for purposes of marriage or business, they kept careful track of who

Fig. 22: The Louis Forman and Naomi Rose Naboshek family

was related to whom and to what degree. Sholom Aleichem wrote about family connections in one of his stories. In "The Bubble Bursts," a stranger who has a familiar appearance calls Tevye, the main character of the story, by name. Tevye asks the man where he comes from and the man answers

> 'I am a relative of yours.' That is, your wife, Golde, is my second cousin once removed. 'Hold on!' I say. 'Aren't you Boruch-Hersh Leah-Dvoshe's son-in-law?' 'You've hit the nail right on the head,' he says. 'I am Boruch-Hersh Leah-Devoshe's son-in-law, and my wife is Sheina Sheindel, Boruch-Hersh Leah-Dvoshe's daughter. Now do you know who I am?' 'Wait,' I say. 'Your mother-in-law's grandmother Sarah-Yenta and my wife's aunt, Fruma-Zlata, were, I believe first cousins, and if I am not mistaken you are the middle son-in-law of Boruch-Hersh Leah-Dvoshe's.'[93]

Although Sholom Aleichem's story was humorous and perhaps not just a little touched with cynicism, I mention it here as an example of the importance that maintaining familial connections had in Europe. The United States is much larger than Ukraine, and its cities and towns have populations many thousands of times larger than the small villages from which my ancestors came. In this country, the family spread out. We are literally all over, from New York to California, from Washington State to Florida, and every point in between. There are Forman and Millonchick descendants still living in New York City as they did when the family arrived more than a hundred years ago. Some of their descendants live within a mile of where our ancestors first settled.

When several Jews find themselves together, they inevitably engage in a game of "Jewish geography." A mid-1990s film, *Six Degrees of Separation*, popularly advanced the theory that all people are six or fewer social connections away from each other. The film was based on a book about the life of a con artist, but the idea of connectivity proved popular. Jews have long recognized the importance of maintaining ties with extended family. There is even a word in Yiddish, *machetanem*, which has no English equivalent but means the in-laws of a person's child. Through language, we form relationships and connections. Just like in Sholom Aleichem's story above, Jews often find themselves in situations where "Jewish geography" assists in establishing interpersonal connections. Although this adventure of finding my family seems endless, each new contact is exciting. Everyone I speak with fills in more details of family life in Europe and the United States.

Where There is a Will, There is a Way

Several years ago, a search at the Brooklyn, New York, courthouse uncovered Tzvi Hersch's will and probate[94] documents. These ultimately proved the identity of his siblings and children and was key in disentangling the misinformation about Tzvi Hersch's siblings and father. When I was walking around Brooklyn one day and thinking of apartments owned by my Forman and Millonchick ancestors, a thought occurred to me about records previously unexplored. I had never considered wills or probate files as a resource for my family's records. I asked Allan Jordan, a genealogist based in New York, to look up the family in the probate records held at the Brooklyn Courthouse. Today, many probate records are available digitally on *Ancestry.com*, but that was not the case at the time.

From the probate documents, it appeared that Tzvi Hersch used more than just the names that we found on the ship manifest, death certificate, and gravestone. Harris apparently used a long list of pseudonyms: Harris Melon, Harris Mellon, Hershel Miller, Harris Miller, Herschel Millen, and Hershel Milianchik! These documents also straightened out family connections and led to additional analysis of the information at hand. Two women, Esther and Anna, previously thought to be Tzvi Hersch's nieces—that is, the daughters of a brother Abraham—turned out to be his sisters. There was no brother Abraham. We had misinterpreted his gravestone and other documents and thought his father was Jacob and that he had a brother named Abraham Jacob, not realizing that his father's name was Abraham Jacob. His will provided not only the names of his beneficiaries but also their relationships to him and their addresses. One sister, Esther, remained in Europe. A document in Russian with an English translation certified that Esther Yakovelevna Bass was the sister of Harris Mellon.

Harris also included in his will the names of his children who had predeceased him and the number of children each of them had. The names of those grandchildren were all mentioned in the probate documents. Information in the will and probate documents cleared up errors about Harris's children and his grandchildren; after all, Harris knew this information firsthand, as did his son Max,

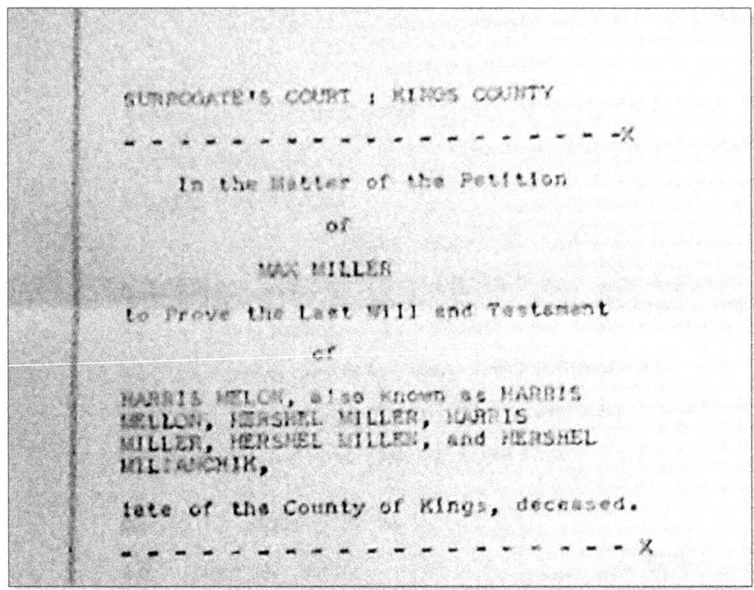

Fig. 23: Tzvi Hersch's aliases[95]

who was his executor. We now knew without question that Harris and Rose had seven children: Esther Leah, Harry, Nathan, Joseph, Charles, Sam, and Max. As mentioned above, the 1910 census reported that Chaya Ruchel (Rose) had given birth to 12 children, six of whom were still living. Although seven have now been identified, all living in 1910, it has not been proven that more children were born before the family emigrated and perhaps did not survive.

Harry married Mina and they had four children: Abraham, Lottie, Nettie, and Sarah. Harry died in 1930. Harris's will stated that his son Harry predeceased Harris and had four children. These were mentioned by name in the probate document. Nettie died before 1942. Because Nettie was included in the will and named in the probate document, we know that she died after Harris's death in 1934.

Nathan, who also predeceased Harris, married Rebecca, and the will included their three children, also named in the probate document: Murray, Sam, and Max. My records indicated that Nathan and Rebecca had four children, but it is likely that the fourth died in childhood.

Research and the discovery of information are never-ending. Thanks to DNA matches and social media, I have connected with someone from each branch of the families of Tzvi Hersch's siblings and his children. I cannot imagine accomplishing these connections in years gone by. When I queried my mother or

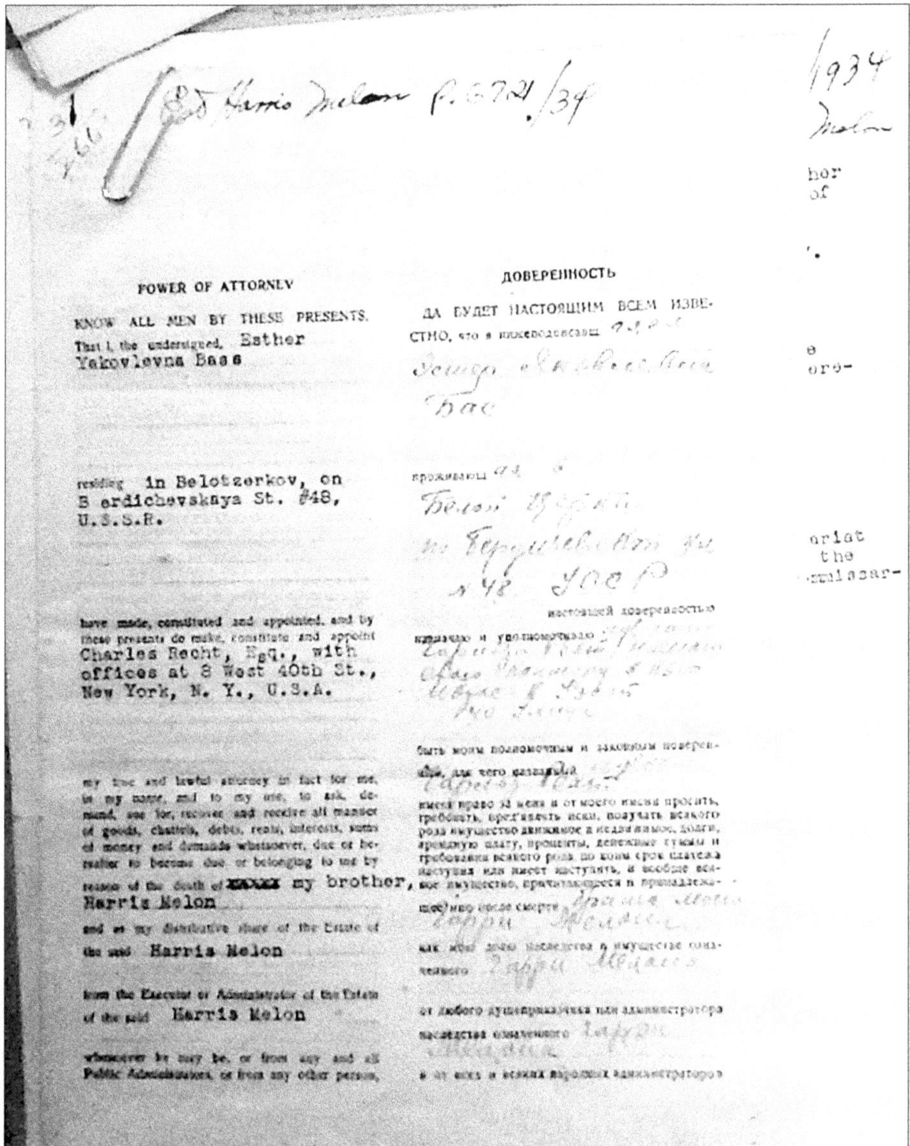

Fig. 24: Esther Bass's affidavit of relationship[96]

her sisters about people in their extended families, I find myself mentioning names unfamiliar to them, for the most part. Every once in a while, however, there is some recognition, and after thinking for a short bit, one of them retrieves a story they heard long ago or a memory of something they haven't thought about for perhaps 70 years or longer. This research not only satisfies a need in me to identify family but provides a mechanism to connect with my own parents, siblings, aunts, uncles, and cousins by sharing these stories. It also does something else—provides a bridge to give to my own children, Arielle Silver and Efrem Weiss, to connect them to their history.

According to the will, Harris's son Sam had two children. Clara and Jennie are named in the probate document, which referred to Jennie with the surname of Cohen. That most likely meant that Jennie had married. According to the document, Jennie and her sister Clara lived at 435 Herzl Street in Brooklyn, New York. If she still lived at that address in 1940, she, along with her husband and any children they might have had, should have appeared in the pages of the 1940 census.[97][98,] To find the address on the census, I did several things. First, using Google Maps,[99] I located the street address.

Then, I went to the Steve Morse One-Step tool, which has an address-to-enumeration district converter. I entered the address and the cross streets of

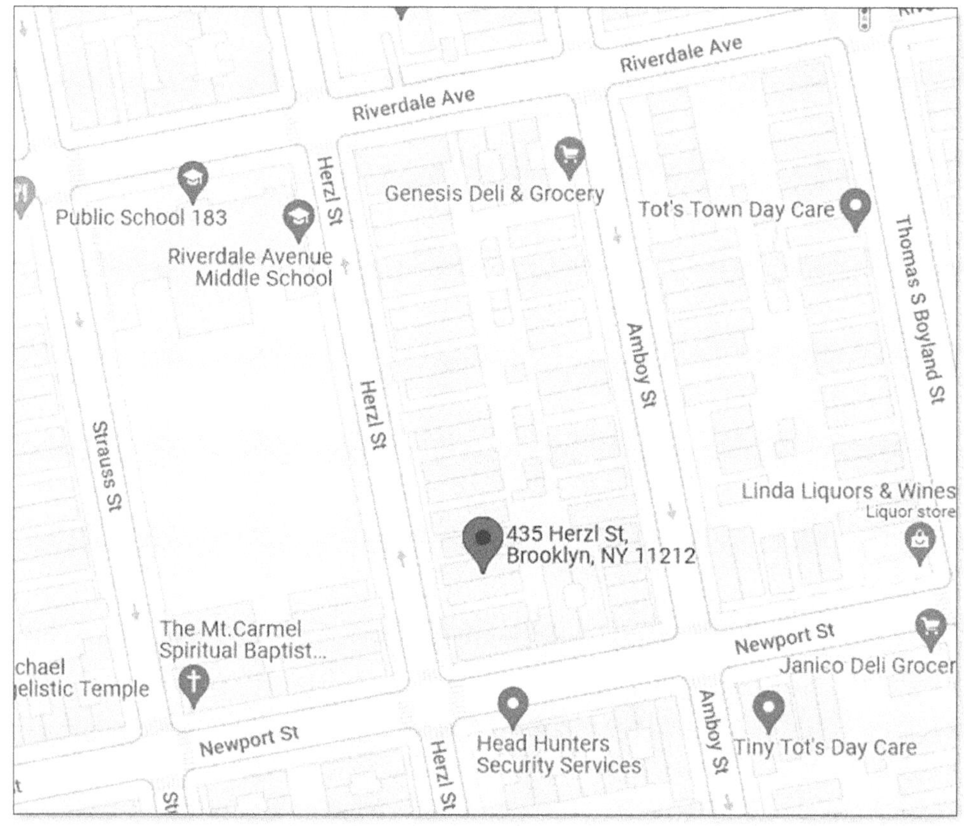

Fig. 25: Address of Jennie and Clara according to Harris's will

Riverdale Avenue and Newport Street. These details matched with Enumeration District 24-2178. Going to the enumeration district through a link on the Steve Morse One-Step tool brought me to the 35 pages of that enumeration district to the census on *Ancestry.com*. On page 12, I located 435 Herzl Street. Four families were listed at the address. None of the four families—Kravitz, Wolf, Groff, or Wosker—included anyone with the first names of Jennie or Clara. I continued perusing the balance of the pages of the enumeration district, paying close attention to the families on Amboy Street in addition to those on Herzl, since the family owned property on Amboy Street. I did not find anyone who matched Sam Miller's daughters. Then, I looked for the 1930 census enumeration district, which I located at Enumeration District 24-796. Armed with that information, I went to *Ancestry.com* and, through the card catalog, found the 1930 U.S. Federal Census. I put the state, county, and city names in the search criteria and opened the 1930 census for that enumeration district.[100] There were 29 pages. I found the address easily enough on page 11 but still could not locate the sisters.

Finding the probate records gave us more insight into the aliases by which Harris was known, and thus, other names to use in our searches for him and the family. The probate records also included aliases by which some of his children and grandchildren were known. We found the New York State 1925 census[101] showing Harris and Rose Millon as occupants of a Hopkins Avenue address in Brooklyn, New York. In the 1910 census,[102] they are listed as Harris and Rosy Mellon; in 1920,[103] as Harry and Rose Millin; and in 1930,[104] as Harry and Rose Mellon. Some of the differences in spelling could be due to the enumerator's understanding of the name, considering the accents of the respondents, but given the probate record, it is probable that the enumerator understood exactly what s/he was told. From 1910 until 1930, they lived at 232 Hopkins Street in Brooklyn. At the time of Harris's death in 1934, he lived at 137 Bristol Street in Brooklyn.[105] At Rose's death, two years earlier, they still lived at the address on Hopkins Street.[106] Max's brother-in-law Sam Goldberg owned the Bristol Street Building and lived there in 1930.[107]

To date, the family has not been identified in a 1900 U.S. Federal Census or 1905 New York State Census. Because of the changes in surname, it is difficult to identify the family clearly. More research is needed to find census records for Harris and Rose, marriage records for some of their children in the United States, and birth records for their grandchildren.

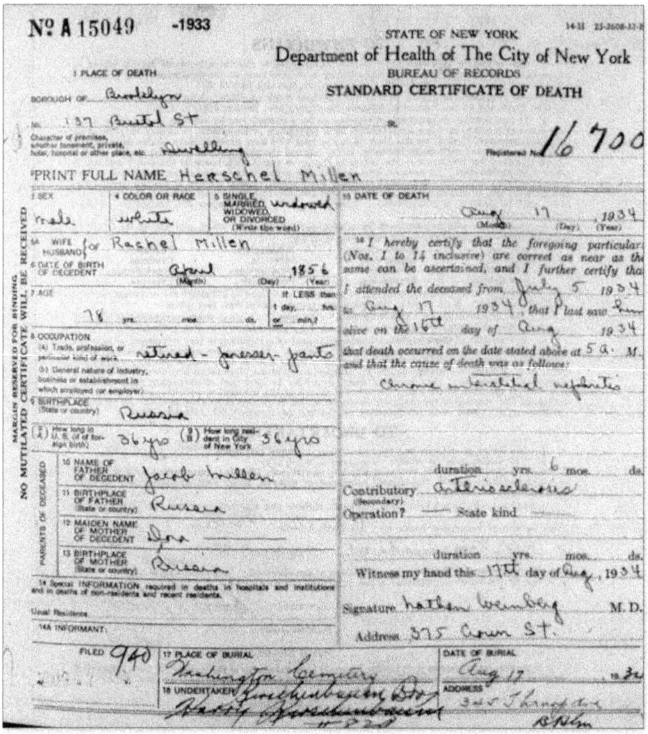

Nº A 15049 -1933

STATE OF NEW YORK

Department of Health of The City of New York

BUREAU OF RECORDS

STANDARD CERTIFICATE OF DEATH

1 PLACE OF DEATH

BOROUGH OF Brooklyn

No. 137 Bristol St St.

Character of premises, whether tenement, private, hotel, hospital or other place, etc. Dwelling

Registered No. 16700

2 PRINT FULL NAME Herschel Millen

3 SEX male | 4 COLOR OR RACE white | 5 SINGLE, MARRIED, WIDOWED, OR DIVORCED (Write the word) widowed

5A WIFE or HUSBAND of Rachel Millen

6 DATE OF BIRTH OF DECEDENT April 1856 (Month) (Day) (Year)

7 AGE 78 yrs. mos. ds. If LESS than 1 day, hrs. or min.?

8 OCCUPATION (a) Trade, profession, or particular kind of work retired - presser - pants

(b) General nature of industry, business or establishment in which employed (or employer)

9 BIRTHPLACE (State or country) Russia

(A) How long in U.S. (if of foreign birth) 36 yrs (B) How long resident in City of New York 36 yrs

PARENTS OF DECEASED

10 NAME OF FATHER OF DECEDENT Jacob Millen

11 BIRTHPLACE OF FATHER (State or country) Russia

12 MAIDEN NAME OF MOTHER OF DECEDENT Dora

13 BIRTHPLACE OF MOTHER (State or country) Russia

14 Special INFORMATION required in deaths in hospitals and institutions and in deaths of non-residents and recent residents.

Usual Residence.

14A INFORMANT:

15 DATE OF DEATH Aug 17, 1934 (Month) (Day) (Year)

16 I hereby certify that the foregoing particulars (Nos. 1 to 14 inclusive) are correct as near as the same can be ascertained, and I further certify that I attended the deceased from July 5 1934 to Aug 17 1934, that I last saw him alive on the 16th day of Aug 1934 that death occurred on the date stated above at 5 a. M. and that the cause of death was as follows:

Chronic interstitial nephritis

duration yrs. 6 mos. ds.

Contributory (Secondary) Arteriosclerosis

Operation? —— State kind

duration yrs. mos. ds.

Witness my hand this 17th day of Aug, 1934

Signature Nathan Weinberg M.D.

Address 375 Crown St.

MARGIN RESERVED FOR BINDING. NO MUTILATED CERTIFICATE WILL BE RECEIVED

FILED 940 | 17 PLACE OF BURIAL Washington Cemetery | DATE OF BURIAL Aug 17 1934

18 UNDERTAKER Kirschenbaum Bros | ADDRESS 345 Throop Ave

Harry Kirschenbaum | Bklyn

Above: Fig. 26: Herschel "Harris" Millen's death certificate[108]

Fig. 27: Rose Mellon's death certificate[109]

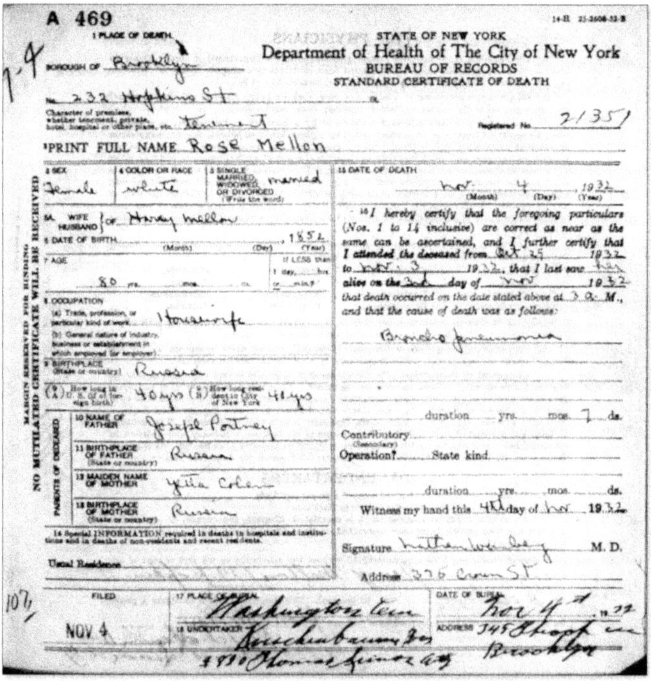

A 469

STATE OF NEW YORK

Department of Health of The City of New York

BUREAU OF RECORDS

STANDARD CERTIFICATE OF DEATH

1 PLACE OF DEATH

BOROUGH OF Brooklyn

No. 232 Hopkins St St.

Character of premises, whether tenement, private, hotel, hospital or other place, etc. Tenement

Registered No. 21351

2 PRINT FULL NAME Rose Mellon

3 SEX female | 4 COLOR OR RACE white | 5 SINGLE, MARRIED, WIDOWED, OR DIVORCED (Write the word) married

5A WIFE or HUSBAND of Harry Mellon

6 DATE OF BIRTH (Month) (Day) 1852 (Year)

7 AGE 80 yrs. mos. ds. If LESS than 1 day, hrs. or min.?

8 OCCUPATION (a) Trade, profession, or particular kind of work Housewife

(b) General nature of industry, business or establishment in which employed (or employer)

9 BIRTHPLACE (State or country) Russia

(A) How long in U.S. (if of foreign birth) 40 yrs (B) How long resident in City of New York 41 yrs

PARENTS OF DECEASED

10 NAME OF FATHER Joseph Portney

11 BIRTHPLACE OF FATHER (State or country) Russia

12 MAIDEN NAME OF MOTHER Yetta Cohen

13 BIRTHPLACE OF MOTHER (State or country) Russia

14 Special INFORMATION required in deaths in hospitals and institutions and in deaths of non-residents and recent residents.

Usual Residence

15 DATE OF DEATH Nov. 4, 1932 (Month) (Day) (Year)

16 I hereby certify that the foregoing particulars (Nos. 1 to 14 inclusive) are correct as near as the same can be ascertained, and I further certify that I attended the deceased from Oct 29 1932 to Nov. 3 1932, that I last saw her alive on the 3rd day of Nov 1932 that death occurred on the date stated above at 3 a. M., and that the cause of death was as follows:

Broncho pneumonia

duration yrs. mos. 7 ds.

Contributory (Secondary)

Operation? State kind

duration yrs. mos. ds.

Witness my hand this 4th day of Nov 1932

Signature Nathan Weinberg M.D.

Address 375 Crown St

MARGIN RESERVED FOR BINDING. NO MUTILATED CERTIFICATE WILL BE RECEIVED

FILED NOV 4 | 17 PLACE OF BURIAL Washington Cem | DATE OF BURIAL Nov 4th 1932

18 UNDERTAKER Kirschenbaum Bros | ADDRESS 345 Throop Ave Brooklyn

Probate and Wills as Research Tools

Ancestry.com offers insight about research techniques, suggesting that:

...[c]ourt, land, and probate records are an often overlooked but important part of genealogical research. For example, court cases can often involve dozens of litigants and defendants, many of whom may be related. Land records, such as deeds, are among the most important documents available for tying a specific person to a specific place; especially in those cases where time, place, and circumstances have made vital records difficult to research. Probate records can supply interesting details, such as the total value of estates and lists of surviving family members. ... These types of records can help you locate ancestors' residences, determine occupations, find financial information, establish citizenship status, or clarify relationships between people...[110]

Probate court records may or may not contain a will, depending on whether the decedent executed a will. If the executor of the estate filed the will as part of the probate court records, the clauses in that will can provide useful information. Luckily for us, the wills of both Levi S. Forman and Tzvi Hersch Milontzik are part of the probate records.

Kurenitz:[111] The Name of Still Another Town

Levi S. Forman's will named as beneficiaries several Jewish organizations whose addresses were in Europe. One beneficiary, *Talmud Torah of Kurenitz,* puzzled us. A few details of the school and its pupils appeared in a letter from an official at the school to Levi's widow in 1936. Among other information, the letter stated that the Kurenitz Talmud Torah housed and schooled 40 orphans. Reading further into the file, I came across a document with a message that was very sad and troubling. It was a 1950 petition to the Surrogate Court of New York in the matter of funds disbursed from Levi S. Forman's estate. The document indicated that further payment to the Talmud Torah in Kurenitz, Russia, could not be made because of the destruction of that institution in World War II. There was one other legatee from Europe, Menachem Mendel Shulman of Naiko, Russia, who remains a mystery. I have been unable to locate a place called Naiko in Russia or in territory once held by Russia. Perhaps Menachem Mendel Shulman originally lived in Kurenitz—there are several people mentioned in a *Yizkor book*[112] from Kurenitz.[113]

One of the many misunderstandings held about our ancestors' lives in Europe involves their ability to relocate. Then, as now, people relocated for many reasons. Often, genealogists searching for records of their Jewish families in Europe insist on only looking in one place for evidence that their family lived there. My research showed the error of that assumption. We instruct our students in genealogy classes to suspend belief. Just because a name appears with one spelling somewhere does not mean it will appear in all records in that form. So, too, birth dates and years appear unclear, as do places where our ancestors may have lived. The name of the town, village, or city in which our ancestors lived may not appear on many written records, but the name of the place became part of the stories they told. The name might have been distorted by an accent, by the language in which they knew the name, or by the particular way it was referred to by its inhabitants. Cities were known by different names in

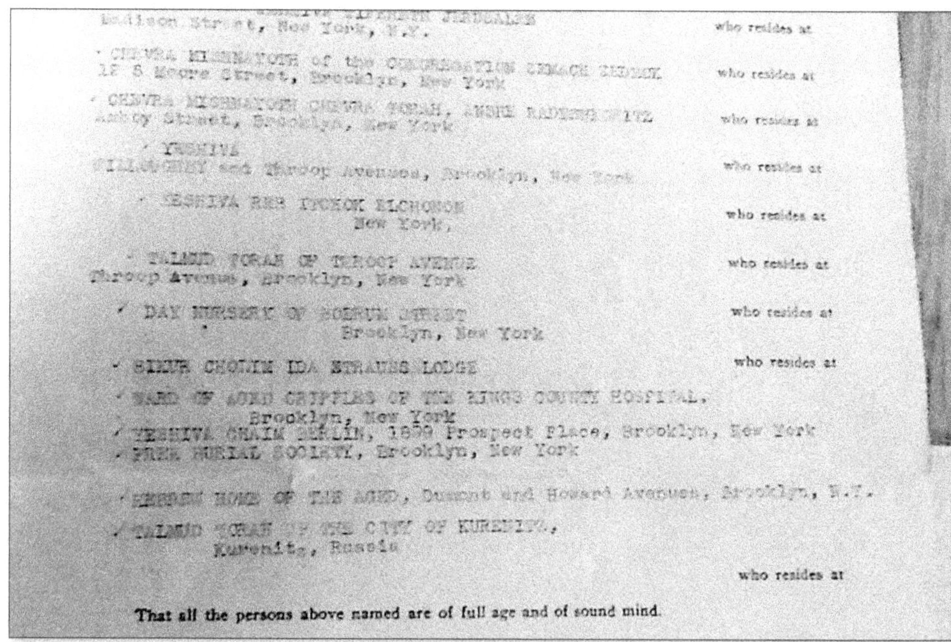

Fig. 28: Beneficiaries listed in Levi S. Forman's will[114]

June 25, 1936

To the same charitable lady
Father Forman
Max Miller
Sarah Miller

No address

It is a long time that we did not write to you, and we did not receive any letter from you because there was nothing to write.

Now we are able to write to you that your Talmud Torah is in the same frame as it has been managed when your husband and father, God bless his soul, lived. There are forty children, poor orphans, and two instructors teaching them God's learning, as it was wished of the great philanthropist, God bless his soul. Father and husband, he shall be in heaven; that during his life planted in the town of Kurnits, an institution where forty Jewish children are learning the great holy enterprise being undertaken. His wife shall live long with his kindhearted children who are watching to take care and help our Talmud Torah, place of learning. That the Talmud Torah excels them all.

Fig. 29: Portion of 1936 letter from Talmud Torah school in Kurenitz[115]

different languages. Today's city Lviv in Ukraine was known as Lwów in Polish, L'vov in Russian, and Lemberg in German.

Until we found the Talmud Torah beneficiary in Levi S. Forman's will, I had never heard of Kurenitz. I did not know if the Formans lived there or whether they had a relationship with the school beyond one of philanthropy. Kurenitz today is Kurenets, Belarus. Like so many other Eastern European cities, it had an ever-changing border. When Levi S. emigrated from Europe, the area was Kurenets, Vilejka District, Vilna Province, Russian Empire. When he died, it was Kuraniec, Wilejka County, Wilno Voivodeship, Poland.[116] Obviously the *shtetl* and Vilejka did not move, and yet politics made it difficult to locate. The clue of a connection to Kurenitz was my discovery that it was in Vilejka District, the place Sylvia told me her family was from. Up until that point, I had not looked for the death record of Levi S.'s wife, Esther. I had heard stories about her from my mother and my aunts. They remembered her and knew where she lived and died. We knew where she was buried. It had just not occurred to me to look for other documentation. As soon as I read her death certificate, I understood the connection to Kurenitz.[117] That was her birthplace. She was born about 1849 and died 4 November 1943. She lived in New York for 50 years, and at the address at which she died, 467 Kosciusko Street, for 25 years. Her father was Abraham Dinerstein and her mother was Sarah, maiden name unknown. Ida Roth, her youngest daughter, was the informant, and the physician who signed the certificate was Dr. Harry Gruber, the family's doctor for many years. She was buried at Washington Cemetery on 5 November 1943.

By the time the Kurenitz *Yizkor* book was written in 1956, both Esther and Levi were long gone, and they and their children had left Europe more than 60 years earlier. Although there are people mentioned in the book with the Dinerstein and Forman surnames, the family has no memory of siblings of either of them or any other information besides the names of their parents—Eliyahu, Charna, Abraham, and Sarah. Most of the records from Kurenitz have been indexed, and although I searched through them, I cannot identify any of the people in those records. I spoke directly with the archivists, in Lithuania and Belarus, who reported that they were unable to find any records pertaining to Levi's and Esther's ancestors or to their marriage and the births of their children. Levi's will included a list of beneficiaries, but the only relatives listed were his wife and children. If Esther left a will, it has not been found.

The legacy of *Yizkor* books is that researchers today can uncover information about cities destroyed during World War II and people murdered during the Holocaust.

Yizkor (Memorial) Books are some of the best sources for learning about Jewish communities in Eastern and Central Europe. Groups of former residents, or landsmanshaftn, have published these books as a tribute to their former homes and the people who were murdered during the Holocaust. The majority of these books were written in Hebrew or Yiddish, languages that many contemporary genealogists cannot read or understand. Yizkor books were written after the Holocaust as memorials to Jewish communities destroyed in the Holocaust. They were usually put together by survivors from those communities and contain descriptions and histories of the community, biographies of prominent people, lists of people who perished, etc. They are often embellished with photos, maps, and other memorabilia. Yizkor books are valuable to genealogists, since the books may include biographies or photographs of relatives, or may include family members in a list of people who perished. Yizkor books also give important background information about the history and Jewish life in a particular community.[118]

JewishGen is an important resource for *Yizkor* books and their translations. Many *Yizkor* books can be found at the *Dorot Jewish Division* of the main branch of the New York Public Library on 42nd Street.[119] Another wonderful resource for *Yizkor* books is the Yiddish Book Center, which working together with the New York Public Library digitized over 650 Yizkor books from the collections of the two institutions. The YIVO Institute for Jewish Research is a valuable repository of material that illuminates Jewish life in Europe before World War II.[120] In the Kurenitz *Yizkor* book, I discovered that the murder of most of the Jewish population occurred on 9 September 1942.[121] In the memoir of the town—a chapter in the *Yizkor* book—Baruch Zuckerman wrote that:

Unlike most shtetls in Lithuania and Belarus, Kurenitz was mainly Ḥasidic. It had three synagogues and two minyans. And from this, only one synagogue belonged to the "mitnagdim"... The town was blessed with a large number of unique teachers. They were not credentialed...Then came the days that the flame of enlightenment spread around the town. Stronger yet were the effects of the unstoppable radical socialist movement. The firebrands that tried to evoke hate to the tsarist regime did not need to use much persuasion. Their job was done by the evil, deeply anti-Semitic authority. But neither the spirit of enlightenment nor the revolution would affect the town's spirit. Externally, things changed, but the deeper essence stayed the same till the arrival of Zionism that let yet unique new expression and longing surface. New tunes and ideals were heard in the hills and the valleys—Hebrew schools, beloved teachers that only spoke Hebrew, Zionist organizations like Histadrut, youth movements like hachaloot, and Hashomer Hatza'ir. But in some ways it was a new tune for an old song. Old wine in a new bottle...The size of the population hardly changed. Many immigrated, but new births replenished the

The *Yizkor* book was a wealth of information, but I could find no institution
formally called *"Talmud Torah,"* although the words and the phrase are familiar,
taken from a phrase in *Mishnah Peah 1:1: Talmud Torah k'neged kulam*–"the study
of Torah is equal to them all."[123] This is certainly a worthwhile name for a Jewish
center of learning and study but hardly a unique name. I could not identify the
specific *Yeshivah* to which Levi's will referenced.

The Stories Continue, and
They Continue to Confuse

It amazes me how, like the game of telephone, information morphs quickly into
misinformation. In 2017, I was contacted by a descendant of one of the great-
grandchildren of Tzvi Hersch who found me through a DNA match. She said her
father was Max and her grandfather was Nathan and her father had a brother,
Samuel. Before I confirmed the branch from which she descended, I needed
to know when her grandfather died, since her branch, like so many others in
the Millontzik family, abound in the names Max, Nathan, and Samuel. After
her descent was confirmed, I read and reread her comments several times. She
wrote that her grandfather Nathan married Bertha Kiel, whom his parents did
not approve of, and the couple was cut off from the rest of the family. A review of
the probate documents proved that the children of her grandfather Nathan, who
predeceased his father, Harris, were bequeathed the same amounts of money that
was granted to Harris's other descendants.

The story in the retelling may have been conflated with other facts, but I found
that the name of her grandfather's wife, Bertha Kiel—the mother of his children—
was incorrect. Since her grandfather was 24 years old at the time of his marriage,
it is possible that he was previously married, although his 1911 marriage record
indicated that this was his first marriage.[124] Bertha's gravestone indicated that her
Hebrew name was Rivka, the equivalent of the English Rebecca, and her father

L to R (standing): Sharyn Reisberg, Arielle Silver, Shari Levy, Samantha Reisberg, Susan Lipsky Rahban, Iris Reisberg, Roberta Bernstein, Charlotte Miller
L to R (seated): Joshua Reisberg, Jenna Levy (both held by Phyllis Lipsky), Sylvia Moldofsky, and Bella Gold

was Mordechai.[125] On the marriage record, Rebecca's father was named Max and Rebecca's maiden name was Meyer. Max may have been the Americanized version of Mordechai. Mordechai is often Americanized to Max, Milton, Marvin, and other names beginning with the letter "m." Although Rebecca appeared with that first name on censuses before the 1923 death of her husband, her name became Bertha after his death, beginning with the 1925 New York State census.[126] On that census, Bertha's mother, Sarah Meyer, was a widow living with Bertha and her three sons. If Bertha remarried during the long years of her widowhood, from 1923 until her 1963 death, it is not indicated on her gravestone, so there is no indication of where the surname Kiel might have originated.

Endnotes

1. Sylvia was born in 1906 in Brooklyn, New York, and died in 1991 in the Bronx, New York.

2. *The Donna Reed Show and Leave it to Beaver* were television shows that aired in the 1950s. The shows' female leads were Donna Reed playing middle-class housewife Donna Stone and Barbara Billingsley as June Cleaver, respectively. The two roles came to be the embodiment of the role women should hold—housewives who spent their days cooking, cleaning, and waiting for their children to return from school and their husbands from work.

3. There are several spellings and differences in its name and pronunciation depending on which of the many languages common in the area are used to refer to it: Vileika, Vilejka, Belarusian: **Вілейка**, Russian: **Вилейка**, Polish: Wilejka, Lithuanian: Vileika. The city itself was at times in the Vilna (now Vilnius, Lithuania) province and sometimes in the Minsk (now Minsk, Belarus) province. Both provinces were in the Russian Empire.

4. The region of Russia/Poland was broken down into political subdivisions called *gubernya*. In 1914, there were 15 *gubernyas* in the Jewish Pale: Bessarabia, Chernigov, Ekaterinaslav, Grodno, Kherson, Kiev, Kovno, Kurland & Lifland, Minsk, Mogilev, Podolsk, Poltava, Tavrich, Vilensk (Vilna), and Vitebsk. There were another 10 in the Kingdom of Poland: Kalisz, Kielce, Lomza, Lublin, Piotrkow, Plock, Radom, Suwalki, Siedlce (Sybolitz), Warszawa (Warsaw). The *gubernyas* were subdivided into uezds. Often, the main town had the same name as the gubernya or the uezd.

5. "Census: Vileyka Uezd," Census, *The History of Belarussian Jewry* (http://www.beljews.info), accessed January 2012.

6. Kalman Farber and Joseph Se'evi, editors, "Memoirs and Family Stories: The Story of Vileyka," KehilaLinks, *JewishGen* (https://jewishgen.org), accessed January 2012.

7. Whatever building the Formans lived in or in which their grocery store was located, it is no longer there. A Google Earth search yields a picture of what may be New York City housing projects or other apartment houses. Although the buildings appear to be old, they are neither as old as they would need to be for the Formans to have resided there nor are they of a style consistent with the 1890s and early 1900s.

8. "Forman Family Photo," photograph, circa 1902; researcher's copy.

9. Stephen P. Morse, "Ellis Island & Castle Garden Search Forms and Ship Arrivals," *One-Step Webpages* (http://stevemorse.org), accessed August 2012.

10. Stephen P. Morse, "Ship Lists: Searching for Ships in the New York Microfilms in One Step," *One-Step Webpages* (http://stevemorse.org), accessed January 2012.

11. Warren Blatt in FAQ #10 "Passenger Lists" on *JewishGen.org* wrote, "These passenger lists were filled out at the port of embarkation by the ship's purser and checked by U.S. customs or immigration authorities upon arrival. Thus, the names on these lists are the European, pre-Americanized versions of names. The names were written down the way that they sounded. Do not expect to find your ancestor's name spelled as it is today—realize that your immigrant ancestor wouldn't be able to recognize the written name even if it were shown to him/her if they read only Russian and/or Yiddish/Hebrew." Found at "JewishGen FAQ – Frequently Asked Questions," InfoFiles, *JewishGen* (http://www.jewishgen.org), accessed February 2018.

12. The first of the outbound manifests to be digitized and widely available were those of the Hamburg American Line. *JewishGen.org*'s FAQ #10, "Passenger Lists," written by Warren Blatt, included a section "Hamburg Passenger Lines," in which he wrote: "The port of Hamburg, Germany, maintained lists of emigrating passengers for 1850-1934. About 40% of Eastern European Jewish immigrants (Polish, Russian, Hungarian, etc.) left via Hamburg. These lists contain the emigrant's town of origin. They are indexed by year and the first letter of each passenger's surname, so some searching is required." Found at "JewishGen FAQ – Frequently Asked Questions," InfoFiles, *JewishGen* (http://www.jewishgen.org), accessed February 2018.

13. Many outbound ships heading for the United Kingdom and the United States have been digitized and transcribed at "Immigration," *Gjenvick-Gjonvik* (https://www.gjenvick.com), accessed February 2018.

14. Kings County (New York) County Court, Declarations of Intention, p. 86, Levi Selig Forman, dated 12 April 1895; digital image, "New York, U.S., State and Federal Naturalization Records, 1794-1943," *Ancestry* (http://www.ancestry.com), accessed April 2022

15. Eastern District (New York) District Court, Naturalization Petitions, Volume 35, p. 386, Levi Selig Forman, naturalized 5 August 1901; digital image, "New York, U.S., State and Federal Naturalization Records, 1794-1943," *Ancestry* (http://www.ancestry.com), accessed April 2022.

16. "History of Brooklyn," *The WNET Group* (http://www.wnet.org/brooklyn/history/history2.html), accessed August 2012.

17. Federal Writers' Project (N.Y.), New York City Guide: A Comprehensive Guide to the Five Boroughs of the Metropolis: Manhattan, Brooklyn, the Bronx, Queens, and Richmond (New York: Random House, 1939), p. 3; researcher's copy.

18. "Brooklyn History – An Overview from Breuckelen to Brooklyn," *TripSavvy* (http://brooklyn.about.com/od/historicbrooklyn/a/History.htm), accessed February 2018.

19. Samuel Philip Abelow, *History of Brooklyn Jewry* (Brooklyn, New York: Scheba Publishing Company, 1937), p. 5; researcher's copy.

20. Martin Henry Weyrauch, *The Pictorial History of Brooklyn: Issued by the Brooklyn Daily Eagle on Its Seventy-fifth Anniversary, October 26, 1916* (New York: Brooklyn Daily Eagle, 1916), p. 8; researcher's copy.

21. Hasia R. Diner, *The Jews of the United States, 1654 to 2000* (Berkeley, California: University of California Press, 2004), p. 105; researcher's copy.

22. Elizabeth Bogen, *Immigration in New York* (New York: Prager Publishers, 1987), p. 11; researcher's copy.

23. Diner: pp. 106-107.

24. Irving Howe and Kenneth Libo, *World of Our Fathers* (New York: Harcourt Brace Jovanovich, 1976), p. 131; researcher's copy.

25. Abelow: p. 12. Mention of this association can also be found in *The American Jewish Yearbook* (Philadelphia, Pennsylvania: Jewish Publication Society of America, 1919), vol. 21; digital image, *Google Books* (http://books.google.com), accessed February 2018.

26. Jacob Rader Marcus, *United States Jewry, 1776-1985* (Michigan: Wayne State University Press, 1990), p. 135; researcher's copy.

27. Leonard Dinnerstein, *Antisemitism in America* (New York: Oxford University Press, 1995), p. 53; researcher's copy.

28. Robert A. Rockaway, *Words of the Uprooted: Jewish Immigrants in Early Twentieth-Century America* (Ithaca, New York: Cornell University Press, 1998), p. 1; researcher's copy.

29. Found at "Russ & Daughters: Appetizing Since 1914," *Russ and Daughters* (http://russanddaughters. com/whatisappetizing.php), accessed February 2018.

30. "467 Kosciuszko St," street view, 2012; digital image, Google (https://maps.google.com), accessed April 2022.

31. "Sarah Forman, Milton Silverman, and Rhoda Moldofsky," photograph, June 1949; researcher's copy.

32. Blintzes are paper-thin crepes stuffed with cheese or potatoes, rolled into a "package," and then baked or fried. Cheese blintzes are often served with sour cream and jam or fruit compote.

33. Gefilte fish is an Eastern European Jewish tradition. It is made of fish that is ground or chopped and mixed with carrots, onions, spices, and eggs. At one time, this mixture was probably stuffed back into the fish skin and baked. Today, the mixture is generally not stuffed into the fish skin, but baked as a loaf or made into balls and boiled, or, in some communities, fried. Gefilte fish can either be sweet or savory. Carp is a common fish used for gefilte fish.

34. "Sylvia and Abraham Herbert," photograph, circa 1958; researcher's copy

35. Marian L. Smith, "American Names: Declaring Independence," 8 August 2005, *Immigration Daily* (http://www.ilw.com/articles/2005,0808-smith.shtm), accessed February 2018.

36. *Matzevah* is the Hebrew term for "gravestone." *Matzevot* is the plural form.

37. The Hebrew word *bas* is the same as the Hebrew word *bat* with a different pronunciation. They both mean "daughter." In Ashkenazic accents, the Hebrew letter *taf* ת sometimes appears with a dot (called a dagesh) in the center of the open space. Ashkenazic pronunciations differentiate between the letter with and without the dagesh – with the dagesh, the letter is pronounced "t" and without "s." In modern Hebrew, there is no differentiation, and the letter is always pronounced "t." Since this is a softer sounding "t" than another letter called a tet sometimes transliterations of the taf with a dagesh is rendered "th."

38. Grave marker of Harris Millonchick (died 17 August 1934), Washington Cemetery, Brooklyn, Kings County, New York, photograph, 2010; researcher's copy.

39. Grave marker of Rose Millonchick (died 4 November 1932), Washington Cemetery, Brooklyn, Kings County, New York, photograph, 2010; researcher's copy.

40. According to records of Chaya Ruchel's children in the United States, her maiden name was either Cohen or Portnoy. Marvin wrote in *Zhid* that Chaya Ruchel and Chaim Czidovetsky were first cousins, and that Chaya Ruchel arranged for her daughter Esther to marry Sam. From this, it is possible that Marvin assumed that Chaya Ruchel's maiden name was Jitovsky, which he probably only heard and never saw written down, and that Marvin did not make the connection between the names because of their different appearance.

41. Marvin A. Goldberg, Zhid: A Russian Odyssey (New Jersey: Xlibris, 2007), pp. 35-45; researcher's copy.

42. United States, Department of Justice, Immigration and Naturalization Service, Passenger and Crew Lists of Vessels Arriving at New York, New York, 1897-1957, SS *Karlsruhe*, arrived 25 November 1898, p. 215, Lines 27-29, Menasche, Ester, and Shaic Zidowetzky; digital image, "New York, Passenger Lists, 1820-1957," *Ancestry* (http://www.ancestry.com), accessed February 2018.

43. Chaim Freedman, *Beit Rabbanan: Sources of Rabbinic Genealogy* (Petah Tikva, Israel: Chaim Freedman, 2001); digital image, "Difficulties in Researching Rabbinical Families," InfoFiles, JewishGen (https://www.jewishgen.org), accessed February 2012.

44. Skvira is located in the Kiev oblast in north-central Ukraine, at 49°44'0"N, 29°40'0"E.

45. United States, Treasury Department, Customs Service, Passenger Lists of Vessels Arriving at New York, New York, 1820-1897, SS *Palatia*, arrived 25 July 1896, Lines 4-6, Herschko, Schmul, and Mordche Molontzik; digital image, "New York, Passenger Lists, 1820-1957," *Ancestry* (http://www.ancestry.com), accessed February 2018.

46. An oblast is a municipal division, often translated as a "region" or "province."

47. Marvin A. Goldberg, *Zhid: A Russian Odyssey* (Philadelphia, Pennsylvania: Xlibris, 2007), p. 24; researcher's copy.

48. "Skvira," *Jewish Virtual Library* (https://www.jewishvirtuallibrary.org), accessed January 2022.

49. Ibid.

50. Goldberg, 2007: p. 38.

51. Goldberg, 2007: p. 25.

52. "Russia Virtual Jewish History Tour," *Jewish Virtual Library* (https://www.jewishvirtuallibrary.org), accessed January 2022.

53. Abelow: p. 3.

54. Abelow: p. 3.

55. Spector and Wigoder: p. 1197 reports the 1897 population as 2,184. The Jewish Virtual Library lists that same number from an 1847 Jewish population census. It is likely that this was the number used in the information found in *The Encyclopedia of Jewish Life Before and During the Holocaust*. The Jewish Virtual Library reports an 1897 Jewish population of almost 9,000. "Skvira," *Jewish Virtual Library* (https://www.jewishvirtuallibrary.org), accessed January 2022.

56. Goldberg, 2007: p. 38.

57. Rottenberg: p. 47.

58. Goldberg, 2007: p. 38.

59. Ukrainian: **Біла Церква**, Polish: Biała Cerkiew, Russian: **Белая Церковь**, literally White Church. It is located at 49°47' N, 30°07' E.

60. Seymour Spector, editor, *The Encyclopedia of Jewish Life Before and During the Holocaust* Typed a note (New York: New York University Press, 2001), p. 99; researcher's copy.

61. "Bogdan Chmielnicki," Jewish Virtual Library (https://www.jewishvirtuallibrary.org), accessed January 2022.

62. Geoffrey Treasure, *The Making of Modern Europe, 1648-1780* (London, United Kingdom: Routledge, 2003), p. 533; researcher's copy.

63. Lawrence Fine, "Contemplative Death in Jewish Mystical Tradition," *Sacrificing the Self: Perspectives on Martyrdom and Religion* (New York: Oxford University Press, 2001), p. 100; researcher's copy.

64. Isaac Bashevis Singer (translated by Jacob Sloan), *Satan in Goray* (New York: Noonday Press, 1955); researcher's copy.

65. Meyer Levin, "A False Messiah," 13 November 1955, Web Archive, *The New York Times* (https://www.nytimes.com), accessed January 2022.

66. Singer: p. 5.

67. 1910 U.S. Federal Census (Population Schedule), Manhattan, New York County, New York, ED 505, Sheet 1A, Dwelling 2, Family 4, Sam Goldberg household; digital image, "1910 United States Federal Census," *Ancestry* (http://www.ancestry.com), accessed October 2015.

68. Grave marker of Harris Millonchick (died 17 August 1934), Washington Cemetery, Brooklyn, Kings County, New York, photograph; digital image, "Find Records," *JewishData* (https://jewishdata.com), accessed January 2022.

69. It is possible that the job of "bell lamp inspector" was related to railroad inspections. There were many ways in which lanterns were used in connection with the operation of railroads. "[R]ailroad lanterns served a very important purpose: they communicated signals at night between trains and stations. Sometimes, a timely lantern signal meant the difference between life and death." It is possible that he inspected these types of lanterns. Or, he could have been an inspector who used lanterns to check the safety of trains. "[A] main type of lantern is the inspector's lantern, which was more utilitarian in design. Inspectors used these lanterns to examine train cars, so they had reflective surfaces designed to focus the globe's light. Inspector's lanterns were generally made from sheet metal so they would be durable." He also could have been an inspector of lamps used by railroads for another purposes. "Marker lamps, for example, were hung on the last car to signal the end of the train. Classification lamps on a locomotive indicated what kind of locomotive it was. Other kinds of lamps included semaphore lamps, switch lamps, and crossing-gate lamps." "Antique Railroad Lanterns and Lamps," *Collectors Weekly* (http://www.collectorsweekly.com/railroadiana/lanterns), accessed January 2022.

70. Goldberg, 2007: pp.35-36.

71. "Buckboard," *Werner Wagon Works* (http://www.wernerwagonworks.com), accessed January 2022.

72. Goldberg, 2007: p. 37.

73. Slivovitz is a potent brandy made from damson plums.

74. Goldberg, 2007: p. 38.

75. The *kahal* is the community. Leaders of the community were expected to collect taxes and function as the liaison between the civil authority and the populace.

76. Goldberg, 2007: p. 40.

77. A discussion of the shift from the Julian to the Gregorian calendar can be found in part 1, chapter 1.

78. I spoke to several other of Tzvi Hersch's great-grandchildren, none of whom recollect any of these stories. These other great-grandchildren are descendants of Esther Leah's siblings rather than Esther herself. They all expressed astonishment at hearing or reading the stories, and said that if they were true, they surely would have heard them, too.

79. Goldberg, 2007: p. 42.

80. Vladislav Soshnikov, "Jewish Genealogical Research in the Imperial Russian Empire," *Avotaynu: The International Review of Jewish Genealogy* XVI (Summer 2000); researcher's copy.

81. Goldberg, 2007: p. 43.

82. Aubrey Newman, "Patterns of Late 19th- and Early 20th-Century Migration and Transmigration from Europe," *Avotaynu: The International Review of Jewish Genealogy* XVII (Fall 2001); researcher's copy.

83. "Milyontzik Family," photograph, circa 1902; researcher's copy.

84. United States, Treasury Department, Customs Service, Passenger Lists of Vessels Arriving at New York, New York, 1820-1897, SS *Palatia*, arrived 25 July 1896, Lines 4-6, Herschko, Schmul, and Mordche Molontzik; digital image, "New York, Passenger Lists, 1820-1957," *Ancestry* (http://www.ancestry.com), accessed February 2018.

85. 1910 U.S. Federal Census (Population Schedule), Brooklyn, Kings County, New York, ED 505, Sheet 2A, Dwelling 6, Family 22, Harris Mellon household; digital image, "1910 United States Federal Census," *Ancestry* (http://www.ancestry.com), accessed February 2018.

86. 1920 U.S. Federal Census (Population Schedule), Brooklyn, Kings County, New York, ED 311, Sheet 12A, Dwelling 80, Family 258, Harris Millin household; digital image, "1920 United States Federal Census," *Ancestry* (http://www.ancestry.com), accessed February 2018.

87. 1925 New York State Census, Brooklyn, Kings County, Block 2, ED 4, AD 6, p. 12, Dwelling 232, Harris Millon household; digital image, "New York, State Census, 1925," *Ancestry* (http://www.ancestry.com), accessed February 2018.

88. 1930 U.S. Federal Census (Population Schedule), Brooklyn, Kings County, New York, ED 24-326, Sheet 7B, Dwelling 73, Family 163, Harris Mellon household; digital image, "1930 United States Federal Census," *Ancestry* (http://www.ancestry.com), accessed February 2018.

89. The information on the census is based on what a person tells a census taker or, more recently, writes on the census form. There is no documentation required to verify the information, nor is enough information asked to allow the information to be verified. A person was asked for the year of their immigration. They were not asked for the name of the ship on which they sailed. Their country of origin appears on the census, but not the city or region.

90. Marvin Goldberg's father, born in Skvira in 1897.

91. Sholom Aleichem was the pen name of Solomon Naumovich Rabinovich (1859 – 1916), one of the best-known Yiddish authors. His works have been translated into many languages, and his stories about Tevye the milkman and his daughters are best known from the Broadway musical and movie *Fiddler's Roof*.

92. Sholom Aleichem (translated by Julius and Frances Butwin), "The Bubble Bursts," *Favorite Tales of Sholom Aleichem* (New York: Avenel Books, 1983), p. 392; researcher's copy.

93. "Probate records relate to a deceased person's estate, whether that estate is "testate" (through a will) or "intestate" (without a will). Whether the decedent left a large estate or just some personal property, there's a good chance that a probate file exists in a local court that oversaw distribution of property, the guardianship of a minor, or payment of debts." Definition found on "New York, U.S., Wills and Probate Records, 1659-1999," *Ancestry* (https://www.ancestry.com) accessed February 2018.

94. Kings County (New York) Surrogate's Court, Probate File of Harris Miller, File No. 6721, 1934; Kings County Surrogate's Court, Brooklyn, New York.

95. Kings County (New York) Surrogate's Court, Probate File of Harris Miller, File No. 6721, 1934; Kings County Surrogate's Court, Brooklyn, New York.

96. "1940 Census FAQs," Research Our Records, *National Archives* (https://www.archives.gov), accessed February 2018.

97.   Censuses which have been digitized and indexed, as the 1940 census has, can be searched through various means. One way is to search for a surname or for the first names of people living together. Another way, if the address at which they lived is known, is to search census pages for that address and see who lived at that address. To find where they lived in the many thousands of census pages there are for a county or town, the enumeration district must be identified. Through Steve Morse's One-Step search engine, it is possible to easily identify enumeration districts. Stephen P. Morse, "Unified Census ED Finder," *One-Step Webpages* (http://stevemorse.org), accessed February 2018.

98.   "Google Maps," *Google* (https://maps.google.com), accessed February 2018.

99.   "1930 United States Federal Census," *Ancestry* (https://www.ancestry.com), accessed February 2018.

100.   1925 New York State Census, Brooklyn, Kings County, Block 2, ED 4, AD 6, p. 12, Dwelling 232, Harris Millon household; digital image, "New York, State Census, 1925," *Ancestry* (http://www.ancestry.com), accessed February 2018.

101.   1910 U.S. Federal Census (Population Schedule), Brooklyn, Kings County, New York, ED 505, Sheet 2A, Dwelling 6, Family 22, Harris Mellon household; digital image, "1910 United States Federal Census," *Ancestry* (http://www.ancestry.com), accessed February 2018.

102.   1920 U.S. Federal Census (Population Schedule), Brooklyn, Kings County, New York, ED 311, Sheet 12A, Dwelling 80, Family 258, Harris Millin household; digital image, "1920 United States Federal Census," *Ancestry* (http://www.ancestry.com), accessed February 2018.

103.   1930 U.S. Federal Census (Population Schedule), Brooklyn, Kings County, New York, ED 24-326, Sheet 7B, Dwelling 73, Family 163, Harris Mellon household; digital image, "1930 United States Federal Census," *Ancestry* (http://www.ancestry.com), accessed February 2018.

104.   City of New York (New York) Department of Health, Bureau of Records, Standard Certificate of Death, Certificate 16700, Herschel Millen, died 17 August 1934, in Brooklyn; FSL Microfilm 2079140.

105.   City of New York (New York) Department of Health, Bureau of Records, Standard Certificate of Death, Certificate 21351, Rose Mellon, died 4 November 1932, in Brooklyn; FSL Microfilm 2070585.

106.   1930 U.S. Federal Census (Population Schedule), Brooklyn, Kings County, New York, ED 24-570, Sheet 9B, Dwelling 31, Family 195, Samuel Goldberg household; digital image,

107.   "1930 United States Federal Census," Ancestry (http://www.ancestry.com), accessed October 2015.

108.   City of New York (New York) Department of Health, Bureau of Records, Standard Certificate of Death, Certificate 16700, Herschel Millen, died 17 August 1934, in Brooklyn; FSL Microfilm 2079140.

109.   City of New York (New York) Department of Health, Bureau of Records, Standard Certificate of Death, Certificate 21351, Rose Mellon, died 4 November 1932, in Brooklyn; FSL Microfilm 2070585.

110.   Ancestry® Family History Learning," *Ancestry* (http://www.ancestry.com), accessed April 2022.

111.   Kurenitz is known in many different languages with slight variations of pronunciation—Russian: **Куренец**. Yiddish: קורעניץ. Belarusian: **Куранец**. Hebrew: קורניץ. It is located three miles north of Vileika and 66 miles east of Vilnius (Vilna). In 1897, there were slightly more than 1,600 Jews living there.

112.   *Yizkor books* are memorial books written about life in towns whose Jewish populations were

murdered during World War II. The books often include a history of the town as well as brief biographical sketches of people who lived there. They include firsthand accounts of what life was like before the war. The authors of these books are usually groups of people who were from the town.

113.   A. Meyerowitz (translator), "The Scroll of Kurzeniac (Kurenets, Belarus)," Yizkor Books, *JewishGen* (https://www.jewishgen.org), accessed February 2018.

114.   Kings County (New York) Surrogate's Court, Probate File of Levi S. Forman, File No. 1367, 1935; Kings County Surrogate's Court, Brooklyn, New York.

115.   Mendel Cepelowicz and Moses Alperoowitz, of Kurenitz, to Esther Forman, Max Miller, and Sarah Miller letter, dated 25 June 1936, Fundraising plea from Kurenitz community; Probate File of Levi S. Forman, File No. 1367, 1935; Kings County Surrogate's Court, Brooklyn, New York.

116.   Kurenets, Belarus, is located at 54°33′N / 26°57′E

117.   City of New York (New York) Department of Health, Certificate and Record of Death, Certificate 22391, Esther Forman, died 4 November 1943, in Brooklyn; FSL Microfilm 2134861.

118.   "Yizkor Book Project: Frequently Asked Questions (FAQ)," Yizkor Books, *JewishGen* (http://www.jewishgen.org), accessed February 2012.

119.   *"[it] is responsible for administering, developing and promoting one of the world's great collections of Hebraica and Judaica."* Found at "About the Dorot Jewish Division," Locations, *New York Public Library* (http://www.nypl.org), accessed February 2012.

120.   "Founded in 1925 in Vilna, Poland (Wilno, Poland, now Vilnius, Lithuania), as the Yiddish Scientific Institute...dedicated to the history and culture of Ashkenazi Jewry and to its influence in the Americas. Headquartered in New York City since 1940, today YIVO is the world's preeminent resource center for East European Jewish Studies; Yiddish language, literature and folklore; and the American Jewish immigrant experience." Found at "History of YIVO," About, *YIVO Institute for Jewish Research* (https://www.yivo.org), accessed February 2012.

121.   Baruch Zukerman (translated by Carmel Levitan), "Our withered town, Kurenitz, Villeyka County, Vilnus District," Yizkor Books, *JewishGen* (http://www.jewishgen.org), accessed February 2012.

122.   Zukerman.

123.   The full translation of the verse reads: "These are the things that are without measure: charity, first fruits, pilgrimage to the temple, righteous deeds, and studying Torah. These are things that a man can eat of their fruits in this world, but their true fulfillment is in the world to come: honoring one's parents, righteous deeds, bringing peace between a man and his friend. Studying Torah is equal to them all."

124.   City of New York (New York) Department of Health, Certificate and Record of Marriage, Certificate 615, Nathan H. Millon and Rebecca Meyer, married 17 January 1911, in Brooklyn; FSL Microfilm 1613366.

125.   Lainie Cat, grave marker of Bertha Millon (22 May 1892–15 September 1963), Beth David Cemetery, Elmont, Nassau County, New York, photograph, uploaded 2014; digital image, "Bertha Millon," memorial 132044158, *Find A Grave* (http://www.findagrave.com), accessed February 2018.

126.   1925 New York State Census, Brooklyn, Kings County, Block 1, ED 2, AD 5, p. 3, Dwelling 666, Bertha Millon household; digital image, "New York, State Census, 1925," *Ancestry* (http://www.ancestry.com), accessed February 2018.

127.   Milton Silverman, "Five Generations of Forman and Milontzik Descendants," photograph, 1987; researcher's copy.

It Started With a Box: The Silberman and Buchbinder Families

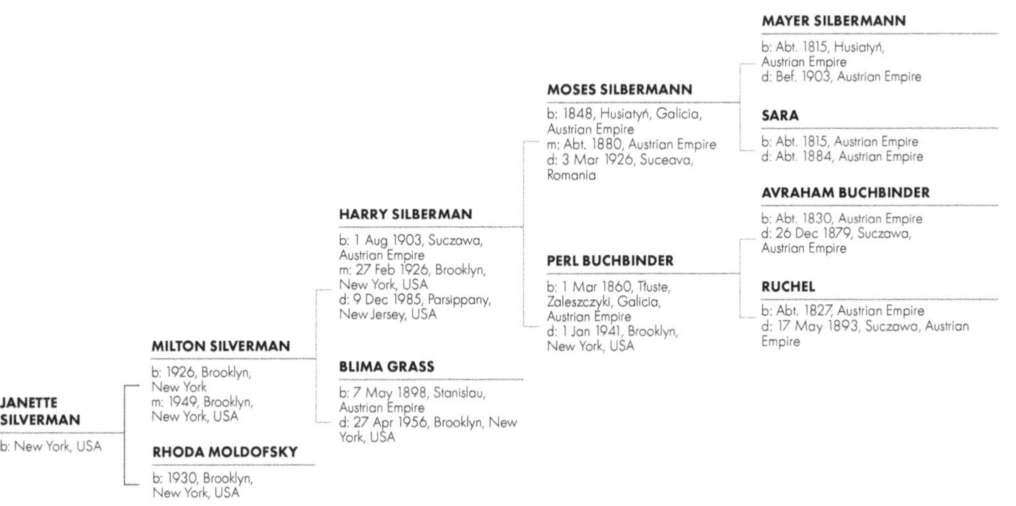

It Started With a Box:
Silberman and Buchbinder

Reflecting on the way I began researching the history of all my grandparents' families, I am struck by the very different paths the search took, and how my grandparents, in very different ways, provided the keys and the direction my investigations would take. The two grandparents I knew best were my maternal grandmother, whose family was previously discussed, and my paternal grandfather. Both knew of my interest in finding out about their families before they arrived in the United States, and both were equally reticent about answering questions regarding the lives of their families in Europe. Part of my grandmother's refusal or inability to answer my questions may have been because, by the time she was born, her family had been in the United States for almost two decades. My grandfather, however, arrived in the United States as an adult. I think he just

Fig. 1: Harry Silberman with his oldest great-grandchildren,
L to R: Jenna Levy, Arielle Silver, and Efrem Weiss[1]

wanted to speak about other things. Perhaps he didn't understand the purpose of my questions or how much of the story of his own family and that of of my paternal grandmother's would die with him.

My grandfather, Harry Silberman, died in December 1985. After he died, my parents, sisters, and I found boxes filled with receipts, letters, lists, photos, and scraps of paper in his apartment. The boxes proved to be a treasure trove once we figured out how to decipher the material. The letters were written in Yiddish, German, Romanian, Polish, Italian, and French, languages none of the immediate family members spoke fluently or read with any degree of comprehension. The receipts included money orders to someone in Palestine and, later, in Israel—Gershon Buchbinder.[2] None of us knew who he was.

Also in the box were money orders to one of Harry's brothers, Norbert. Norbert remained in Europe after the rest of his siblings immigrated to the United States. Among the papers, we found hospital receipts for the births of Harry's two sons—my father, Milton, and his younger brother, Stanley. Harry's mother, Perl Buchbinder, emigrated from Europe in 1928 and the receipt for her steamship passage was in the box. Almost two years after the death of her husband, Moshe Silberman, in Romania, she joined her adult children in New York and Pennsylvania.

We were fortunate, for many reasons, that Harry lived into his mid-80s. For me, memories of him are clear. I can still hear the sound of his heavily accented voice in my memory. He lived in the United States for most of his life, and retained the accent and cadences of his native language, although it was never clear what that language was! He spoke Yiddish and German, and he said he learned enough Russian to speak with Russian soldiers in World War I. He probably read and spoke Romanian, since documents in the box from that period are in Romanian, but I'm just guessing. I don't recollect ever asking. In fact, until I wrote this, it didn't occur to me that this was a question. I'm fortunate because my parents have excellent memories of their parents. I asked my dad, and he said he didn't know. It wasn't a question that occurred to him to be curious about, either.

We knew that Yiddish was the language he spoke at home, but what did he speak on the street or in school? I wish he had told me more about his childhood and his family. The stories he told included little detail. Among the memories he shared were some about a cousin, Julius, who was older and who fled Romania sometime before World War I. Julius would sometimes sneak back to town. Each time Julius returned, he climbed through a window long after dark or just before dawn. In celebration, Perl roasted a leg of lamb. Harry said Julius eventually took up permanent residence in England and served in Parliament as a member of the House of Commons. I did not know then that I should have asked more questions. Was Julius a Silberman or a Buchbinder? Who were his parents? I have not yet identified a Julius Silberman or Buchbinder in England that fits Harry's description.

The stories my grandfather told me during the last year of his life were unverifiable at that time. Some of them remain so, at least for now. His stories drove my imagination and ultimately directed some of my research. Before I began to investigate the Silberman family, my dad and I knew certain things: my grandfather's name in Yiddish was Mayer Hirsch. He was known as "Harry" in English. By his own admission, he was born with the name Max Heinrich, which he said he hated. After arriving in the United States, he became "Harry" when the opportunity presented itself. Harry told us that his father's name in Hebrew was "Moshe," and my father, born soon after Harry's father, Moshe, died, was named after him—Milton in English, Moshe in Hebrew, Moishe in Yiddish. Harry's father's secular name was Moses. Many Jews in the Diaspora have a Hebrew or Yiddish name used for ritual purposes and a secular name used in daily life. So, it appears, did Harry and his parents. Harry's mother was "Perl." Her Yiddish name and secular name were the same. Harry's father Moshe was called Moses.

Alexander Beider, a noted authority of Jewish names, commented that, beginning at some point in the Middle Ages, Jewish men in Europe, Asia, and northern Africa typically had both a sacred name and a secular name. The sacred name, bestowed at circumcision, was used at his bar mitzvah, when he was called to the Torah, at the time of his marriage, and at his death. These names included not only traditional Hebrew names found in the Bible but also names used since ancient times, like Alexander, that became incorporated into Hebrew. Secular names were non-Hebrew or Aramaic names, often taken from colloquial names and nicknames. Frequently, no distinction was made between names for women, since they were not, traditionally, called to the Torah. A woman's secular name might appear on her marriage contract written in Hebrew letters.[3] In some Jewish communities in Poland, more than 40% of Jews had double given names by the nineteenth century. One of the two names was their sacred name and the other a secular name, often a secularized version of the sacred name.[4]

Fig. 2: Moses and Perl Silberman, circa 1920[6]

Milton knew his grandmother Perl well. Two years after Moshe's death in 1926, Perl came to the United States and lived with Harry and his family for part of the time. At other times, she lived with her daughter—Harry's older sister, Leah—in Pennsylvania. When Harry arrived in the United States in 1920, he was a bookbinder. That was a family craft, passed down through many generations. Perl's father was a bookbinder and her maiden name, Buchbinder, attested to that. Moshe, the story goes, was apprenticed to Perl's father from the time she was a small child. When she grew up, the two married and raised a family in Suceava, Romania.[5] When I asked Harry how long the family lived in Romania, he said his grandparents—that is, his father's parents—arrived there from somewhere farther east. Beyond that, he did not know where the family had resided or why they moved to Suceava. Unfortunately, I neglected to ask any further questions about Perl's parents or her siblings.

Our research began with these few names and facts. In early 1986, we began to look through Harry's papers. One document in his boxes was a black-bordered sheet written in Romanian, on which we could clearly read the name "Moses Silbermann."[7] It told us he was a "binder of books" who died in March 1926. The document appears to be contemporaneous—that is, issued at the time of his death. It was a notice of his funeral. The information on the page informed us that he was

Asociaţia meseriaşilor Grupa V-a

aduc trista ştire despre trecerea din viaţă a valorosul...   ...membru, a domnului

MOSES SILBERMANN

legător de cărţi

care după o lungă şi grea suferinţă a decedat în etate de 73 ani.

Înmormântarea va afla loc Joi 4 Martie a. c. la orele 3 p. m., la care

sunt invitaţi a lua parte toţi membrii asociaţiei.

SUCEAVA, în Martie 1926.

Fig. 3: Moses Silberman's 1926 death notice[8]

73 years old at his death and, although it did not provide the cause of death, it reported that he died after a long illness. Perl brought this page with her when she came to the United States. We understood this document perfectly. Well, let me amend that statement—we understood it perfectly once we translated it since the language of the document was not in English.

The next document we examined proved troublesome. It was written in German, so the language was less of an issue, but the subject was, at least initially, very confusing, and took us many months of research to understand. The document was dated 1908 and granted Moses Silbermann a license to practice business as a bookbinder.[9] According to this document, he lived or worked at House Number 15, Suceava. The information verified what we knew of Moses Silbermann—that he was a bookbinder and lived in Suceava. The troubling information included on the document was that he was born in Husiatyn, Galicia. I cannot even begin to describe our confusion when confronted with this place name. Today, an internet search would bring an immediate answer, but in 1986, there was no easy way to find information. At that time, the only Galicia I had heard of was in Spain, and that was clearly not the area of Europe to which these records referred. The terms *Litvak* and *Galitzianer* meant little to me except that some Jewish families were divided along those lines, and the references had something to do with customs. Before 1986, it had not occurred to me that the terms actually referred to geographic places.

Additional issues we confronted when beginning our research into Husiatyn and Galicia were due to language. Both Husiatyn and Galicia appear in different documents as Gusiatyn and Halicia. These differences arise from a linguistic issue. Cyrillic is the alphabet that both Russian and Ukrainian use. However, the Cyrillic letter "r" is pronounced "h" in Ukrainian and "g" in Russian. The transliteration of the city of Husiatyn[11] and the Province of Galicia[12] are words

Fig. 4: Gewerbe-Schein, 1908[10]

which, in Cyrillic, both have the same initial letter. In Polish—a language written in the Latin alphabet—and in Ukrainian, the city is known as Husiatyn. In Russian, it is called Gusiatyn. A city called "Husi" exists which is not the same city as Husiatyn. Husi was in Moldavia, now Romania. Today, Husiatyn is in the Tarnipol *oblast* of what is now Ukraine. Prior to World War I, it was in Galicia Province, Austrian Empire, and during the interwar period between World War I and World War II, it was part of Poland. Husiatyn is located at 49°04' N 26° 13' E and is 214 miles west-southwest of Kyyiv.

Husiatyn is located on the west bank of the Zbruch River. In the nineteenth century, the Zbruch River formed the boundary between Austria-Hungary and the Russian Empire. During the interwar period in the twentieth century, it formed the boundary between the Republic of Poland and the Soviet Union. Jews lived in Husiatyn since its formation in the sixteenth century. At that time, Jews primarily worked as farmers. In the early seventeenth century, three Jewish farmers in Husiatyn were accused of killing Christian children, and the farmers were tortured and killed. Over the years, many different political entities conquered and ruled the area. Among the conquerors were Cossacks, Turks, and Poles.

By 1772, the Kingdom of Poland controlled this area, which, by 1795, would be partitioned between Russia and Austria with Husiatyn partly in the hands of Austria. Most Jews in Husiatyn lived in Galicia, the side of the partition controlled by Austria. In 1765, shortly before the first partition of the Polish-Lithuanian Commonwealth, 1,444 Jews lived in Husiatyn. According to *The Encyclopedia of Jewish Life Before and During the Holocaust,* Jewish life there flourished, and the town became a center of trade. The arrival of Ḥasidic rebbes and their followers further boosted the economy and its importance in Jewish Galicia.[17] Among these were Rabbi Naḥman of Bratislav and his devotees. By 1861, a Ḥasidic rabbinic court was established, with Mordechai Shraga Feivish Friedman, son of Rebbe Israel of Ruzhin, at its head. The Ḥusiatyner rabbinic dynasty continued for four generations of rebbes. After World War I, the second Ḥusiatyner rebbe relocated to Vienna, joining other rebbes of the Ruzhiner dynasty. From there, in 1937, he went to Tel Aviv. The last Ḥusiatyner rebbe died in Tel Aviv in 1968.[18] The Ḥasidic branches are often known by the towns from which a rebbe and his followers originated. These towns have "-er" appended to the name of the town, thus Ḥusiatyner from Husiatyn, Ruzhiner from Ruzhin, etc.

Relationships developed with the local noble who was in a position to protect the community, and with such protection, the Jewish community grew and thrived. Marquis Golokhovski Aronson wrote that "[n]ew synagogues were built, as were ritual baths, hospitals, and old-age homes. The town supported new industries, including a Jewish-owned factory to make fountain pen nibs, print shops and paper merchants, as well as doctors, lawyers, and other professionals."[19] By 1882, a train route had been established that provided connections to Stanisławów,[20] also in Galicia. The distance between Husiatyn and Stanisławów was probably

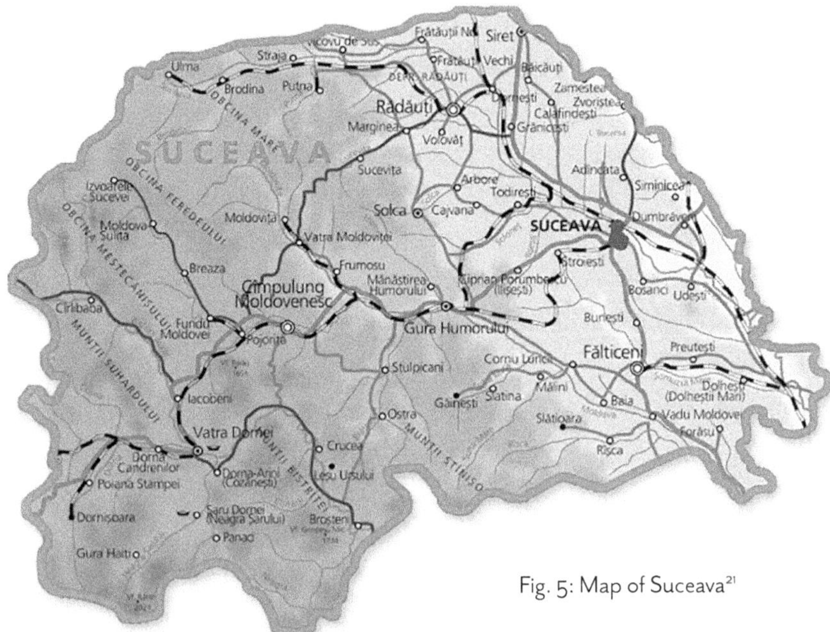

Fig. 5: Map of Suceava[21]

about 80 miles. The distance from Ḥusiatyn to Suceava, where Harry's family relocated, was under 150 miles.

Milton Silverman, the eldest son of Harry Silberman, remembers his grandmother Perl, née Buchbinder,[22] very well. He theorized that the family's move to Suceava from their former home in Husiatyn was based in religious sensibilities, not politics. Milton said he thought the family moved due to their religious practices more than anything else. As Ḥasidic influences became greater in Husiatyn, the family wanted to live in a place where there was less control and oversight by neighbors and a formal religious society. They were probably *mitnagdim*[23] and valued not only religious but secular education. Although they were observant, and remained so even after immigrating to America, they were not necessarily followers of any rebbe, nor did they want to be in that position.

Suceava, Romania, is not far from Husiatyn, but it appears to have been home to a very different type of Jewish community in the nineteenth century. Suceava is in the Bucovina district and is a slightly older city than Husiatyn. It was first settled in the fourteenth century and already had a Jewish presence by the fifteenth century. It was, politically, part of Moldavia[24] at that time and served as the Moldavian capital from 1380 until circa 1565.[25] Jews rose to prominence as bankers:

As occurred elsewhere in Europe, laws regulating and restricting interactions
between Jews and Christians were enacted by the mid-seventeenth century.

By the end of the seventeenth century, Transylvania left its association with the
Ottoman Empire and became part of the Austro-Hungarian Empire.[28] Similarly to
other places in Europe, blood libel charges were brought in the eighteenth century.
Unlike other European communities with similar anti-Semitic ritual murder charges,
the Moldavian Jewish community and the surrounding Christian areas remained
calm. By 1776, 55 families lived in Suceava, with a total of 300 Jews.[29]
Prince Mihail Sturdza, an early-nineteenth-century Romanian nobleman,
granted the Jews a 140-acre tract of land to be held by them in perpetuity.[30]
During the nineteenth century, Jews were permitted to immigrate to Moldavia
from Galicia and Bucovina. Many Ḥasidim took advantage of this liberal policy.
By 1808, the chief occupation of the Jews in Suceava was the production and
serving of brandy, beer, and alcohol.[31] By 1845, more than 85,000 Jews lived in
Moldavian cities. The 1847 petition of the government by a group of *maskilim*[32] to
force Moldavian Jews to abandon Ḥasidic dress and to allow a modern Jewish
school to open makes the liberal leanings of the area clear. The school opened in
1855, the same year that the first Yiddish journal was published in Iași.[33]

Moldavia and Husiatyn were on two different paths. Husiatyn would become known as a Ḥasidic stronghold, while Suceava would have a strong Ḥasidic presence but an equally strong and vibrant one comprised of other segments of Judaism. More than one-third of the total population of 10,000 was Jewish by 1880. By the time my grandfather was born in 1903, almost 7,000 Jews lived in the city of Suceava and an additional 1,500 Jews lived in the Suceava district.[34] The *History of the Jews in Bukowina, Geschichte der Juden in der Bukowina* includes a wonderfully detailed description of the composition of the community and some of its activities during the nineteenth century, when my great-grandparents relocated there:

[T]he "Beth Hamidrasch" was built in 1860 by Hersch Langer and Jakob Beer Weidenfeld. The two rabbis Hager and Jankale Moskowitz had their own prayer houses. In the great synagogue, the cantor Spektor officiated, the prayer reader was Srul Awner, a well-known Talmudist. The trustee of the great synagogue was Mendel Eisenberg. Members of the leadership were: Imperial Council, Hermann Beiner, who was an active captain in the Austrian army, leather factory owner Salomon Sternlieb, the iron dealer Schaje Langer, Mendl Bogen, Meier Rosenstock, Markus Kahn, Eisik Gruenberg, Alter Gruenberg, Lipa Fraenkel, Feibel Holdengraeber, and Hersch David.

The prayer house "Chewrath Thilim" was built by Mosche Matian, the "tailor school" by Eisig Rothkopf, the "Wiznitzer Klaus" by Mordche Tennenhaus, the Sadagurer Klaus by Mordche Leib Safran, Jonas Schwalbach, and Wolf Sigal, who contributed the land.

The community supported a Talmud Torah whose building was contributed by Itzig and Regine Vogel. Before the First World War, there was a Bible school where Grünseid, Moses Rosenstrauch, Kupferberg, and Wolf Gerson Langer served as teachers.

The first Jewish organization in Suceava was the "Chowewe Zion," whose founder Schaje Langer died in Transnistrien. His wife, Charlotte Langer, was founder of the woman's organization, "Ruth," which carried on significant social and cultural activities. The Zionist organization "Theodor Herzl" was founded by Dr. Adolf Gabor, who died in Schargorod Transnistrien, and Dr. Abraham Schapira, who also died in

Transnistrien. Schaje Langer and Avrum Aron Tennenbaum were effective members. The "Jüdische Gewerbe und Krankenunterstützungsverein," whose president was Karl Scherzer, should also be mentioned here.

As representative of the Suceava Jews, the physician Dr. Weidenfeld sat in the Bukovina parliament. Later, he was a lecturer at the university in Vienna. In the city government of Suceava, in 1907/8, the lawyer Dr. Baruch Schaffer was the first deputy mayor of Suceava and chairman of the Social Democratic Party of the Suceava district, under whose leadership a sewer system and electricity was installed, and second deputy mayor was the lawyer Dr. Heinrich Rohrlich Horowitz, who died in Schargorod of typhus. The Jewish city council members were: estate owner Hersch Sperber, lawyer Dr. Heinrich Lupul; Mosche Sternlieb; physician Dr. Benjamin Sperber; lawyer Dr. Adolf Gabor; Bernhard Kern; Leon Rothkopf; lawyer Dr. L. Bogen; lawyer Dr. Meir Teich, etc.

For decades, R. Mosche Hager served as rabbi in Suceava and Gerschon Stettner served as rabbinical court judge. His court in the "Long Street" was a center for thousands of his Chasidim who came to him out of the neighboring villages of the "Old Kingdom,"—Falticeni, Botoschani, Dorohoi, etc. After his death, his son, Chaim Hager, followed him in the rabbinate.

No less well known as a performer of wonders was a woman, the "Schotzer" rebezin. Her son was Rabbi Jankale Moskowicz, a well-known benefactor in the city. He welcomed in his house in the Itzkaner Street every poor person who came to Suceava and provided him with food and money. Thousands of Jews made pilgrimages to the graves of his father and mother, lit candles there, and left kwittlach with their wishes. People often came with Torah rolls and prayed by the graves. In memory of the Schotzer rabbi, a schotzer prayer house was erected in Chernivtsi. On July 28, 1914, in the house of the Rabbi Mosche Hager, the double wedding of his two oldest daughters was held.[35]

The Buchbinders in Suceava

I t is unclear exactly when Perl Buchbinder and Moses Silberman relocated to Suceava and why, but by the time they moved there, Perl's parents and at least one of her siblings were already there. Avraham Yosef Buchbinder, Perl's father, died on 26 December 1879. His death record only states the bare facts and does not include his parents' names, although other death records in the record book have more details. Perhaps the records with more extensive information are of people who were born in the area. There are no birth records in Suceava for Perl's oldest two children—David, born in 1880, and Lea, born in 1882. However, her third child, Chaya Ettel, was born in December 1883 in Suceava. She was the first of at least four of the children born to Perl to die in infancy.

By the time Perl and Moses moved to Suceava, at least one of Perl's siblings was already living there. Perl's sister Golde married there before 1878, divorced within a few years after the 1878 birth of her daughter Chaje, and married again before 1884. Another sister, Sura Lea, was there by the 1883 birth of her oldest child.

We know very little about Perl and Moses and the rest of the family in Suceava except the few details included in vital records. Perl and Moses's marriage and that of Perl's sister Sura Lea were registered there, decades after the actual marriages occurred. Quite surprisingly, our insight into the delayed

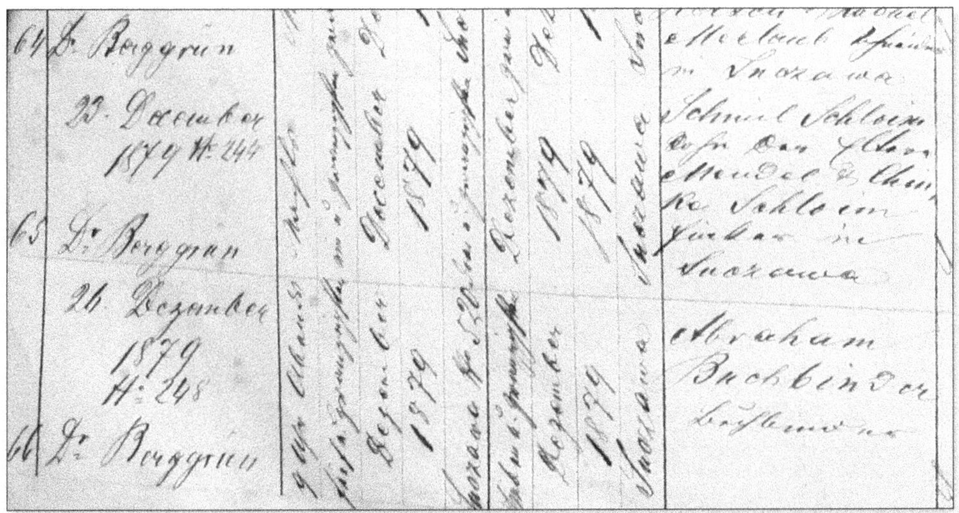

Fig. 7: Item 66, 1879 death record of Abraham Buchbinder[36]

marriage registration, which we considered to be an oddity, was not from records we found in the Suceava archives or the boxes of papers in Harry's apartment. Rather, it was something literally in plain sight hanging on a wall in my sister's house. It was a piece of "memorabilia" Harry had given to her many years earlier. After Harry's death, we began to examine it and discovered its significance.

The certificate is in German, dated 1913, and called *"Familien-Auskunfts-Bogen"*—Family information sheet. The caption on the page informed us that the document originated from Bukovina Crown Lands in the Austro-Hungarian monarchy. The document itself is part of the "Jewish District Register of Suzcawa." The page includes a preprinted label that the document is "for military purposes only" and was issued "in accord with the register of the Jewish registration authority." It contains information about 13 people—Moses and Perl Silberman and 11 children. Missing is a 12th child, David, who immigrated to the United States in 1905. Two of the 11 children on the document no longer lived with the family. The document includes details of their whereabouts. It reports that son Abraham had recently left for America, and son Yudel served in the military. There is no explanation of why they appear on the document and David does not. The address is "house number 15 in the town of Suczawa." This was the same address that appeared on Moses's work application. Although the certificate includes Moses's birth year, 1848, and the birth year of most of his children, it does not include one for Perl or for their oldest daughter, Lea. Moses, it confirms, was born in Husiatyn, in Galicia. The spelling in Romanian on the document makes it clear how both these names were to be pronounced: Husiatyn with an "H" and Galicia with a "G." By the time Perl left Suceava in 1928, either the houses had been renumbered and street names established, or she had moved. According to the voucher for her ship ticket in 1928, she resided at 19 Regina Maria Street, Suceava, Bukowina-Romania, not "house number 15 in the town of Suczawa." Houses were numbered as they were built, and without a street name, it is difficult to determine where the house was.

Examining the "family information sheet," we laughed both in amusement and confusion, noting that the marriage date for Moses and Perl was 20 May 1899 and, for Lea, was 30 May 1899. By 1899, Moses and Perl had 10 children. Of course, at that point, early on in our investigation of the family's history, we didn't understand the context of the information. Lea's marriage date was confirmed later through her descendants. She married Abraham Hersh Barasch in May 1899. Their first child, Rose, was born in June 1900. We have found no other

Israelitisches Geburts-Matrikenamt Suczawa

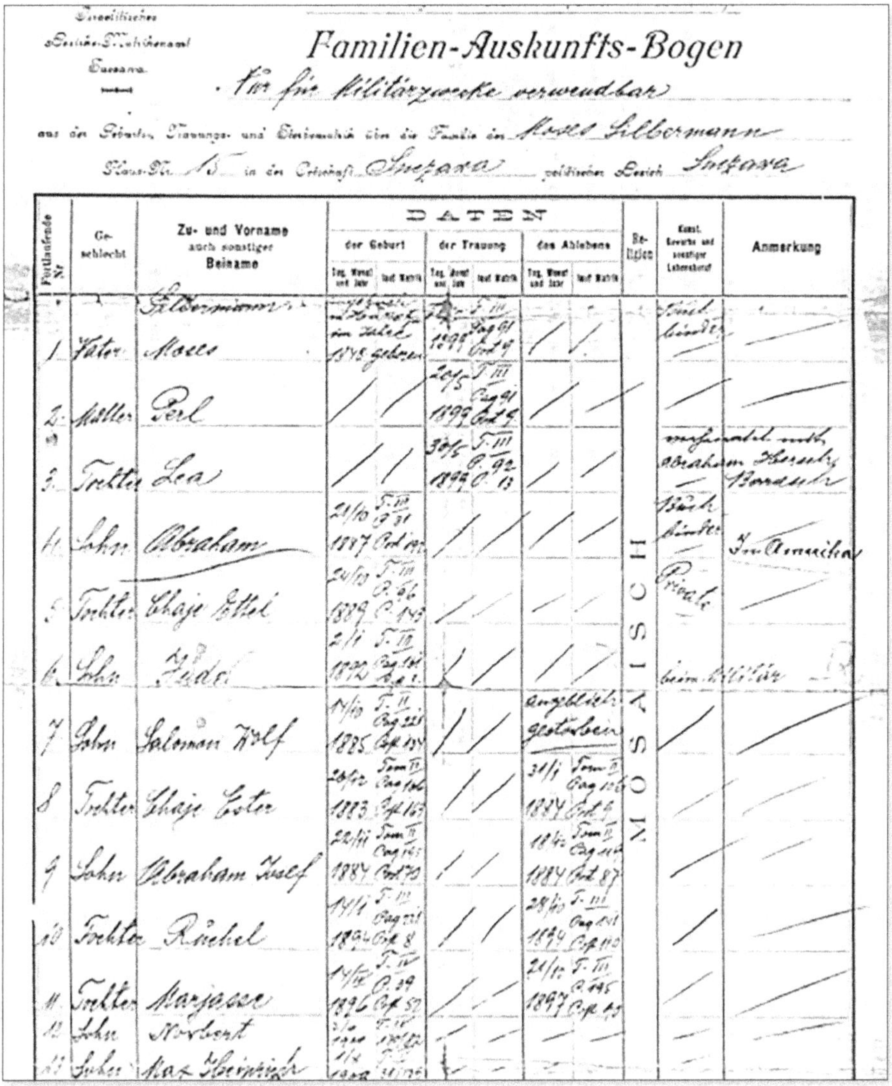

Familien-Auskunfts-Bogen

Nur für Militärzwecke verwendbar

aus den Geburts-, Trauungs- und Sterbematriken über die Familie des Moses Silbermann

Haus-Nr. 15 in der Ortschaft Suczawa politischer Bezirk Suczawa

Fortlaufende Nr.	Geschlecht	Zu- und Vorname auch sonstiger Beiname	DATEN der Geburt: Tag, Monat und Jahr	der Geburt: laut Matrik	der Trauung: Tag, Monat und Jahr	der Trauung: laut Matrik	des Ablebens: Tag, Monat und Jahr	des Ablebens: laut Matrik	Religion	Kunst, Gewerbe und sonstiger Lebensberuf	Anmerkung
1	Vater	Silbermann Moses	im Jahre 1848 geboren		20/5 1899	T. III Pag 91 Post 19	/	/	MOSAISCH	Buchbinder	
2	Mutter	Perl	/	/	20/5 1899	T III Pag 91 Post 19	/	/			
3	Tochter	Lea	/	/	30/5 1899	T III P. 92 Post 13	/	/		verehelicht mit Abraham Herzig Bonduch	
4	Sohn	Abraham	21/10 1887	T. III P. 31 Post 192	/	/	/	/		Buchbinder	In Amerika
5	Tochter	Chaje Ettel	24/10 1889	T. III P. 66 Post 143	/	/	/	/		Private	
6	Sohn	Juda	2/1 1892	T. III Pag 164 Post 1	/	/	/	/		beim Militär	
7	Sohn	Salomon Wolf	14/10 1885	T. II Pag 225 Post 134	/	/	angeblich gestorben			/	
8	Tochter	Chaje Ester	20/12 1883	Tom II Pag 104 Post 163	/	/	31/1 1884	Tom II Pag 106 Post 4			
9	Sohn	Abraham Josef	22/11 1887	Tom II Pag 141 Post 70	/	/	18/12 1884	Tom II Pag 114 Post 87		/	
10	Tochter	Rachel	1/1 1894	T. III Pag 221 Post 8	/	/	28/10 1894	T. III Pag 141 Post 110		/	
11	Tochter	Marjasse	14/12 1896	T. III P. 39 Post 57	/	/	24/12 1897	T. III P. 245 Post 45		/	
12	Sohn	Norbert	1900	[illegible]	—	—	—	—			
13	Sohn	Max Heinrich	1902	[illegible]	—	—	—	—			

Fig. 8: Family information sheet

document that records the marriage of Moses and Perl, such as a *ketubah*, a Jewish marriage contract. At the time, we knew that we were missing some crucial information about social or legal conventions. We assumed that the norm was not to wait to get married until after the births of 10 children. Jewish communities regulated themselves based on Jewish law and custom, which meant, among other things, prohibitions against unrelated unmarried adults of different genders living together or having children out of wedlock. The Jewish community would have maintained birth, marriage, and death information for Jewish legal purposes.

Among these would be proper records of marriages, deaths, and divorces to allow children to prove their legitimacy and marry within the Jewish community. When there was a disadvantage imposed by the government, such as conscription or taxation, government records might not reflect actual dates or even the existence of marriages.

The reasons for recording the marriage of Moses Silbermann and Perl Buchbinder at the same time as that of their eldest daughter is unknown; however, we can speculate based on historical information. The reason Perl and Moses's marriage wasn't recorded at the time of the actual event was probably due to the Austrian Empire's restrictive family laws directed at the Jewish community. Registering their marriage at the time they did was most likely driven by their children's desire to emigrate. Writing about the period between 1795 and 1918 in Austro-Hungarian Galicia, genealogist Jeffrey K. Cymbler commented that:

...only one son in each Jewish family was allowed to marry. In addition, only those couples who possessed between 500 and 1,000 florins and who paid 10 percent of their wealth as a marriage tax could marry. Galician Jews who had fewer than 500 florins could not apply for permission to marry at all; those with more than 1,000 florins had to pay a higher marriage tax. The result was that most Galician Jews married religiously only.

The marriages were never recognized nor recorded by the civil authorities; the children of such unions often were recorded as illegitimate and required to adopt their mother's maiden name as their own surname.[37]

Although Suceava was in the Austrian Empire, it was not in Galicia, it was in the Bukovina province. Laws for Jews in Galicia would not have applied to the Silberman family once they relocated to Suceava. However, those laws in effect for the Jews of Galicia would have affected the family before they relocated. Many places in the Austrian Empire had a cap on the number of Jews and the number of Jewish families permitted residency. Not only was the oldest son the only male child permitted to marry, but he was required to live in the same locale as his father did. If a vacancy occurred because of a death or emigration of a family, the authorities could prevent that vacancy from being filled.[38] The law also stated that when a couple did not register their marriage with the civil authorities, a child was not permitted to use the father's surname, and the child was registered as illegitimate at birth. Children of unregistered marriages were not only illegitimate, but they were not legal residents. They were prohibited from certain occupations and were not permitted to travel.[39] Laws were repealed and then issued again with slightly different wording and sometimes with harsher terms. For example, although in 1869, some of the restrictive marriage laws were eased, in 1875 civil registration of marriages was enforced. This new law said that all official documents for a child whose parents did not have a registered marriage, could only show the surname of a mother, and that child could not inherit from the father. Illegitimate births were recorded in large numbers on Jewish records all over Galicia until the late nineteenth century. At the very end of the century, many marriages were registered. It is probable that prior to the enactment of the laws regarding a child's illegitimate status, the practice of not registering marriages in the Jewish community was widespread. Laws are rarely, if ever, enacted to regulate something that is not already a practice.

The reasons for Moses and Perl not recording their marriage might have been to avoid the tax or because Moses was not the first son in his family to be married. It might even have been that the law was no longer in effect but the custom established by the law may still have been followed. Another possibility for the lack of records was that:

> ...[m]arriages were performed under Jewish law and [Jews] saw no need for registration with the civil authorities. Also, there were many marriages within families, with cousins or nieces, which are permitted under Jewish law but not under civil law. These weren't registered, thus causing the non-Jewish authorities to wonder at the number of Jewish "illegitimate" births. Still...not every Jew in Hungary changed his family name, and many family names were used for hundreds of years.[40]

Although Perl and Moses registered their marriage long after the fact, it is unclear why they did. Children born to non-registered couples were given their mother's surname at birth and suffered under other restrictions. Not all the children of Moses and Perl were born in Suceava, but those that were had the name Silberman, not Buchbinder, at birth. An example of this is Fig. 9, the record of the 1889 birth of Chaya Ettel, the third child born to Moses and Perl. Chaya Ettel

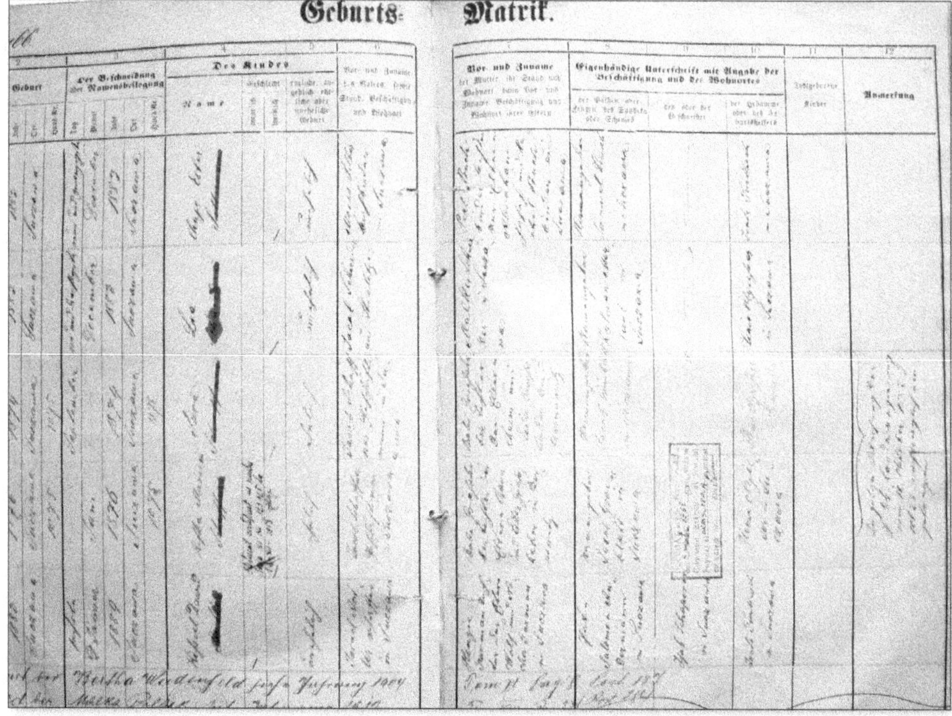

Fig. 9: 1889 birth record of Chaya Ettel[41]

tragically died when she was less than a month old. Although it appears to modern eyes as though her surname was crossed out, this kind of marking is true for all the births on the page, and I believe the names were highlighted, not crossed out.

Since it was not only in Austro-Hungarian Galicia or even among Austro-Hungarian Galician Jews that vital records were not always maintained, it is important to consider the question raised by ChaeRan Y. Freeze. Speaking about Czarist Russia, Freeze asked: "what onerous state laws impelled so many Russian subjects (not just the Jews) to evade registration at all costs?" As she pointed out, there was a need for new legislation after the partitions of Polish-Lithuanian Commonwealth. She wrote that the laws were:

...to establish order in its newly annexed borderlands and to define the social and legal obligations, rights, and privileges of its subjects. That, however, proved to be extremely complicated: the diverse population of Jews did not really fit into the existing structures and legal categories. The result was a plethora of contradictory and confusing legislation.

Nevertheless, registration was one means to enable the government to integrate the Jews into its administrative system, and, indeed, the state had instruments for inscribing and tracking its Jews.[42]

The government's intention may well have been benign, but the taxation, regulation, and conscription that followed such registrations proved otherwise. Consequences due to the "illegal" status of religious-only marriages and the children born of them took the form of fines, imprisonment, or even banishment from a community by the authorities. Many ramifications particularly affect researchers concerning the surnames of children born to couples with unregistered marriages. We had a lot to learn about how these names were ultimately recorded on birth, marriage, or death records. Research becomes complicated when it is unclear whether the surname used at the time of immigration was that of the immigrant's father or mother. Since immigrants often changed their names shortly after arriving in their new homeland, another question that arises is whether the choice of a new surname could relate to a name by which they were known in Europe. Identifying the surnames of both of a person's parents thus becomes a necessary tool in research.

German Surnames

As previously noted, some of the documents found in Harry's apartment were in German. These documents were from the days of Austrian rule over Suceava. Moshe and Perl lived in the Tarnopol[44] area of Galicia before they went to Suceava. Perl was born in Tluste, Zaleszczyki District[45] Galicia, not far from Stanisławów. We have no records of the lives of Perl Buchbinder and Moshe Silbermann before they were in Suceava. The records we have indicate that they came from Husiatyn. We cannot, however, document that their surnames came with them from Husiatyn, although we believe that the family was known by Silbermann in Husiatyn. *JRI-Poland's* databases provide information that there were families with the surname of Silberman living in the Tarnopol[46] region in the mid- and late 1800s. There was a Moshe Silberman in Tarnopol who married Dobrisch Wachs in 1857. We are certain this is not our Moshe, but due to other similar names repeated in branches of that family, which also appear in ours, we believe there is a strong possibility that they are related to our Moshe. Our Moshe's parents were Mayer Hersh and Sara, and our Moshe was born in 1848, he would have been too young to marry in 1857. We speculated that Mayer Hersh had a brother named Yitzchak and that the Moshe who married Dobrisch might be the son of Yitzchak. Their surname was written as Zylberman. This spelling more accurately reflects the way the name Silberman was pronounced by German speakers. *JRI-Poland* databases include 92 records of Buchbinders in the Tarnopol region. None of these records can be definitively linked to Perl or her parents, Avraham Yosef and Rose Ruchel. Before we figured out that the Moshe who married Dobrisch was not "our" Moshe, we hypothesized that Perl was his second wife and that my dad had a lot of half-uncles and aunts—and, of course, cousins. When identifying information that seems at odds with other known facts, I find that if I hypothesize different scenarios, ultimately it helps to narrow the field of possibilities and the issue gets resolved.

In July 1787, Josef II[47] mandated that the entire population of Eastern Galicia adopt German given names and surnames prior to 1 January 1788.[48] In 1789, legislation was passed to enforce Josef II's decree. Before this time, most Jewish families in the area did not have surnames, with the exception of rabbinic dynasties.[49] In 1795, the Polish territory known as West Galicia was absorbed into the Austrian

Empire[50] and, by 1805, the Jews of that area were also required to adopt names as mandated by the 1787 law.[51] According to Wynne, those Galician families who carry non-Germanic surnames migrated to Galicia and brought their names from elsewhere.[52] In both Prussia and Austria, the official language was German. Beider wrote that, in Prussia, unlike Galicia, Jewish surnames formed from masculine given names were common, as were surnames formed by modifying original Jewish given names. In the Russian Empire's Pale of Settlement, surnames often had a toponymic origin. He continued by commenting that:

> Differences in official languages had important influences on the languages used in creating Jewish surnames. In Galicia and Prussia, the official language was German, and in both areas, the entire surnaming process was managed by Christian clerks. Almost all names are derived from German. A few names are derived from Hebrew or Polish, but a large proportion of Jewish names from Galicia and Prussia sound like German names. In Congress Poland, the situation is more nuanced. We have two different layers of names. In the first, oldest layer, the names were German, assigned by either Austrian or Prussian authorities between 1797 and 1809, during the time when the area that later become Congress Poland belonged partly to Prussia and partly to Austria. When the Polish government issued a law forcing Jews in Congress Poland to establish their surnames in 1821, a large number just took the same names that had been assigned to them 20 years earlier by either Prussian or Austrian authorities.[53]

Wynne pointed out that, in spite of the use of Germanic surnames, Polish name endings were often appended to the German name.[54] Those Polish name suffixes often differentiate between gender, such as the masculine "ski" and the feminine "ska." They also used feminine endings that indicated whether a woman was unmarried, like "owna" or "anka," or if she was married or a widow, like "owa" or "yna."[55] Mandating that Jews have German surnames was a way to integrate Jews into Austrian society and bring them "closer to an appreciation for what Austria had to offer."[56] In other words, make the Jewish people not Jewish. The American practice of Indian boarding schools founded to eliminate traditional Native American ways of life and replace them with what was considered mainstream American culture, is an example of a similar practice by a ruling body attempting to wipe out a minority group. The surname mandate was part of a larger scheme beginning with a 1784 mandate requiring civil registration of births, marriages, and deaths. Prior to the name mandate, most Jews were known by their patronymic names. The Germanic-sounding surnames of Silberman and Buchbinder may have resulted from this legislation. We know the Buchbinder surname referred to the family's occupation as bookbinders. Of all the surnames carried by various branches of my family, that is the only one whose origin is clear.

In the United States, Silberman took a variety of forms. Some of Harry's brothers spelled their names with a double "n"—Silbermann. It is possible that they used a variety of other spellings, including an initial "Z" instead of an "S." Although Harry and his wife, Blima, spelled the name "Silberman," their two sons, Milton and Stanley, spelled their names "Silverman." The story related to me was that the hospital misspelled Milton's name when he was born and his parents decided to leave the spelling the way it was. When Stanley was born, they supplied the spelling with the "v" and kept their own names spelled with a "b," although changing the spelling of their names might have been easy to accomplish at that time, since Harry was naturalized after Milton's birth. I wonder why Harry and Blima did not change the spelling of their surname then. Milton said he recalled that, when his mother registered him in kindergarten, there was an argument because her name and that of her son were not the same.

The papers we found in Harry's apartment included letters from his niece Erika and her father, Norbert Silberman. Norbert was the only one of my grandfather's siblings who remained in Europe after the beginning of the Nazi takeover. One afternoon in the summer of 1985, shortly after my grandfather's diagnosis with terminal cancer, he and I looked through old photo albums. Perhaps his illness made him uncharacteristically talkative. We came to a photo that he identified as his brother Norbert. I had never before heard of this brother. He told me that Norbert died during the war. Finally, he told a story of Norbert's death outside Mauthausen, a concentration camp. Harry said that Norbert attempted to bribe guards to gain the release of his youngest daughter, Erika, from the camp, but the guards shot him. According to my grandfather, Norbert's wife, Ella, was a beautiful woman. As an actress in Yiddish theater, she caught the eye of a Nazi officer, who arrested her and took her into his home as his mistress. After several years, she

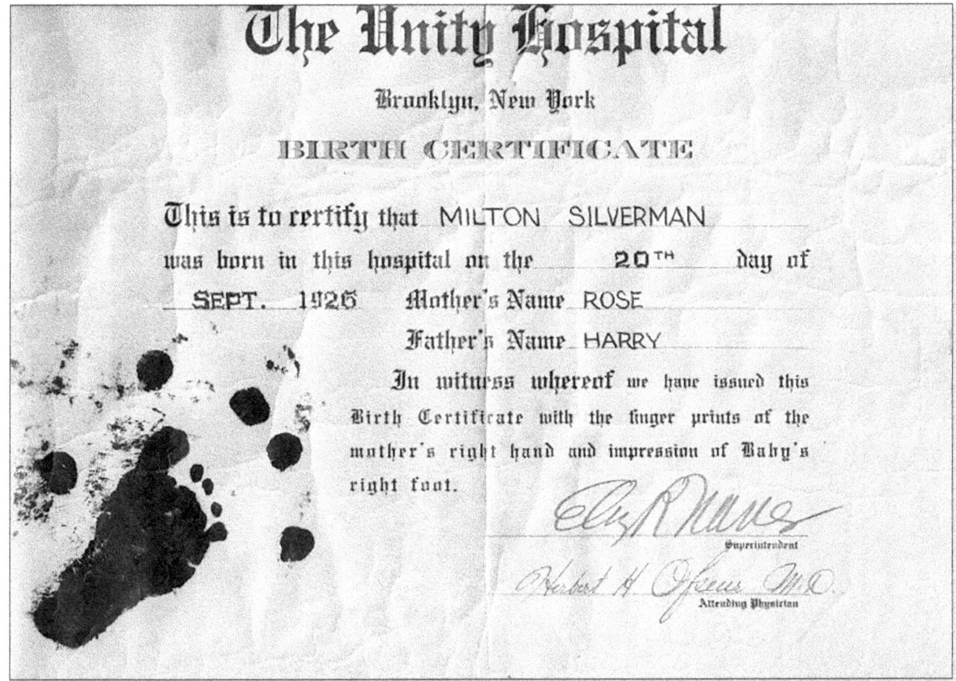

Fig. 10: Milton Silverman's 1926 birth certificate[57]

was released and committed to a mental institution. The officer took Ella's younger daughter, Erika, in her stead. Norbert, frantic to get Erika out, bribed a guard. When he went to exchange the money for his daughter, the friendly guard was not there, and other guards shot and killed Norbert. The story was tragic.

Yad Vashem and Holocaust Records

Among the papers were letters from Erika to my grandparents during and after the war. From Erika's letters, it does not sound as if the story Harry told us was true. Norbert did die at Mauthausen, just not the way Harry said it transpired. I discovered the records of his incarceration and death at Yad Vashem. One day in the summer of 1997, I was at Yad Vashem looking through their indices of names. Endless hours of poring through lists of survivors in all parts of Europe yielded no results for anyone of whose fate we were uncertain that I could name at that time. In the middle of the day, I started looking through some records from the concentration camps and discovered the intake and death records for Norbert. Although I knew he died in or near a camp, seeing the record shook me. I suppose that was a normal reaction to the confirmation of a death in such awful circumstances.

I visited Israel for the first time in 1966. As part of that visit, I toured Yad Vashem, the Shoah memorial center in Israel that was established in 1953 to memorialize all those murdered during the Holocaust and perpetuate their names.[59] In addition to their extensive grounds and exhibits, there was a massive microfilm library in 1997. At the time, I did not understand the implications of that library but was grateful that it was available for research. Today, research in the Yad Vashem databases can be conducted not only on-site in Israel, but also through their digital collection of records and materials at http://www.yadvashem.org. In addition to their database of names of victims, submitted by survivors, families, and friends of victims and gathered from lists of names maintained by the camps, Yad Vashem serves as a repository of copies of the archives originally held by the International Tracing Service (ITS) in Bad Arolsen, Germany. The microfilm record I found in 1997 was part of the ITS records. The cryptic note on the bottom of the index card that recorded Norbert's information reads "ITS Master Index."

At that time, I had no idea about the value of the ITS master index or what the letters "ITS" meant. The letters "ITS" stand for "International Tracing Service." In 1943, a tracing bureau was formed under the auspices of the British Red

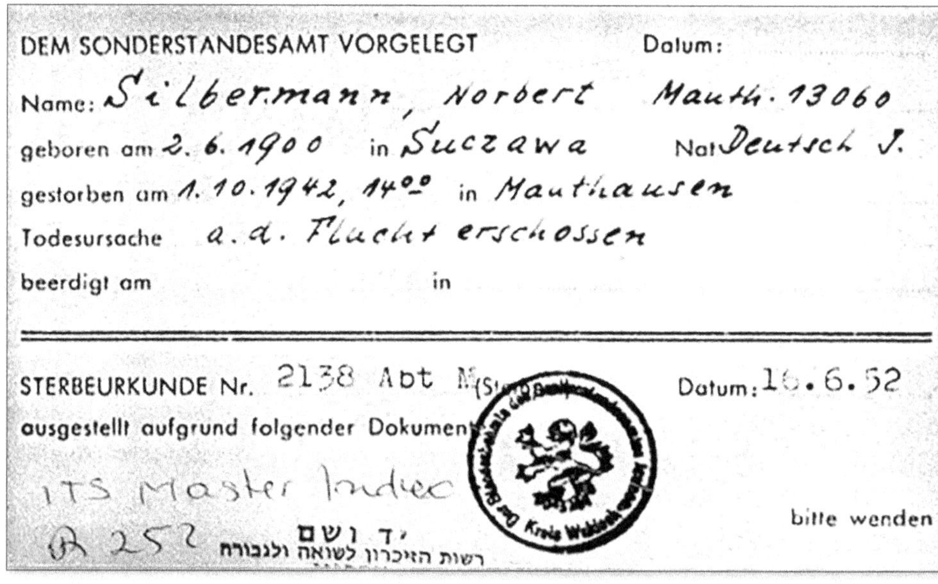

Fig. 11: Norbert Silbermann's Mauthausen record[58]

Cross. Its purpose was to trace and register missing persons. To that end, it began collecting documents held by the Nazis, including information from orphanages, hospitals, concentration camps, and refugee camps. The files the ITS held ultimately contained information on nearly 18 million people from concentration camps or who were refugees after the war. The material is not comprehensive. There is little information in these records, for example, about the people murdered on the streets in Eastern Europe by the *Einsatzgruppen*.[60]

The founding of the ITS was not intended specifically to aid Jewish families that were split up during the war. People of all nationalities had their lives disrupted during the war, and many people throughout Europe were looking for family members. The ITS also was not intended to become an archive—its primary purpose at its inception was that of a tracing service. Although the ITS was not open to the public, its employees responded to written requests for information about missing people.

The ITS morphed into an archive as the need for tracing missing people diminished. After the war, in 1955, the ITS came under the umbrella of a coalition of 11 nations including the United States, France, Israel, and Great Britain and was administered by the International Committee of the Red Cross. The governance of the ITS by the Red Cross ceased in 2012. At that time, the German Federal Archive took over its administration. Since 1956, Yad Vashem has held much material from the ITS archives, such as the records I searched in 1997. Beginning in 2007, digitized ITS holdings were released to organizations in each of the 11 countries responsible for the archives. Some of the databases can now be searched online through the websites of many of the repositories. More research can be done in person or by submission of written requests to one of the repositories.[61] In April 2019, the name of the ITS was changed to the Arolsen Archives-International Center on Nazi Persecution. The name change emphasizes its new goals as an archive. The Arolsen Archives offers the public projects, exhibitions, and education on the consequences of anti-Semitism, discrimination, and racism, in addition to continuing to make available the collection of documents from concentration camps and ghettos.[62]

In 2012, I spoke with Zvi Bernhardt (1962-2020), then Deputy Director of Reference and Information Services and Deputy Director of the Hall of Names at Yad Vashem.[63] He told me that the Nazis did not write down names and information about all the people murdered in the camps. He said that records of western Europeans and of people who lived for a short period in the camps were created at deportation points. Records such as the ones I found for Norbert only existed when the person to whom the records referred was admitted to the camp. If a person was murdered immediately, no record was created, and that person's name would never appear on any camp record. Bernhardt said that 85% of the people who arrived at Auschwitz were murdered within a day of their arrival and their names were not recorded! What we know from this record is that Norbert was not murdered outside the camp, as Harry's story indicated.

Among the Yad Vashem documents I searched through were lists of people. It is difficult to describe the lists and the effort needed to look through them. There was little organization in their compilation, as could be expected in a time before the internet. Each list was created according to the city of a person's birth or residence. Some were handwritten, some typed. The records I looked at were the originals dating from just after the end of the war. Europe was in chaos, and the records were never reorganized. Indices were created only recently, making an electronic search of digitized records possible. The compilation of names was intended to help people find those who were missing after the war. To find someone, it was necessary to look through the records in each city and country unless you knew in which country or city they lived after the war. The hours I spent searching through the microfilm records at Yad Vashem proved invaluable, and I learned a lot. Finding a record for Norbert was more by chance than anything else. Looking at lists of names with scribbled notes containing tidbits of information about the people gave me a feeling of hopelessness and loss. I read each name carefully, hoping that I, 50 years after the end of the war, might still find a record of someone in my family. I cannot imagine how survivors must have felt when looking at these same lists in the days, weeks, and years immediately following the devastation. Once I found Norbert's name, I requested the record. The friend who accompanied me that day said she thought I was going to pass out when I found him. This was the first record I found in my research—I had never looked through Shoah records prior to that day. Since then, I have not stopped reading lists of names and searching for people. Although it is obviously impossible to restore those who were victims of the Shoah to life, we can restore them to memory.

Norbert died in Mauthausen on 1 October 1942. We have several letters from him, all written in German[64] dated in 1937, 1938, and 1941. His last letter was from Zurich dated 17 July 1941. In it, he asks about his daughter, Charlotte, living in New York. He commented that only two countries in Europe would permit mail to be sent to the United States,[65] and that it was for the purpose of sending and receiving mail that he was staying in Switzerland. He did not mention any specifics about his situation or where he had been or what he was doing. His greeting mentioned that he had not heard from the family in many months. Since none of the letters to which he refers remain, it seems likely the full correspondence from him to his mother and brother were not preserved. I had hoped that the missing information might be included in letters he wrote to other relatives, but descendants of his other siblings had no letters from him. Norbert's daughter Charlotte lived in South Florida for many years and would not speak of her father. In July 1941, Norbert wrote:

I am fine and still alive, which is very important, even after everything, during the war-time situation. After what I have overcome and what we've experienced, I don't believe that I'm still alive. We have no other aim than just live on, and only God knows if we'll live to the end, as we're living in Europe, in the world full of blood and tears. Nothing but blood, tears, horrors, and estrangement.

I have no knowledge of what happened to him between the date of this last letter and the date of his death. The Mauthausen record does not include the date of his incarceration.

On 12 March 1938, Germany invaded Austria. The invasion had been carefully planned. Just before it happened, the press reported rioting and a call by the Austrian populace for German troops to assist in restoring order. The propaganda was part of an orchestrated attempt to get Austrian Chancellor Kurt von Schuschnigg to resign his post and to influence a vote that would permit the banned Austrian National Socialist Party to participate in the government. Schuschnigg, conscious that help would not be forthcoming from France and England, resigned his post, leaving the way clear for the invasion and the subsequent annexation the following day. The troops encountered no resistance.[66]

Mauthausen is located about 12.5 miles from the Austrian city of Linz near the Danube River. It was built by prisoners from Dachau sent to Mauthausen on 8 August 1938, only a few months after the Anschluss of Austria,[67] for the express purpose of building a new concentration camp. Mauthausen is not only

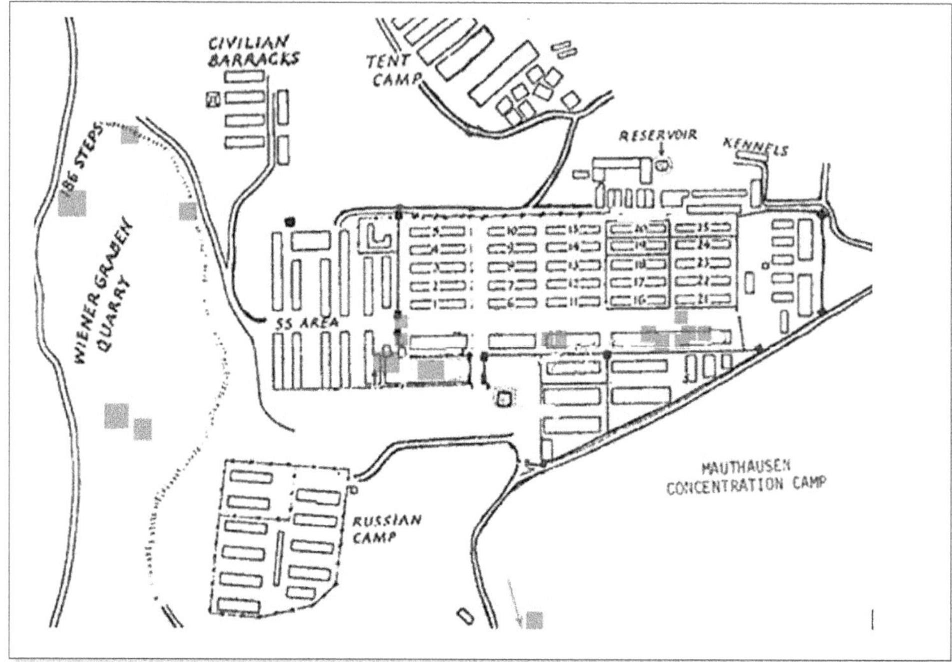

Fig. 12: Mauthausen map

the name commonly used for the mother camp, but it is also the name applied to the entire complex that grew out of the mother camp.[68] The prisoners worked in an abandoned stone quarry that would literally provide the building blocks for the physical plant.[69] The designation of the Mauthausen concentration camp as a Category III camp indicated that it was intended to serve as a camp with a harsh regimen.[70] Guenter Lewy, a professor emeritus of political science at the University of Massachusetts Amherst, wrote that "inmates as a rule were not expected to emerge alive."[71] Between 8 August 1938 and 5 May 1945, about 195,000 people were delivered to these camps.[72] By 1945, the Mauthausen complex was comprised of almost 60 sub-camps.

The main camp included 32 barracks surrounded by electrified barbed wire. Eventually, the fields around it also came to be enclosed by electrified barbed wire. In this wire-surrounded enclosure, prisoners who were primarily Hungarian Jews and Russian soldiers stayed in the open all year round.[73] Gordon Horwitz wrote that its inmates "were deemed incapable of being rehabilitated and hence not qualified for eventual release. In practical terms, the issuance of an order to Mauthausen represented a life term or death sentence for the inmates."[74]

Dr. Konnilyn Feig, a researcher and teacher of the Holocaust, referred to the production that resulted from the labor of the inmates there as a "sideline, a byproduct of the killing process."[75] I wish we knew when Norbert was sent there and how much time he spent there. I hope it was not long.

Fred Zimmak wrote in a message that appeared on the Austria-Czech Special Interest Group (SIG) Digest listserv in December 2011[76] that, while incarcerated in Auschwitz, Birkenau, and Ravensbruck concentration camps, his mother both sent and received letters. The letters his mother received do not appear to be similar to those described in a message by John Freund in response to Fred Zimmak's comments. Freund described postcards inmates wrote at Birkenau just before they were killed.

Birkenau was a camp located in Auschwitz, within sight of the gas chambers. Here, the Nazis created a 'Family Camp' (September 1943) with inmates transported from Terezin. In March 1944, six months after arrival, all those still in the camp (many died here before) were killed in the gas chambers. A few days before, all those in the Family Camp (there was another transport from Terezin in December 1943) were handed postcards to mail to Terezin or to anyone outside of camps. The message was "we are well and together"...the date given was several weeks later. By then, only inmates that arrived in Birkenau from Terezin in December 1943 were in the family camp (other than those who died there). Several messages hinting that all was not as written were passed on, but none were recognized by the reci[]pients. For example, some signed the postcard as 'DEATH' in Hebrew. NONE of these postcards show the address of the camp as Auschwitz. The usual address given was 'Birkenau bei NeuBerun.'

As far as we know, Norbert wrote no letters, as described by Zimmak, nor postcards, as described by Freund. The July 1941 letter is the last communication from him I could find.

Norbert's Family and Yiddish Theater

Erika's letters to Harry, in which she spoke of Norbert, her father, sounded as if she barely knew him. She intimated that he had abandoned the family when she was a baby! Her letters included mysterious-sounding allegations about bank accounts in Zurich and references to possibly well-known family stories that nobody remembered any longer. As I wrote this, I thought about *midrashim*[77] that developed fill-in-the-blanks in biblical stories and references in the Bible to material that must have been well known at the time the Bible was written or edited but which are no longer understood. Jewish literature is replete with attempts to explain gaps in the biblical text. An example of this type of *midrash* are the stories built around Genesis 29:17—"And Leah's eyes were weak; but Rachel was of beautiful form and fair to look upon." It is easy to imagine how Rachel looked, but the first phrase "Leah's eyes were weak" is more difficult. Did that mean that she couldn't see well, tears freely flowed from her eyes, that she squinted, or that her appearance was unpleasant? The authors of the biblical text may have known and understood what they wrote, and it is likely that its listeners understood the term when the story was told and retold. Later, its meaning was unclear, and stories developed to explain it in the context of the relationship between the sisters and Jacob's choice of Rachel for his wife. Similarly, contemporary family stories lose some of their meaning when they contain references to unidentified people and are not specific about events. Our inclination is to make sense of incomplete stories and offer speculation about their meaning or intent.

We knew that Norbert, Harry's brother, married a woman who was an actress in the Yiddish Theater. My father said that his cousin Charlotte Silberman, Norbert's older daughter, was an actress in Yiddish theater. Charlotte, with whom my father had sporadic contact, filled in some information about her mother and her sister, Erika. Erika died about 1995 in Europe, where she had remained after the war. Charlotte settled in the United States, having arrived from Europe under the sponsorship of a Jewish vaudeville group in 1938. The ship manifest from the docking of the *Ile de France* on 5 September 1938 lists her among the passengers. She gave the name of her grandmother Rosa Siegler in Vienna as her European contact and listed a person she called her "director," named Fiszon, as her U.S. contact on West 48th Street in New York City. The director has not been definitively identified, but it could have been Misha Fiszon, who is mentioned as an actor and director in many biographical sketches of actors in Yiddish theater in Europe and the United States.[78] It is likely that the 1938 visa allowing her to come to New York fell under the Immigration Quota Act of 17 March 1932,[79] where "Such aliens shall not be considered artists or professional actors under the terms of the Immigration Act of 1917, and thereby exempt from the contract labor laws, unless they are recognized to be of distinguished ability and are coming to fulfill professional engagements corresponding to such ability."[80]

Further investigation proved the story about the connection to Yiddish theater an understatement rather than an embellishment. It revealed that Charlotte's maternal grandfather was Maurice Siegler, also known as Moshe Beltzer, an actor and director. Charlotte's grandmother, the "Rosa" on the manifest, was Rosa Channa Rozenshteyn, a singer from Iași, Romania. Rosa and Maurice had three daughters: Adella, also known as 'Ella'; Erna; and Sevilla. All three became prominent figures in live Yiddish theater. Ella was Charlotte and Erika's mother. In May 1998, Charlotte told Milton that her grandfather Moshe Siegler was with the family in Vienna when the *Anschluss* occurred in 1938. He went to Czechoslovakia and tried to obtain exit visas for Ella, Charlotte, and Erika. During that period, the family lived in the Stephanie Hotel in Vienna.

Fig. 13: Erna Siegler and Sevilla Pastor, 1936[81]

Steve Lasky, creator of the online Museum of Family History[82] and translator of the "Lexicon of the Yiddish Theatre Biographies," summarized the role of the Sieglers for me in an email exchange in 2009. At that time, his website with the translations was not as well developed, as it is today, and the full translation of the lexicon had not been completed.

In the 1930s, the Pastor-Siegler troupe gave frequent guest performances at the Jüdische Künstlerspiele, with Sevilla Pastor as a celebrated "star." Rosa Siegler was a singer and actor; she married the actor Maurice Siegler around 1900 and came to Vienna with him in 1909. Until 1915, Maurice Siegler was the director of the Jüdische Bühne, and in the 1920s, he and Rosa appeared with the Freie Jüdische Volksbühne. In the 1930s, the Siegler family, consisting of Maurice and Rosa Siegler, their daughters Erna Siegler (Vienna 1911–unknown) and Sevilla Pastor, and their son-in-law Muniu Pastor, gave successful guest performances in Vienna. Erna Siegler, who debuted as early as 1920, took part in the troupe's performances in the 1930s in the role of the romantic lover; after 1938, she fled to the USA. Sevilla Pastor had married the actor Muniu Pastor in 1926; her specialty and greatest success with audiences was in trouser roles.

Howe and Greenberg explained the importance of Yiddish theater:

...[b]eginning with the wandering troupes of Eastern Europe, and particularly Rumania, the Yiddish theater quickly became a popular institution—in fact, the major cultural outlet for the Jewish masses. Not only did professional playwrights like Abraham Goldfaden and Jacob Gordin write for it, but many Yiddish poets and novelists were tempted by the mass audiences it could provide in such centers as Warsaw and New York. To be sure, the Yiddish theater was often sentimental, crude, and melodramatic, but at its occasional best, it released an enormous creative and emotional energy.[83]

Theater and plays have long provided a way of entertaining the masses and informing the public. In Jewish culture, there is a tradition of the *Purim shpiel*—the retelling of the Purim story often acted out in costume. Dramatic presentations were also traditionally acceptable at *Ḥanukkah* and weddings, even though "rabbinic tradition disapproves of theater, which is alluded to in the very first psalm as *moshav letsim*, the 'seat of scoffers.'"[84] Roger I. Simon, a noted educator, described the beginnings of Yiddish theater when he wrote:

The inception of Yiddish theater must be understood as a fundamentally radical event in the process of a Jewish cultural revolution. Jews had historically lacked any theater tradition. Such practices were considered vulgar and to be shunned within a life devoted to God, community, and family. While a form of Jewish theater had flourished since the Renaissance in the guise of the purimspiel, such performances were limited to one brief yearly holiday and were most often loosely organized within what from outside the culture might be called a type of Rabelaisian carnival. Thus Yiddish theater was located within an emerging discourse that emphasized "the new," "the modern," and which (with various degrees of ambivalence) broke with what many at the time saw as a sense of limitation and suffering attached to traditional Jewish life.[85]

Although amateur Yiddish theater existed before 1876, it was in that year, in Iași, Romania,[86] that the first professional performance occurred. Iași was not too far from the birthplace in Suceava of Harry Silberman and his siblings. It is easy to imagine that the family may have seen plays or heard about the Yiddish theater as they were growing up.

These first plays were performed by Avrom Goldfadn at the Green Tree wine gardens in Iași. His performances did not initially begin as plays but as poetry readings, and after their success, he began performing simple plays.[87] Simon referred to Yiddish theater as a "revolutionary cultural form."[88] He pointed out that, while Avrom Goldfadn may not have performed professionally until 1876, he appeared in 1862 in the "first known production of any modern Yiddish play"—a comic melodrama performed at his school.[89] Brigitte Dalinger, in an article on actresses in Yiddish theater, commented that most female performers in Yiddish theater were either the daughters or wives of performers.[90] The Dora Teitelboim Center for Yiddish Culture website referred to Charlotte (Silberman) Cooper as: "a third-generation Yiddish actress who began performing as a child with her grandfather's troupe originating in Vienna, the Ziegler Troupe."

Charlotte was still performing in 2008 in Miami, Florida. Their website contains an interview with her in which she discussed some details of the Yiddish theater in Europe.[91]

Violence Born of Political Change: Russian Empire

In 1882, at the time Yiddish theater was under threat in the Russian Empire, the first Yiddish theater production opened in New York. In Russia, however, Yiddish theater was on the verge of being prohibited. The March 1881 assassination of Czar Alexander II was followed by a wide series of pogroms. His son Alexander III took the throne and almost immediately began to abrogate the more permissive policies instituted by his father. By August 1883, Yiddish theater was on the list of prohibited activities.[92] In general, Jewish life in Russian territories under the rule of Alexander III took a turn for the worse. Prohibitions and violent actions against the Jews had a profound effect that would be felt for decades. David Vital wrote about the connections of three important dates in European history: 1789, 1881, and 1933. He commented that the French Revolution, along with the fall of the Bastille in 1789, was the point at which "the long, final history of the Jews of Europe begins in earnest. The seizure of power in Germany by the National Socialist Party [in 1933] marks that at which the chapter draws to its end."[93]

Events, of course, do not occur in a vacuum, but at times, some events that appear to be widespread have their biggest impact on a small group within the whole. Such was the aftermath of the assassination of Alexander II and the ascension to the throne of Alexander III. Vital wrote that, unlike the events of 1789 and 1933, the 1881 events "did not form a landmark of such supreme importance in the general historical evolution of Europe as a whole."[94] However, it was a different story for the Jews of Russia.

> [T]he year 1881 marked a turning point as significant in retrospect as 1789 and as sharp and dramatic and as fraught with initially incalculable but profound consequences as 1933...If 1933 and the years immediately subsequent to it mark European Jewry's culminating agony, 1881 marks the first great milestone on the road towards it.[95]

The Jews, under the relatively lenient and liberal policies of Alexander II, hoped that they would find equality. With his ascension to the throne in 1855 after the death of Nicholas I, some of the harsh policies of Nicholas were almost immediately relaxed and reversed. Among these policies were censorship and restrictions on travel. The number of years required for military service was reduced from 25 to six, and universities were opened to all Russian citizens, including Jews. Although all Russians were ostensibly equal under the law according to an 1861 declaration by Alexander II, some Russians, it appeared, were less equal than others. Jews were expected to work at earning their civil rights. Many Jews, such as artists, were granted the right to live and work outside the Pale.[96] This freedom of movement for artists, including playwrights and authors, partially accounted for the success of Yiddish theater.

In the period immediately following the assassination of Alexander II, the Jewish future seemed hopeful, with Czar Alexander III receiving some prominent Jews. Sanders, quoting an unnamed news report, wrote that it was "the first time a Jewish deputation has been admitted to the presence of a Russian emperor.[97] However, the realistic acknowledgment was that change, and not for the better, was on the horizon. The 18 March 1881 *Jewish Chronicle* reported that:

> *...in the reaction which is sure to come on the murder of the Czar, the Jews will lose some of the privileges gained during the reign of Alexander II...God help them if but the faintest shadow of suspicion rests upon any Jews for complicity in the regicide conspiracy.*[98]

Those fears were realized when a Jewish woman, Hessia Meyerovna Helfman, was among those arrested for the assassination. Although she was sentenced to death, her execution was postponed because she was pregnant, and her sentence was later commuted to life in prison following widespread protests from abroad. It is unlikely that Helfman took part in the assassination. Because of her documented background as a revolutionary and propagandist, Helfman became an easy target for blame when anti-Semitic groups attempted to assign responsibility for the assassination to the Jews.[99] She died shortly after giving birth in 1882.

The period immediately following the assassination and continuing until 1884 was marked by waves of pogroms[100] that Vital categorized as "the most severe and sustained that Europe had known for a very long time." But, he continued, pogroms "were not foreign to Jewish experience."[101] By 1883, it appeared as if the policies of Alexander III might be more liberal for the Jews than had been anticipated. The official, albeit belated, coronation of Alexander III in May, which could have, according to Russian tradition, brought with it "various privileges and alleviations for different sections of the Russian population,"[102] ignored the Jews. The appointment of a High Commission for the Revision of Current Laws Concerning the Jews under the direction of Count **Peter Ludwig von der** Pahlen provided a glimmer of hope for the possibility of reform.[103] That potential was never realized. During its five years of existence, the commission passed countless restrictions on Jewish activity and movement without going through legal channels to become law.[104] Among the many newly restrictive policies adopted were quotas on Jewish enrollment in gymnasia and universities. Within the Pale, Jews could not constitute more than 10% of the students in secondary schools and universities. Outside the Pale, the quota stood at 5% except in Saint Petersburg and Moscow, where it was 3%.[105] The rationale was "that the growing influx of the non-Christian element into the educational establishments exerts, from a moral and religious point of view, a most injurious influence upon the Christian children."[106] Other restrictions prevented Jews living in the Pale from freely relocating from village to village, even when the villages were contiguous. In practice, this rule was even more restrictive than it appears to be. Not only was a Jew suddenly bound to a place of residence, but a relative—even a parent—who resided in another town could not be brought to live with a person. Nor could someone inheriting a place of business or residence take possession if the new owner lived in another village.[107] Against the backdrop of these restrictions and pogroms, so began a major wave of immigration from Eastern Europe to the United States, the *goldeneh medinah*.[108]

1920: An Immigrant in New York City

In the years following the assassination of Alexander II, Harry Silberman's parents possibly contemplated a move south to Suceava, where they ultimately settled, as discussed above. Based on the little information Harry provided, it seems to be the right period and would have taken them from an area bordering the Russian Empire to an area fairly distant from that border. There is no indication that Perl and Moshe contemplated a transatlantic journey. However, five of their

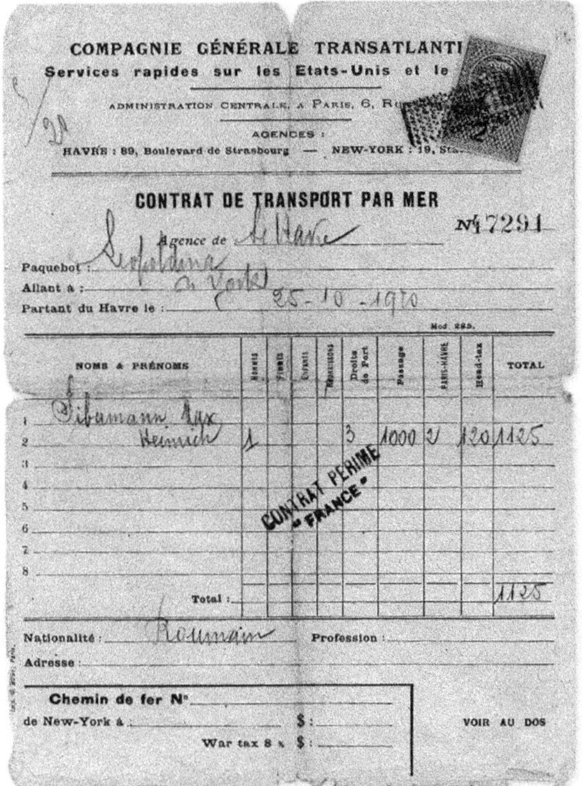

Fig. 14: Max Heinrich Silbermann's ship contract[109]

children immigrated to the United States, and, after Moshe's death in 1926, Perl ultimately followed them. Only one of their children who survived infancy and childhood remained in Europe after Perl left in 1928. That was Norbert, who died in Mauthausen, as discussed previously.

When Harry left Europe as Max Heinrich Silberman, he was not traveling into the unknown. Harry sailed on the French ship line *Compagnie Génerale Transatlantique*, leaving from Le Havre in 1920. Between World War I and World War II, the French line offered promotional packages that "included rail transport to Le Havre and accommodations in a hotel constructed specifically for passengers awaiting embarkation," because "the French passenger trade was limited."[110] Perhaps Harry purchased one of these packages. The hotels provided a venue for the shipping line to conduct medical examinations and prepare all the documentation the immigrants needed to bring with them. Although this seems costly, it made more fiscal sense for the shipping line than bearing the cost of

Fig. 15: Dining room at hotel for immigrants in Le Havre[112]

Fig. 16: Gerald Milton Silverman's birth record[114]

transporting immigrants who were refused entry at Ellis Island back to Europe.[111] After 1903, a fine of as much as $100 was imposed for each passenger who was refused entry by United States immigration officials.

Several of Harry's siblings preceded him, immigrating to the United States and settling in New York and Pennsylvania. Between 1907 and 1922, his older brother Avraham,[113] who became Adolph Arthur in the United States, traveled from Europe to America and back again several times. Adolph initially married Jetta Hofrichter in New York not long after his first arrival, and had three children with her in Suceava and New York, the youngest born in 1913. They either divorced or he abandoned her. In 1930, he and Minerva Salzman had a child, Gerald Milton Silverman, in Syracuse, Onondaga County, New York. I found and conversed with Jetta Hofrichter's children and several of their relatives. Among the papers in Harry's boxes was a copy of Minerva's son's birth certificate, but we knew nothing else about him. From connections with Adolph's grandchildren, I slowly, over several years, made contact with one of Gerald Milton's children and discovered that my inability to identify him earlier was due to several name changes. Descendants of that branch of the family no longer use the surname Silberman or Silverman. Adolph, I discovered during conversations with one of his great-grandchildren, was estranged from most of his children and grandchildren. My father, who was close to some of Harry's siblings, only recalls seeing Adolph once, in the mid-1930s. Discussions with a descendant of Gerald Milton revealed that, for some reason, although he lived with his mother, one summer he lived with Adolph, who needed Gerald's birth record to register him in a program. This might explain the 1944 date on the record certifying Gerald's 1930 birth.

People often ask me why I keep some information about my family online, where it can be viewed publicly. Miraculous discoveries that took place in September 2012 clearly demonstrate the wisdom of that. In 2009, I traveled to Ukraine and maintained an online travel blog at http://unknowntravels. wordpress.com/. That site not only has details of my three weeks of Ukrainian travel, but also has some details of each branch of my family. A good and persistent researcher can use that information to find more complete details of my family's history. One of Adolph's great-granddaughters, Lynn, did just that, and then sent me an email identifying herself. She told me that she thought she had tracked down Minerva Salzman and her son. Following the clues, I found details of Minerva's life in the 1940 census, and then of her career as a lawyer. Minerva died in 1990 and her obituary names her son, Jay M. Stanley.[115] This name aligns with the name his children and grandchildren told me he adopted.

Adolph married one more time, to a woman from New Orleans named Edyth Bilger Ott. She owned an antique book shop, and he set up a bookbindery in the back. Harry drove from New York to New Orleans every year from 1957 until the year before his death in 1985 to help collect and bind books. After Adolph's 1967 death, Harry continued to work with his sister-in-law. Strangely, Adolph claimed to have no knowledge of bookbinding. Adolph also made other claims his grandchildren shared with me—most notably, that he was a spy for the United States government and traveled to Europe with his small children as a foil. Another story said that he was a graduate of medical school in Vienna and sold pharmaceuticals all over Europe. According to his grandchildren, his children said he left them with his female friends while he traveled around.

Families have stories of all sorts, but it is rare to come across one such as Adolph's, filled with so many statements contradicted by documentation. A 1980 newspaper article commemorated the closure of Edyth's bookstore, the Southern Book Mart located at 742 Royal Street in New Orleans, Louisiana.[116] The article quoted a 1938 newspaper interview with Adolph. He was said to be "a native of Vienna and a graduate of the University of Vienna's medical school. He arrived in the U.S. in 1920 and was a wholesale druggist. He learned the art of bookbinding from a bookbinder he hired when he set up an addition to Edyth's store, called Adolphus Bindery." Adolph wasn't born in Vienna. He was born in 1887 in Suceava—I have his birth record.

He did, on one of his trips from Europe, arrive in New York in 1920. The ship manifest identified his occupation as a "merchant" and reported that he was

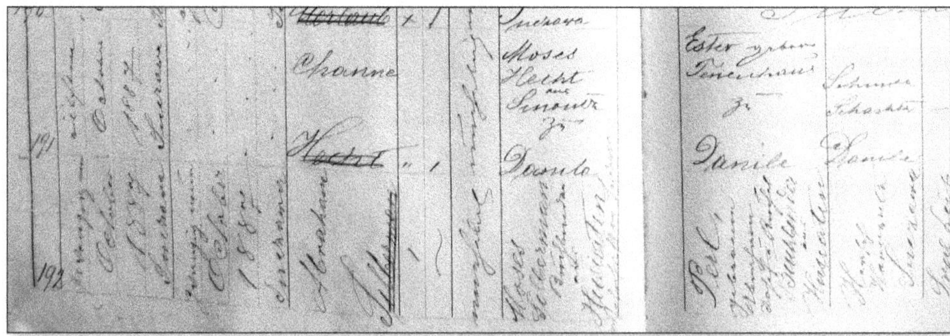

Fig. 17: Record of the 1887 birth of Abraham [AKA Adolph] Silberman in Suceava[117]

Fig. 18: 14 June 1913 arrival of Adolf Silberman on the SS *Volturno*[118]

single. However, his destination in the United States was the home of his wife, "Jetty Silbermann!" A previous arrival in 1913 also identified the home of that same wife as his destination, and his oldest son, Phillip, was born in New York in 1909—I also have his birth record. On the 1913 ship manifest, his occupation is given as "bookbinder." A family list from Suceava in the same year also identifies his occupation as "bookbinder." Adolph submitted his Declaration of Intention in 1922, followed by his Petition to Naturalize in 1926. In them, he used the 1920 arrival date but said his son, Phillip, was born in 1909 in New York. His other two children, Anne and Harry, were born in Europe in 1911 and 1913, respectively. It is not, of course, impossible that Harry was born in January 1913 in Europe, but when Adolph arrived in New York in June 1913, his wife in the United States was listed as his destination. It's possible that she returned to the United States with infant Harry before June 1913. It is also possible that Harry was born in New York, but birth records after 1909 are not yet accessible to the public.

Adolph, like many of his siblings and his mother, was a bookbinder. Perl's family were bookbinders and Adolph's parents met because Moses was apprenticed to Perl's father. When Perl came to the United States in 1928, she repaired and bound books for local synagogues. Adolph's reimagined life story is extremely elaborate, and if one didn't know the background or have access to the documents, it would be all too easy to believe!

Because genealogical research can be never-ending and obsessive, I went searching for more information about Adolph. To my surprise, I found another marriage for him. This, more than any of the other documents truly shocked me. It seems that, in 1922, while still married to Ethel—known in Yiddish as Jetti— he married Dora Jakobson Brenner. It was her second marriage. She was a widow, and the marriage record from 28 December 1922 included her maiden name. Adolph's father is recorded as Morris, which is incorrect, but his mother was correctly noted as Perl Bookbinder. The record reported that he was born in "Suzawa, Roumania," proving that this was, in fact, the ancestral Adolph. Although he was still married to Ethel and had three children with her, he is listed as single.

I emigrated to the United States of America from   Havre France

on the vessel   Rochambeau   ; my last
(If the alien arrived otherwise than by vessel, the character of conveyance or name of transportation company should be given)

foreign residence was   Austria   ; I am   married; the name

of my wife is   Ethel   ; she was born USA

and now resides at   with me

It is my bona fide intention to renounce forever all allegiance and fidelity to any foreign prince, potentate, state, or sovereignty, and particularly to

    Ferdinand 1st King of Rumania and or Austria of whom I am now a subject;

I arrived at the port of   NY   , in the

State of   NY   , on or about the   13th   day

of   October   , anno Domini 1   920: I am not an anarchist; I am not a polygamist nor a believer in the practice of polygamy; and it is my intention in good faith to become a citizen of the United States of America and to permanently reside therein: So HELP ME GOD.

(Original signature of declarant)

Subscribed and sworn to before me in the office of the Clerk of said Court at New York City, N. Y., this 11 day of   December

[SEAL]

anno Domini 19 22

Fig. 19: 1922 naturalization document for Adolph Silverman[119]

The address at which he lived, 1649 Washington Avenue, is very close to the address on the ship manifest for his 23 October 1920 arrival—1699 Washington Avenue. In August 1922, four months before his marriage to Dora, his destination on his arrival manifest was his wife, living at 128 Graham Avenue, Brooklyn, and on that voyage, he traveled with two of his children, Phillip and Anna. On 11 December 1922, when he filed his Declaration of Intention, the first papers for naturalization, his wife was recorded as Ethel! There is no question as to whether this is my grandfather's brother—the ship arrival information was correct, and the signature matches others!

It is improbable that a divorce would have moved through the courts in New York between the 11 December 1922 declaration and his 28 December 1922 marriage to Dora. At the time, and for many decades after, there were few grounds for divorce in New York, one of them was adultery. It was possible, of course, for couples to separate and never divorce, but if they remarried, those marriages would generally take place in another state. However, in 1926, Adolph filed his Petition for Naturalization, naming Ethel, born on 13 December 1892, as his wife, and stating that she and their three children all lived with him in Brooklyn! The only conclusion I can draw is that this was proof of his life as a bigamist. If there was another reason for the documentation, it has thus far eluded me. I searched the 1925 New York State Census for Dora, Ethel, and Adolph and came up empty-handed. I searched for that same census under the children's names and did not find anything. I was hoping that, if I saw who was in each household, I might achieve clarity and understand Uncle Adolph and his life more thoroughly. I found Ethel in the 1930 census, living with her children and enumerated as both head of household and married. Divorced or separated women at the time when such status carried shame might claim to be married or widowed. By 1940, Ethel lived with her daughter Anna and son-in-law Joseph Chazkel and their children. She was enumerated as widowed.

Speculating, hypothesizing, and creating a *midrash*[120]—such as I did about whether Adolph was a bigamist—are helpful ways to help me discover new paths to search. Finding a storyline that fits the documentation when there are holes in the sequence leaves me open to errors in my analysis of the data. In Jewish tradition, *midrashim* were created to interpret and understand text, often filling in gaps for better understanding.

Harry's oldest brother, David,[122] emigrated in 1905. David first married Bertha Feder in 1906, and, after her 1916 death, married Lena Paula Knobler, another émigré in New York, and remained there. Milton fondly recalled David, and in 2012 wrote that:

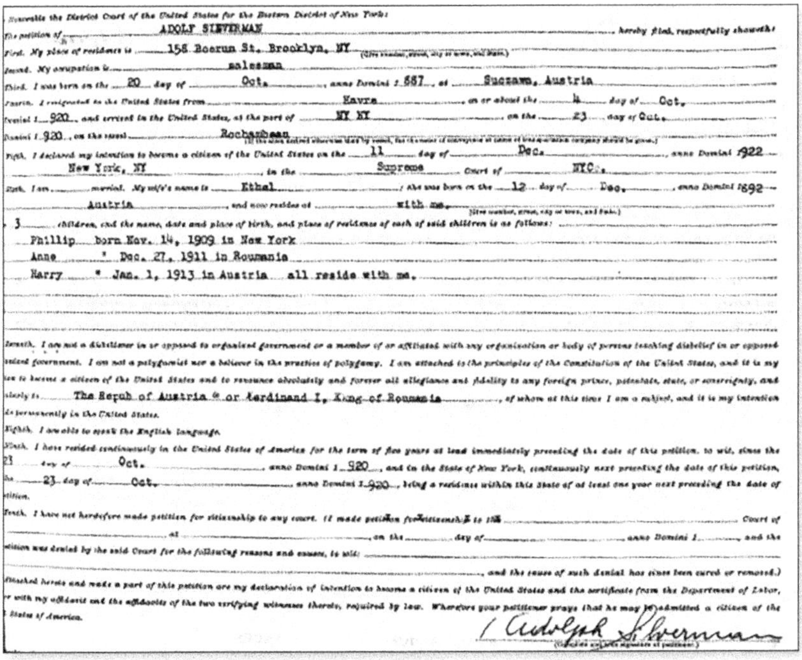

Honorable the District Court of the United States for the Eastern District of New York:

The petition of ADOLF SILVERMAN hereby filed, respectfully showeth:

First. My place of residence is 158 Boerum St. Brooklyn, NY (Give number, street, city or town, and State.)

Second. My occupation is salesman

Third. I was born on the 20 day of Oct. anno Domini 1887, at Suczawa, Austria

Fourth. I emigrated to the United States from Havre on or about the 4 day of Oct. anno Domini 1920, and arrived in the United States, at the port of NY NY on the 23 day of Oct. anno Domini 1920, on the vessel Rochambeau

Fifth. I declared my intention to become a citizen of the United States on the 11 day of Dec. anno Domini 1922 at New York, NY, in the Supreme Court of NYC.

Sixth. I am married. My wife's name is Ethel; she was born on the 12 day of Dec. anno Domini 1892 at Austria and now resides at with me. (Give number, street, city or town, and State.)

I have 3 children, and the name, date and place of birth, and place of residence of each of said children is as follows:

Phillip born Nov. 14, 1909 in New York

Anne " Dec. 27, 1911 in Roumania

Harry " Jan. 1, 1913 in Austria all reside with me.

Seventh. I am not a disbeliever in or opposed to organized government or a member of or affiliated with any organization or body of persons teaching disbelief in or opposed to organized government. I am not a polygamist nor a believer in the practice of polygamy. I am attached to the principles of the Constitution of the United States, and it is my intention to become a citizen of the United States and to renounce absolutely and forever all allegiance and fidelity to any foreign prince, potentate, state, or sovereignty, and particularly to The Repub of Austria or Ferdinand I, King of Roumania, of whom at this time I am a subject, and it is my intention to reside permanently in the United States.

Eighth. I am able to speak the English language.

Ninth. I have resided continuously in the United States of America for the term of five years at least immediately preceding the date of this petition, to wit, since the 23 day of Oct. anno Domini 1920, and in the State of New York, continuously next preceding the date of this petition, since the 23 day of Oct. anno Domini 1920, being a residence within this State of at least one year next preceding the date of this petition.

Tenth. I have not heretofore made petition for citizenship to any court. (I made petition for citizenship to the Court of at on the day of anno Domini 1 and the petition was denied by the said Court for the following reasons and causes, to wit: and the cause of such denial has since been cured or removed.)

Attached hereto and made a part of this petition are my declaration of intention to become a citizen of the United States and the certificate from the Department of Labor, together with my affidavit and the affidavits of the two verifying witnesses thereto, required by law. Wherefore your petitioner prays that he may be admitted a citizen of the United States of America.

Adolph Silverman
(Complete and true signature of petitioner.)

Fig. 20: Adolf Silverman's 1926 Petition for Naturalization[121]

He was called and addressed with a Yiddish pronunciation, Duvid. He and his family were the most frequent family visitors, and we to his apartment in the Lower East side. He was the businessman, an entrepreneur applying the bookbinding skills to manufacture office supplies—cardboard files, desk blotters, and other items that would be strange in the modern world.

There was a time when he formed a business partnership with my father and his son Sol (who was my father's age). I was not aware of this arrangement until we found the partnership contract after my father's death. It is my impression that though they all were compatible as family, the business interactions were bad.

My first real job was in Uncle David's shop in Spring Street, Lower East Side, one summer. I think I was 15 at the time. For that job, I had to obtain "working papers" and sign up for Social Security. It paid 40 cents an hour. When I told my friends [that] I had a "real" job and earned $16 a week, they were in awe.

Since, Uncle David was [more than] 20 years older than my father, I looked upon him as almost a grandfather. To me, he was friendly and understanding. He gave me T'fillin[123] and a siddur[124] for my Bar Mitzvah, which I still have.

The second-oldest sibling, Lea,[125] emigrated in 1907 to join her husband, David Barasch, in Philadelphia. They lived in Philadelphia and New York. Another brother, Julius,[126] also emigrated. My search for Julius's manifest covered the period of 1913 to 1936. All I knew initially was his military status from the 1913 Suceava family information sheet and that he married Lilly Lehrer in New York in 1936. For many years, I could not locate immigration information for him. Then, in September 2012, while looking closely at the manifest for the October 1920 sailing of the SS *Rochambeau*, one of the ships Adolph sailed on, I realized that Julius was also on that ship but on a different page of the manifest. His name on the manifest is Jude Silberman. He was on page 23, while Adolph was on page 15.

Milton remembered Julius's wife as Gussie, and his ship manifest indicates that his destination was the home of his wife, Gussie, in New York. We searched through the 1920 census for the address at which the ship manifest indicates she lived in October 1920. We searched through the enumeration district and located

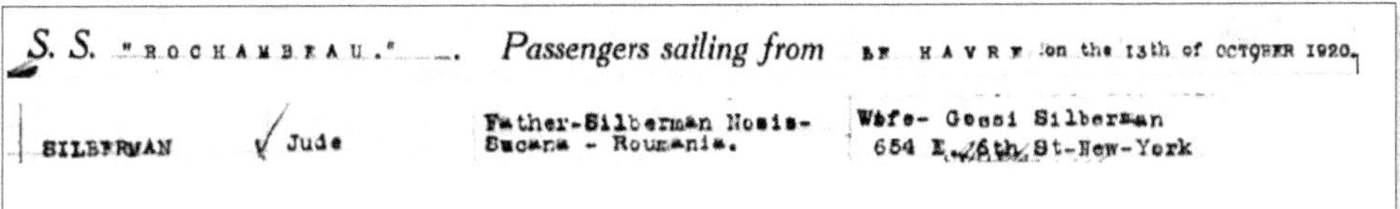

Fig. 21: Jude Silberman, line 7, List 23[127]

the address, but Gussie did not live there at the time the census information was recorded. Although it was common for families to arrive separately, it was most common for a man to emigrate first, sometimes with older children, and later send for his wife and the rest of the family. It was not common for a woman to arrive first. Perhaps this is an indication that Julius, like his brother Adolph, traveled back and forth from Europe to the United States, although one of the questions on the ship manifest was whether the traveler had ever been in the United States prior to this trip, and Julius answered "no." Considering all the alternative truths Adolph provided on various records, it would not be surprising to find that his brother reported information similarly. On all these documents, the mother's name, Perl Buchbinder or Bookbinder, and birthplace of Suceava (with many different spellings), Austria (or Romania), is consistent. The father's name is generally Moses, also with varied spellings. There is no doubt that these all refer to the same family. Although Gussie didn't die until 1946, Julius married Lily Lehrer in 1936! No record of a divorce has been located and in the 1940 census, Julius was enumerated with Gussie. No record of a 1940 census enumeration with Lily has been identified to date.

Harry was the youngest of Perl's children.[129] Norbert[130] remained in Europe after the rest of his siblings left and died in Mauthausen. When Perl left Europe, she traveled in greater style than her children had on their initial journeys from Europe. Harry sent her a second-class ticket. The ship's manifest indicates that she could neither read nor write. Initially, I thought this must be incorrect. I thought that comments made by both her son Harry and grandson Milton indicated that she was literate. She was a bookbinder, like Harry, Adolph, and Moses. Harry's mother, Perl, lived with his family and also with Lea's family across the street. Milton said that she attended a morning service every day of her life—not at the synagogue next door, but at the one she preferred a block or two away. She also did bookbinding for the synagogue, repairing old prayer books and other sacred texts. However, two letters Norbert sent from Europe indicate the possibility that she could not write. A 1936 letter from Norbert to Harry questions why he did not

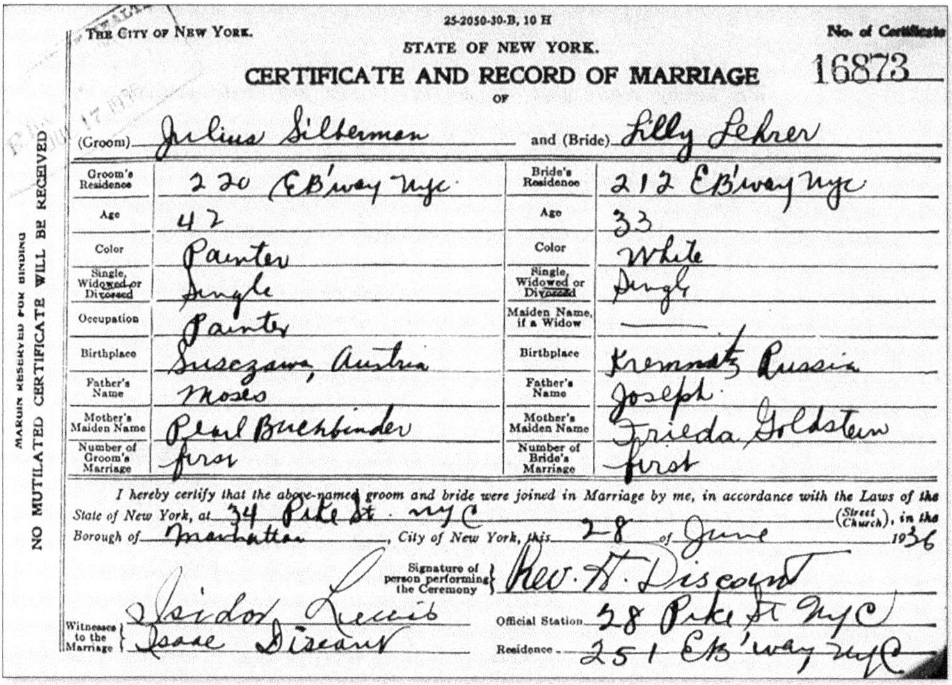

THE CITY OF NEW YORK. 25-2050-30-B, 10 H No. of Certificate 16873

STATE OF NEW YORK.

CERTIFICATE AND RECORD OF MARRIAGE

OF

(Groom) Julius Silberman and (Bride) Lilly Lehrer

Groom's Residence	220 E B'way Nyc	Bride's Residence	212 E B'way Nyc
Age	47	Age	33
Color	Painter	Color	White
Single, Widowed or Divorced	Single	Single, Widowed or Divorced	Single
Occupation	Painter	Maiden Name, if a Widow	—
Birthplace	Susczawa, Austria	Birthplace	Kremnatz Russia
Father's Name	Moses	Father's Name	Joseph
Mother's Maiden Name	Pearl Buchbinder	Mother's Maiden Name	Frieda Goldstein
Number of Groom's Marriage	first	Number of Bride's Marriage	first

I hereby certify that the above-named groom and bride were joined in Marriage by me, in accordance with the Laws of the State of New York, at 34 Pike St. NYC *(Street, Church), in the Borough of* Manhattan*, City of New York, this* 28 *of* June *1936*

Signature of person performing the Ceremony: Rev. H. Discount

Witnesses to the Marriage: Isidor Leewib, Isaac Discount

Official Station: 28 Pike St NyC

Residence: 251 E B'way NyC

MARGIN RESERVED FOR BINDING

NO MUTILATED CERTIFICATE WILL BE RECEIVED

Fig. 22: Record of the 1936 marriage of Julius Silberman and Lilly Lehrer[128]

receive responses to earlier letters.[131] Norbert wrote a letter to Perl in 1937 asking who wrote the letter she sent him because he did not recognize the handwriting.[132] When I first read these letters, I thought that perhaps, in the first instance, Perl didn't have the time, and in the second instance, since the handwriting was not Perl's, Norbert wondered whose it was. Perhaps, though, she could read but not write. The possibility is that she could do neither and that letters she received were read to her. It is more likely that she had limited writing skills than that she could not read. As a bookbinder, she would have needed to read titles of books and duplicate the titles on the newly bound books. Milton said, in a February 2012 conversation, that he thinks his mother, Blima, wrote Perl's letters to Norbert. But, he said, he never gave it much thought. The letters were in German, so perhaps Perl did not write German. Maybe she wrote only in Yiddish. We do not know why Norbert's letters were written in German, not Yiddish.

Second-class travel was much different than traveling in steerage on transatlantic crossings. In 1928, the passage for Perl's second-class transport cost $153—a veritable fortune. Harry's 1920 steerage steamship passage cost ₣1000, the approximate equivalent of $45.50 today.[133] That was less than one-third the

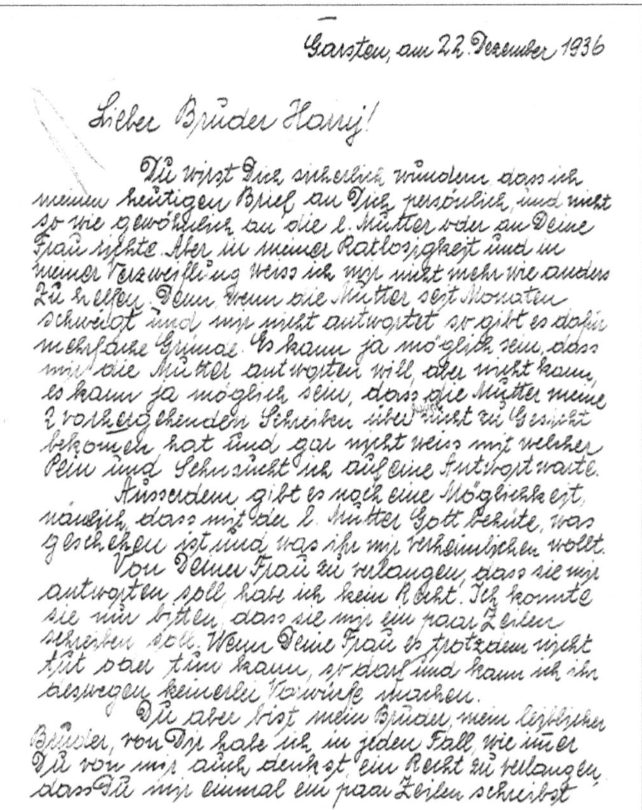

Fig. 23: 22 December 1936 letter from Norbert to Harry

cost of Perl's second-class ticket eight years later. Harry was a house painter by the time Perl arrived in the United States. Although he was rarely out of work, her fare may have represented a huge portion of his annual income. Perl traveled on the SS *Hamburg*, a new ship that made its maiden voyage in 1925! Allan Jordan, a maritime historian, told me in February 2012 that:

Second class in the 1920s and 1930s was sort of like the Holiday Inn versus the Ritz. It was ok—nothing fancy but comfortable travel. Ships in the 1920s worked generally on three classes—first, second, and third, sometimes called tourist, tourist third, etc. (Remember, steerage went out with World War I and the end of the great immigration. Steerage became third, or tourist, in the 1920[s] and that lasted till the mid-1930s, when the whole system was upset by the Depression.) Each class was a step down from the prior one and, on most ships, people did not mix between the classes at all. Second-class cabins would have been comfortable but likely without a private bath. [A bath] might have been shared between two cabins or, more likely, [was] down the hall. Most of the cabins would have had a wash basin in the cabin itself or, if you got a really nice cabin, it might have had a toilet, too, but no tub. Tubs would have been in a bathing room for which you would make a reservation. There was often a bathing steward or stewardess who supervised and could be a very strict, by-the-rules type.

Food would have been simple but reasonably good. The lavish meals were only in first class. The German ships were very Teutonic in style. Formal, regimented, marching bands, [and] that type of stuff. Second class [was] less formal than first but still clearly a step above tourist, or third. No dormitories in second class. No fancy entertain[ment] like the modern cruise ships. Passengers mostly amused themselves in the 1920s with very little organized activity. A May crossing might have had ok seas, but the air temperature would have been cool on the way across so people were likely mostly indoors. No sunbathing, [unless] maybe outside [on a] deck chair with a blanket.

The Hamburg was introduced in 1926, so in 1928, she was still a new ship. She was mid-sized for the industry and very much a working ship. The ship would not have been the fastest nor most luxurious afloat, but it was far from the dismal experience of the immigrants, either. Before World War I, Hamburg America (HAPAG) had built big ships, but everything went to the Allies at war's end and HAPAG rebuilt its fleet in the 1920s with more mid-sized, hard-working ships. HAPAG did not get back into the race with the great superliners of the 1920s and 1930s. The Hamburg was part of a class of ships, and she carried around 200 in first class [and] close to 500 each in second and third class. The class of ships was called the Ballin class for Albert Ballin, who had run HAPAG before the war and was a real visionary [at] improving conditions for immigrants, setting up the rail line links to the dock, opening a ship line hotel for the immigrants on the dock in Hamburg, etc.

Modern European historians Lorraine Coons and Alexander Varias wrote that, although some people "cruised" on ships for pleasure, "for the masses of

PURCHASER'S RECEIPT AND CONTRACT
(To be retained by the Purchaser of the Ticket)

HAMBURG-AMERICAN LINE

2nd CLASS
(INDICATE CLASS)

Good for one year
from date of issue

PREPAID No. 319851

Received from the purchaser named at the foot hereof the amounts set forth below for transportation of the following passengers, but subject to all the terms and conditions of the contract on the reverse side of this receipt and of the west-bound passage contract to be hereafter issued to said passengers; and also subject to the rules and conditions of all other carriers over whose lines said passengers may be forwarded.

NAMES OF PASSENGERS (Write Plainly)	AGE
Perl Silberman	63

ADDRESS: *Suceava St., Regina Maria 19 Bukowina — Roumania*

FROM *Hamburg* TO *New York*
DESTINATION IN U. S. OR CANADA

	Class	Full	Half	Infant	Free	Rate		$
EUROPEAN RAIL FARE								
OCEAN FARE OR THROUGH RATE	2	1				145		145
AMERICAN RAIL FARE								
U. S. HEAD TAX								8
LANDING MONEY								
OTHER CHARGES								
PAYMENTS TO PASSENGERS								

AMOUNT PAID $ 153

PURCHASER MUST READ CAREFULLY AND SIGN CONTRACT ON REVERSE SIDE

Purchaser should forward "Passenger's Notice" direct to the Passenger and advise him not to leave his home for the port of embarkation until advised to do so by the Company.

NAME AND ADDRESS OF PURCHASER: *Harry Silberman 7073 Union St. Bklyn N.Y.*

AGENT'S NAME AND ADDRESS: Public National Bank & Trust Co., Pitkin Ave. Branch, Pitkin Ave. & Watkins St. FOREIGN DEPARTMENT

DATE ISSUED JUN 13 1927 19

Fig. 24: Perl's pre-paid ticket[134]

people traveling on [a] ship, necessity was the main impulse."[135] Beginning in the late 1920s, steamship lines became cognizant that an untapped market for transatlantic voyages might be single women and began marketing to attract them.[136] Their marketing goal was to develop a tourist market. The advertising was not directed to people like Perl, one of the large numbers of Jews leaving Europe by steamship to join her family in America. The Red Star Line, a steamship line from Antwerp, Belgium, required that "all female immigrants be supervised by a female officer at the expense of the steamship company" at the insistence of the Canadian government. This supervisory position was added in 1925. The Red Star Line advertised that this employee was on board "for the benefit of all ladies traveling alone."[137] I found no similar reference to such a requirement by the U.S. authorities, nor are there any family stories about Perl's voyage. However, women traveling on their own were frequently detained when they arrived in the United States if a male relative was not at their port of arrival.

First- and second-class travelers were permitted to leave the ship when it docked in New York City; they did not need to experience the intimidating interviews and examinations at Ellis Island to which steerage passengers were subjected with the possibility of being detained there or deported back to Europe. The steerage compartment provided the barest minimum of accommodations and services, with as many passengers crowded into the space as humanly, not humanely, possible. The total revenue collected from these steerage passengers in effect afforded the steamship lines the ability to offer luxurious accommodations in first class, becoming slightly less luxurious in second and third class, and still turn a nice profit.[138] Did Perl's son purchase a second-class ticket so that his mother could travel in more comfortable circumstances, was this a safer way for her to travel, or was he perhaps trying to impress her with his ability to have her travel in "style?"

An excerpted 1998 article from the catalog "Hamburg Emigration Port," part of an exhibition from the State Publicity Department of the City of Hamburg, described part of the voyage. According to the article, the trip itself, for steerage passengers leaving from Hamburg, was as intimidating as when they arrived in New York. During certain periods, steerage passengers were quarantined for as long as two weeks in Hamburg before being permitted to board a ship. The shipping line claimed this quarantine was to avoid epidemics on board and when they landed in the United States and other ports.[139] Of course, the underlying reason was to avoid the fine for attempting to land passengers who could not pass the physical or mental examinations.

Perl's family provides a couple of clear examples of how a family can lose touch within one generation. In the early 1980s, Harry asked me to do something for him. He handed me an envelope his mother received while she was still in Europe. The return address was of "I. Goldenzweig, 4000 Colonial, Montreal, Canada." He asked me to find this family. He didn't know who they were, but said they were important to his mother. At the time, I had no idea how to find them.

Several years later, I was in Montreal and tried looking in phone books and for the address but had no luck finding anyone named Goldenzweig. Among the letters in the boxes left by Harry were several Yiddish letters. It was decades after his death before I found someone who could read the handwritten Yiddish. Among these letters were several from Montreal. The translations shook me. The letters from Montreal were from Bertha (Breine in Yiddish) Goldenzweig, who turned out to be Perl's sister!

Bertha never lived in Suceava. She married Issie Goldenzweig, and they left Europe in 1905 for Canada. I have not yet discovered a record of their marriage in Europe or found any other information about them before their arrival in Canada. They arrived at about the same time as Issie's brother and sister-in-law, Nathan and Fanny Goldenzweig. Although Nathan and Fanny had several children, Bertha and Issie remained childless. In a 1927 letter to Perl, Bertha complained of an illness that resulted in a hospitalization. Bertha expressed a desire to see Perl's children in the United States and aggravation that, although Perl's husband, Moses, had died a year previously, her children had still not sent her a ticket. Bertha died in May 1929. Perl arrived in the United States a year earlier, in May 1928. Harry, with whom she lived, had no idea that the Goldenzweig his mother wanted to find was her sister.

Bertha, it turned out, wasn't the only one of Perl's sisters who arrived in North America. In 2018, to my surprise, I found that her sister Golde had immigrated in 1902 and settled in Philadelphia, where she lived until her death in 1918. DNA is an amazing tool, and when paired with documentation from traditional genealogical research, it can open doors. In 2018, I received an email from someone claiming to be a third-cousin match with me. Eastern European Jews have huge numbers of third- and fourth-cousin DNA matches, most of whom are difficult, if not impossible, to place on a family tree. This is due primarily to endogamy, the practice of marrying within a community. In Eastern Europe, Jews often married first and second cousins. Descendants resulting from these marriages appear to be more closely related than they are, in DNA results. If two first cousins marry, their children will only have six great- grandparents rather than eight!

I try to respond to all the inquiries I get from my DNA matches, but, as has been the case time after time, the matches are too distant, and I never expect to be able to find our most recent common ancestor. Due to endogamy, most Eastern European Jews are related to each other, and our DNA matches typically can be

NAME	RELATION	Sex	Color or race	Age at last birthday	Whether single, married, widowed, or divorced	Number of present marriage	Mother of how many children		Place of birth of this Person
							Number born	Number now living	
Hass Max	Head	M	W	53	M	27			Austria (Pol) Gal
— Goldy	Wife	F	W	53	M	27	7	5	Austria (Pol) Gal
— Myar	Son	M	W	24	S				Austria (Pol) (Ger)
— Hyman	Son	M	W	18	S				Roumanian
— Benjamin	Son	M	W	14	S				Roumanian
— David	Son	M	W	12	S				Roumanian

Fig. 25: 1910 household of Golde (Buchbinder) Huss with her husband and children[140]

in the hundreds of thousands. I always begin my response by asking for surnames
that appear in the family and where they lived in Eastern Europe. None of the
names from this third-cousin match were familiar to me. By way of response, I sent
her my family surnames. She immediately recognized one, Huss, as this was her
great-grandparents' surname before they changed it after arriving in Pennsylvania.

My newfound third cousin, Glori, had no idea that her great-grandmother
had any siblings, nor did she know anything about the family's background. I
knew from records in Suceava that Golde married Aron Leib Kolber and had
one daughter, Chaje, with him before they divorced. Golde went on to marry
Mordche Leib Huss, and I knew of three children born to them: Abraham Jossel in
1884, Maier Hersch in 1886, and Marie in 1888. I lost track of them after 1888.
Glori (named after Golde) told me that Golde and Mordche, who became Max,
emigrated from Bucharest. They must have left Suceava after Marie was born and
before the 1892 birth of another child, Hyman, in Bucharest. Through discussions
with Glori, it became clear that Golde had a total of seven children, four whom I
had previously identified and then had another three after relocating to Bucharest.
Glori only knew of five.

The 1910 census informed us that she had had seven children, of whom only
five were still living. The two girls, Chaje and Marie, didn't survive. On 11 May
1907, Mordche began the process of naturalization by filing his Declaration of
Intention to Naturalize. On that and on his 1909 Petition for Naturalization, he
reported he left the port of Hamburg on 6 June 1902 and arrived at the Port of
New York 18 June 1902, on board the vessel SS *Bluecher*. On the manifest, his

name appeared as Markus Huss, and he traveled with 16-year-old Maier (this was Mordche Leib and his son Maier Hersch). Their destination was Philadelphia, where they planned to join Markus's nephew, whose last name was Weiss. It is unclear when Golde arrived. If her manifest could be found, the children with whom she was traveling might clarify whether the two girls died before the family left Europe. I wonder if Golde's son Maier Hersch and my grandfather whose Yiddish name is the same, were perhaps named after the same person. My grandfather was named after his paternal grandfather. If Golde's son and Perl's son were named after the same person, it would mean that the Silberman and Buchbinder families had other intra-family relationships. Since neither Perl's mother's maiden name, nor Moshe's mother's maiden name have been identified, it is possible there is a relationship through their line.

Golde died in November 1918 in Philadelphia. Her sons all married, and although one moved to Michigan, the others remained in Philadelphia. Perl's daughter, Lea (Golde's niece), and her husband, Abraham Barash, arrived in the United States in 1907 and settled in Philadelphia. With them came their two daughters, born in 1900 and 1902 in Europe. They were contemporaries of Golde's children. When I asked Lea's grandson Yossel if he remembered cousins in Philadelphia, he said they had no relatives in Philadelphia. By the time Perl arrived in New York in 1928, it appears that all contact between the sisters and their families had been lost.

Endnotes

1. Janette Silverman, "Harry Silberman, Jenna Levy, Arielle Silver, and Efrem Weiss," photograph, 1985; researcher's copy.

2. Some of the earliest money orders and notes were sent to "Palestine," the name of Israel in its pre-1948 statehood days. Material sent to the same person after statehood were sent to "Israel."

3. Alexander Beider, "Discontinuity of Jewish Naming Traditions," *Avotaynu: The International Review of Jewish Genealogy* XXVIII, no. 2 (Summer 2012): pp. 43-44; researcher's copy.

4. Alexander Beider, "Names and Naming: Personal Names," *YIVO Encyclopedia* (http://www.yivoencyclopedia.org), accessed February 2022.

5. Suceava is located at 47°39′05″N 26°15′20″E. It is 221 miles north of Bucureşti (Bucharest). Before World War I, it was in the Bukovina province of the Austrian Empire, and after World War I, it was part of Romania.

6. "Perl and Moses Silberman," photograph, circa 1920; researcher's copy.

7. The original document, entitled "Asociaţia meseriaşilor Grupa V-a," dated 4 March 1926; researcher's copy.

8. Asociaţia Meseriaşilor Grupa V-a (Suceava, Bucovina District, Romania), Deaths Notice for Moses Silberman, dated 4 March 1926; researcher's copy.

9. The original document, with the title "Gewerbe-Schein," is dated 16 June 1908 and refers to a form filled out on 28 April 1908; researcher's copy.

10. Suczawa District (Bukovina Province, Austrian Empire) District Authority, Business License, Number 14716, Moses Silbermann, dated 16 June 1908; researcher's copy.

11. In Cyrillic, Husiatyn is written as **Гусятин**.

12. In Cyrillic, Galicia is written as **Галиция**, while in Ukrainian, it is written as **Галичина**, pronounced Halychina.

13. "**Гусятин** Husiatyn, **Гусятинського району, Тернопільська область, Україна**," Haapalah / Aliyah Bet, *Wertheimer Family and Relatives* (https://www.wertheimer.info/family), accessed January 2012.

14. Seymour Spector (editor), *The Encyclopedia of Jewish Life Before and During the Holocaust* (New York: New York University Press, 2001), p. 536; researcher's copy.

15. George Aronson, "A Brief History of the Jewish Community in Gusyatin, Ukraine," *JewishGen KehilaLinks* (http://kehilalinks.jewishgen.org), accessed December 2011.

16. Spector: p. 536.

17. Spector: p. 536.

18. Susanna Leistner Bloch, "The Husiatyn Chasidic Dynasty," *JewishGen KehilaLinks* (http://kehilalinks.jewishgen.org), accessed February 2022.

19. Aronson.

20. Information about Stanisławów, a place that figures prominently in my paternal grandmother's Kreisler-Gras family, can be found in the next chapter, entitled "Return to Sender."

21. Dean Echenberg, "Suceava Judet (County) Today," map, undated; digital image, "Suceava Romania," *JewishGen KehilaLinks* (https://kehilalinks.jewishgen.org), accessed February 2022. Permission granted by Dean Echenberg.

22. *Hasidism* is a movement that started in Eastern Europe in the 1700s by Rabbi Israel ben Eliezer. This movement emphasized the ability to grow closer to God through everything we say, do, and think rather than through intellectual pursuits.

23. *Mitnagdim* means "opponents." This is the term applied to a religious movement among the Jews of Eastern Europe that resisted the rise of Hasidism in the eighteenth and nineteenth centuries.

24. Moldavia refers to a region in Romania, not to the Republic of Moldova. What was once the expansive region of Moldavia is now split between three counties – the western half is in Romania, the eastern portion is in the Republic of Moldova and the northern and southeastern portions are in Ukraine.

25. "Moldavia," Browse, *The YIVO Encyclopedia of Jews in Eastern Europe* (https://www. yivoencyclopedia.org), accessed December 2011.

26. "Moldavia," Browse, *The YIVO Encyclopedia of Jews in Eastern Europe* (https://www. yivoencyclopedia.org), accessed December 2011.

27. "Moldavia," Browse, *The YIVO Encyclopedia of Jews in Eastern Europe* (https://www. yivoencyclopedia.org), accessed December 2011.

28. Ladislau Gyemant, "Sources of Research for Jewish Genealogy in Transylvania," *Avotaynu: The International Review of Jewish Genealogy* XI (Summer 1995): p. 13; researcher's copy.

29. Hugo Gold (editor), Dr. N. M. Gelber, Martin Hass, Dr. Chaim Kupferberg, and Jerome Silverbush (translator), "Geschichte der Juden in der Bukowina: Suceava (Romania)," Yizkor Books, *JewishGen* (https://www.jewishgen.org), accessed February 2022.

30. Spector: p. 1260.

31. Hugo Gold (editor), Dr. N. M. Gelber, Martin Hass, Dr. Chaim Kupferberg, and Jerome Silverbush (translator), "Geschichte der Juden in der Bukowina: Suceava (Romania)," Yizkor Books, *JewishGen* (https://www.jewishgen.org), accessed February 2022.

32. *Maskilim* are "enlightened ones," or proponents of the *Haskala*—the Jewish Enlightenment—which was an intellectual movement among the Jews of central and Eastern Europe.

33. "Iași," Browse, *The YIVO Encyclopedia of Jews in Eastern Europe* (https://www.yivoencyclopedia. org), accessed December 2011.

34. Hugo Gold (editor), Dr. N. M. Gelber, Martin Hass, Dr. Chaim Kupferberg, and Jerome Silverbush (translator), "Geschichte der Juden in der Bukowina: Suceava (Romania)," Yizkor Books, *JewishGen* (https://www.jewishgen.org), accessed February 2022.

35. Hugo Gold (editor), Dr. N. M. Gelber, Martin Hass, Dr. Chaim Kupferberg, and Jerome Silverbush (translator), "Geschichte der Juden in der Bukowina: Suceava (Romania)," Yizkor Books, *JewishGen* (https://www.jewishgen.org), accessed February 2022.

36. Jewish Community of Suczawa (Suczawa District, Bukovina Province, Austrian Empire), Deaths 1877-1887, p. 40, Number 66, Abraham Buchbinder, died 26 December 1879; Suceava County Branch Archive of National Archives of Romania, Suceava, Romania.

37. Jeffrey K. Cymbler, "Polish-Jewish Genealogical Research—A Primer," *Avotaynu: The International Review of Jewish Genealogy* IX (Summer 1993): pp. 4-12; researcher's copy.

38. Wilma Abeles Iggers, *The Jews of Bohemia and Moravia: A Historical Reader* (Detroit, Michigan: Wayne State University Press, 1992), p. 57; researcher's copy.

39. Wynne: p. 57.

40. Rabbi Meir Wunder, "About Galicia," *Avotaynu: The International Review of Jewish Genealogy* II (October 1986); researcher's copy.

41. Jewish Community of Suczawa (Suczawa District, Bukovina Province, Austrian Empire), Births 1887-1894, p. 100, Number 143, Chaje Ettel Silberman, born 24 October 1889; Suceava County Branch Archive of National Archives of Romania, Suceava, Romania.

42. ChaeRan Y. Freeze, "To Register or Not to Register: The Administrative Dimension of the Jewish Question in Czarist Russia," *Avotaynu: The International Review of Jewish Genealogy* XIII (Spring 1997): pp. 6-11; researcher's copy.

43. Freeze: p. 10.

44. Tarnopol is now known as Ternopil, Ukraine.

45. Tluste is now known as Tovste, Ukraine.

46. Ukrainian: **Тернопіль**, translit. Ternopil', Polish: Tarnopol, German: Tarnopol Russian: **Тернополь**, translit. Ternopol'.

47. Josef II was the Holy Roman Emperor from 1765 to 1790 and ruler of the Austrian Habsburg lands—initially co-ruler with his mother, Maria Theresa, and then, after her 1780 death, the sole ruler. Maria Theresa and Josef ruled Austria when the first partition of Poland occurred in 1772 and formed East Galicia from the land ceded to Austria.

48. Alexander Beider, "Jewish Surnames in Russia, Poland, Galicia and Prussia," *Avotaynu: The International Review of Jewish Genealogy* XIX (Fall 2003); researcher's copy.

49. Wynne: p. 35.

50. Wynne: p. 39.

51. Beider: (Fall 2003)

52. Wynne: p. 35.

53. Beider: (Fall 2003)

54. Wynne: p. 38.

55. Susana Leistner Bloch, "Polish Patronymics and Surname Suffixes," *JewishGen KehilaLinks* (http://kehilalinks.jewishgen.org), accessed March 2012.

56. Wynne: p. 40.

57. The Unity Hospital (Brooklyn, Kings County, New York), Birth Certificate, Milton Silverman, born 20 September 1926; researcher's copy.

58. Mauthausen Concentration Camp (Mauthausen, Austria), Death Report, Norbert Israel Silbermann, died 1 October 1942; International Tracing Service, Bad Arolsen, Germany.

59. Zvi Bernhardt, "Using the International Tracing Service Material (Yad Vashem)," International Association of Jewish Genealogy Societies Conference, Paris, France, July 2012.

60. The *Einsatzgruppen* were death squads who followed the German army into Poland in September 1939 and into the Soviet Union in June 1941. They conducted mass murders principally by shooting Jews and others, often engaging the local civilian population and police to assist them. Information taken from "Einsatzgruppen (Mobile Killing Units)," Holocaust Encyclopedia, *United States Holocaust Memorial Museum* (http://www.ushmm.org), accessed August 2012.

61. Zvi Bernhardt, "Using the International Tracing Service Material (Yad Vashem)," International Association of Jewish Genealogy Societies Conference, Paris, France, July 2012.

62. "01/02/2019 News," Latest News, *International Tracing Service* (https://www.its-arolsen.org), accessed January 2019.

63. Bernhardt and I attended the International Association of Jewish Genealogy Societies held in Paris in July 2012.

64. The letters were translated from the German by Ella Mintsys in Ukraine and by Milton Silverman in New York. Often, I had both of them translate the same material to see if there were nuances in the translations that might convey different meanings. The differences were slight, but often, one of them would be unable to translate a word that the other understood.

65. Norbert didn't name the other country.

66. "*Anschluss & Extermination: The fate of the Austrian Jews,*" German Occupation, *Holocaust Education & Archive Research Team* (http://www.holocaustresearchproject.org), accessed February 2022.

67. The word *Anschluss* means a "union."

68. Konnilyn G. Feig, *Hitler's Death Camps: The Sanity of Madness* (New York: Holmes & Meier, 1981), p. 116; researcher's copy.

69. "Mauthausen (Austria)," The Camps, *JewishGen* (http://www.jewishgen.org/ForgottenCamps), accessed January 2012.

70. "Austria," Holocaust Encyclopedia, *United States Holocaust Memorial Museum* (http://www.ushmm.org), accessed January 2012.

71. Guenter Lewy, *The Nazi Persecution of the Gypsies* (Oxford, England: Oxford University Press, 2000), p. 170; researcher's copy.

72. "Mauthausen," *Remember.org* (http://remember.org/camps/mauthausen/mau-introduction.html), accessed January 2012.

73. "Mauthausen (Austria)," The Camps, *JewishGen* (http://www.jewishgen.org/ForgottenCamps), accessed January 2012.

74. Gordon J. Horwitz, *In the Shadow of Death: Living Outside the Gates of Mauthausen* (New York: Free Press, 1990), p. 10; researcher's copy.

75. Feig: p. 116.

76. The Austria-Czech Discussion Group was part of the SIG system of moderated listservs set up through *JewishGen*. Fred Zimmak's message was written on 30 December 2011 and John Freund's response, which included the original message, appeared as message number one in the Austria-Czech Discussion Group Digest on 4 January 2012. These Special Interest Groups are now called Research Divisions and rather than separate discussion groups, they are all under the umbrella of JewishGen Discussion group. An archive holds all the messages previously submitted through the individual SIGs.

77. In its traditional sense, *midrash* (plural *midrashim*) refers to biblical exegesis which goes beyond the literal meaning of the text to try to offer commentary or interpretation of the text. It is often, as used here, a story that fills in the gaps to offer potential explanations for something that has no clear meaning.

78. "The Remarkable Zalmen Zylbercweig and his Lexicon of the Yiddish Theatre," Museum of the Yiddish Theatre, *Museum of Family History* (http://www.museumoffamilyhistory.com), accessed January 2019.

79. Many of the injustices caused by immigration quotas were reversed in 1965 with President Lyndon Johnson's signing of the Hart-Celler Act. This new act repealed a system of national origin quotas that had, in effect, discriminated against immigrants from almost all of Asia, Africa, and southern and eastern Europe." Elizabeth Bogen, *Immigration in New York* (New York: Prager Publishers, 1987), p. 3; researcher's copy.

80. U.S. Citizenship and Immigration Services, "Immigration Legal History Legislation 1901-1940," *ilw. com* (http://www.ilw.com), accessed January 2012.

81. "The Lexicon of the Yiddish Theatre," "Erna Siegler and Sevilla Pastor," photograph, 1936; Theatre, *Museum of Family History* (http://www.museumoffamilyhistory.com), accessed January 2019.

82. "The Lexicon of the Yiddish Theatre," Museum of the Yiddish Theatre, *Museum of Family History* (http://www.museumoffamilyhistory.com), accessed January 2019.

83. Irving Howe and Eliezer Greenberg (editors), *A Treasury of Yiddish Stories* (New York: Viking Press, 1954), p. 45; researcher's copy.

84. Nahma Sandrow (editor and translator), *God, Man, and Devil: Yiddish Plays in Translation* (Syracuse, New York: Syracuse University Press, 1999), p. 2; researcher's copy.

85. Roger I. Simon, *Teaching against the Grain: Texts for a Pedagogy of Possibility* (New York: Bergin & Garvey, 1992), p. 104; researcher's copy.

86. Iaşi was known in various languages as Yas [Yiddish], Jassy [German and Polish], Jászvásár [Hungarian], and Iassy [Russian]. Before World War I, it was in the Moldavia province, Romania, and today is Iaşi, Romania, located at 47° 10' N 27°36' E, 202 miles NNE of Bucureşti. It is the second-largest city in Romania and the seat of the county by the same name.

87. Sandrow, 1999: p. 5.

88. Simon: p. 103.

89. Simon: p. 104.

90. Brigitte Dalinger, "Yiddish Theater in Vienna," Encyclopedia, *Jewish Women's Archive* (http://jwa. org), accessed January 2019.

91. greenmentch, "Charlotte Cooper Yiddish Theater Memories," posted 5 March 2014, *YouTube* (https://www.youtube.com), accessed January 2019.

92. Simon: p. 105.

93. David Vital, *A People Apart: A Political History of the Jews in Europe 1789-1939* (New York: Oxford University Press, 2001), p. 181; researcher's copy.

94. Vital: p. 181.

95. Vital: pp. 181-182.

96.   Phyllis Goldstein, *A Convenient Hatred: the History of Antisemitism* (Brookline, Massachusetts: Facing History and Ourselves National Foundation, 2012), p. 218; researcher's copy.

97.   Ronald Sanders, *Shores of Refuge: A Hundred Years of Jewish Emigration* (New York: Henry Holt and Company, 1988), p. 4; researcher's copy.

98.   *Jewish Chronicle* report was quoted in Sanders, 1988: p. 5.

99.   "Helfman, Hessia Meyerovna," Encyclopaedia Judaica (Detroit, Michigan: Macmillan Reference USA, 2007), vol. 8, p. 783; researcher's copy.

100.   Vital described pogroms as "anti-Jewish riots consisting of violence against persons and the pillage and looting of their property." Vital: p. 289.

101.   Vital: p. 289.

102.   Simon Dubnow, *History of the Jews in Russia and Poland, from the Earliest Times until the Present Day* (New Jersey: Avotaynu, 2000), p. 373; researcher's copy.

103.   Sanders, 1988: p. 141.

104.   Dubnow: p. 373.

105.   Sanders, 1988: p. 143.

106.   Dubnow: p. 373.

107.   Dubnow: p. 375.

108.   The "golden country"—a land of opportunity where the streets were paved with gold.

109.   Compagnie Générale Transatlantique (Paris, France), Contrat de Transport par Mer, Number 47291, Max Sibermann, dated 25 October 1920; researcher's copy.

110.   Lorraine Coons and Alexander Varias, *Tourist Third Class: Steamship Travel in the Interwar Years* (New York: Palgrave MacMillan, 2003), p. 10; researcher's copy.

111.   "Le patrimoine maritime bâti de 1850 à nos jours," *lehavre.fr* (http://lehavre.fr), accessed September 2012.

112.   "Hotel de la Rue Phalsbourg, Salle a Manger," photograph; researcher's copy.

113.   Avraham, born in 1887, was the sixth of Perl's 12 children.

114.   New York, Department of Health, Certification of Birth, Certificate 3893, Gerald Milton Silverman, born 16 November 1930, in Syracuse, Onondaga County; researcher's copy.

115.   "Minerva Salzman Henkin," *The New York Times*, New York, New York, 22 May 1990, p. 11, col. 2; digital image, "Times Machine," The New York Times (https://timesmachine.nytimes.com), accessed February 2022.

116.   "'All Good Things Must End,' As Final Chapter of Southern Book Mart Comes to a Close," *The Times-Picayune*, New Orleans, Louisiana, 19 October 1980, p. 16, col. 1; researcher's copy.

117.   Jewish Community of Suczawa (Suczawa District, Bukovina Province, Austrian Empire), Births 1887-1894, p. 35, Number 192, Abraham Silbermann, born 21 October 1887; Suceava County Branch Archive of National Archives of Romania, Suceava, Romania.

118.   United States, Department of Justice, Immigration and Naturalization Service, Passenger and Crew Lists of Vessels Arriving at New York, New York, 1897-1957, SS *Volturno*, arrived 14 June 1913, p. 203, Line 15, Adolf Silberman; digital image, "New York, U.S., Arriving Passenger and Crew Lists (including Castle Garden and Ellis Island), 1820-1957," *Ancestry* (http://www.ancestry.com), accessed April 2022.

119. United States, Department of Labor, Naturalization Service, Declaration of Intention 296760, Adolph Silverman, dated 11 December 1922, in the Supreme Court of New York County, New York; digital image, "New York, U.S., State and Federal Naturalization Records, 1794-1943," *Ancestry* (http://www.ancestry.com), accessed April 2022.

120. *Midrash* is a form of literature that offers interpretation and commentary of biblical verses. The plural is *midrashim*. In its broadest sense, though, the term *midrash* can be applied to any interpretation of text. I use it here as a generic term to explain what I did in my search for understanding.

121. United States, Department of Labor, Naturalization Service, Petition for Naturalization 61704, Adolph Silverman, naturalized 16 September 1926, in the District Court for the Eastern District of New York; digital image, "New York, U.S., State and Federal Naturalization Records, 1794-1943," *Ancestry* (http://www.ancestry.com), accessed April 2022.

122. David, born in 1880, was the oldest of Perl's 12 children.

123. Phylacteries are worn by observant Jews during morning prayer services every day except on the Sabbath and holidays.

124. A prayer book.

125. Lea, born in 1883, was the fourth of the 12 children.

126. Julius, born in 1892, was the eighth of the 12 children.

127. United States, Department of Justice, Immigration and Naturalization Service, Passenger and Crew Lists of Vessels Arriving at New York, New York, 1897-1957, SS *Rochambeau*, arrived 23 October 1920, p. 189, Line 7, Jude Silberman; digital image, "New York, U.S., Arriving Passenger and Crew Lists (including Castle Garden and Ellis Island), 1820-1957," *Ancestry* (http://www.ancestry.com), accessed April 2022.

128. City of New York (New York) Department of Health, Certificate and Record of Marriage, Certificate 16873, Julius Silberman and Lilly Lehrer, married 28 June 1936, in Manhattan; FSL Microfilm 1674581.

129. Two of the children whose names appear on the census from Suceava—Solomon Wolf, born in 1885, and Chaya Ettel, born in 1889—do not appear in any other records or documents we have located.

130. Norbert, born in 1900, was the 11th of the 12 children.

131. Norbert Silbermann, of Garsten, Austria, to Harry Silberman, of Brooklyn, New York, letter, dated 22 December 1936, news from Europe; researcher's copy.

132. Norbert Silbermann, of Garsten, Austria, to Perl Silberman, of Brooklyn, New York, letter, dated 13 December 1937, news from Europe; researcher's copy.

133. Although exact currency conversion between 1920 French francs and United States dollars is difficult to find, I found that, in 1920, ₣22 would purchase 2.341 grams of gold. The price of that amount of gold in 1920 was $1.547. "Historical Currency Converter," *Historical Statistics.org* (http://www.historicalstatistics.org), accessed January 2019.

134. Hamburg-American Line, Purchaser's Receipt and Contract, Number 319851, Perl Silberman; researcher's copy.

135. Coons and Varias: p. XVI.

136. Coons and Varias: p. 32.

137. Coors and Varias: p. 118.

138. Coons and Varias: p. 9.

139. [No Author], "Emigration from the Port of Hamburg, Germany," *Avotaynu: The International Review of Jewish Genealogy* XIV (Winter 1998): p. 19; researcher's copy.

140. 1910 U.S. Federal Census (Population Schedule), Philadelphia, Philadelphia County, Pennsylvania, ED 166, Sheet 3A, Dwelling 28, Family 37, Max Hass household; digital image, "1910 United States Federal Census," *Ancestry* (http://www.ancestry.com), accessed February 2022.

Part 2, Chapter 2
Return to Sender: The Kreisler/Zweifler and Grass Families

Janette Silverman

b: New York, USA

Milton Silverman

b: 1926, Brooklyn, New York
m: 1949, Brooklyn, New York, USA

Rhoda Moldofsky

b: 1930, Brooklyn, New York, USA

Harry Silberman

b: 1 Aug 1903, Suczawa, Austrian Empire
m: 27 Feb 1926, Brooklyn, New York, USA
d: 9 Dec 1985, Parsippany, New Jersey, USA

Bilma Grass

b: 7 May 1898, Stanislau, Austrian Empire
d: 27 Apr 1956, Brooklyn, New York, USA

Selig Gras

b: 1866, Halicz, Austrian Empire
m: Bef. 1896, Stanislau, Austrian Empire
d: 12 Dec 1920, Stanisławów, Poland

Chana Kreisler

b: 21 Aug 1875, Stanislau, Austrian Empire
d: 12 Oct 1941, in Stanisławów, Poland

Jakob Gras

b: Bef. 1846, Austrian Empire

Ruchel

b: Bef. 1846, Austrian Empire

Shimon Kreisler

b: 1846, Austrian Empire
m: Bef. 1871, Austrian Empire

Tova Zweifler

b: 1846, Nadwórna, Austrian Empire

Looking Back, Looking Forward

I am writing this in the early part of 2023, a full year after Russia's leaders woke from their slumber and continue their attempts to take over land that doesn't historically belong to them. I am looking forward, anticipating the end of this unjustified war initiated by Russia in its attempt to subjugate Ukraine. My hope is, of course, that Russia will be forced to withdraw and go home. As I write looking forward to the end of the hostilities, I am also looking backward to other strife in these same places. This area, Ukraine, is the place where most of my family came from. Eastern Ukraine, including the capital, Kyyiv, was once part of the Russian Empire. Western Ukraine, where this chapter has its roots, was part of the Austrian Empire. Both were, before that, part of the vast Polish-Lithuanian Commonwealth.

Return To Sender: Kreisler-Grass Family

In April 1956, my paternal grandmother, Blima Rosa (Grass) Silberman, died of pancreatic cancer. As I grew older, I often thought of her. I reinforced early memories by reflecting on conversations with other relatives and the few photographs we had of her. Until my paternal grandfather, Harry Silberman,[1] died in December 1985, those memories surfaced most often during visits to his apartment at 78 East 94th Street in Brooklyn, New York. My grandparents moved into this small apartment in about 1928, and Harry and Blima's two sons grew up there. At times, Harry's mother, Perl (Buchbinder) Silberman, or her granddaughter Charlotte Silberman lived with them. Harry occupied this apartment until his death in 1985. Although often sick during the years preceding her death, Blima managed to cook my favorite foods when we visited. As an adult, I still remembered the taste of her stuffed cabbage. Even though I experimented, trying to duplicate that recipe—which, of course, she never wrote down—I came close but never quite succeeded. I remember my grandmother's pedal-driven sewing machine and her hand-stitched embroidery. Somewhere, I still have the tattered remains of a

Fig. 1: Blima Rose Grass, circa 1915[2]

yellowing apron she made for me. I did not, however, remember what she looked like, the feel of her skin, or the scents that surrounded her. I have only a very vague memory of her European-accented voice.

Harry didn't often speak about her. Although, as the birthdays of their grandchildren approached, he said he dreamed vividly of her. Those dreams always reminded him of the upcoming birthday of one of their five grandchildren. She only lived long enough to meet two—my sister Shari, who was a baby when Blima died, and me. Harry never spoke of his family who remained in Europe when he immigrated and he did not know Blima's family in Europe. Even though he never met any of those European relatives, he surely would have known of them. But his response to questions was that no one remained in Europe. At the time, I thought he meant no one stayed behind. Now, though, I know better, and I realize he meant no one survived the Holocaust. He did not want to speak of the fate of those who died. Memories of the Holocaust loomed over Blima's family, and, as it did for so many other families, shut down the flow of stories about family members lost in the war.

Shortly after Passover 1985, Harry was diagnosed with terminal cancer. Perhaps, being aware of the short time left to him, he grew more willing to identify people in photographs and to speak about their fate. About my grandmother's family and where they were from, he only said a few words, and those few words spoke volumes: "In October 1941, they were rounded up and shot on the streets or herded into the synagogue and burned alive." Of course, those words horrified me, and for the first time, the Holocaust became very personal. Although he may have known stories of Blima's siblings, parents, aunts, uncles, and cousins, he did not share those. Only after his death did we gain insight into the identities of those people.

When I began researching my grandparents' stories, I thought there would be very little to discover. Harry identified some people in old pictures as being siblings of his or Blima's. After Harry's death, my father, Milton; his younger brother, Stanley; and I visited Harry's apartment on several occasions to go through his personal effects. There were stacks of letters in the boxes of papers we found in his apartment. Initially, the large number of pages and photographs seemed overwhelming. We soon developed a plan. We began by sorting letters into stacks according to the writer or recipient. The letters in the largest stack were addressed either to or from Samuel Leon Gras, who lived on Lenina Street in Stanisławów,[3] Poland. These letters were all written in Polish. In the stack were letters in sealed envelopes from Blima in the United States to Samuel in Stanisławów. The envelopes bore postmarks from the 1940s, and all had an official stamp. My father commented that it was odd to find such long correspondence between my grandmother and a brother with whom she had had a falling out years earlier. He made that comment before we examined the letters and their envelopes more closely and realized the significance of the postmarks.

When we started examining the envelopes, we saw that the ones addressed to Samuel were all stamped "retour parti"—the equivalent of "return to sender." That led to a comment that I believe I made, something to the effect of how sad

Fig. 2: 1946 envelope returned to sender[4]

it was that my grandparents had been writing to someone who was already
dead—killed in the Holocaust. At that point, we had not noticed the postmarks on
the envelopes sent to my grandparents. Most of the envelopes lacked postmarks
because my father—and, later, my father and I—collected stamps. We neatly
cut out the area from envelopes that held a stamp and soaked the stamp off the
envelope backing so it could be mounted in a stamp album. It never occurred to us
that the information surrounding the stamp might someday prove to be invaluable.
We found it possible to match the names on some of the letters with the names of
people in photos previously identified. Samuel gained a face and was about to
have a voice, as well. Our initial assumption was that Samuel had been murdered
by the Nazis in 1941 along with the remainder of his family in Stanisławów. We
thought, therefore, that the letters were logically being returned as undeliverable.[5]

Samuel, Diana, and Eugene

Blima's oldest son—my father, Milton—told me about the events of 1 September
1939, the day of the Nazi invasion of Poland. He said he remembered being
at the New York World's Fair that day, just before his 13th birthday and his bar
mitzvah. He was with his mother and his younger brother, Stanley. In a 2010
email, Milton wrote:

Fig. 3: Map of Ivano-Frankivsk and Suceava[6]

My imperfect recollection is that, on that day, my mother, brother, and I attended the New York World's Fair in Flushing Meadow Park. One of the buildings had an electric moving sign board—just like the one on the old NY Times building in Times Square. The news came flashing around the building and caught my mother's attention. To naïve, 13-year-old me, I was not alert enough to understand her startled, perhaps stressed, reaction to the news as the lights went around and around carrying other news as well: Wall Street stock market, tennis tournament results, and probably other items not in my memory.

The Fair, we were told, was to encourage friendship among countries by having many countries providing outreach by way of their own buildings and exhibits. Well, looking back, it certainly was not the time or place. But, of course, it might be said that, in an era of appeasement of international tensions, it was typical—see no evil.

At that time, I had a Polish secretary who agreed to translate the letters and did so over several months,[7] in no particular order. In fact, the most important of the letters turned out to be one of the last ones she translated. To my surprise, she was not moved at all by the contents of that letter, or of its implications, and was as matter-of-fact about it as the ones containing more mundane discussions. Much later, I wondered why she and her parents left Europe in the late 1940s and what they had been doing during the war. Her reaction of course may have been benign— perhaps since the events about which she was reading happened long ago, and because she didn't know the people, she was unaffected.

That last letter said, in summary, that Samuel; his wife, Diana; and their son, Eugene,[8] were the only ones in Blima's large family who survived the war. They were frantic to get in touch with Samuel's family in America, who they hoped had survived the widespread devastation in Europe.[9] Later letters pleaded with Blima and Harry to reply to the letters. The hope they had of reconnecting with their American relatives diminished as time passed.[10] The stack of letters included several from one of Samuel's friends who had fled Poland, asking my grandparents why they did not respond to Samuel's letters. We do not know whether Harry and Blima answered the letters written by Samuel's friend. We do know they replied to Samuel's letters, but it was clear that the letters they mailed to him were returned. Initially, we had no idea why that happened. Later, we discovered that Stanisławów remained in the Soviet sector after the war, and letters from the United States were not being delivered. It amazes me, looking back after all these decades since I first found our family, that we were all so naïve. We knew nothing.

We quickly realized that we had another geographical mystery. These letters and papers referred to Stanislau, Stanisławów, Stanislav, and Lwów. Were all these places the same or did they reference different cities? Using an atlas, we discovered that the names Stanislau, Stanislav, and Stanisławów referred to the same city in different languages. Lwów[11] was a completely different place, located not too far from Stanisławów. Of course, cities nearby with similar names complicate the issue. We found Stanislavchik in the Vinnitsa district, Stanislawzyk in the Tarnopol district, and even a Stanisławów in the Mińsk Mazowiecki district not far from Warsaw. This latter location was more than 320 miles from our Stanisławów! Many cities, town, streets, and buildings are named after Saint Stanislaus, the patron saint of Poland. The city in which our family lived is Stanisławów, now called Ivano-Frankivsk. It is located in the district by the same name. At its 300th anniversary in 1962, the city was renamed for the Ukrainian poet Ivan Franko.

In 1997, after a trip to Ivano-Frankivsk, Susannah R. Juni wrote that Stanisławów:

Fig. 4: Stanisławów map, circa 1905[12]

...was not a small shtetl; rather, it was a city of 150–200 thousand people...before World War I, it was officially known by its German name, Stanislau, and it was located in the region of the Austro-Hungarian Empire called Galicia. Because of the large ethnic Polish population, the Polish town name, Stanisławów, was colloquially used by many people in its shortened version of Stanislaw (pronounced Stanislav). The Austro-Hungarian Empire (and the province called Galicia) ceased to exist after the end of World War I, and the city found itself within the borders of newly formed Poland, with the official name of Stanisławów.[13]

According to *The Encyclopedia of Jewish Life*, the city of Stanisławów was established in the mid-seventeenth century, and Jews were among its first residents.[14] The original population was comprised of Armenians, Ruthenians, Poles, and Jews.[15] In 1662, a few years after the settling of the city, "the Jews of Stanislaw were given the right to permanently stay in the city[16] for trading and doing crafts, and to be free from any taxes for leaving the city."[17] This right was initially granted for a period of 20 years. They were also allowed "three houses for communal affairs."[18] Among these was a synagogue, a wooden building.[19] The wooden synagogue[20] was not an anomaly; many churches, houses, and commercial buildings were constructed of wood.[21]

The Jews of Stanisławów had the freedom to engage in commercial transactions and to conduct business in their homes on all days but Christmas and Easter. On other Christian holy days, they had permission to conduct commerce after the conclusion of that day's church services.[22] By the eighteenth century, Jews had attained the status of leading merchants, a position previously held by Armenians.[23] This change resulted from economic hardships suffered by Armenians in the wake of wars at the beginning of the eighteenth century in Poland. Initially, Armenians petitioned the owner of the city to curtail the commercial rights of Jews to regain their own economic advantages, but even with this change in privileges, the Armenians still struggled and finally left the city. At that point, in the 1730s, the mercantile center housed 19 Jewish merchants and five Armenians.[24] By the late 1700s, the Jews built a larger synagogue, this time out of stone and wood. That synagogue stood until World War II.[25]

During the nineteenth century, the Jewish population in Stanisławów grew rapidly. At the beginning of the century, there were 151 non-Jewish artisans and 69 Jews. By century's end, there were 690 Jewish artisans and a little more than 300 non-Jews.[26] By the mid-1800s, only 14 of the 730 sellers and merchants were non-Jews.[27] In the nineteenth century, Jewish artisans outnumbered non-Jewish artisans two to one. Tailors comprised one-third of those. Jews owned two-thirds of the factories in the district. One of the Jewish families held the salt monopoly for all of Galicia and served in local political offices; they also held office in the Austrian parliament. By 1910, when my family began to leave the area, the Jewish population numbered more than 15,000, almost half of the total population. Forty synagogues existed, including the one previously mentioned that dated to the late 1700s. Jewish schools in the area served not only the local Jewish population but also attracted Jewish students from all over Galicia. In addition to Orthodox *yeshivot*, there were Zionist programs and a Reform temple. Jews owned almost all the 800 stores in Stanisławów by 1921. Jewish lawyers and doctors and Jewish owners of factories and welfare services abounded in Stanisławów.[28] Jews held prominent positions in this thriving city.

Nechama Tec, a Holocaust survivor and Professor Emerita of Sociology at the University of Connecticut, wrote: "[l]ittle is known about the Jews of wartime Stanisławów, their lives, resistance, and deaths."[29] The history of the Jews in Stanisławów came to a very violent and bloody end in October 1941. The United States Holocaust Memorial Museum described that end:

On October 12, 1941, they [the Nazis] demonstrated how they meant to "solve" the "Jewish Question" in the area. This day was later called "Blutsonntag" ("Bloody Sunday"). Unlike the other districts of the General Government, in the region of Stanislawów the local German administration did not wait until the extermination camps had been established. Thousands of Jews were gathered on the market square; then the German forces escorted them to the Jewish cemetery, where mass graves had already been prepared. On the way, the German and Ukrainian escorts beat and tortured the Jews. At the cemetery, the Jews were compelled to give away their valuables and show their papers. Some of them were then released, but the majority had to remain. The men of the Security Police (SiPo) then started the mass shootings, assisted by members of the German Order Police (Ordnungspolizei) and also the railroad police. Krüger personally took part in the shootings. The Germans ordered the Jews to undress in groups and then proceed to the graves, where they were shot. They fell into the grave or were ordered to jump in before being shot...Some survivors have described the massacre in detail, revealing the incredible brutality applied by the German forces. Many survivors remember how bravely Dr. Tenenbaum of the Jewish council went to his death. Krüger, the head of the Gestapo, offered to set him free, but Tenenbaum said that he rejected this offer from a murderer and that he wanted to die with his brethren. In the evening, those Jews still alive were allowed to leave the cemetery. The German forces shot between 8,000 and 12,000 Jews on that day. Seibald, the chairman of the Jewish council, survived the massacre but lived in hiding afterwards. Most probably he was also killed later on. On the day after the bloodbath, Lamm was called to the Gestapo headquarters, where they informed him that he would be the new chairman of the Jewish council. Among the members of the Jewish council in the ghetto was the engineer Julian Feuerman, who wrote a personal testimony in 1943 while he was in prison but did not survive the war.[30][31]

According to records in the Ivano-Frankivsk archives,[32] Chana Jetta Kreisler Grass grew up at the same address at which she raised her children: 24 Sapizhinska Street in downtown Stanisławów. From records at the archives in Ivano-Frankivsk in 2009, we noticed that several Landsman and Kreisler families lived at numbers 20 and 22 Sapizhinska Street. Many of those names were familiar to us. On that October day in 1941, the first people summoned out of their homes were those who lived in the area near the market square. Our relatives were probably in that group. In the photo below, an arrow points to a large, white, gray-roofed building. There are several smaller buildings on the street above it. Those smaller buildings are what seem, from the exterior, to be charming residences. The white building is the municipal tax office. That tax office stands where 20, 22, and 24 Sapizhinska Street once stood. It is the only place where original houses no longer stand. In the photo, what appear to be strange indentations in the middle of the street are areas of grass, bushes, and flowers in a park-like median. It is quite beautiful and is like other old parts of the city and its parks.

Fig. 5: Sapizhinska Street[33]

Finding the Family

From the tone of the letters written by Samuel, his friends, and Diana's brother,[34] it did not appear that Samuel and Diana ever received any response from Blima or heard news of their American family. Sofie Caplan attempted to locate remnants of her family from Kalusz in the Stanisławów district following the war. She wrote of her frustrations with letters having been returned to her stamped "unknown at this address." She eventually learned of their fate from surviving family members who "spent the war years in Asiatic Russia"[35]—perhaps in circumstances similar to those Samuel and Diana experienced.

During the days and weeks following the stunning news of the survival of Samuel, Diana, and Eugene, the family spoke often, attempting to figure out what exactly transpired in the days and years following the war. Locating corroborating evidence often is the most difficult part of research.[36] Finally, after questioning officials at different agencies including Yad Vashem[37] and the Red Cross, we identified the "Search Bureau for Missing Relatives" in Jerusalem as a potential source for locating my missing relatives. Batya Unterschatz, the volunteer running the organization at that time, disclosed that, 20 years earlier in the 1960s, someone in New York had been searching for the same family. The address Batya sent me was the same address at which they had lived prior to the war and the address to which my grandparents had unsuccessfully written.[38]

I mailed a letter to the family at that address. What transpired shocked me. They had moved years earlier, and the name of the town had changed,[39] but this time, unlike in the years after the war, the letter was delivered. Within a month, I received a response. Samuel, Diana, and their son, Eugene, were still alive in 1986. Eugene's daughter, Ella, was an English professor at a university in Ukraine, and it was she who wrote the reply. Their response was a tearful one, as they had despaired of ever hearing from their American relatives and thought everyone in the family was long dead. They needed to be told that Blima and her sister Fanny died in the mid- and late 1950s, respectively. We sent them copies of letters and, more importantly, family photos that predated the war, along with four decades' worth of news. All remembrances of Samuel's and Diana's families had been lost to them during the war, so they were grateful to receive the copies. In those days, a photocopy produced a negative, so for each page and each photograph, two copies needed to be made.

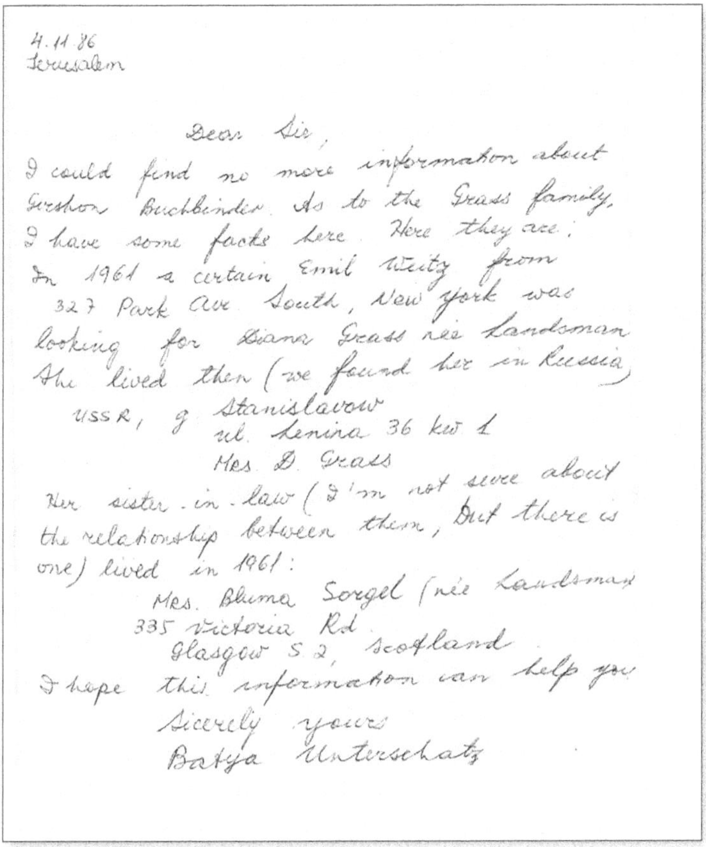

4.11.86
Jerusalem

Dear Sir,
I could find no more information about Gershon Buchbinder. As to the Grass family, I have some facts here. Here they are:
In 1961 a certain Emil Weitz from 327 Park Ave South, New York was looking for Diana Grass née Landsman. She lived then (we found her in Russia)
USSR, g. Stanislavow
ul. Lenina 36 kw 1
Mrs. D. Grass
Her sister-in-law (I'm not sure about the relationship between them, but there is one) lived in 1961:
Mrs. Bluma Sorgel (née Landsman
335 Victoria Rd
Glasgow S. 2, Scotland
I hope this information can help you
Sincerely yours
Batya Unterschatz

Fig. 6: Letter from Batya Unterschatz[40]

In the early days of our correspondence, Ella wrote what her grandmother Diana dictated to her. The language was stilted, not because of Ella's lack of proficiency with English, but because of restrictions imposed by the then-Soviet government on what she could easily write and mail to the United States. We were told by others with more experience writing to people behind the Iron Curtain that we needed to be cautious and not make any political comments. We discovered that many, if not all, letters going into the Soviet Union were subject to censorship. There were strict guidelines to follow for mailing packages, too.

Despite the restrictions, we learned that Samuel had been in the Russian army. As a pharmacist, he initially was sent to the front but, due to poor eyesight, he was sent to Kazakhstan, where a job awaited him. Unbeknownst to Samuel, Diana used family connections to get herself, Eugene, and her father, Abraham Landsmann, relocated to Kazakhstan for the duration of the war. While there, they

Fig. 7: View in 2010 of Samuel and Diana's pre- and post-war apartment[41]

found Samuel. Diana's father died while they were in Kazakhstan but she, along with Samuel and Eugene, returned to their home in Stanisławów after the war.

Samuel and Diana died within a couple of years of that initial correspondence, and Eugene died in 2008. Ella's daughter, Julia, is now an adult and has a child, Ilya. Encouraged by our continued correspondence and the limited information that Ella sent in those early years, I began to search for records of the family and to try to understand what their lives had been like. The answers came slowly and not without a great deal of frustration. It took more than two decades to develop a rudimentary understanding of the information and to begin to put the pieces of the puzzle into their proper places.

1920 Immigration

Blima arrived in the United States with her sisters Fanny and Clara in 1920. Clara, the oldest of nine siblings, was born in 1896, Blima in 1898, and Fanny in 1900. Fanny and Blima remained in the United States, married, and had

Fig. 8: Ella, standing next to her father, Eugene (L), and her grandfather Samuel (R), with her grandmother Diana in front[42]

families, but Clara returned to Europe, probably about 1925. The story we were told decades later (and the story Samuel wrote from Europe through Ella) was that Clara returned to Europe to marry her childhood sweetheart. Years later, the ship manifest and a *yahrzeit* list shed a potentially different light on the story of their arrival in the United States. The sisters did not travel to the United States together but on two separate ships arriving in New York within a few days of each other, from two different ports![43] Blima left Europe on 28 November 1920,[44] while her sisters left on 23 November.[45] Blima landed in New York on 7 December and Clara and Fanny on 4 December. The difference in the sailing time may have been due to the different ports from which they left—Clara and Fanny from Rotterdam, Netherlands, and Blima from Le Havre, France.

Zelig Gras, their father, died within two weeks after the sisters' ships docked in New York. Since we knew Clara returned to Europe, before we had more information, we explored a *midrash* to explain her return. We decided that "Clara returned to Europe a few days after her father's death to assist her mother, Chana, with her younger siblings." This contradicted what Samuel said and what Harry

Fig. 9: 1925 New York State Census[48]

told us, but for a long time, that was our story, and we seemed to be wedded to it—satisfied with that explanation. Thankfully, we didn't disregard other information. A careful examination of Blima's notebook from a night-school class she took in Brooklyn from about 1922 to 1924 showed two addresses on the cover;[46] one was her own and one was Clara's. Both addresses were in Brooklyn, New York! Milton was surprised at Blima's home address, 619 Rockaway Avenue, because, as he told me, that was where Fanny and her husband, Willie Ostrofsky, lived. Milton said he was unaware that his mother lived with them or that Willie and Fanny married before his own parents. A search through the New York marriage records revealed that Fanny and Willie married in January 1921, just a few weeks after the sisters arrived in New York. The 1925 New York State Census[47] provided the information that Blima still resided with Fanny and Willie in that year. The census indicated that Willie had arrived in the United States long before the Grass sisters—when he was only 16!

Clara did not live with them, and, to date, no evidence has been found that she was still in New York. To our surprise, we discovered that, in 1913, several years prior to the immigration of his daughters, Zelig visited the United States, or at least planned to visit. On his ship manifest, he indicated that his destination was the home of his brother-in-law Isak Kreisler and that his closest relative in Europe was his wife, Chane Grass. Did Zelig really come to the United States? No one in the family remembers any mention of this.

The manifest covers two pages, and one thing is clear: there is a line through his name that goes across both pages. His is the only passenger entry that has a line like that. Was Zelig's name crossed out because he didn't make the sailing? We have found no evidence of him in the United States, nor would we anticipate

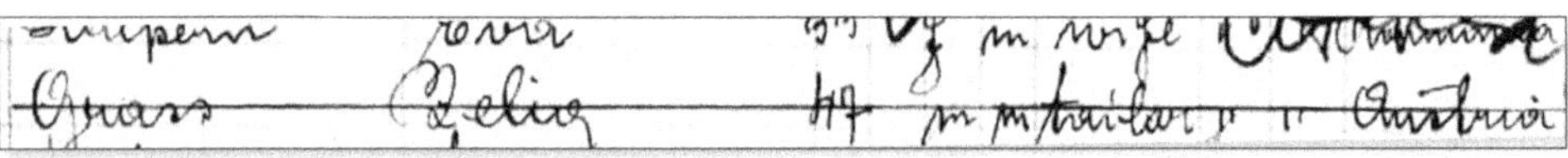

Fig. 10: August 1913 arrival of the SS *Imperator*[49]

Fig. 11: L to R: Chana, Moshe, Zelig, Blima with Fanny in the front [50]

records from someone who didn't remain. Records are only left if someone does something notable—is born, marries, dies, resides, establishes a business, is arrested, winds up in a newspaper story, etc. The average person might never leave a documentary footprint. From the evidence on the manifest, it looks like Zelig planned a trip and, for whatever reason, did not take it. Many times, when someone missed the boat (literally) you can find them on another sailing a few days later, but not in this case. This, of course, opens the nasty "what if" drawer— what if he had made that trip and sent for his wife and children to join him? If that had happened, then the history of my family would have been much different.

Information from the Ivano-Frankivsk archives provided the date of Clara's marriage to Zygmunt Weber in 1924. My original understanding of the sequence of events has now been revised. I understand the truth of the original story that Clara returned to Europe to marry her childhood sweetheart. She did not return to Europe to assist her mother with the younger children after her father's death but remained in New York for a few years. Clara was murdered with her husband and children, her siblings, and their spouses and children, along with her mother, Chana, in a Nazi round-up and massacre in Stanisławów on 12 October 1941.[51] This was the end of the Sukkot holidays and men who were in the synagogue that morning to observe special rituals were locked in the building, which was then torched. All inside were burned to death.

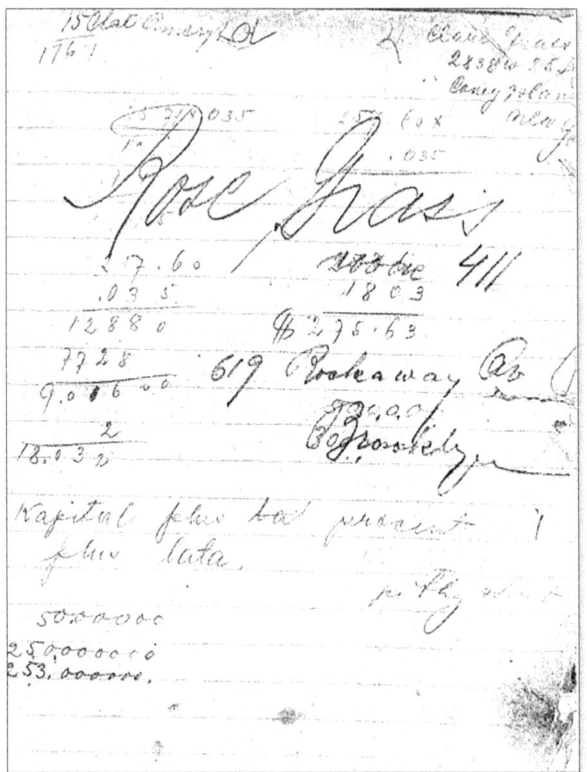

Fig. 12: Cover of Blima's citizenship class notebook;
her address is in the center of the page and Clara's name and
address are in the upper right corner[52]

Several interesting facts can be found on the manifests from the two ships on which the sisters traveled from Europe to the United States. First, the ships departed Europe within five days of each other from two different ports. Blima left on the SS *La Lorraine* from Le Havre while her sisters traveled on the SS *Rotterdam* leaving from Rotterdam. The second page of the manifests shows Blima planned to stay with a cousin, Charles Zweifler, in the Bronx, and her sisters listed their uncle Peter Zwerin in Manhattan as their destination. At the time we found the ship manifests, we had seen the names Zweifler and Zwern/Zwerin/Zwirn on European records from Stanisławów but had no idea of the extent of the familial connections. Once we found these manifests and other records through Jewish Records Indexing-Poland,[53] we could draw lines connecting them. Peter's wife, Rose, was Chana Jetta's younger sister!

In an odd turn of events, there was another encounter, years later, with a descendant of Peter and Rose, who lived in New York for many years. They later

Fig. 13: Peter Zwirn and Rose Kreisler[54]

relocated across the United States to California sometime after the 1940 census and before Peter's 1951 death. All six of their children were born in New York. Their second-youngest, Herbert Leo, was born in June 1920. When he was 6 months old, Fanny and Clara stayed with the family. Herbert died in New York in 2009. He and his wife lived on the east side of Manhattan, not far from the United Nations. For a few years, my son, Efrem, lived on the east side, not too far from the United Nations. New York is a big city with a large population. However, coincidences abound. This was one of them. About 2007 or 2008, Efrem was putting some furniture out at the curb. An elderly couple stopped by and commented on the chairs Efrem had just put out. They chatted for a while and exchanged contact information. They stayed in touch for a while. Several years later, Efrem was going through one of my long descendant reports and came across Herbert's name. It was then that he told me he had met and become friendly with him. Neither Efrem nor Herbert knew of the familial relationship. My daughter, Arielle, moved to California years ago. Many of the Zwirn descendants live there. It is possible that at some point, she, too, will meet a member of the extended family.

Transatlantic Travel

A 1910 Senate Immigration report clearly stated that newly arrived immigrants are expected to be met at Ellis Island by friends or relatives already in the United States. A person who lands and whose relative or friend fails to meet them can be held for up to five days while they await their arrival. Should their sponsor not arrive, the immigrant can be sent back to Europe or released to a representative of a philanthropic or religious group that has government authorization to serve in that capacity.[55] There is no reason to believe that the Zweifler or Zwerin sponsors did not meet their charges, since none of the sisters appear on the detention pages of the manifest.

Something I find of endless interest is how memories or even records of events that occurred within modern memory have so many different versions. Stories abound about names being changed, stowaways on vessels, exchanges of identity, and how names were entered or transcribed from manifest to manifest. For ships departing from Europe, two sets of manifests were prepared before a ship left Europe: one, the departure manifest, became part of the shipping company's records and the other, an arrival manifest, used the manifest form required by the United States Immigration Services.[56] Thus, as information was copied from one place to another, names might have been spelled differently by the clerk. If an arrival and departure manifest can be found for the same sailing, it is possible to compare the names on both and to determine how the name was recorded.

It is not too surprising, given the large number of Jewish immigrants coming to the United States from Eastern Europe between 1881 and 1924, that a lot has been written about them. Despite the volumes of material, it is sometimes difficult to determine the differences in the journeys undertaken by immigrants at any point in time during those 40-plus years. It is easy to see what the changes in immigration laws accomplished on the American side of the transatlantic journey, but since that has little bearing on the European outbound journey and many borders were involved, the only way to know is through descriptions provided by immigrants. Therefore, the descriptions of emigration presented here may not be the exact experiences of Blima, Feige, and Chaja.

Foreign exit document requirements varied widely by country. For example,

Russia required male emigrants to obtain an exit permit before they could leave; to get one, they had to have completed their required military service. The Russian government also had an understanding (if not a formal agreement) with the railroads and shipping companies not to sell tickets to anyone who could not produce an exit permit showing military service. Hence, a common story was of young men who bought or otherwise obtained someone else's military papers to get an exit permit. Once they did so, they had to buy the ticket under that assumed name. Thus, the U.S. manifest would appear with that name. There was, of course, no impediment for the newly arrived immigrant to change his name once he left Ellis Island or another port of arrival. If someone took a different name and there was no documentation with both names, it would be impossible to find the immigrant on the boat, and potentially impossible to find the person back in Europe prior to emigration. I am frankly relieved that, in all my own family's research, this was not one of the issues we encountered.

Passenger lists or manifests were created by the shipping office at the time of ticket purchase, not at the time passengers boarded the ship. There was possibly one more stop to make before a passenger boarded the vessel—at a police station where there might be official paperwork to complete. If a passenger list had not already been created, it might be created at this point. If there was already a passenger list, a potential emigrant would be checked against the list and permitted to board. If the information had not already been obtained, the emigrant might be asked at the police station who had purchased the ticket for them, along with their occupation, destination, and a contact in their hometown. Sometimes a person's name and details are on several different manifests for ships leaving Europe days or weeks apart. In these cases, the passenger's name will have a line through it for each of the sailings the passenger missed.

Why did Blima and her sisters travel on two separate ships? The answer to that question may remain unresolved. To try to find the answer, or at least suggest possible scenarios, I decided to ask other genealogists, thinking that some of them might have encountered something similar. When I posed the question to the *JewishGen* Discussion Group, a suggestion was made that:

> *...[t]ickets for train and ship travel were often purchased in the US by the 'sponsor' relative; they could set up any route for the person to get from their town to a port using the extensive rail system in Europe at*

the time, and if two different people brought parts of the family they probably did not coordinate and set up different routes. Tickets were often purchased through immigrant banks. Philadelphia immigrant bank records survive and show how one relative purchased tickets for groups of family members to travel, supplying names, ages, address in Europe, as well as steamship line, which determined the port of departure and arrival.[57]

So, according to this suggestion, different relatives might have purchased the tickets, and those relatives were unable to coordinate travel arrangements.

Banks were often created by affinity groups. In New York, the Emigrant Savings Bank was founded by Irish immigrants. Jews also set up banking systems to aid immigrants to the United States and provide a way for newly arrived people to send money back to Europe. In the port cities on the East Coast of the United States in the late nineteenth and early twentieth centuries, many charitable organizations aided immigrants arriving from Europe. The Hebrew Immigrant Aid Society (HIAS) was one of those organizations. Port cities also offered so-called "ethnic" or "emigrant" banks, conveniently located in Jewish neighborhoods where newly arrived immigrants tended to settle. These banks were commercial enterprises started mainly by established German Jews as a place where recent immigrants could save money and arrange to purchase steamship tickets to bring their families to the United States. In Philadelphia, Pennsylvania, HIAS preserved the original records of four immigrant banks formerly operating in the city.[58]

In a January 2012 email, Phyllis Kramer, then Vice President of Education at *JewishGen.org*, shed some light on the process and the banks. She wrote:

The question often arises: "how did the immigrant get his ticket?" A common method in both Eastern Europe and U.S. cities was to purchase tickets, often on the installment plan, through agents hired by banks...in 1868, Sender Jarmulowsky established a bank in Hamburg for the express purpose of purchasing tickets in low season and reselling them in the spring at a higher price. Jarmulowsky contracted with agents who travelled the shtetls throughout Eastern Europe. When the shipping lines established their own network of agents,

Fig. 14: Advertisement for the Sender Jarmulowsky Bank[59]

Jarmulowsky moved to New York and opened his bank in 1873, erecting the landmarked building that still stands at 54 Canal Street.

These banks in New York and Philadelphia were cooperative, not chartered by the state; they did not make loans, [but] instead, they sold tickets to immigrant families and arranged for monies to be transferred to families in Europe. There are no records surviving from the Jarmulowsky Bank[60] in New York, probably because it went bankrupt, but it's an interesting story. When World War I was imminent, immigrants rushed to their bank[s] to send money to their families in Eastern Europe; this rush overpowered the bank, as it had heavily invested in real estate in East Harlem; these investments were not liquid, so the bank could not meet its obligations.

To date, no proof has been found that this is how tickets for Blima and her sisters were purchased, but it is a reasonable possibility. There are other possibilities, too. In some years and for some ports, it is easier to quickly see how and where tickets were purchased. On those manifests, there is a question asking whether the traveler or someone else purchased the tickets. The manifests for Blima and her sisters did not provide this information.

Another possibility is that Blima decided to leave after her sisters began their trip and did not have time to join them, so she took the next available ship, which left from a different port. She could have also been traveling with friends or relatives who have not yet been identified. Unless some correspondence or other documentation becomes available that sheds some light on this, we may never know the answer. Clara and Fanny were on the same sailing as their aunt, Sara Lea Pfeffer Kreisler. Interestingly, Sara Lea, who was married to Chana Jetta's brother Samuel, traveled under the surname of Zweifler, not Kreisler. The name of Samuel and Chana Jetta's mother was Gitel Tova Zweifler, also known as Sheindel, and her husband was Shimon Kreisler. Samuel, who arrived in 1913, sailed under the surname Kreisler!

How Do We Know What to Call Her? Pick a Name, Any Name...

Blima's mother was Chana Jetta Kreisler. The family knew this before we began our research. In the archives in Ivano-Frankivsk, we found the death record for Blima's father, Zelig Grass. The record reads, in translation: "Selig Gras died December 12, 1920—[he was] a tailor, [his] wife was Chana Yetta Zweifler, [he] lived at 24 Sapizhinska—minor children: Rachel born January 12, 1909; Penina born December 20, 1905, Osias born June 19, 1911, Sala born December 23, 1917. Children who reached majority: Samuel Leon Gras." Only his children who were living with them were noted. Blima, Fanny, Clara, and Mundek were all living elsewhere at the time of his death.

Above, I noted two contradictory statements—that Blima's mother was both Chana Jetta Kreisler and Chana Jetta Zweifler. This discrepancy will be discussed below. What followed our initial discovery of Chana Jetta with two surnames posed difficulties in comprehending the information and sorting it out because there were many people in the family with similar discrepancies in their records. Chana Jetta's father was Shimon Kreisler, and her mother was who? Tova Gitel, Gizella Tova, or maybe it was Shaindel? How about Chana Jetta—was her surname Kreisler or Zweifler? Were these the same people? Boris Feldblyum has done extensive research on Jewish given names. He wrote that a given name for Jews was one of the most important facets of their identity because it connected them to the past and to their ancestors.[61] As an example of the corruption and distortion of given names, he wrote:

> *A common "Russian" example is Elieser, which means "my God has helped" (to escape the sword of Pharaoh), Exodus 18:4. In Russia, this name also produced a plethora of names: Bukish, Buksh, Dliezer, Elazar, Elezer, Elezerek, Eliazar, Eliazer, Fabuli, Fajv, Fajvish, Fuks, Iozibl', Krup, Laza, Lazan, Lazar, Lazar', Lazarus, Lazer, Lazl, Lazor, Lejzl, Lejzor, Lejzor, Lezl, Liber, Liberman, Lipa, Lipko, Lipman, Litman, Lozer, Lozor, Luzer, Lyajzer, Lyazer, Lyuzer, Papu, Vajv, Vajvish, Zalman, Zisman, Zusa, and Zusman.[62]*

In summary, he wrote that "[a]long with adopting new names, Jews changed a number of Jewish names, either adapting them to local tongues or accepting local variants of old Jewish names."[63]

Feldblyum commented further that it was a common practice at different junctures of a person's life to assign new or additional names—in other words, to change their "real" name. Sometimes the new name would be used only for a short time, sometimes for many years. A person might have no knowledge of their own official or legal name, the name given to them by their parents at birth and under which they were registered.[64] People often had hyphenated names, one in Yiddish and one in Hebrew, but sometimes other names would also be appended.

Rabbi Asher Bar-Zev was well known for his extensive research into his family's history and wrote that his father was called Menachem Ze'ev, Menachem Volf, and Menachem Mendel. The Volf/ Ze'ev change is understandable: one is the Yiddish equivalent of the other, a Hebrew name. Adding the Mendel is not easy to understand. Menachem Mendel was a popular name combination after several famous rabbis who bore that same double name.[65] After researching the name Mendel, Bar-Zev discovered that it might have been formed as a diminutive from Menachem. Someone with the first name Menachem might have had it shortened to "Men" and then had a German diminutive ending, "del," added to it. Then, people who were used to double names called him by the full name, Menachem, and the nickname, Mendel, combining the two to form a new, two-name combination.[66]

The late Professor G. L. Esterson and David Curwin wrote that "[o]ur nineteenth-century Eastern European Ashkenazi ancestors had numerous Yiddish and European secular names that they used for different purposes."[67] In an effort to clarify the preponderance of formal and informal names by which our ancestors were known, Esterson designed the "Given Names Database (GNDB) Project." This is one of hundreds of databases available through *JewishGen.org*. The database includes names used by Jews in 14 European countries between 1795 and 1925. Esterson described how names were used in the Jewish community, writing that:

In European countries, the rabbis recognized Primary-Subsidiary double given names (like Aleksander Ziskind or Yehuda Leyb) as the legal names for recording women and men in Jewish legal documents (Get,[68] ketuva,[69] and other Jewish contracts), and for calling a man to the Torah for an aliya.[70] In addition to their Primary name, many Jews had a Subsidiary (i.e., Yiddish or European secular) name which was commonly linked to their Hebrew Primary name, like the Yiddish names Yudl or Leyb, to Yehuda. Most also had other simple Non-Subsidiary names (which were not written in a Get), like names of endearment (e.g., Yiddish name Yidele) and diminutives (Yudye or Itke), and others. And European emigrants to foreign countries adopted many foreign vernacular names (like Joseph or Rebecca). In some cases, Jews collected as many as 35 given names in some of these categories, depending on regional European and foreign name popularity and usage.[71]

The information accumulated for these databases was taken from many sources, including rabbinic records, *matzevot*, *yizkor* books, and archival European records. A major utilization of the GNDB occurs when:

...archival research has yielded a Yiddish name for an ancestor, then a search of the GNDB supplies all other possible Jewish names that the ancestor may have used in his or her European country of residence, as well as the possible corresponding vernacular names used in a number of foreign countries. All of the given names in each of the above categories depend on the particular European country of origin and the particular foreign country of immigration.[72]

It often seems as if our ancestors deliberately used all these names so that we, their descendants, would be incapable of finding them. More likely, there was no malevolence attached to the practice, or, if there was, it was directed at the Russian government, to ensure an inability to be identified for tax or conscription purposes. A search in the GNDBs for "Gitel," one of the names Chana Jetta's mother was known by, yielded the following results:

> *Legal/Hebrew: Gita / Gitl / Gitsha / Guta / GutlGutlin / Tova*
> *Legal Origin: < German, Gut 'Good'*
> *Yiddish: Gite / Gitshe / Gute / Tove*
> *Yiddish Origin: < Yiddish calque < Bunya*
> *Yiddish Nickname: Gides / GITELe / Gitl / Gitla / Gitle /*
> *Gitlye / Gitse / Gitsye / Guste / Gusti / Gusye / Gutl / Gutlye*
> *US Name: Bertha / Carrie / Geitel / Gertrude / Gisela / Gisella /*

It is clear that both "Tova" and "Gitel" mean the same thing and that Gizella, although identified as a name from the United States, is also linked to these names. The "Yiddish calque" referred to under "Yiddish Origin" is identified by Koenig as:

> *...a translation. For example, the French name Bonhomme has essentially the same meaning as the German name Guttmann, 'a good man.' In Yiddish, Guttmann becomes Gutman, and Bonhomme is reduced to Bunem. One is a calque of the other.[73]*

Superstition often dictated how a person would be known. Some name changes occurred when an individual was an only child, as a protection from evil forces. Other name changes came about when someone was ill, to fool the angel of death. In some places, it was considered bad luck for two people in the same town to have the same name, for a man to marry a woman with the same name as his mother, or for a woman to marry a man with the same name as her father.[74] Imagining a town where no two people held the same first name is difficult, but in places with small populations, it may have been common. We know that Sheindel was one of the names Chana Jetta's mother, Tova Gitel, was called, and that her mother was also called Sheindel, and that Tova Gitel's brother Shimon married a Sheindel Devorah. We further know that all three of these women cannot be the same person because of the differences in birth years and some other verifiable facts. Chana Jetta's mother, Tova Gitel, was born in 1846. Sheindel Devorah was born in 1854. Tova Gitel's mother, Sheindel, was born about 1820—her son Shimon, Tova Gitel's brother, was born in 1840. Perhaps one or more of them was called Sheindel to describe her as being pretty. Descriptive terms were common— big Fanny and little Fanny, for example.

The Z's—Zweifler and Zwern/ Zwiern/Zwerin/Zwirn

What about Tova Gitel's maiden name? Was it really Zweifler? Shouldn't a name be straightforward? Actually, in the case of Jews living in Stanisławów in the late nineteenth century, the response to that last question is a resounding "no." Not only did Jews have a civil or secular name but they also had a Yiddish name and were frequently called by a nickname. Any of these names could and often did show up on records. This makes disentangling people from others with similar names difficult at the very least, and sometimes impossible. Birth records usually recorded a mother's name in a variety of forms, and a father's name may also appear on the record. Sometimes the child had the mother's surname, not the father's. On death and marriage records, both parents' names may be recorded. However, sometimes names would not be identical on each of these records. The spelling might be different, a first and middle name might appear in a different order, or the surname on two consecutive records for the same person might not be the same.

Originally, attempting to straighten out my confusion regarding the multiplicity of names, I created lists on spreadsheets. I went through the indices that Jewish Records Indexing-Poland (*JRI-Poland*) had compiled and searched for a particular surname in Stanisławów. I recorded all the people connected to that surname and then sorted the list in several ways—by the person's name, the mother's first or last name, or the father's name—and tried to create pairs of parents from these lists whenever possible.

In the indices of birth and death records from Nadworne of people with the surname Zweifler,[75] several issues can be noted from which conclusions were drawn and may, at some point, be proven incorrect. One of the positives of looking at a name such as Zweifler is that the name appears to be relatively uncommon—there are not many people with the surname. These two lists (see figures 15 and 16) are the complete lists of births and deaths for Zweiflers in Nadworna between 1866 and 1897. Comparing the two lists helped to isolate and verify names. For example, there are several records for a couple with the first names of Schloma and Judiss or Judes. In some instances, both people are given the surname of Zweifler, but in some, Judiss was referred to as Tellering. Are these two different couples or are they the same? In some records, Schloma Zweifler is paired with Rifke Tellering. Is Rifke the same person as Judiss, or a different person? Other information is very clear. A comparison of the births and deaths shows that Chanzie Bochner and Isak Juda Zweifler had a daughter named Malka who was born in 1891. There was a Malka who died in 1891 at 4 weeks whose parents were Chancie Bochner and Itzak Juda Zweifler. These are clearly the same parents for the same child despite spelling differences.

Sometimes it is possible to figure out relationships if some basic information is known, even if the names are not clear. For example, in 1902, a child named Benzion was born to Israel Schaffer and Debora "Kreisler r Zweifler." I knew that Chana Jetta had a sister named Deborah—was this the same person and, if so, what did the "r" in the record between Kreisler and Zweifler mean? It wasn't until I conducted thorough research on the Yad Vashem website that I discovered that this Debora Kreisler r Zweifler married to Israel Schaffer with a son Benzion with a slight spelling difference—Bentzion—was the same person as Chana Jetta's sister Deborah. Yad Vashem and Bentzion Schaffer's Pages of Testimony are discussed at length below.

Some double surnames in the records have "f" between the names. Was this the same as "r"? Research provided the answer. "R" stands for recte, meaning "legally" or "corrected," and "f" is short for "false." Both additions to names were a result of the complexities of religious and secular life in Galicia. In both cases, the problem is the same—the issue of so-called "religious marriages" in Galicia. Austrian authorities put a very high fee/tax on official registration of Jewish marriages in the eighteenth century, restricted the number of Jewish families in some towns, and even prohibited more than one son in a family from marrying. To get around these laws, Jews often married only under the *chupah*,[78] without registering their marriage with the civil authorities. By law, these marriages were not considered to have taken place. These children were labeled "illegitimate" on

Surname	Givenname	Year	Type	Akt	Page	Signature	Event	Sex	Father	Fathersurn	Town	Mother	Mothersurn	Tow
	Sacharye	1867	B		17	940		M	Schlome	ZWEIFFLER		Judes	ZWEIFFLER	
	Henzia	1869	B		25	940		F	Josel	ZWEIFLER		Mariam	LAMPEL	
	Chaim Hersch	1871	B		33	940		M	Herzil	LEITTNER		Malka	ZWEIFLER	
	Menasche	1872	B		39	940		M	Josel	ZWEIFLER		Mariem	ZWEIFLER	
	NN	1877	B	17		941		M	Schloma	ZWEIFLER		Judiss	TELLERING	
	Machle	1878	B	153		941		F				Rifka	ZWEIFLER	
	Schmil Jankel	1879	B	35		941		M				Reisel	ZWEIFLER	
	Brany	1881	B	3		941		F				Reisel	ZWEIFLER	
	Herzel	1883	B	90		941		M				Reissel	ZWEIFLER	
	Rachel	1885	B	68		942		F				Reisel	ZWEIFLER	
	Mordko Joseph	1886	B	209		942		M				Reisel	ZWEIFLER	
	Sumer	1887	B	132		942		M	Jossel	ZWEIFLER		Chaje Sura	SCHULMAN	
	Jekil	1889	B	92		942		M	Zeldi	ZWEIFLER		Chancie	BACHNER	
	Abrahm	1890	B	142		942		M	Schloma	ZWEIFLER		Beile	KATZ	
	Malka	1891	B	153		942		F	Isak Juda	ZWEIFLER		Chanzie	BOCHNER	

Fig. 15: List of Zweifler births[76]

Surname	Givenname	Year	Type	Akt	Signature	Page	Age	Sex	Living	Town	Father	Fathersurn	Mother	Mothersurn	Comments
ZWEIFLER	Itzig	1868	D		944	3	69 y.	M							
ZWEIFLER	Sacharia	1869	D		944	7	2 y	M							
	stillborn	1877	D	3	945			M			Schloma	ZWEIFLER	Judiss	ZWEIFLER	
ZWEIFLER/JÄGER	Margule	1878	D	3	945		67 y.	F			Irre	ZWEIFLER	Reise	ZWEIFLER	
	Judiss	1878	D	108	945		3 m.	F			Schloma	ZWEIFLER	Judiss	TALLERING	
	Naschel	1881	D	16	945		5 y.	M			Johsel	ZWEIFLER	Mariam	GERLER	
ZWEIFLER	Herzel	1881	D	133	945		55 y.	M			Srul	ZWEIFLER	Henie	ZWEIFLER	
	Itzig	1883	D	17	946		7 m.	M			Schloma	ZWEIFLER	Rifka	TELLERING	
	Hudie	1883	D	28	946		3 y.	F			Schloma	ZWEIFLER	Rifka	TELLERING	
BRUM	Beile	1885	D	19	946		50 y.	F			Isak	ZWEIFLER	Chane Rosa	ZWEIFLER	
	Jacob	1886	D	116	946		7y.,10m.	M			Moses	SCHWAGER	Reisel	ZWEIFLER	
	Herzel	1888	D	46	946		1 y.	M			Isak Juda	ZWEIFLER	Chanzie	BOCHNER	
	Rachel	1888	D	101	946		7 m.	F			Moritz	SCHWAGER	Reisel	ZWEIFLER	
ZWEIFLER/PALSER	Malke	1891	D	54	946		63 y.	F			Jakob	PASSLER	Rifka	PASSLER	
	Malke	1891	D	102	946		4 w.	F			Isak Juda	ZWEIFLER	Chanzie	BOCHNER	

Fig. 16: List of Zweifler deaths[77]

their birth records and bore the name of their mother, not their father. Illegitimate children were like illegal aliens and had many restrictions imposed on them, including having certain occupations forbidden to them, not being able to get travel documents, and not being permitted to inherit their father's estate. There was the so-called "alleged legitimization" of children, a process whereby the father of a child declared his paternity, which was then confirmed by two witnesses. Notes in the birth record provide this information. Those children, given their mother's name at birth and a correction noted in records later, when they grew up, may have used both last names. Thus, the name might appear as Kreisler r Zweifler, where Kreisler was the mother's family name and, after the marriage was registered, the legal name became Zweifler, the father's family name. The name could also appear as Kreisler f Zweifler, which would indicate that Zweifler was the father's name but the legal name was the mother's name, Kreisler. Zweifler might, of course, be the surname of the paternal grandfather or grandmother, depending on the marital situation of the child's grandparents, and the same could be said of Kreisler on the maternal side. Of course, even if the parents had their marriage registered before the birth of the child, it is possible that the grandparents had not registered their marriage.

As if this was not already complicated and confusing enough, the whole matter increased in complexity if a person's parents registered their marriage later in life. This frequently occurred when their children were adults, perhaps to

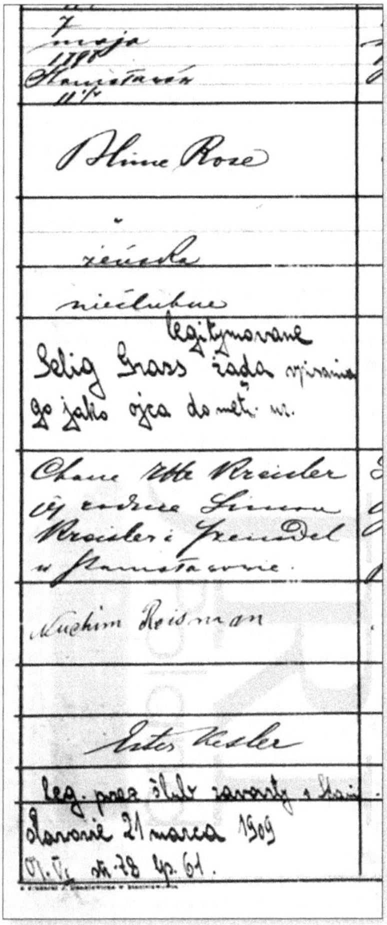

Fig. 17: Blima's birth record[80]

secure the inheritance of the child or prior to emigration. When this resulted in a change of the child's family name, the new information was added to the birth register. Children from such marriages could also go to court or apply to an official to change their name in the form of a decree. Blima's birth record[79] notes that she was illegitimate and that her father, Zelig Grass, "requests to enter his name as father in the birth certificate." That same record indicates that it was amended in 1909. On it is written "Marriage certificate, registered in Stanisławów March 21, 1909 VI N61." The points that had long puzzled me were clarified in 2009 by the archivist in Ivano-Frankivsk and by Ella's translation of Blima's birth record in 2012.

Our records include many more pieces of confusing and conflicting information. From the archives in Ivano-Frankivsk, the following was noted, in the

translation of a document in which Sara Lea applied for permission to immigrate
to America:

*Sara Lea Zweifler v[81] Kreisler born in 1884 in Buczacz living at 22
Sypazinska is applying for a passport to immigrate to America with her
children Malki Zweifler Kreisler born in 1907, Moses Zweifler Kreisler
born in 1910, Simon Zweifler Kreisler born in 1913, Paula Zweifler Kreisler
born in 1914. Her parents were Schulem and Perl and her husband was
Samuel. This is registered May 12, 1920.[82]*

We knew Sara Lea was born to Perl Pfeffer and Sholom Schuster in Buczacz
in 1884, and she married Samuel Kreisler. From Paula's birth certificate,[83] we
learned that Sara Lea's surname was Pfeffer. Sara Lea's father was Shulim
Shuster and her mother was Perl Pfeffer from Buczacz District, Galicia Province.
The information was recorded by Nuchim Reisner, and the midwife's name was
Reisa Loifer. Paula's parents, Sara Lea and Samuel, were married in Buczacz
on 16 January 1906. The birth record also indicated that Paula's father was in
America at the time of her birth.

According to a certificate issued in 1920,[85] Sara Lea was permitted to live in
Buczacz. It is unclear why Sara Lea, a native of that area, needed permission to
continue to live there in 1920. It is possible that she needed this document to apply

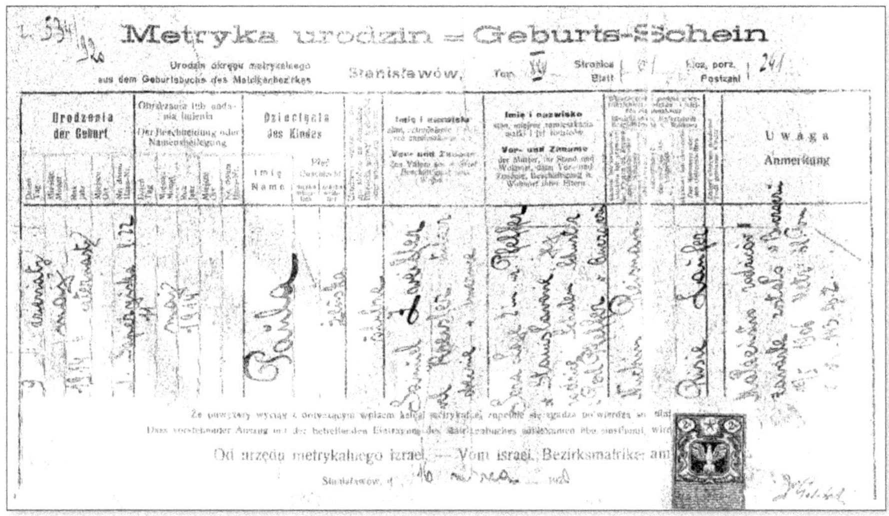

Fig. 18: Paula's birth record[84]

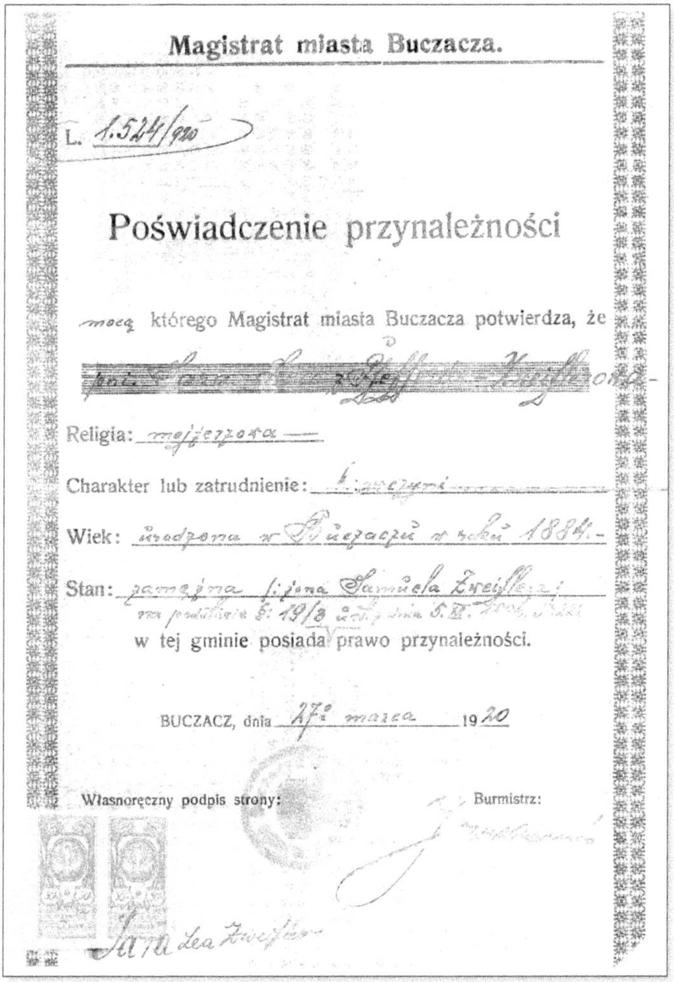

Magistrat miasta Buczacza.

L. 1.524/920

Poświadczenie przynależności

mocą którego Magistrat miasta Buczacza potwierdza, że

Religia:

Charakter lub zatrudnienie:

Wiek: urodzona w Buczaczu w roku 1884.-

Stan:

w tej gminie posiada prawo przynależności.

BUCZACZ, dnia _______ marca _____ 1920

Własnoręczny podpis strony: Burmistrz:

Fig. 19: Residency permit, 1920[86]

for a passport to leave, since the passport application is dated 12 May 1920, shortly after the certificate of residency was issued. The translation of the certificate reads:

This is to certify, by the magistrate of Buczacz, that Sara Lea, seamstress, born in Buczacz in 1884, married to Samuel Zweifler is given permission to be resident of that area, according to record 19/3. Buczacz, March 22, 1920.

In a brief examination of any one of the documents, the information appears to be simple and straightforward. However, when reviewing and analyzing all the

Fig. 20: Sara Lea's passport cover[87]

documentation, the entirety becomes very confusing. Adding to the confusion—
and, as yet, unresolved—is information from Sara Lea's ship manifest where she
appears with her children traveling from Europe to New York to join her husband
and their father, "Sam Zweifler." The Sam referred to on Sara Lea's marriage
certificate is a Kreisler, not a Zweifler. Sara Lea's passport has the Zweifler and
Kreisler but not the Pfeffer or Schuster names on it. On the document, "vel" before
Kreisler indicates that Kreisler is an alternate surname!

At a Boston genealogy conference in 1996, Lauren Davis spoke of reasons for
alternate names:

*1) A man may take on the wife's surname, particularly if she is from
a more prestigious family. 2) Some records may identify people by
their occupation rather than surname. Although this is an error, not a
variant surname, it can lead to the same sort of confusion in research. 3)
Someone can be identified by patronymic from their father's given name,
rather than a surname.*

She added that the term "vel" is also used when a family adopted a new
surname. Although Davis's comments did not refer to the Stanisławów area, there
is no reason not to conclude that something similar occurred in Stanisławów.[88]
Another cryptic mark attached to names on documents is "z" or "z d."[89] These are
from "z domu," which is literally "from the house of" and is the woman's maiden
name. The letter "z" by itself could be a short form of "z domu" and means "from."
The placement of the "z" or "z d." is found, like "vel," between two surnames.
These abbreviations are often used in the same way "née" is used to indicate a
maiden name. Another link between names is the German "geb," which stands for
geboren, meaning "born." The name following "geb" would be a person's birth
name. "Vel," "geb," "z d.," "false," and "recte"[90] are found on Galician records,
indicating differences between a birth name and a name by which a person might
be known later in life. However, it is very likely that records for many people do
not indicate that there was an alternate surname by which they were known. To
figure out the exact identity of a person, it is sometimes necessary to compare
records, such as I did with the Zweiflers from Nadworne. The results may be only
a "best guess." I was researching a family from Kraków, also in Galicia, not long
ago and, quite by accident, found out the family names. I knew the name of a man
who married into the family of interest. I had no idea that the woman he married
didn't have her father's surname. Documents I found for her and her father in
the twentieth century never hinted that her maiden name wasn't the same as her
father's. I didn't find her birth record, but I did find her marriage record, which
identified her parents and the name she used at the time of her marriage, which
was her mother's surname. Without that record, I never would have known to
search for her under a different last name.

Ship Manifests—
Clues to Relationships and Questions

Sara Lea Zweifler's passenger manifest, which shows her arrival in New York, and the detention notations on the manifest link her to the Grass (Grasz) family in Stanisławów, her birth in Buczacz, to Samuel Zweifler in New York, and to Peter Zwerin! She and her children were held in detention waiting for Sam Zweifler to meet them, which he ultimately did. Ship manifests may include a great deal about the passenger. Since many of them are handwritten, they can be difficult to read. Sara Lea's arrival manifest is typed, although the detention list is handwritten.[91] She and her children—Malka, Moses, Simon, and Paulo (Pauline)—traveled together. Sara and her oldest child, 11-year-old Malka, were both noted as able to read and write Yiddish. No other language was indicated for any of them. They were all Polish citizens; their race, or people, was Hebrew. They last lived in Stanislaw, Poland, and the name of their nearest relative in Poland was Grasz in Stanislaw. Their destination was New York, joining "husband and father Sam Zweifler c/o P. Zwirn at 347 E 5 St., New York City." Sara Lea's birthplace was Burchacz[92] and her children were all born in Stanislaw.

The detention list that was filled out at Ellis Island to account for all those who were not immediately admitted indicated that Sara and four children were held until her husband, Sam Zweifler, came to meet his family. There is a column on the detention list labeled "manifest" that provides a group and number cross-referenced to the passenger list. The group is the page, and the number is the line number. Detention pages are at the end of the manifest. The family does not appear to have remained in detention for long. The last columns on the detention page indicate how many meals the detained aliens consumed, and none are noted for Sara.

A close look at Sara Lea's manifest reveals that she and her children were travelling on the SS *Rotterdam*. They left the port of Rotterdam on 23 November 1920. This record is on pages 131 and 132 of the manifest. Her nieces Chaja and Feige travelled on the same ship, and their records are on pages 117 and 118! Perhaps the mystery behind the sisters' travel to the United States on two different ships from two different ports five days apart is easy to resolve, but, of course, any resolution is based purely on speculation pending documentation. Considering the

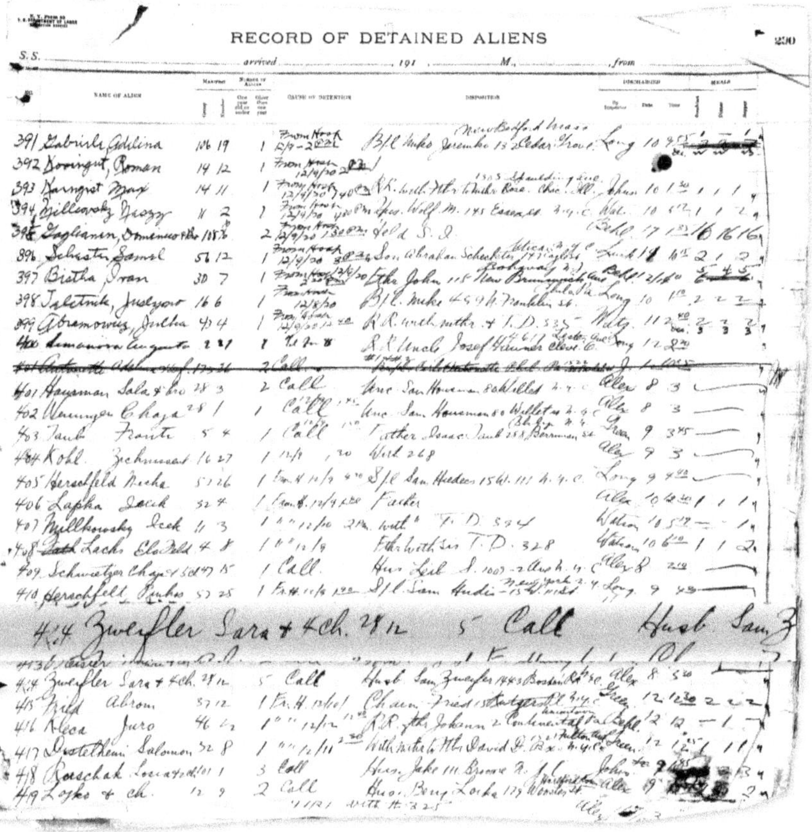

Fig. 21: Sara Lea's detention record[93]

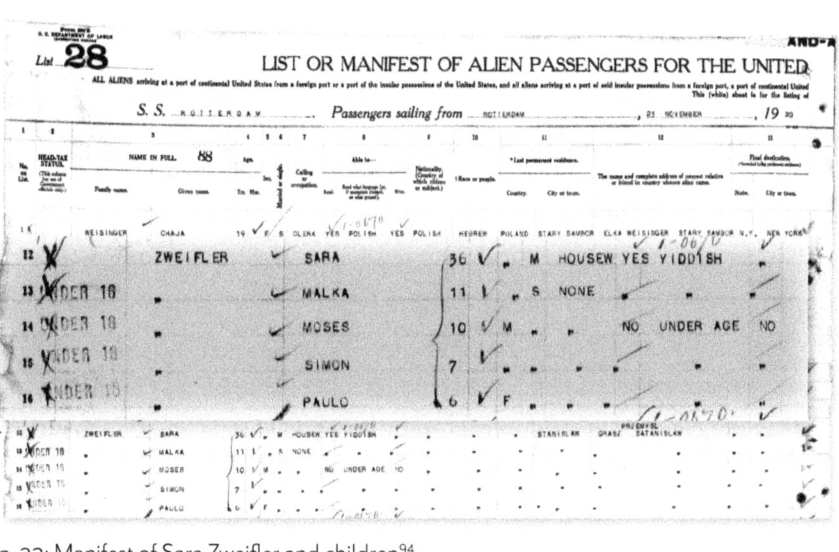

Fig. 22: Manifest of Sara Zweifler and children[94]

various possibilities provides several scenarios. Perhaps Chaja, Feige, their aunt, and her four children made plans to come to the United States and booked their tickets, and then, after the plans were already made, Blima decided to go, as well? For some reason, she was unable to book passage on the same ship. Maybe she left too late to board the ship, or maybe the tickets were sold out. Instead, she left five days later. Again, it is possible that none of these suppositions are what transpired, but they are simple and reasonable explanations, and until more plausible ones are suggested, these will become part of the family narrative. This voyage of the SS *Rotterdam* made one stop in Boulogne-Sur-Mer, where additional passengers boarded the vessel. In addition to listing all the passengers, the manifest also indicates various ports at which the ship docked *en route* and who boarded the ship at each of those stops. The number of stops affected the number of days the transatlantic crossing took.

In addition to the pages listing the names and other pertinent information about aliens bound for the United States, the manifest also listed United States citizens. The bulk of the passengers on this crossing of the SS *Rotterdam* boarded in Rotterdam, and the ship took on only a few new passengers in Boulogne-Sur-Mer.

The ship Blima traveled on, *La Lorraine*, had fewer passengers, and all boarded in Le Havre, France. There are no pages in the manifest that indicate that any passengers were U.S. citizens. It is possible that the ship stopped at other ports and that the only people boarding the ship at those ports were cabin passengers. If they were cabin passengers, then those pages of the manifest might not have been preserved. Not only did Blima travel on a different ship, but she also left Europe from a different port. She left from Le Havre while her sisters, aunt, and cousins left from Rotterdam. Did she go to Le Havre because the French shipping lines were offering free transport to the port and accommodations while travelers awaited a ship[95] or was it because the next available ship was leaving from there? It is interesting to note that Blima left for the United States from Le Havre on 28 November 1920, a little over a month after Harry Silberman left from that same port. Blima and Harry, according to family stories, met in New York. Perhaps they met in Europe. There is no information to date that informs us of how long either Blima or Harry was in Le Havre before their ships departed. The harbor area was probably crowded with people awaiting passage or arriving in France, and it is probable that their paths did not cross, or at least not in Le Havre. It is easy, more than 100 years after the fact, to speculate and conjecture a potential relationship between them in Europe that resulted in her following him to America, although there is nothing that supports this speculation.

Le Havre, *La France, La Lorraine:*
A City and Her Ships

In July 2012, I visited Le Havre. The city was a bustling harbor then, as it was in 1920. Le Havre, like Rotterdam and Hamburg,[96] was devastated during World War II. Rotterdam was bombed heavily by the Germans in May 1940 while Hamburg's losses were primarily in 1943, resulting from Allied bombing. Le Havre was a focus of the Battle of Normandy in 1944, and its losses were due to air attacks by Allied forces while the city was occupied by the Germans. Although most of the city was destroyed by bombs in World War II and rebuilt, there are still many older buildings standing. I thought visiting the archives there might be interesting. My expectations were minimal—I didn't think I would find any information about my grandmother, since I assumed that she was only in the city long enough to board a ship. I thought perhaps the archives might hold some information about the ship or the city during that period so I could have a better understanding of another aspect of my grandmother's life.

The archivists and other personnel at the archives were very kind about helping and trying to follow my halting French. I told the first archivist I spoke with that I was looking for information about *La Lorraine* and that my grandmother had left France on it in 1920. She looked through some huge books and came up empty-handed. She called for another archivist whom she said was an expert on the ships. This archivist asked a few questions and told me that he would have no information about people in transit because a lot of people came through the area with the sole purpose of boarding a ship. It took a few minutes before I was able to communicate that it was not information about my grandmother that I wanted, but rather, information about the ship in 1920. First, he told me that *La Lorraine* was not carrying passengers in 1920. I showed him Blima's ship manifest, and, with great reluctance, he said that their records were incomplete. I was amazed there were as many records as there were, given the history of the area. I did not ask him about *La France,* the ship on which Harry sailed. There is a website for the French Lines,[97] which, when I first examined it in 2013, appeared to include passenger lists from 1864 to 1936. Since Blima and Harry, as well as some other family members, traveled during those years,

Fig. 23: Street near the archives in Le Havre[98]

I thought I would look at the manifests to see if additional information was
included on departure manifests from France, since I already had manifests
for their United States arrival. Manifests for only three sailings of *La Lorraine*
appeared on the site: 1902, 1903, and 1918. The only manifest of *La France*
included on the website was of a sailing in 1930. For whatever reason, manifests
from other sailings of these two ships were not available. Those manifests are no
longer on the website, and most of the pages at the time of this writing, appear
to be "under construction."

The fleet of passenger ships belonging to the Compagnie Général
Transatlantique included *La France* and *La Lorraine. La Lorraine* sailed from Le
Havre to New York from 1899 to 1923 and *La France* from 1912 to 1932. Both
served as warships during World War I. Following the war, they were refitted
and resumed passenger service in 1919. During a 2012 visit to the tourism office
in Le Havre, I found some basic information about the city and its history. Le
Havre is an old city, first founded in the sixteenth century as Le Havre de Grace
on the site of an earlier fishing village. It was established as a harbor to replace

224

Fig. 24: La France[99]

Fig. 25: La Lorraine[100]

older ports that had silted up and were no longer useable. By the nineteenth century, it had become a primary port for emigrants sailing to the United States from France. Today, the harbor is bustling, the city hosts many events, and the destruction of the mid-twentieth century is not readily apparent.

Relatives and Relationships

Anyone who has ever done genealogical research has probably noted that it is not only complex, but rarely does the research lead from point A to point B without diverting to points Q, D, T, X, and Z before winding up at B. Often, we find ourselves going back over and over again to the same charts and documents in an effort to find out where people fit into our tree. This means that someone whose documentation was dismissed as not having a place in the larger family tree frequently must be revisited as more is learned about the family. Figures 15 and 16 are charts of births and deaths in Nadworne from 1866 to 1897 for people named Zweifler. The couple Chancie Bochner and Itzak Juda Zweifler are one of the pairs of parents on these charts. In the way of complex, interwoven discoveries, I discovered a close relationship between Chancie and Itzak Juda and Charles Zweifler, whose home was Blima's New York destination.

Chancie Bochner traveled to the United States on at least two occasions— once in 1909 and the other in 1921. Each time, she traveled with several of her nine children. The exact years of her travel back to Europe are unclear, as is the length of her stay there. These can only be guessed at based on documentation about her in the United States. On neither of the arrival manifests did she indicate that her destination was the home of her husband, Itzak Juda. It is possible that Itzak Juda remained in Europe at the time of her first trip. By her second trip, he was deceased. On the 1921 manifest, she is listed as a widow, but in 1909, the

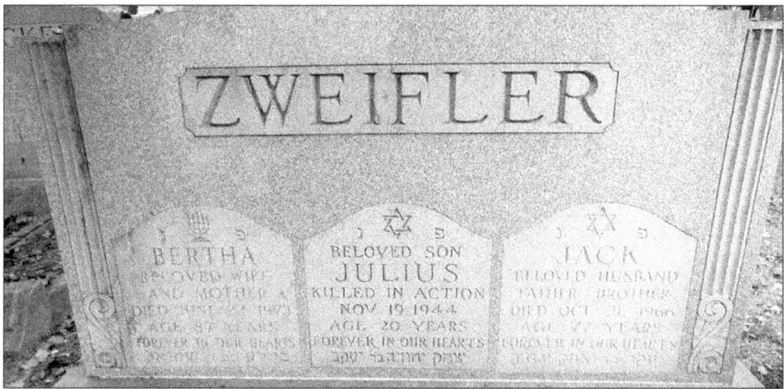

Fig. 26: Gravestone of Julius (Yitzchak Yehuda, son of Ya'akov) and Jack (Ya'akov, son of Yitzchak Yehuda) Zweifler[101]

manifest indicated her status as "married." In the United States, Chancie became known as Hannah or Anna. In 1921, on her second trip to New York, she planned to join her brother, whose surname was Bochner. Her son "J. Zweifler," living in Vienna, was listed as her nearest relative in Europe. Since she only had two sons whose first names began with a "J," and "Josef Haras"—who was born in 1904 and became "Joseph Harry" in the United States—was traveling with her, an older son, Jack, born in 1889, must have been the son living in Vienna. Jack ultimately made his way to the United States. This is clear from the birth of his son, Julius, born in 1923 in

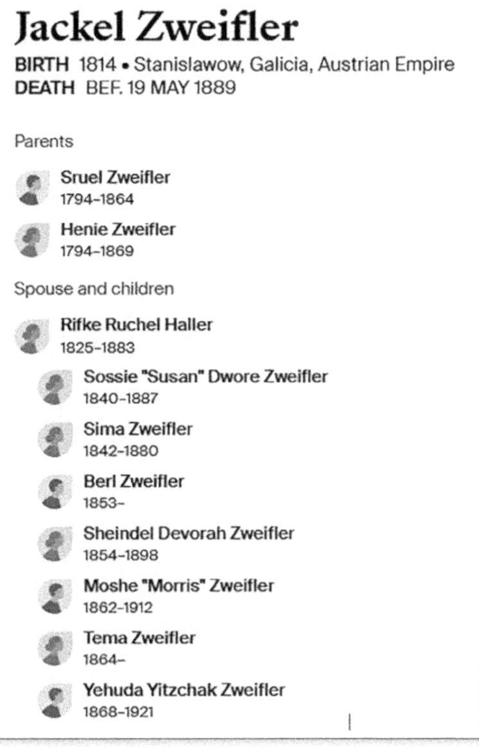

Fig 27: Jackel Zweifler's parents, spouse, and children

New York. Julius was named after his deceased grandfather, Yitzchak Yehuda. His gravestone, with its Hebrew inscription, tied him to Chancie's husband.

Chancie's husband, Itzak Juda, also listed on some records as Juda Itzak, was a son of Jackel Zweifler and Ruchel Haller. One of his sisters was Sheindel Devorah Zweifler, who married Sumer Zweifler Braunstein, Tova Gitel's brother. Another of Itzak Juda's brothers was Morris Moshe Zweifler, who married Cirl Rieger. One of their children was Charles Zweifler, born in Stanisławów in 1896. Charles's draft registration dated June 1918 conclusively demonstrates that he lived in the United States before the arrival of his mother and brothers.

Charles and Tillie probably married before 1921, when their first child was born. Tillie's maiden name has not yet been identified. Charles's World War I draft registration has a Fallsburg, New York, address. Fallsburg is in Sullivan County, outside New York City. Since their marriage certificate does not appear in the New York City marriage records, there are several possibilities as to when and

Serial No. .... O★39   Registration No. **66**

1. Name in full: Charles Zweifler — (Given name) (Family name) — Age, in yrs. 21
2. Home address: Fallsburg N.Y. — (No.) (Street) (City or town) (State)
3. Date of birth: August 24 1896 — (Month) (Day) (Year)
4. Where were you born? Galicia Austria — (City or town) (State) (Nation)
5. I am {
   1. A native of the United States.
   2. A naturalized citizen.
   3. An alien.
   4. I have declared my intention.
   5. A noncitizen or citizen Indian.
   (Strike out lines or words not applicable)
6. If not a citizen, of what Nation are you a citizen or subject? Austria
7. Father's birthplace: Galicia Austria — (City or Town) (State or province) (Nation)
8. Name of employer: Sigmund Heyman
   Place of employment: Fallsburg New York — (No.) (Street) (City or town) (State)
9. Name of nearest relative: Rosie Krell
   Address of nearest relative: 1317 Wilkins Ave Bronx N.Y. C.N.Y. — (No.) (Street) (City or town) (State or Nation)
10. Race — White, Negro, Indian, or Oriental — (Strike out words not applicable)

I affirm that I have verified above answers and that they are true.

Charles Zweifler
(Signature or Mark of Registrant.)

P. M. G. O.
Form 1 (blue)

REGISTRATION CARD.

Fig. 28: World War I draft registration of Charles Zweifler[102]

where their marriage took place. By the time Blima arrived in the United States, her cousin Charles Zweifler, whose home she listed as her destination, was living at 263 East Street in the Bronx. The street number was not on the manifest.

According to the 1930 census,[103] Charles and Tillie both immigrated to the United States in 1913. It is possible but unlikely that they married before their immigration, since he was only 17 years old, and she was 14. Perhaps they married in Sullivan County. It is also unlikely that they married before Charles's 1918 draft registration since Tillie is not listed as his contact on that form. However, by the 1930 census, they were living in Brooklyn and had two children. On Charles's World War II draft registration,[104] he used his mother's name, Reiger, as well as the surname Zweifler. Both surnames are in parentheses, and there is no note of explanation for the parentheses, which is not common. It is possible that these are meant to indicate that he used both. Milton pointed out that:

...since the draft card record of his residence was in the "Borscht Belt" area of Fallsburg, NY, it is possible that Charles was working at one of the summer resort hotels there. That fact aligns with the listing of his occupation as a waiter in a restaurant in the 1930 census. Then, again, in another [document],[105] he is listed as working at Ratner's, a Kosher Jewish restaurant on the Lower East Side.

Using documents such as those described above, it is possible to begin to recreate families and link people to one another. These types of documents may provide sufficient information to validate previously unverified family stories. Although I have not yet discovered Charles's birth record, I have identified records of eight children born to his mother, Cirl (or Zirl) Rieger, daughter of Josef Hirsz and Chaje Rieger. Moshe, their father's name, is not listed on the birth records, but he appears on death records of two of the children who died in childhood.

The Catskill Mountains: A Jewish Retreat

The "Borscht Belt," is located about 100 miles northwest of New York City in Sullivan and Ulster counties in the foothills of the Catskill Mountains. Beginning in the 1800s, it provided a respite from city life for Jews. As early as the 1870s, Jews began visiting the area and found many hotels closed to them due to anti-Semitism. Irwin Richman, Professor Emeritus of American Studies at Pennsylvania State University, and a historian of the Catskills, noted that, beginning with the 1883 purchase of 60 acres by Charles Fleischman and his subsequent construction of a luxurious summer home, Jews flocked to the region.[106] The Fleischman estate and those of his friends and relatives were soon joined by small bungalows and rooming houses, some catering to the wealthy but most appealing to the working class.[107] The lower Catskills were located close to New York City, which had the country's largest Jewish population. Accessibility, due to the ease of railroad transportation, made the area very attractive, just as stagecoach and canal transportation had been responsible for access to the upper Catskill areas decades earlier. The towns of the lower Catskills included Liberty, Monticello, Ellenville, Woodbourne, Hasbrouck, South Fallsburg, Livingston Manor, Fallsburg, Loch Sheldrake, Greenfield Park, Mountaindale, Accord, Ulster Heights, Kiamesha

Lake, Kerhonkson, Swan Lake, Glen Wild, Hurleyville, Ferndale, White Sulphur Springs, Rock Hill, Parksville, Woodridge, and White Lake. Many resorts that were off-limits to Jews were in the upper Catskills. Lavender and Steinberg called it poetic justice that the same advertising brochures used to attract a non-Jewish clientele to the upper Catskills were employed to attract Jews to the lower Catskills, substituting "Kosher Cuisine Featured" for "No Hebrews Accommodated."[108]

A 2009 *New York Times* article noted that Sullivan, Orange, and Ulster counties were home to a booming resort business that engaged local farmers and out-of-town businessmen in the nineteenth century. Local farmers had hotels as new customers and opened their own small boardinghouses.[109] Eventually, most of the farmers realized that renting rooms to visitors was more profitable and gave up farming. The Catskills as a summer Jewish resort began as one of the Baron de Hirsch's agricultural projects in the early twentieth century.[110] De Hirsch carried on his family's legacy of Jewish philanthropy. The records of the Baron de Hirsch Fund, established in the late 1800s, show:

> *Its objective was to promote the development of Jewish settlements as well as trade schools. The Jewish Agricultural Society was a subsidiary of the Fund and was chartered in New York in 1900 to provide agricultural training for East European immigrants. The JAS acquired land in New York, New Jersey, Pennsylvania, and Connecticut...*[111]

When Jews began farming in the area that ultimately became a popular Jewish summer resort, an established Christian farming community existed there. Jewish famers joined them, and it was there "that the largest and most successful Jewish farm settlements developed. The lower Catskills were relatively close to New York City, an important factor in the survival of the Jewish farmers."[112] At this late date, perhaps no record exists of what Charles Zweifler was doing in Fallsburg in June 1918, at the time of his draft registration, but it does not take much imagination to put him in one of the many hotels working as part of their summer waitstaff, given his occupation in 1930 and 1942. Much to my surprise, as I was researching the Catskills, I received an email from a woman named Beth Friedman Smile who is related to me through the complexities of marriage and who summered in the Catskills every year while she was growing up. Beth is a descendant of the son-in-law of Harry Silberman's sister, Lea. Beth is the daughter of Rosalie Saslow (originally Zaslowsky) and Alan Friedman. Rosalie was the daughter of Irving Zaslowsky and Lena Goldstein. Irving's sister Fannie married Samuel Bernstein, whose daughter Florence married Nathan Maltz. Nathan was the son of Eugene Maltz and Clara Richlas. Eugene's second wife was Fay Barash, whose mother, Lea Silberman, was my grandfather, Harry Silberman's sister.

When I was a child, growing up in Far Rockaway, Queens County, New York, a couple of miles from the Atlantic beaches, going to "the mountains" meant going to the Catskills, and it seemed so exotic. We went for a weekend or a week, generally with relatives. When I was a teenager, youth group conventions were often held at a hotel in the Catskills. As an adult, we went skiing and ice skating in the winter, and to hang out by the pool and do family "things" in the summer. My parents' synagogue held fundraising weekends there, and my sisters and I, our spouses, grandparents, and, often, in-laws would all go with my parents for noisy, food-filled, bonding time. I never imagined that my genealogical research would discover that our family had other ties to the Catskills.

Back to The Zwirns

Feige and Chaja, Blima's sisters, listed the home of Peter Zwirn as their destination on their ship manifest.[113] Peter was married to Rose Kreisler, one of Chana Jetta's sisters. From various ship manifests, it appears that Peter traveled back and forth to Europe at least twice. It is not clear how much time he spent in America after his 1907[114] arrival, but in 1910,[115] Peter came to the United States with Rose. They appear to have married in 1909 in Stanisławów, before emigrating. Their six children were all born in New York between 1910 and 1923. The names of their children were initially identified from the 1930 census.[116] However, from time to time, the surname would appear in my research efforts, and little by little, I learned more about the family.

In 2006, I found a family tree on *rootsweb.com*[117] belonging to Alan Whitney Thrailkill, Jr. This tree was called "Thrailkill-Zwerin Relations." Alan had put it online about three years earlier, and on it, I found several Zwerins who seemed to be identical to people already on my tree related to Peter. However, there were enough differences in the details to make me question whether I was looking at the correct family. In 2008, Milton got an email notice from *JewishGen* Family Finder that someone named Lynn Squire had added a name that might be the same as one we were researching. Milton contacted Lynn and we began a three-way correspondence. After we looked at material Lynn sent, it became clear that Alan's connection to the Zwerin family is through his wife, Rita Zwerin, and that Lynn and Rita shared great-grandparents Gershon Zwerin and Rivka Weitz. For several weeks, Lynn and I discussed the "correct" spelling of Zwerin. Although she and other descendants of Gershon's settled on this spelling, Gershon's brother Chaim Leib's descendants spell it Zwern or Zwirn. Peter's ancestor is Chaim Leib. Lynn's maiden name was Zwerin, and over the years, she and I met many times, mostly at genealogy

Chaim Leib Zwirn

BIRTH 1840
DEATH BET. 1914–1918

Spouse and children

Channah Sarah Knoler Blau

Jacob Zwern
1875–1875

Pessie Zwirn
1876–

Pincus "Peter" Zwirn
1877–1951

Pearl Zwern
1879–

Moses Zwern
1881–1883

Rachel Zwern
1884–

Jakob Zwirn
1886–1887

Ester Zwern
1888–1889

Stillborn Zwern
1892–1892

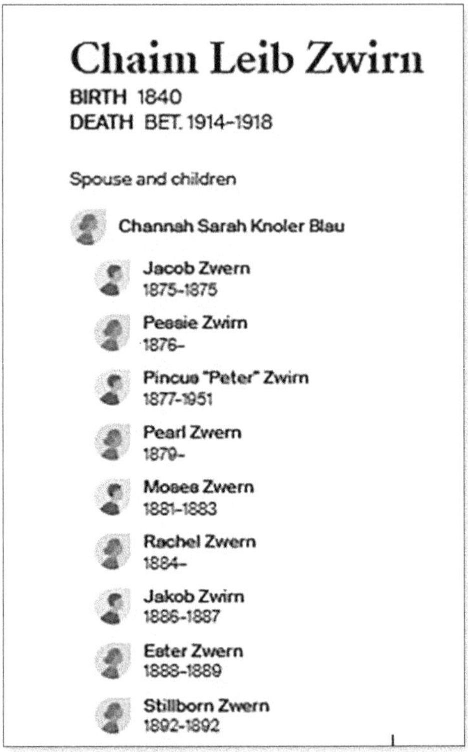

Fig. 29: Peter Zwirn and his siblings and parents

conferences. In 2016, Lynn was living in North Carolina, and joined my family for a seder. It was a very emotional experience for all of us—bringing the descendants of families together for the first time in almost 100 years. Lynn, sadly, died in December 2022.

A Word (or Two) About Spelling

Lynn was definitely not alone in her feelings about the way her name was spelled. Names are deeply personal and our connections to them are emotional. Many of our immigrant ancestors came from places where records were kept in Russian, Polish, German, and Hebrew, as Lynn's and mine did. Russian uses the Cyrillic alphabet, which has 33 letters. Hebrew (and Yiddish) use an alphabet with 22 letters; vowels in this alphabet are additions, and most written Hebrew does not include vowels. Polish, based on the Latin alphabet, has 32 letters, including some with diacritics: the *kreska* or acute accent (ć, ń, ó, ś, ź); the overdot or *kropka* (ż); the tail or *ogonek* (ą, ę); and the stroke (ł). The Polish language also eliminates the q,v, and x found in English.[118] German, which also uses Latin letters in addition to the 26 letters found in English, has three umlauts (Ä, Ö, Ü) and one ligature (ß).[119] All of these languages include sounds that are not found in English. The point is that, when names in their original forms are written in another language and then transliterated into English, there will be many spelling variations. Sometimes these variations are caused as someone tries to write the sounds they are hearing, and depending on the scribe and what that person's native language is, will often influence their interpretation of the sounds. Sometimes, as immigrants became integrated into their new home environment and its language, they changed the way they spelled their name. Perhaps they wanted it to appear to be more like other American names—take the difference in appearance of the name *Müller*, which might change to Muller and then to Miller. More complex names might undergo changes to make the spelling and pronunciation of the name easier. It is likely that we will never know the reasons why our immigrant ancestors changed their names or why siblings each chose different names. What we can do, however, is keep an open mind when investigating the history of our families, looking not at spelling, but at the sounds of the names and the variations in the sounds caused by differences in dialects to attempt to identify the original names.

Return to the Zwirns

The first intersection of my family with the Zwirn family occurred in my great-grandmother's generation. It is probable, but has not yet been discovered, that there were earlier connections between the two families. Eastern European Jews often married first and second cousins—people whose backgrounds the family knew—so it would not be unusual to find a connection prior to the earliest one we have now identified, which happened in the nineteenth century. This is probably true for most Jewish families who lived in the same towns and regions for many generations. Among the pitfalls when doing Jewish genealogical research is sorting out which people are descended through which branch and who their common ancestors are. Although the internet has made records easily accessible, it has also opened the door to the possibility of compounding errors. We first identified the connection between the Kreisler and Zwirn families with the discovery of the note on a 90-year-old ship manifest.

In early February 2012, I found a tree that had recently been uploaded to the internet. It included the Zwirn family, and the author of the tree was someone with whom I was unfamiliar. The information on her tree, was, at least according to my research, correct and yet incorrect. She had apparently not recognized that there were two Jacob Zwirns—one born in 1833 and one in 1865. She assumed the Jacob Zwirn born in 1835 was married to Sosia Arbeit, born about 1870. I queried her about that match, thinking that a 35-year difference in age between a husband and wife was not so unusual and perhaps I had my facts wrong. Rather than engaging in a conversation comparing facts, this other researcher just changed her information to conform with what I had! Did she investigate to know that there were two Jacob Zwirns or did she just accept the new information as correct?

Many researchers decide to put trees online and allow other people not only access to see their trees but also the ability to add or change information. Collaboration with other researchers, especially with family members who have an interest in the research, is important. However, allowing unrestricted access to data can cause the perpetuation of poor research. It is more constructive to maintain a database that only grants permission for "read"—not "write"—access and allow them to compare trees. This means that a "visitor" to the site can see what data is contained in the tree but does not have an option of making changes or additions to that tree. I believe that it is only proper to merge data after checking it against corroborating documentation and ascertaining that it does not cause a conflict with data already in the file. To resolve any conflict that arises, the researcher, like with all good research, must examine the new and old data and determine which information is most likely to be correct if there is no documentation to prove or disprove the facts.

The few times I searched for "Zwirn" on the internet using Google or genealogy websites, I noted that there seemed to be two distinctly separate families—one Jewish and one non-Jewish, perhaps German. I was able to roughly tie together all the Jewish people carrying the name. The non-Jewish family lived in Indiana and seemed to be a discrete group with strong ties to Christianity. There was a minister named John Zwirn. To my surprise, I received an email from John Zwirn one day in 2008. He identified himself as the grandson of Peter and Rose

Zwirn, one of three children of their son Seymour. I was floored. This was the first I had heard of this family, despite having been in close touch with other Zwirn relatives, including other descendants of Peter and Rose. John's niece Amie, his sister Judith's daughter, emailed me just a few weeks after my initial contact with John, apparently independently and without knowing I had heard from John. My contact with John after those initial emails has been minimal, and most of my contact with that family continues through Amie and, occasionally, her mother, Judith. Amie told me that her grandfather Seymour married the daughter of a Christian minister in 1947 and converted to Christianity. The rest of the family, as was the custom in traditional families, treated Seymour as dead. In 2008, in Seymour's old age, his granddaughter wanted to bring the family back in touch with him. Seymour was the last surviving child of Rose and Peter, and Amie has contacted his siblings' descendants and met many of them. Seymour died just after his 100th birthday in August 2023.

Sorting Out Surnames and Other Record Challenges

R ecords of long-deceased people are difficult to locate. There are many challenges compounding the difficulty of the passage of time in the search for records in Europe. Those include the distance of the records from where the researcher is based, translating records from multiple languages, understanding the conventions of what types of records were made at different times, and locating the archives where the records were kept. We know for example, that:

> *[Vital events (i.e., birth, marriage, divorce, [and] death records), however, were almost always recorded in the registers of the towns where these events took place, not in the town [where their family might be registered]. From an exhaustive analysis of the vital records of the 19th-century Czarist Empire, we learn that more than 75 percent of the people were born, married, divorced, or died in towns other than those where they or their parents were registered. We know this because in each registration entry, the government official also listed the town where the individual or his father was registered.[120]*

Even when the record can be located and a translator can be found who can read the handwriting, there is always the issue of what the names are that are being researched. In the United States, the naming convention for surnames has been, with few exceptions until the late twentieth century, that the child carries the surname of the father. Sometimes this was the case in Eastern Europe, but sometimes it was not. The possibility existed that a child might bear the mother's or even a grandmother's surname. There were many different naming patterns: all the siblings in a family could use one surname, sometimes the siblings had different surnames, sometimes their surnames were the same as one or the other of their parents, and sometimes the surname did not bear any resemblance to that of their parents. Then there are those instances, just in case the situation was not confusing enough, where the same person is known by many different surnames. When comparing written records, we may be examining records in which the surnames are the same but the spelling so dramatically different that the name appears to have changed from one record to another. A research challenge is to maintain as much objectivity as possible so that the researcher does not fall into the trap of insisting that a name or date is what it appeared to be in a specific record. Probably the first rule of thumb for a genealogist is to suspend belief. Anything that is "known" needs to be put in a category of alternatives; in other words, if a date in one place is 1853 and it is recorded as 1857 elsewhere for the same person for the same event, both dates must be accepted as potential alternatives until some record is found that unquestionably proves one or the other or even both of the previously "known" dates incorrect. So, too, are surname conflicts resolved.

Earlier, I mentioned challenges identifying Tova Gitel/Gizel/Sheindel as one person. Her brother Sumer, or Simon, carried the surnames of both Braunstein and Zweifler, although Tova Gitel was only listed on records as Zweifler. Sara Lea was known as Pfeffer, Zweifler, or Kreisler. Although I have not found records in which she is known as Schuster, since that was her father's surname, it is possible such a record will be found. In Galicia, where the Kreisler and Grass families resided, recording marriages had other implications. Gary Mokotoff[121] wrote that:

It is well known that during the 19th century in Galicia, if a husband and wife were only married by a rabbi, that is, they were not married civilly, when they went to register the birth of their children, the children were given the surname of the mother by government authorities because they were considered "illegitimate."[122]

In 2010, as part of a discussion about parents' names in birth records in Galicia being seemingly included (or excluded) erratically, Mark Halpern[123] responded by writing:

...the answer is that it depends on where the record was recorded, when it was recorded, and possibly who was the registrar. In Galician records, 1877 is an important date. Starting in that year, the names of the mother's parents were required, but the names of the father's parents were not. In the Bialystok records (Russian Pale of Settlement), names of the parents were not required but the mother's and father's patronymic (father's given name) was usually provided. For Russian/Congress Poland, the names of parents were not required, but many times the patronymic was recorded.[124]

Expanding on this, Mark wrote as part of another discussion in November 2010 that:

...[i]n my experience with these Galician records, the recording of the information was anything but consistent. The information varied from town to town, from period to period, and from registrar to registrar (in the same town).

I am sure you will find many examples of children's death records where the parents did not have a civil marriage where the father's surname was used. Also, you will find many examples of children's death records where the parents did have a civil marriage and still the mother's surname was used.

What I am suggesting is that the recording of a surname on a child's birth or death record is not enough evidence to determine whether or not his/her parents had a civil marriage before the birth.[125]

Laws Affecting Births and Marriages

It is difficult to follow all the legislation that affected the Jewish community. In addition to changes in jurisdictions, many of which imposed laws that were either nullified or modified as political boundaries changed or a new ruler ascended a throne, there may be contradictory information in resources. Reconciling these differences may be possible with intense study of the laws themselves.

Pre-dating the partitions of the Polish-Lithuanian Commonwealth and, thus, the establishment of Galicia, the Austrian legal system included restrictions on Jewish marriage, at least by 1726. The 1726 law permitted only one male in a Jewish family the legal right to establish a household. The number of households within a Jewish community were also strictly dictated by a set quota. Even households established within that quota were subject to taxes. These legitimate households were registered, and it was only with the death of the head of a legitimate household that another household from that same family was permitted. Further legislation in 1736 set the minimum marriage age of a Jewish bride at 15 and a groom at 18. Their ages had to be documented with a registered birth or circumcision.[126]

By 1783, after the first partition, legislation was passed that mandated civil marriage for all Austrians as part of the separation of church and state regarding family law.[127] However, the Jewish community, which regarded marriage as a strictly religious matter, resisted compliance. In 1791, requirements from the 1726 laws were reaffirmed. Additionally, a part of the 1736 law that had been largely ignored by the Jewish community requiring births, marriages, and deaths within the Jewish community to be registered with the Catholic parish was then going to be enforced.[128] Marriage laws became harsher over time. An 1810 order restricted Jewish marriages by subjecting prospective brides and grooms to an examination, based on the writings of Herz Homberg.[129] Any Jewish couple who wanted to register their marriage with the civil authorities was required to pass this examination.[130]

Almost 100 years later, in the 1870s, the lack of registration of Jewish births, marriages, and deaths was still an issue in the Austrian Empire. Laws were passed mandating how births and deaths were to be recorded, so names of parents previously missing in records of births and deaths were included. The registration of a child's birth was required to be done with the name of the mother if there was no civil registration of the parents' marriage, unless the father attested to his paternity in the presence of witnesses. Children whose parents did not have their marriages registered with the civil authorities were illegitimate, and, among other things, were not entitled to inherit from the father.[131]

So, even for births and marriages, events that we might have thought of as having consistency in recordkeeping within a geopolitical area, different laws and customs dictating the types of records and their format can be found. In addition, individual registrars might have had their own way of doing things, all contributing to inconsistent record keeping. As part of a discussion about Galician birth records lacking a father's name, Mark Halperin expanded on earlier comments by writing:

[A] Galician birth entr[y] without the father's name listed is not uncommon. The lack of a father's name in a birth record is the result of Austrian laws that require a civil recorded marriage to exist for the child to be considered legitimate in the eyes of the Austrian Crown.

First, let's talk about civil marriages. The Hasidic movement spread rapidly throughout Galicia in the 18th century. Hasidic leaders wielded great power in the community. Roughly 6 of 7 Galician Jews were Hasidim. Marriage was an area of great contention between the Crown and the Hasidic leadership of the Jewish community. The Crown designated and paid one Rabbi in each district to perform marriages. These Rabbis were usually more secular than the majority Hasidim of the community. So, it was normal for the Jews to resist the mandate for civil marriage.

Jews were married under a Chupa in a purely religious ceremony, which was not ever registered with the Crown...

For births considered out of wedlock by the Crown, regulations specified how the father's name was to be recorded. His name was not to be recorded unless he officially acknowledged paternity. So, every time our grandparents—bubbe and zeyda—had a child, zeyda would go to the vital records registrar and swear in front of witnesses that he was indeed the father. This meant that his name could be listed on the birth record in the remarks column, but the Crown still assigned bubbe's maiden name to the child.

*The above was the law, but in practice the recording of birth
events of a couple without a civil marriage was very inconsistent.
In some cases, the mother's maiden name was recorded for the
child. In some cases, the father's surname was recorded for the
child. In many cases, no surname was identified for the child. For
illegitimate births, sometimes the father's name was recorded in
the column for father, sometimes in the remarks column with or
without a sworn statement of paternity, and sometimes the father's
name was not recorded at all. It depended on the town and the
registrar...The lack of any father's name on a birth record could
mean that the father did not report the birth in person. In other
words, another family member or friend reported the birth.*[132]

In addition to issues regarding names on birth certificates and later documents,
there are other challenges due to the timing of recording a birth. Warren Blatt
wrote about the custom of registering births after the fact and how those delayed
registrations might lack the accuracy of registering something concurrent with the
event itself, even shortly afterward. He wrote:

*Many births were registered long after the event ("delayed registrations"),
and it was only the word of the registrant and his/her witnesses that
determined what was recorded. How often have we heard a grandparent
say that his/her mother was never sure of the real birthday...She just
said that it was "three days before Purim," etc. This does not lend itself to
accurate record-keeping.*[133]

Delayed registration of births was not only something we encounter in Europe. In
the United States, legislation requiring births to be recorded was passed or enforced
at different times in each state, usually not until the late nineteenth or early twentieth
centuries. Births at home were the norm during that period, and it was not uncommon
for a midwife to register a birth days or weeks after the fact, or to not have the
birth registered at all. My maternal grandmother's birth record was, according to
her family, destroyed in a fire in a local New York City repository. In cases where
a birth certificate is needed later for a passport or social security registration, the
individual might bring witnesses or documentation to attest to a birth at a particular

time. A census, for example, would prove a person was living by a certain date. Sometimes in research, I have encountered amusing birth records. I found a delayed birth record filed in the 1930s for a man claiming to have been born in the early twentieth century, in the United States with letters supporting this from his parents. The delayed birth was duly registered. Twenty-first-century research revealed that the man was born in Europe before the family's emigration, and he was on the ship with his parents. What did the false delayed birth record do for him? It established his citizenship. Recently I discovered a 1921 delayed birth record in Canada for a man ostensibly born there in 1909. The 1911 Canada census however, said the family arrived in Canada in 1909, and the person who received the 1921 birth record was four years old at the time of the census. He was born in Europe two years earlier than the delayed birth record claimed.

The Archives: An Adventure

In the spring of 2009, Ella contacted an archivist in Ivano-Frankivsk to begin the process that would grant us permission to visit the State Archives of Ivano-Frankivsk Oblast. The archives in Ivano-Frankivsk are the repository for records not only from the town but also from the entire oblast/province. The records in Ivano-Frankivsk are not complete—they only date from the mid-1800s. Earlier records are primarily held in Lviv. Some records may also be held in Kyyiv, Warsaw, or even in Kraków! Ella's contact at the Ivano-Frankivsk archives, Lyuba Solovka, was the lead archivist in charge of the Department of Information of the Ivano-Frankivsk Regional State Archives at the time. She has since retired. Lyuba's original assignment at the archives involved organizing the holdings of the Jewish community of Ivano-Frankivsk. At the onset, she knew nothing of the community's existence or of its destruction during World War II. She told me she grew fascinated with the events of the Holocaust and wanted to document what happened. She began to research the subject, with little encouragement from her employers. In fact, she was overtly discouraged from pursuing this line of inquiry. When Ella contacted Lyuba and told her why we wanted to come to the archives and a little about the work I was doing, Lyuba became excited. She quickly understood that, just as she could provide me with access to records, I could help with her research efforts by sending her books and other information to which she either had limited access or could not locate. Unlike today, the Ivano-Frankivsk Archives were not readily open to the public in 2009. Special permission was needed to enter and access records. Lyuba granted us that permission. Although I brought a small computer with me, I was instructed that it had to be quickly hidden if anyone else came into the room in which Ella, Lyuba, and I were working. I also had to remain quiet so that it would not be obvious that a non-Ukrainian occupied a seat in the archive. Unlike archives I visited in Tarnopol and Zhytomyr, no foreign visitors were permitted to visit the archives in Ivano-Frankivsk at that time. In Zhytomyr and Tarnopol, the archives were crowded with researchers. Here, there were none. By late 2011, reports from non-Ukrainian researchers indicated that obstacles to gaining access to the archives in Ivano-Frankivsk had been removed. Discussions I heard made it clear that the obstacles were based on local decisions and were probably against national policy. Despite the restrictions imposed on me during the several days I visited the archives in 2009, my research experience was very pleasant, and Lyuba was a great help.

In advance of our visit, Lyuba did a massive amount of research, locating records. This, too, was very different from my experiences in archives elsewhere in Ukraine. Unlike those other archives, we could not come and go as we pleased. Lyuba needed to be present and had to remain in the room with us. I cannot praise the work Lyuba did on our behalf too highly. Ella and I spent more than 20 hours in the archives over several days. Lyuba spent much more time than that locating all the documents. She brought out stacks of record books and ledgers for us to examine. There were so many ledgers, books, and documents that Ella and I were overwhelmed and disorganized in how we examined the material on the first day.

To find records in an archive, it is helpful to know their location in the archive. Records in the archives in Ukraine generally have three or four numbers like 232-1-2097 or 232/1/2097. The first group is the *fond*, written фонд in the Cyrillic alphabet. This is the top level of organization. Different fonds are in different archives. The second number is the *opis*, or опись. The *fond* includes a number of *opisi* (plural of opis). The *opis* contains many files—that, is the third number, or *delo* (дело). If there is a fourth number, it may pertain to the individual document or page in the *delo*.

Because it was not possible in 2009 to get copies of the records, we tried to look at each book and take careful notes of the contents of the record. As we discovered, we were not careful enough, due to time constraints regarding how long we were allowed to spend in the archives on any one day. Consequently, translations and examinations of the documents were not done as carefully or as fully as we might have desired under other conditions. It would have been preferable if we had copies of the documents to study at our leisure, but copies of each document at that time cost almost $8, and as a result, we ordered very few. Photographing the documents ourselves carried the same cost. Although I have not returned to the archive, Ella has gone back many times, even after Lyuba retired. She has been able to get copies of the records much more easily. I have now been in many archives all over Eastern Europe, and without exception, submitting requests in advance to the archives results in books and records waiting for us on our arrival. There are still obstacles in some places that require scheduling a visit long in advance, filling out forms to gain access to records, and being restricted in the number of record books that can be viewed. That restriction is usually five or six books a day. Other archives have no such restrictions and access is only limited to the hours that the archive is open. Some archives require that, during their lunch period, all researchers leave the building. In many archives, records are held off-site, and when requests are made to look at records beyond those made available at the time of a researcher's visit, another visit might need to be scheduled when the additional records can be retrieved. Off-site record storage is not limited to Eastern Europe. The United States National Archives at New York City located at One Bowling Green no longer holds the vast number of records previously held onsite at the former location on Varick Street, where the National Archives were located until 2012. Many records are held in Philadelphia and take a week or more to retrieve. In 2019, some records were relocated from Philadelphia and New York City to the National Archives at Kansas City.

An example of the material Lyuba gathered for us is shown below. This is a card based on a death certificate for Lea née Greif Kreisler, who died on 9 March 1938 at the age of 79. She lived in Stanisławów at 23 Sloneczna Street. Her son Samuel died in 1931. Listed are her surviving grandchildren: Abraham Moses, age 16; Salomea, 15; Isak, 13; Rachela, 12; Kalman, 11; and their guardian, Izrael Greif.

This card not only provided us with information about an entire family, whose birthdates could then be extrapolated based on their ages in 1938, but also gave us the record number, 232-1-2097, so that we could access the complete file if the information proved pertinent to our research.

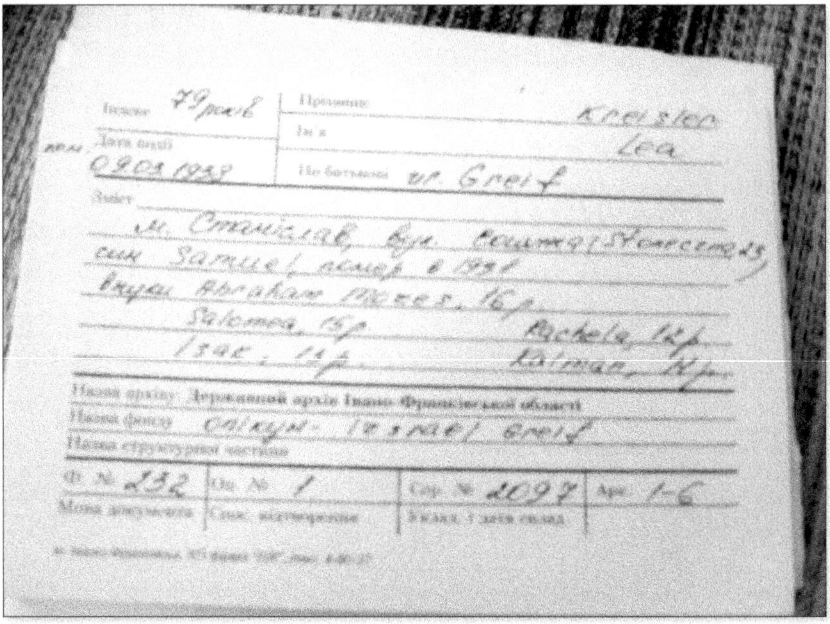
79 років
Прізвище Kreisler
Ім'я Lea
По батькові ur. Greif
Samuel
Salomea
Rachela
Назва архіву: Державний архів Івано-Франківської області
Ф. № 232 Оп. № 1 Спр. № 2097 Арк. 1-6

Fig. 30: Card detailing information about Lea Greif Kreisler[134]

One record catching our attention provided conflicting data regarding Chana Jetta. Before we arrived at the archives, we "knew" Chana Jetta's birthdate. Her nephew Bentzion Schaffer filed a Page of Testimony with Yad Vashem in 1956. In that document, he noted Chana Jetta's birthdate as May 1871.

A 1939 census[136] we examined in the archives showed her birth year as 1874, and an undated list of the inhabitants of 24 Sapizhinska Street listed Chana, three of her children, and one other person, along with their birthdates: Grass, Chana Itta, born August 21, 1875; Ozjas Gras, born June 19, 1911; Rachela Gras, born January 12, 1909; Sala Gras, born December 23, 1917; and Anna Winyk, a Greek Catholic servant residing with them. Although the document itself is undated, the form has a pre-printed date of 1939.

The unusual record to which I referred above is something we misinterpreted and, therefore, misunderstood. While in the archives, we wrote a note that supposedly translated a card saying, "Chana Grass was supervising the prayers at 24 Sapizhinska Street and certified that meetings of political character were not held there in 1884." We thought we took this information from Ivano-Frankivsk record 2-3-1227. The questions that arose all relate to my great-grandmother, a female, being given permission to supervise prayers in 1884 at her residence.

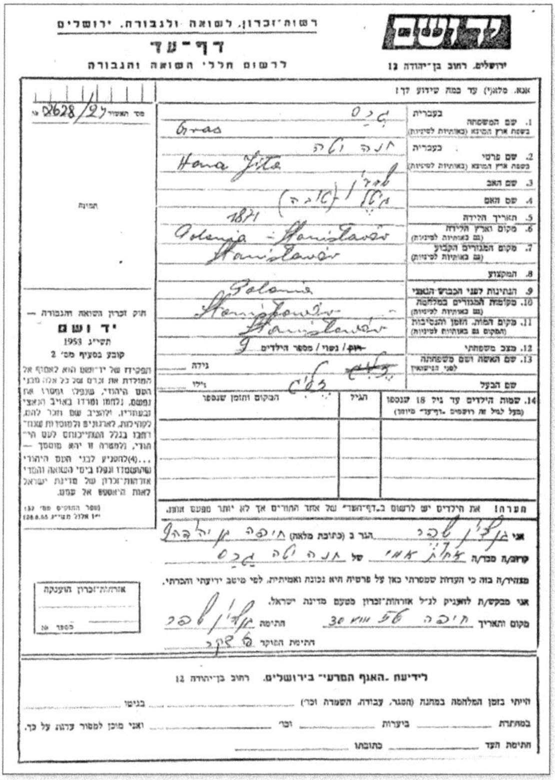

רשות זכרון לשואה ולגבורה. ירושלים

דף-עד

לרשום חללי השואה והגבורה

יד ושם

ירושלים. רחוב בן-יהודה 12

1. שם המשפחה: Gras
2. שם פרטי: Hana Jita
5. תאריך הלידה: 1871
6. מקום הארץ הלידה: Polonja - Stanisławów
7. מקום המגורים הקבוע: Stanisławów
10. מקומות המגורים במלחמה: Stanisławów
11. מקום המות, הזמן והנסיבות: Stanisławów

Fig. 31: Page of Testimony submitted by Bentzion Schaffer[135]

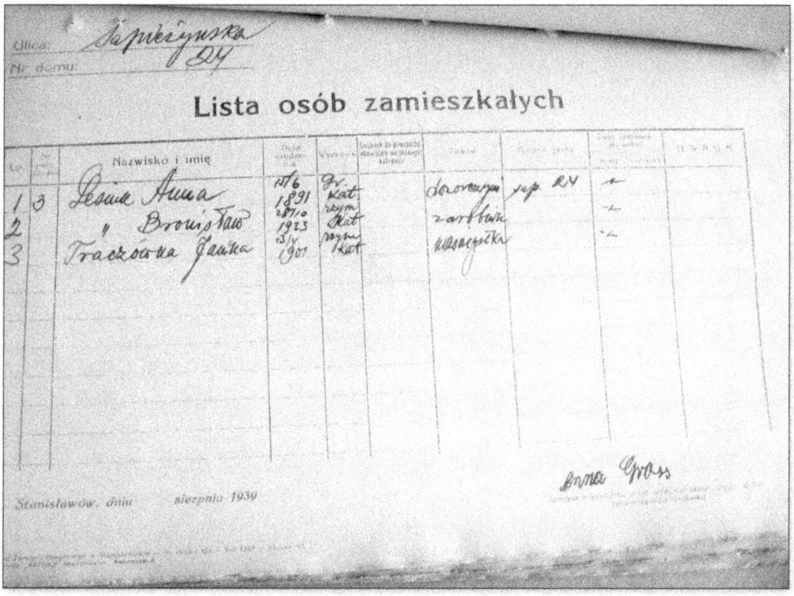

Ulica: Sapieżyńska

Nr domu: 24

Lista osób zamieszkałych

Nazwisko i imię

Stanisławów, dnia sierpnia 1939

Anna Gross

Fig. 32: Record 27-1-742[137]

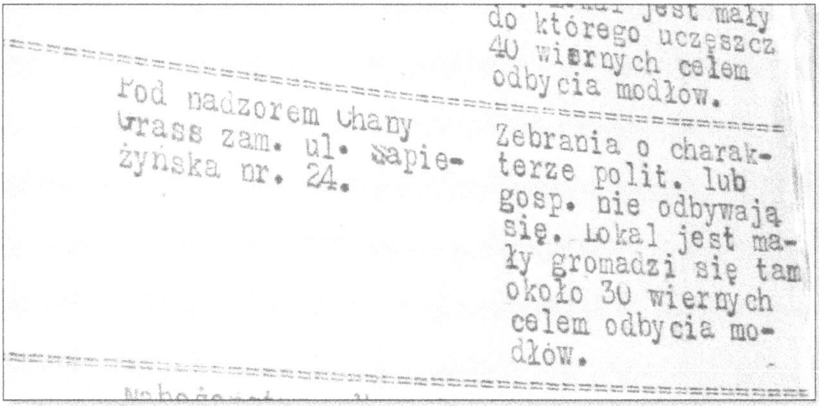

do którego uczęszcz
40 wiernych celem
odbycia modłow.
Pod nadzorem Chany
Grass zam. ul. Sapie-
żyńska nr. 24.
Zebrania o charak-
terze polit. lub
gosp. nie odbywają
się. Lokal jest ma-
ły gromadzi się tam
około 30 wiernych
celem odbycia mo-
dłów.

Fig. 33: Record 2-3-1227[138]

When we looked at her birthdate, which was recorded as 1871, 1874, and 1875 on other documents, we wondered about her age at the time of her marriage, since Grass was her married name and these documents meant that she was 14, 11, or even perhaps 10 years old in 1884. These comments and questions would not have occurred if we had been more careful with our reading of the documents while we were at the archives. After the trip, Ella sent me a copy of the full document 2-3-1227. The apartment at 24 Sapizhinska Street was registered as a place of worship in 1932 and was founded by a Sara Schubert. In that document, Sara Schubert transferred the running of the services to Chana Gras and stated that no political activities were to be held there. This document is part of a registry of religious organizations. All the organizations, according to the document, were founded in 1932, which is unlikely. It is probable that a new rule requiring religious organizations to register went into effect in 1932. It is frustrating to know that my confusion, when confronted with the preponderance of records, caused such sloppiness. I wonder where the note was. Ella and I both remember seeing it.

Although we have not been able to identify the note with the 1884 comment, I speculate that Ella and I inadvertently conflated two separate pieces of information. Our error in translating the document meant that we formed serious errors in our conclusions regarding a young Chana Kreisler Gras. We knew this information could not be correct but did not have the original documents to reassess our impression. I wonder what happened in 1884 at 24 Sapizhinska Street. Perhaps the worship group began meeting in that year. I hope more research at the Ivano-Frankivsk archive will reveal that document's contents, although repeated searches have not been successful to date. This error in my own research skills more than 14 years ago taught me (the hard way) of the necessity of transcribing everything from a record and maintaining an inventory when confronted with extensive numbers of documents resulting from a search.

In 2009, Rabbi Kolesnick told me there were many private synagogues located in residences in Stanisławów before the war. It is not too difficult to imagine that the large Kreisler-Grass family might have had their own place to worship, at least for daily prayers, with attendance at the larger, more formal synagogues in the city used for holidays and perhaps Shabbat. A description of synagogue life in Warsaw includes this: "Most of Warsaw's synagogues were small, often private, prayer houses located in the courtyards or backyards of tenements. One such synagogue was discovered in one of the oldest houses in Praga-Warsaw."[139] Stanisławów is not Warsaw, but this may have been common. We did not locate our relative's home on Sapizhinska Street as the locale for a synagogue in Leo Shtrait's booklet, *Stanisławów's Synagogues.*[140]

Censuses

In the United States, a federal census is mandated to be taken every 10 years, at the decade mark. This began in 1790. Some states conduct censuses in other years. For example, New York State took a census every 10 years from 1825 to 1875, in 1892, and then from 1905 to 1925, while Kansas conducted a census from 1855 to 1925. Censuses throughout the world are taken at times designated by individual government mandates. In Canada, England, and Ireland, there is a 10-year census taken at the years ending in "1"—1851, 1861, etc. In the Austrian Empire, census-taking began in 1869. Johnathan Shea reported on the Austrian Empire's census and described it and the data that was collected:

The 1869 census was the first "name" census, where individual names and surnames of inhabitants were recorded.

In the censuses taken in 1869, 1880, 1890, 1900, and 1910, the actual census form contained nearly identical categories and columns for responses. The only distinctions were the graphic layout of the form and minor details in the instructions.

*The principal columns included the following: (1) Sequence number...
(2) Surname, Name... (3) Sex... (4) Year of birth—in 1900, this was
expanded to year, month, and day of birth.... (5) Place of birth... (6)
Affiliation—the name of the district was entered here, i.e., the district
to which the individual belonged. The Galician district, as an organ
of territorial self-government, was an administrative unit of residents
in effect, and each citizen had to be officially registered in a district...
(7) Religion... (8) Family...Note that the government recognized only
religiously sanctioned marriages and divorces were accorded legal
status only among non-Catholics... (9) Language...Eight languages were
listed as possibilities here: German, Czech-Slovak-Moravian—obviously
considered one language by the census's designers, which in fact is
linguistically imprecise—Ukrainian, Polish, Slovenian, Serbo-Croatian,
Italian, and Romanian. Yiddish is not listed, a language used by the
bulk of the Jewish population. Jews were assigned a language, based
on the dominant language in their area of residence... (10) Vocation
(employment)... (11) Type of job... (12) Other income... (13) Literacy ...
(14) Mental and physical defects ... (15) Present or absent—This question
indicated whether the persons listed in the family unit were actually
residing there or not. In the case of absences, the enumerator was to list
whether the absence was temporary or permanent. It is said that, if aware
of the census date, some individuals absented themselves intentionally for
a variety of reasons. (16) Place of residence of absent persons—Here the
census taker was to indicate the name of the district, if it was in the same
county; the name of the county, if the person was in Galicia or the name
of crownland within Austria-Hungary. For persons living in other nations,
the name of the country was provided. (18) Farm animals.*[141]

Shea reported further that, since it was well known that the census was taken
during the first week of January in the census year, it was a prime time for people
to be away from their homes.

The census pages from 1939 and 1941 on which Chana Jetta and her
children appear were only of Jewish households. The big "X" across their
information on the 1941 household lists may indicate their fate—they were all
murdered in October 1941.

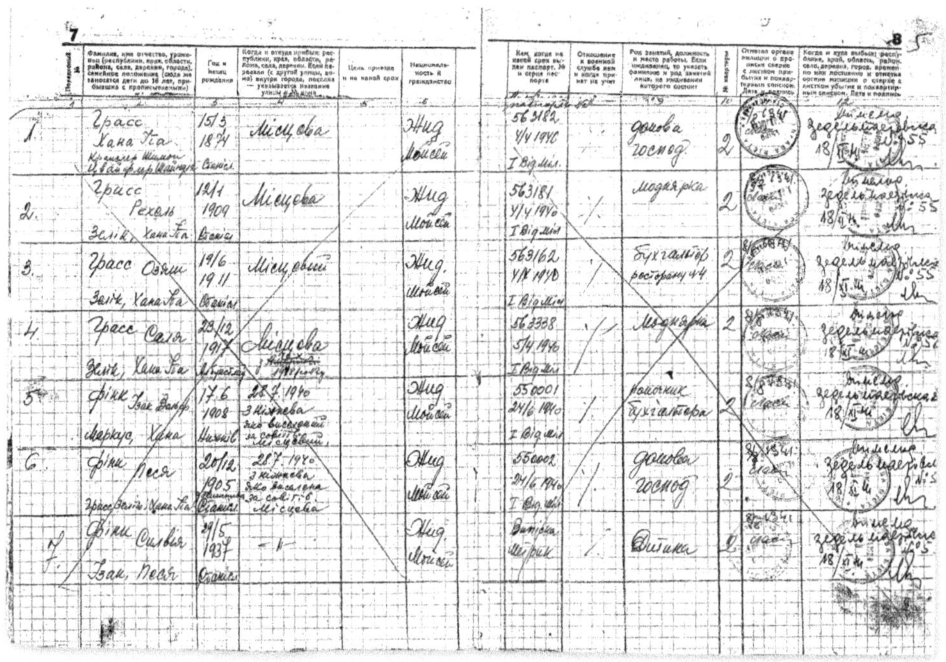

Fig. 34: 1941 Grass family at 24 Sapizhinska Street[142]

Pages of Testimony and Yad Vashem

The fate of many of Samuel's siblings was corroborated through Pages of Testimony filed at Yad Vashem by Bentzion Schaffer. Who was Bentzion? What relationship did he have to our family? Since 1954, Yad Vashem has been collecting the names of Holocaust victims to fulfill its mandate of preserving the memories of the victims of the Holocaust. Their collection is partly comprised of information gathered on what they have termed "Pages of Testimony." Originally, these were yellow pages filled out by hand by survivors and relatives of victims and submitted to Yad Vashem through collection points like synagogues, the Red Cross, and other agencies. Now they can be submitted online at the Yad Vashem website or by printing the form on any color paper and submitting a hard copy to Yad Vashem.

To date, the names of more than five million victims have been collected through Pages of Testimony and other records. Pages of Testimony form the basis of the Central Database of Shoah Victims' Names.[143] Yad Vashem's website provides a portal through which the Central Database can be searched. In 1956, Bentzion Schaffer and his wife, Hencia Arbeit Zwirn, filled out Pages of Testimony for many of their murdered relatives. While searching the database for the names of Blima's siblings in 2006, I discovered that Bentzion Shaffer had submitted the family data. I knew his name from Stanisławów birth records and wire-transfer receipts that were among the many scraps of paper found in Harry's apartment, but until I found these Pages of Testimony, I had no idea of his exact relationship to Blima. He indicated on the "Pages" that his relationship to the Grass siblings was "cousin." One of the search parameters on the Yad Vashem website is to search for other pages filled out by the same person. When I did that, I found out, by examining each of the pages he completed, that his mother was Blima's aunt Devora, Chana Jetta's sister.

Devora and her sister Chana were the only siblings from a family of 10 children who remained in Europe. Devora and Chana were among those murdered in October 1941 on the Stanisławów streets. Pages of Testimony are available in many languages—Hebrew, Russian, German, Polish, French, Spanish, and others. Although a transcribed summary of the information contained in the pages is available online in English, that transcription often has errors regarding relationships or names. It is remarkable that a transcription of these heartbreaking pages is available instead of just an index of the pages.

For many years during the late 1940s and early 1950s, Harry and Blima wired small amounts of money to Bentzion in Israel. From the Pages of Testimony, we learned Bentzion was Chana's nephew—Blima's cousin. These Pages of Testimony gave us clues to some other relatives whose siblings or children had come to the United States years earlier. Some of these people my father, Milton, had met as a child, but their exact relationships to him were never made clear. All this information introduced more questions that we hope to answer someday— either through travel to places in Europe and research in the archives there or though the availability of digital records on the Internet.

Bentzion filled out a Page of Testimony for most of the Grass siblings who remained in Europe. As expected, he did not fill one out for Samuel, who we know survived, but he did fill one out for Samuel's brother Oscar. However, Ella told me of a story she heard from her grandparents: on the day of the round-up and murder of the Stanisławów Jews, Oscar, along with his siblings, mother, nieces, and nephews, went to the market as required. At some point when it became clear what was to happen, Oscar ran away. Initially, he went to Samuel and Diana's home to hide—they were already safe in Kazakhstan.[144] Later, he went from house to house looking for shelter, and finally, he disappeared. Conjecture is that he was turned over to the Nazis and murdered. Since there was no further word from him, it is also possible that he ran away into the woods and died there or joined a partisan group. Although Bentzion filled out a Page of Testimony for him, the possibility exists that he survived the war somehow and took on a new identity. It remains one of the many mysteries that remain even more than 75 years after the end of World War II. It took many years of research before I located the Yad Vashem Pages of Testimony that Bentzion and his wife, Hencia, filled out. Like so much else in this research, there is no straight line from point A to point B. The connections are there but finding them is like navigating a complex maze. The facts are interwoven; the results are not always immediate. It is puzzling to me now, all these years later, as I reflect on what I know and consider how much I do not know and probably will never find out—like how Bentzion found out what happened in Stanisławów.

I started with the wire-transfer receipts and the name of "Benzion Schaffer." His name wasn't familiar to my father, and at first, our question was why my grandparents, who had little money themselves, were sending sums of money to Bentzion Schaffer. My only other clue to this mysterious person was a photograph of a blond-haired little girl hugging a doll—in my memory, but without any proof, I connected that child to Bentzion. The photo was marked "Haifa." Harry must have told me something about her since the photo came from him.

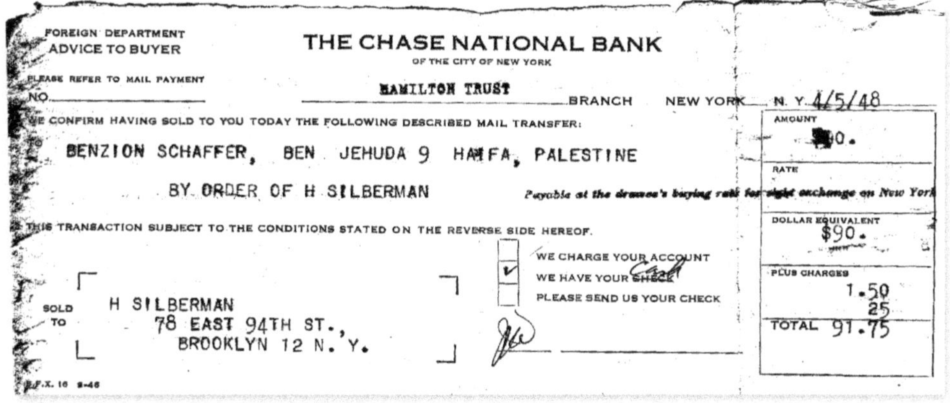

Fig. 35: Money-order receipt, 1948[145]

In 1988, when I was on
a month-long visit to Israel, I
decided to try to find the remnants
of Bentzion's family. A few phone
calls in Israel got me a phone
number for a woman identified
as his daughter, Sarah. When
I called, I understood from a
man who said he was Sarah's
husband that neither he nor
she spoke English. My Hebrew
was not up to a detailed and
extended conversation. He told
me that Sarah's mother, Hencia,
was living with a man who spoke
English, and he gave me their
phone number. From earlier
research, I knew that Bentzion
had died in the 1960s. I called the

Fig. 36: Sarah Schaffer, about 1945[146]

new number and, when I tried to explain my connection, I was told in no uncertain
terms that no one at that number had ever heard of him. Speculation is that Hencia,
knowing that my grandparents had sent money, thought that I was trying to collect,
and I didn't try phoning for another 20 years.

In 2008, I submitted an inquiry to the *JewishGen* Discussion Group. I asked if
anyone knew where Bentzion Schaffer from Haifa was buried. To my delight, not
only did I receive information on where he was buried, but I got a message from
Henriette Podell, who said Bentzion Schaffer married her mother's sister, Hencia
Arbeit-Zwirn. Henriette and I exchanged some information, including photographs
of different family members. After emailing for a while, I decided to try calling
Sarah and her husband again. This time, I asked a friend in Israel to make the
call. Rather than relate the connection to my grandparents, this time I used the
connection to Henriette's mother, Clara, as the tie.

Henriette had fond memories of Hencia, whom she had met as a child, and
had many photos of Sarah. Henriette was anxious to reconnect with Sarah—
the last time she'd had any news of Sarah dated to Sarah's wedding many

Fig. 37: Bentzion and Hencia in Stanisławów[147]

years earlier. My friend in Israel told me of her phone experience. The man who answered the phone said that Sarah was hard of hearing and had been so all her life. The conversation would need to be filtered through the person who answered the phone, Sarah's husband. Although he did not deny the connection to Clara, he did make it clear that the call was not welcome.

A major frustration inherent in genealogical research is an inability to tap into the memory of living people who do not want to share their memories. Often, family stories are not written down. Thus, at the inevitable death of a person who may be the sole heir to the family stories, stories disappear. A unique feature of genealogical research is the utilization of memory as a primary source. Memories are sometimes the key to locating documents and verifiable facts. I am grateful that most of the people I find doing my research are eager to talk about their childhood, their parents, and their families. The Schaffer family shared a portion of their history through their many Pages of Testimony, but other personal stories are irretrievable.

Although the call to Israel was disappointing, I did find out some other connections through the several years of correspondence with Henriette, including the answer to a question about relationships that puzzled my father. Our family dentist, Seymour Schechter, was a cousin; Blima and Harry both had maintained that. But how was "Sy" related? Where did he fit in? It turns out that he was more closely related to Henriette and that his connection to us was as a somewhat distant cousin. Clara came from a large family that left Stanisławów by the early 1930s. By 1934, she and many of her siblings were living in Vienna. One sister, Lily, immigrated to the United States about 1920. She arrived in the United States following her fiancé, Isaac Schechter. They settled in Forest Hills, Queens, and had three children, the oldest of whom was Sy. In August 1939, "Ike" and Lily went to Europe to get Lily's siblings out of Europe. On 15 August 1939, Lily brought all but one of her siblings to the United States. That sister, Sara, was murdered in Auschwitz. Henriette's father was murdered in Buchenwald. It is possible that Sarah Schaffer, born just a few years later, was named after her mother's sister.

Not only was Bentzion married to a woman whose surname included "Zwirn," but in addition to Peter Zwirn, there were two other connections between the Kreislers and the Zwirns. According to Henriette, the girls of Lily and Hencia's generation all carried the linked surnames of both their parents, Jacob Zwirn and Sosia Arbeit. One of their sons, Samuel Zwirn, married Haya Schneier. Their daughter, Sidonie Zwirn, married Bentzion's brother Shimon. We have not yet uncovered Jacob's parents' names and do not know where he fits into our larger Zwirn/Zwerin/Zwern family, but it is probable that he does. Another researcher claimed that Jacob was a brother of Peter. Peter did have two brothers named Jacob. One was born in December 1875 and died shortly after. Another brother named Jacob was born in December 1886 and died in April 1887. The parents of Jacob Zwirn, who married Sosia Arbeit, have been found to be Itzig Zwirn and Rechel Zweifler after years of research. By the time I finish (if ever) dissecting all the information about the Zwirn and Zweiflers from Stanisławów and the area around it, I think I will find that they were all related.

Serendipity

One day in 2006, I was looking at the list of surnames that appears on my own family tree database. There are nearly 18,000 names in the database today. In 2006, there were about 8,000 names. Although I personally entered information about each of the people whose names are included in the database, I often do not remember them unless I have a story about the name or a person.

Fig. 38: Tova Gitel and Shimon, seated[156]

On this occasion, one of the names caught my eye—it was unusual and somehow familiar. After puzzling over it for a while, I realized that I knew someone with a similar surname in college, but the names were not quite the same. The following day, a woman with that same surname[148] posted a message on one of the listservs. I wrote to her, telling her of what I suspected was a familial relationship between us. Her answer confirmed that, and she connected me with another relative, Betty Kreisler Schlissel, in New York who was doing research on that same branch of the family.[149] We ultimately met at my parents' house. My parents and these newly found cousins[150] have lived within five miles of each other for more than 50 years!

During an intense and emotion-laden meeting, we heard, for the first time, the reason Betty's father,[151] Arthur Kreisler, and several of his siblings left Europe for the United States about 1911. Chana, Blima's mother, was the oldest of 10 siblings, at least seven of whom came to the United States. Chana remained in Europe. By 1911, when her siblings emigrated, she was married with many children. According to Betty, Chana's parents, Tova Gitel and Shimon, were wealthy furniture manufacturers.[152] One day, circa 1910, a fire broke out in their home, according to this story. One of Shimon and Tova Gitel's children, a teenager, panicked and slammed a door shut in his rush out of the room. The door jammed and his parents were trapped. The house, a multi-story, wood-frame home, burned to the ground and Tova Gitel and Shimon perished in the fire.[154] Within a year, many of their children left Stanisławów for the United States. Blima arrived in the United States a decade later and briefly connected with her aunts and uncles but didn't remain in close contact with them. Researching in newspapers and police reports in the Ivano-Frankivsk archives, I did not find any evidence of a fire that fit this description. Lyuba, Ella, and I looked through five years' worth of reports without finding any confirmation of the story.

Although I had been searching for ancestors for a long time at that point, I started to look for other cousins in my generation or my father's—people whose parents and grandparents were descendants of Tova Gitel and Shimon. Betty provided an entrée to many cousins who willingly shared their own family stories and photographs with me. Each branch had a compelling story, many of which distracted me from my primary research. I began to develop branches of the trees of my family's *machatunim*.[155] I added a lot of names, relationships, and facts to my tree and realized that I was also filling in the gaps of my understanding of life in Jewish Europe in many places in the nineteenth and twentieth centuries. I began to understand some of the differences in experiences from place to place. Instead of looking at Jewish life in villages and towns as uniform, I looked at the history of each place, the type of work done by Jews, the way Jews lived, how long the Jewish community had been in that place, the way records were maintained, the types of first names and surnames that were passed down, and other cultural facts.

As my research progressed, I discovered something about my family that shocked me and emphasized the importance of their story in the post-Holocaust history of Eastern Europe. I learned that Eugene Gras, who died in 2008, was the last Jew born in Ivano-Frankivsk before the Holocaust who survived and returned to live there. According to the United States Holocaust Museum, only 1,500 Jews from Stanisławów survived the war.[157] Although there were other Jews living in Ivano-Frankivsk by the 1950s, including Eugene's former wife—Ella's mother, Asya—none of their families originated from there. The other Jews, except for my family, were those who Stalin sent as an effort to repopulate western Ukraine after World War II. It is a poignant bit of history, but at least for me, makes the persistence of my family there very significant. I realized that finding information about the background of my own family and others who had died during or before the Holocaust meant that I was almost completely dependent on archival records still in Ukraine, on digitized records and indexes maintained by Jewish

Records Indexing-Poland (*JRI-Poland*), The Church of Jesus Christ of Latter-day Saints, and others. There was very little I would ever actually "know" from firsthand conversations with people of Eugene's age still in Ivano-Frankivsk.

Early Days in New York for the New Immigrants

Blima naturalized in 1954, even though she arrived in the United States 34 years earlier and originally filed her Declaration of Intent in 1924. Blima and Harry married in 1926. Harry naturalized in 1927. Their two children were born in the United States. Why did Blima wait so long to become naturalized? She attended night school to learn English before they were married—her address on her night-school notebook cover is 619 Rockaway Avenue, Brooklyn. Milton recalled that this was the address at which Blima's sister Fanny lived after she married Willie Ostrovsky. He did not know that Blima lived there, too. The Rockaway Avenue address is the one that appears on her 1924 Declaration of Intent. It is the only official document that we have with an address for her in the United States until the 78 East 94th Street address, at which she lived with Harry and their children.

Milton said that Harry and Blima lived on Union Avenue before they moved to East 94th Street. Blima, Harry, and baby Milton moved into the East 94th Street apartment shortly after it was built—before Stanley was born. For a while, Fanny and Willie lived across the street at 79 East 94th Street before moving back to Rockaway Avenue and then to 1880 East 4th Street in Brooklyn, where Willie was the building "super." That building was owned by Willie's brother, Dave. Milton described how they lived.

The Rockaway Ave apt was a real "cold-water" third-floor walk-up flat. Their "bathroom" would qualify as a water-closet—it had only the toilet. The water to flush was in a tank mounted on the wall close to the ceiling. You had to pull on a long chain to release the water. It is my belief that that small room was a retrofit because there was also a toilet room in the hallway for use by all the tenants.

The only other water in the apt was for the kitchen sink—for washing dishes, clothes (no laundromat or washing machines in those days), and

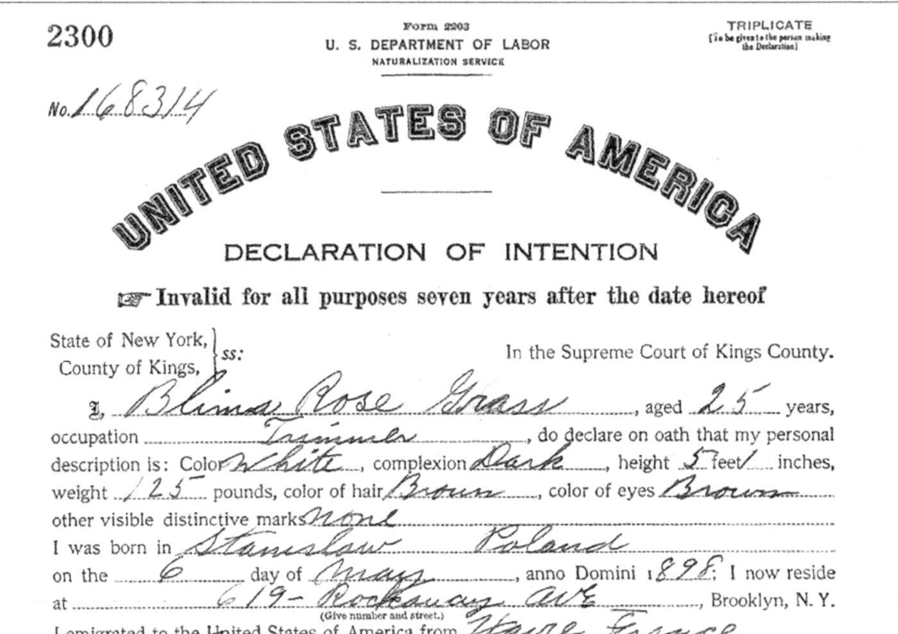

2300

Fig. 39: Blima's 1924 Declaration of Intention[158]

bathing. The bathtub was stored in one of the rooms in the apt and was pulled/pushed into the large kitchen for bathing. The water was heated on the coal/charcoal-burning iron stove on which food was prepared. I have a faint recollection of the installation of a small gas stove while they were there. The only heat for the apartment was from that kitchen stove.

I am sure the rent for the apt was very low. Uncle Willy was out of work frequently, either due to lack of work in the clothing industry or union activity in those Depression days, so that they could not afford more comfortable living arrangements.

Where did Blima live after she landed at Ellis Island? Where did she work? How did Blima and Harry meet? According to data on the 1930 census, Fanny and Willie married in 1921. Their marriage record provides a date in January 1921—a little more than a month after the sisters arrived in December 1920. How did Fanny and Willie meet? Was the marriage arranged? Was that the reason the sisters left Stanisławów? Willie was from Odessa. Not only was that hundreds of miles away from Stanislawów, but Odessa was in the Russian Empire and Stanislawów was in Galicia, part of the Austrian Empire. It is unlikely that the families knew each other in Europe. There are so many questions that are likely to remain unanswered.

Blima wrote in her notebook that she attended nine years of public school and a year of business school while she was in Europe. We have some end-of-year "report cards" for her school years from public school and Hebrew school and also for the year she attended business school in Lwów. Blima described Stanisławów as beautiful with wide avenues and boulevards that were tree-lined and surrounded by mountains with a lot of lakes. For entertainment, there was the cinema, cabaret, theater, and amusement parks. Having visited the city, I can imagine how little certain sections of it have changed in the years since she left. It's difficult to imagine the horrors there two decades later, or the terror that people

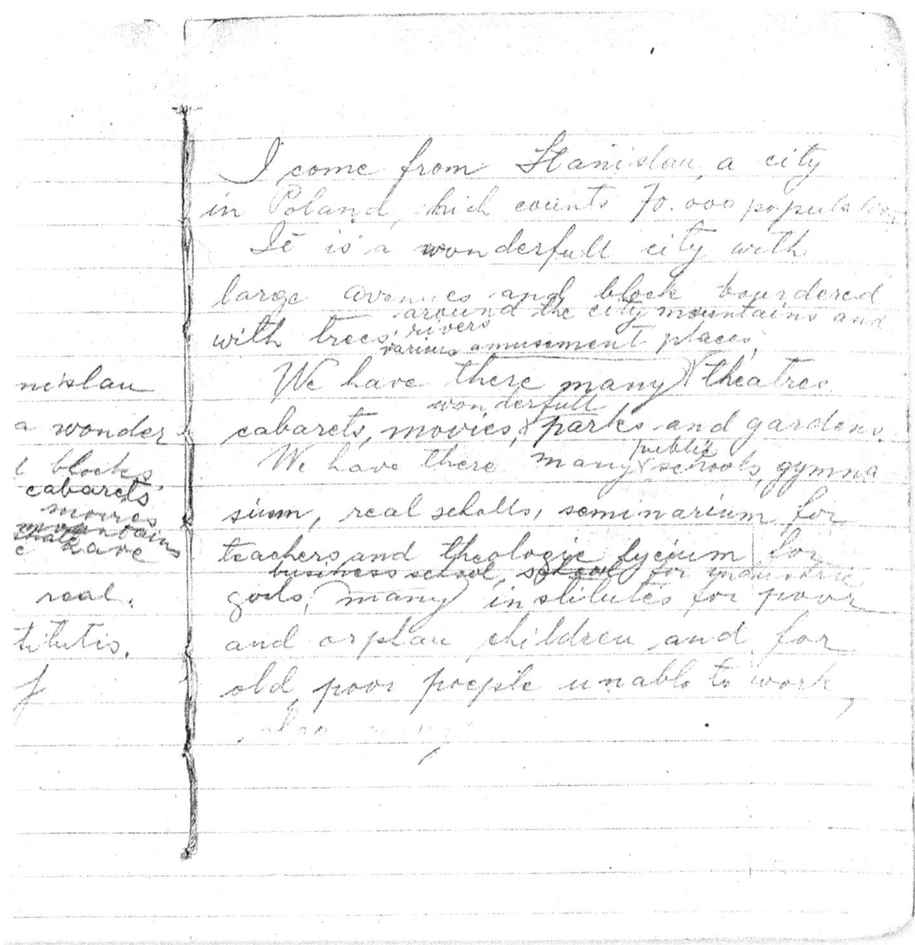

Fig. 40: Page from Blima's notebook[159]

in 2022 and 2023 feel as their city is subjected to occassional shelling. I wonder what life there was like before she left and wish I knew more about her siblings and her parents. Perhaps continued research will reveal more of their lives.

Linked/Unlinked: The Rabbinic Chain

Genealogical research is filled with twists and turns. Sometimes what appears to be a match is discovered to be incorrect. Dr. Byron Sherwin told me years ago that if I could trace my family back to the sixteenth or maybe even the seventeenth century, I would find the link to a rabbinic dynasty. I did not find the link, but what I <u>thought</u> was the link found me. Early in the summer of 2011, I received an email message from Ruth K., who wanted to discuss Blima's father's family with me. Blima's father was Zelig Grass. At the time, I thought Zelig's father was Moses Yakov Gros/Gras and his mother was Ester Hirschhorn. Zelig and his parents were from Skalat, or so I thought. This was the only record of a Zelig Grass I found in Skalat, and I made an error in judgement, thinking that if it was the only one, it must be the right one. Ester's parents were Chaim Isaiah Hirschhorn and Feige Frankel. Ester had several siblings: Malia, Samuel, Bluhme, Hudel, and Aviezer. Ruth and I had a couple of very exciting phone calls—she is a descendant of Malia, who I quickly realized was the Amalia on Ruth's tree. Ruth didn't have my Ester on her tree. There were some minor differences between the names we each had in our records, which we soon realized were due to differences in pronunciation and nicknames handed down by the families.

Then Ruth asked me if I knew of Neil Rosenstein's *The Unbroken Chain*. I knew of the book but had never had occasion to use it and did not have a copy. I purchased a copy of what was, at the time, the most recent edition from 1990 (a newer, more extensive edition is now available). I spent weeks poring over the book and hours tracing the people in Chapter 4, Branch C, attempting to verify information about each of the people I was researching. I found people with surnames of Luria, Isserles, Frankel, Katzenellenbogen, and others—all luminaries in the intermeshed world of rabbinic dynasties. The fascinating thing about "knowing" how my family fit into the pages of history was that the history becomes personally relevant. Just as I connected with the Holocaust through my family's experiences, I formed a personal connection with another segment of

Jewish history in Europe through my family. As interesting as history may be, for me at least, it became more compelling as an objective study when I found a personal connection. I discovered a world of interesting connections and much confusion in the branches, twigs, and leaves that comprise this complex intertwining of families in rabbinic dynastic charts. Given names in any generation and in successive generations within a family are similar, and surnames are often changed, such as when a man who marries into a more illustrious family takes his wife's surname. Some surnames are hyphenated and names on either side of the hyphen are often interchanged. Sometimes one or the other of the names is dropped. As fascinating as this was, I discovered, to my dismay, that this was <u>not,</u> in fact, part of my family's history. That Zelig Grass was not "my" Zelig Grass.

In 1909, Blima's parents, Zelig Grass and Chana Yetta Kreisler, registered their marriage. Zelig's parents, very clearly, were Jakub Grass and Ruchel. I searched, hoping that Ruchel had another name and perhaps was Ruchel Ester or Ester Ruchel and that her maiden name was Hirschhorn. Alas, wishes are not part of exhaustive genealogical research, and the information I found in the record indicated that Zelig was not from Skalat but from Halicz, a town in the Stanisławów district. To date, my attempts to find information about his parents, siblings, or early life have been unsuccessful. So often, documents did not survive. Of course, it's entirely possible that, although he was registered or living in Halicz at the time of his marriage, he could very well have been from elsewhere. Or, more likely, since no records have indicated that he was from anywhere but the Stanisławów district, it may be that records from Halicz are hiding in some other repository, perhaps somewhere as mundane as a box in a basement or attic. If he was from outside the district, I might have found some note in a birth or marriage record from one of his children. Zelig died in December 1920, and his probate records don't have information about his parents or siblings. Marriage records for his children Clara, Blima, Fanny, Mundek, Samuel, and Pepa don't have the names of their paternal grandparents. His three youngest children—Rachel, Oscar, and Sara, all murdered during the Shoah—never married. Perhaps that elusive source holding all these missing puzzle pieces will show up some day.

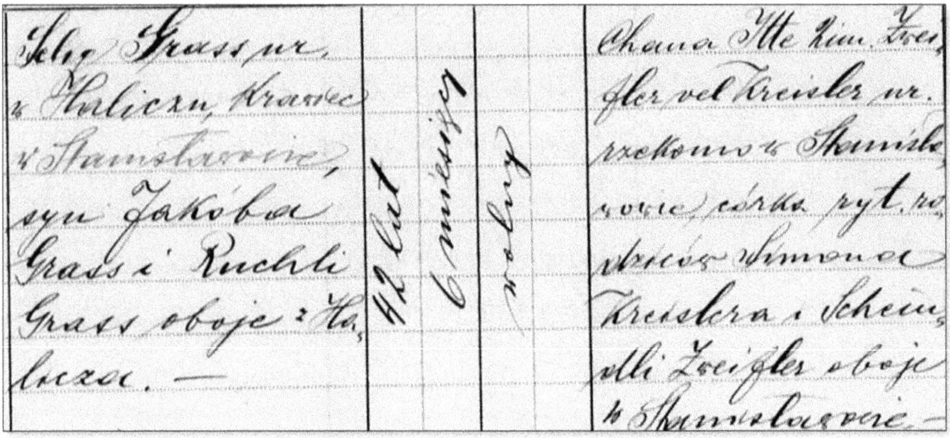

Selig Grass ur. w Haliczu, krawiec w Stanisławowie, syn Jakóba Grass i Ruchli Grass oboje z Halicza. —	42 lat	6 miesięcy	wolny	Chana Itte Zim. Zweifler vel Kreisler ur. rzekomo w Stanisławowie, córka pyt. rodziców Simona Kreislera i Scheindli Zweifler oboje w Stanisławowie —

Fig. 41: Marriage registration of Selig Grass and Chana Itte Zweifler vel Kreisler[160]

Endnotes

1. The Silberman-Buchbinder story is told in the previous chapter.

2. "Blima Rose Grass," photograph, circa 1915; researcher's copy.

3. Stanisławów, now called Ivano-Frankivsk, is located at 48° 53′ 3″ N 24° 41′ 10″ E.

4. Harry Silberman, of Brooklyn, New York, to Samuel Leon Grass, of Stanisławów, Russia, letter, dated 25 March 1946; researcher's copy.

5. In those days, at the beginning of our research, we had not yet thought of our family's history in a larger context.

6. "Google Maps," *Google* (https://www.google.com) accessed May 2022.

7. Thankfully, before giving her the letters, we had the sense to make photocopies of the flimsy wartime paper on which they were written.

8. Referred to in the letters as "Zanek," which we erroneously assumed to be his name.

9. They appear to have not understood how widespread the Holocaust was and feared it had extended to New York.

10. The last letters they had received from the United States were likely in 1942 or 1943, based on their comments.

11. Also written Lwow and known in Yiddish as Lemberg. Today, located in Ukraine, it is known as Lviv.

12. The yellow line is Sapizhinska Street, a main road in the center of Stanisławów where the Grass and Kreisler families lived. "Ivano Frankivsk, Ukraine, 1905 Town Overview Map," Ivano Frankivsk, Ukraine, *JewishGen KehilaLinks* (https://kehilalinks.jewishgen.org), accessed May 2022.

13. Susannah R. Juni, "Ukrainian Research and Ancestral Travels," *Avotaynu: The International Review of Jewish Genealogy* XIII (Winter 1997): p. 33; researcher's copy.

14. Seymour Spector (editor), *The Encyclopedia of Jewish Life Before and During the Holocaust* (New York: New York University Press, 2001), pp. 1233-1234; researcher's copy.

15. Jerrold Landau, "Stanisławów," *Encyclopaedia of Jewish Communities in Poland: Vol. II Eastern Galicia* (Jerusalem: Yad Vashem Martyr's and Heroes' Remembrance Authority, 1980), p. 359; digital image, "Yizkor Books," *JewishGen* (https://www.jewishgen.org), accessed January 2019.

16. Landau put the housing for the Jews as all being located on "the street of the Jews" near the flood bank. I was curious whether that might refer to the modern banks of the river near where my cousin Ella lives today. Her apartment building, less than 10 years old, is at the edge of what was the ghetto built during the Holocaust. The ghetto housed some of the Jews of Stanisławów but was primarily for Jews from nearby towns who were forced by the Nazis to leave their homes and relocate to Stanisławów. I was, however, unable to find a reference to which flood banks these early dwellings were built near. All the sources seem to rely upon (without apparent attribution) this same PINKAS HAKEHILOT: *Encyclopaedia of Jewish Communities in Poland: Vol. II Eastern Galicia*, since they use the exact same language as Landau's translation. Ella lives on Karmelyuka Street **(Вулиця Кармелюка)** near the River Bystrytsia **(Бистриця)**. This river is one of the longest tributaries of the Dnister River, which flows through Ukraine. "Dnister River," *Internet Encyclopedia of Ukraine* (http://www.encyclopediaofukraine.com), accessed January 2019.

18. Landau: p. 359

19. Landau: p. 359.

20. Leo Shtrait, Ivan Monolatiy (editor), **Станиславівські Синагоги** (*Stanislaw's Synagogues*) (Ukraine: **Лілея-НВ**, 2010), p. 14; researcher's copy. Translation from Polish by Ella Mintsys (full translation still in progress).

21. The film, *The Lost Wooden Synagogues of Eastern Europe*, 2000, narrated by Theodore Bikel, provides a great deal of insight into the architecture and use of wooden synagogues in Poland and Lithuania.

22. Shtrait: p. 15.

23. Landau: p. 359.

24. Spector, 2001: pp. 1233-1234.

25. Landau: p. 359.

26. Landau: p. 359.

27. Landau: p. 360.

28. Landau: p. 360.

29. Spector, 2001: pp. 1233-1234.

30. Nechama Tec, *Resilience and Courage: Women, Men, and the Holocaust* (New Haven, Connecticut: Yale University Press, 2003), p. 336; researcher's copy.

31. "Stanisławów," Holocaust Encyclopedia, *United States Holocaust Memorial Museum* (https://www.ushmm.org), accessed February 2022.

32. In 2009, Ella and I visited the Ivano-Frankivsk archives and read a handwritten copy of that diary. I have a copy of Feuerman's untranslated diary in Ukrainian—**щоденник зі станіслава**.

33. Fond 27, Inventory 1, File 742, State Archives of Ivano-Frankivsk Oblast, Ivano-Frankivsk, Ukraine.

34. "Google Earth," *Google* (https://earth.google.com), accessed February 2022.

35. Her brother Isaac had fled to Scotland.

36. Sofie Caplan, "The Quest for the Topf Family," *Avotaynu: The International Review of Jewish Genealogy* III (Fall 1987): p. 6; researcher's copy.

37. Fram discussed some of the issues related to finding information that verified anecdotal information. Edward Fram, "Creating A Tale Of Martyrdom In Tulczyn, 1648" *Jewish History and Jewish Memory: Essays in Honor of Yosef Hayim Yerushalmi* (Hanover, New Hampshire: Brandeis University Press/University Press of New England, 1998), p. 90; researcher's copy.

38. Yad Vashem in Jerusalem is a living memorial to the Holocaust. It was established in 1953.

39. In Stanisławów.

40. Now Ivano-Frankivsk.

41. Batya Unterschatz, of Jerusalem, Israel, to Janette Silverman, of Rockaway, New Jersey, letter, dated 11 April 1986; researcher's copy.

42. Janette Silverman, "Pre- and post-war residence of the Grass family," photograph, 2010; researcher's copy.

43. "Grass family portrait," photograph, circa 1985; researcher's copy.

44. The two ships docked on 4 December and 7 December 1920 in New York Harbor.

45. United States, Department of Justice, Immigration and Naturalization Service, Passenger and Crew Lists of Vessels Arriving at New York, New York, 1897-1957, SS *La Lorraine*, arrived 6 December 1920, p. 274, Line 10, Blima Grass; digital image, "New York, U.S., Arriving Passenger and Crew Lists (including Castle Garden and Ellis Island), 1820-1957," *Ancestry* (http://www.ancestry.com), accessed April 2022.

46. United States, Department of Justice, Immigration and Naturalization Service, Passenger and Crew Lists of Vessels Arriving at New York, New York, 1897-1957, SS *Rotterdam*, arrived 4 December 1920, p. 141, Lines 26-27, Chaja and Feige Grass; digital image, "New York, U.S., Arriving Passenger and Crew Lists (including Castle Garden and Ellis Island), 1820-1957," *Ancestry* (http://www.ancestry.com), accessed April 2022.

47. Fig. 6.11.

48. Fig. 6.9.

49. 1925 New York State Census, Brooklyn, Kings County, AD 18, ED 56, p. 10, William Ostrowsky household; digital image, "New York, U.S., State Census, 1925," Ancestry (http://www.ancestry.com), accessed December 2020.

50. United States, Department of Justice, Immigration and Naturalization Service, Passenger and Crew Lists of Vessels Arriving at New York, New York, 1897-1957, SS Imperator, arrived 27 August 1913, p. 183, Line 12, Zelig Grass; digital image, "New York, U.S., Arriving Passenger and Crew Lists (including Castle Garden and Ellis Island), 1820-1957," *Ancestry* (http://www.ancestry.com), accessed December 2020.

51. "Grass Family Portrait," photograph, circa 1903; researcher's copy.

52. Hoshana Rabba is a holiday on the Jewish calendar, celebrated at the end of the fall holiday of Sukkot. It was on this day, while the men were at prayers, that they were locked in the synagogue and burned to death. The rest of the Jews in town were rounded up and shot in the town center or over graves they were forced to dig for themselves in the woods. It is estimated that more than 40,000 Jews were murdered during this round-up.

53. Blima Grass, Citizenship Class Notebook; researcher's copy.

54. *JRI-Poland* is a searchable database of indexes to Jewish Records of Poland. Many of the indexed items are linked to the actual record. "Search Our Database," *Jewish Records Indexing – Poland* (https://www.jri-poland.org), accessed March 2022.

55. "Peter Zwirn and Rose Kreisler," photograph, unknown year; researcher's copy.

56. Senator William P. Dillingham (Chairman of the Immigrant Commission), Reports of the Immigration Commission: Steerage Conditions; Importation and Harboring of Women for Illegal Purposes; Immigrant Homes and Aid Societies; Immigrant Banks (Washington, D.C.: Government Printing Office, 1911), p. 129; researcher's copy.

57. Nancy Levin Arbeiter, "A Beginner's Primer in U.S. Jewish Genealogical Research," *Avotaynu: The International Review of Jewish Genealogy* XIV (Fall 1998); researcher's copy.

58. The question posed by me was, "My grandmother and her two sisters left Stanisławów (today's Ivano-Frankivsk) for the U.S. in 1921. My grandmother left Europe five days before her sisters—they all docked in NY and they all traveled steerage and went through Ellis Island. My grandmother was on a ship that left from Le Havre. Her sisters left from Rotterdam. Her sisters used the name of a male relative in Manhattan as their destination. My grandmother used a different male relative in the Bronx. We speculate that the difference in who they were going to in the United States may have had to do with sponsorship but we aren't sure that's really the answer. We can't come up with a good guess about why they left from different and distant ports in Europe when they all started out from the same place. If they had left on different ships from the same port, it would have made sense." The answer was suggested by Mark Jacobson, then President of the Jewish Genealogy Society of Palm Beach County (Florida). His response is not <u>the</u> definitive answer. It is just a possibility.

59. "The Lipshutz/Peoples Bank Passage Order Book Records Database for the Port of Philadelphia and Other US East Coast Ports," Databases, *JewishGen* (https://www.jewishgen.org), accessed January 2019.

60. "Sender Jarmulowsky: A Synagogue Founder's Story," *Museum at Eldridge Street* (http://www. eldridgestreet.org), accessed January 2019.

61. "Jarmulowsky's Bank," Educator Resources, *Museum at Eldridge Street* (http://www.eldridgestreet. org), accessed January 2019. This website explains a little more of the history of the Jarmulowsky Bank, the building, and its founder. "Located at 54 Canal Street, this 12-story classical-style bank was built by architects Rouse & Goldstone for Sender Jarmulowsky in 1912....[h]ere, recent immigrants could set up bank accounts, send remittances, and buy steerage tickets for their European relatives—in Yiddish. The bank quickly became a household name among Jews on both sides of the ocean. ... The bank become a testament to Jarmulowsky's success as a businessman and reflected his prominence in the Jewish community of the Lower East Side. Jarmulowsky died in 1912, shortly after the bank was completed, and his sons took over the business. Unfortunately, they lacked their father's business acumen and mismanaged the business. In 1914, at the start of World War I, the bank closed as many depositors made 'runs' on the bank to get money to help their families in Europe. According to the NY Times, 2,000 people demonstrated in front of the bank. 500 people stormed the house where son Meyer Jarmulowsky lived, forcing him to escape across tenement rooftops. Jarmulowsky's sons were indicted for banking fraud and the bank closed. The State of New York took over the bank in May 1917 and auctioned it off. In 2009, Jarmulowsky's Bank building was designated a landmark by the Landmarks Preservation Commission."

62. Boris Feldblyum, "Understanding Russian-Jewish Given Names," *Avotaynu: The International Review of Jewish Genealogy* XIII (Summer, 1997): p. 4; researcher's copy.

63. Feldblyum: p. 4.

64. Feldblyum: p. 6.

65. Feldblyum: p. 7.

66. Asher Bar-Zev, "The Mysteries of Yiddish Given Names," *Avotaynu: The International Review of Jewish Genealogy* XIII (Summer 1997): p. 17; researcher's copy.

67. Bar-Zev.

68. Gerald L. Esterson, and David Curwin. "Ashkenazic European Given Names: Databases for European and Foreign Countries," *Avotaynu: The International Review of Jewish Genealogy* XVII (Summer 2001); researcher's copy.

69. A *get* is a Jewish divorce.

70. A *ketuva*, or *ketubah*, is a Jewish marriage contract.

71. During many Jewish prayer services, a scroll containing the first five books of the Bible is read. This scroll is called a Torah. The entire scroll is written in unvowelized Hebrew and, thousands of years ago, was divided into sections that are read and studied weekly and on holidays. During these readings, people are called up to recite a blessing. This is an *aliya*, which literally means "going up." Traditionally, these were reserved only for adult men, but in many modern Jewish congregations, men and women are treated equally.

72. "The Given Names Data Bases (GNDBs)," Databases, *JewishGen* (https://www.jewishgen.org), accessed March 2022.

73. Esterson and Curwin.

74. James B. Koenig, "Calques, Kinnuim And Couplets: The use of Alternative Names by Jewish Families," *ZichronNote* XXII, no. 2 (May 2002): p. 15; researcher's copy.

75. Feldblyum: p. 7.

76. Births from 1866 to 1897 and deaths from 1868 to 1892.

77. "Nadworna PSA AGAD Births 1866-97," Search Our Database, *Jewish Records Indexing-Poland* (https://www.jri-poland.org), accessed December 2010.

78. "Nadworna PSA AGAD Deaths 1868-92," Search Our Database, *Jewish Records Indexing – Poland* (https://www.jri-poland.org), accessed December 2010.

79. A *chupah* is a marriage canopy under which Jewish religious marriages take place.

80. Fig. 6.18.

81. Stanisławów (Stanisławów District, Galicia Province, Austrian Empire) Civil Registration Office, Jewish Births 1898, Number 276, Blime Rose Grass/Kreisler, born May 1898; digital image, "Księgi metrykalne gmin wyznania mojżeszowego z terenów tzw. "zabużańskich"," *Archiwum Główne Akt Dawnych* (https://agad.gov.pl), accessed July 2018.

82. The letter "v" stands for "vel," meaning "or."

83. See the discussion above about Sara Lea's and Samuel's ship manifests.

84. Fig. 6.21.

85. Stanisławów (Stanisławów District, Galicia Province, Austrian Empire) Civil Registration Office, Jewish Births 1914, Paula Zweifler, born 9 May 1914; researcher's copy.

86. Fig. 6.21.

87. Buczacz (Tarnopol County, Poland) Town Hall, Residence Certificate, Number 524, Sara Lea Pfeffer/Kreisler, dated 27 March 1920; researcher's copy.

88. Poland, Passport, Number 14587, Sara Lea Zweifler v. Kreisler; researcher's copy.

89. Although I was not in attendance at that conference, a colleague was there and shared notes with me.

90. "World Archives Project: Poland, Jewish Holocaust Survivors Registered in Warsaw, 1945-1946 – Abbreviations," *RootsWeb* (https://wiki.rootsweb.com), accessed February 2019.

91. Definitions.net offers many versions of the equivalent of "maiden name" in different languages. "Search," *Definitions* (http://www.definitions.net), accessed February 2019.

92. United States, Department of Justice, Immigration and Naturalization Service, Passenger and Crew Lists of Vessels Arriving at New York, New York, 1897-1957, SS *Rotterdam*, arrived 4 December 1920, p. 155, Lines 12-16, Sara, Malka, Moses, Simon, and Paulo Zweifler; digital image, "New York, U.S., Arriving Passenger and Crew Lists (including Castle Garden and Ellis Island), 1820-1957," *Ancestry* (http://www.ancestry.com), accessed November 2012.

93. This is likely a phonetic spelling of Buczacz.

94. United States, Department of Justice, Immigration and Naturalization Service, Passenger and Crew Lists of Vessels Arriving at New York, New York, 1897-1957, Record of Detained Aliens, SS *Rotterdam*, arrived 4 December 1920, p. 290, Line 414, Sara Zweifler and four children; digital image, "New York, U.S., Arriving Passenger and Crew Lists (including Castle Garden and Ellis Island), 1820-1957," *Ancestry* (http://www.ancestry.com), accessed November 2012.

95. United States, Department of Justice, Immigration and Naturalization Service, Passenger and Crew Lists of Vessels Arriving at New York, New York, 1897-1957, SS *Rotterdam*, arrived 4 December 1920, p. 155, Lines 12-16, Sara, Malka, Moses, Simon, and Paulo Zweifler; digital image, "New York, U.S., Arriving Passenger and Crew Lists (including Castle Garden and Ellis Island), 1820-1957," *Ancestry* (http://www.ancestry.com), accessed November 2012.

96. This was explained in Part 2 Chapter 1 of this book.

97. These are the three port cities from which most of my ancestors left Europe.

98. "Home," French Lines (http://www.frenchlines.com), accessed March 2022.

99. Janette Silverman, "Street in Le Havre," photograph, 2014; researcher's copy.

100. *"La France,"* painting, undated; digital image, "'France': storia di un transatlantico," 20 August 2012, *Miss Jane* (http://missjaneblog.blogspot.com/2012/08/france-storia-di-un-transatlantico.html), accessed August 2014.

101. *"SS La Lorraine,"* photograph, undated; digital image, "Passenger Ships and Images," *Ancestry* (http://www.ancestry.com), accessed August 2014.

102. Grave marker of Julius Zweifler (died 19 November 1944) and Jack Zweifler (died 21 October 1966), Baron Hirsch Cemetery, Staten Island, Richmond County, New York, photograph; researcher's copy.

103. United States, Selective Service System, World War I Selective Service System Draft Registration Cards, 1917-1918, New York, Sullivan County, Local Board for the County of Sullivan, Serial Number 39, Charles Zweifler, born 24 August 1896; digital image, "U.S., World War I Draft Registration Cards, 1917-1918," *Ancestry* (http://www.ancestry.com), accessed January 2012.

104. 1930 U.S. Federal Census (Population Schedule), Brooklyn, Kings County, New York, ED 1175, Sheet 9B, Dwelling 155, Family 155, Charles Zweifler household; digital image, "1930 United States Federal Census," *Ancestry* (http://www.ancestry.com), accessed January 2012.

105. United States, Selective Service System, Selective Service Registration Cards, World War II: Fourth Registration, New York, Brooklyn, Local Board 173, Serial Number 157, Charles Rieger Zweifler, born 24 September 1896; digital image, "U.S., World War II Draft Registration Cards, 1942," *Ancestry* (http://www.ancestry.com), accessed January 2012.

106. Charles Zweifler's World War II draft registration reports that he is employed at Ratner's.

107. Irwin Richman, *Borscht Belt Bungalows: Memories of Catskill Summers* (Philadelphia, Pennsylvania: Temple University Press, 1998), p. 2; researcher's copy.

108. Richman: p. 3.

109. Abraham D. Lavender and Clarence B. Steinberg, *Jewish Farmers of the Catskills: A Century of Survival* (Gainesville, Florida: University Press of Florida, 1995), p. 31; researcher's copy.110.

110 Jennifer Mascia, "Few Laughs Left in a Catskill Town Struggling to Revive," published 18 December 2009, *The New York Times* (https://www.nytimes.com), accessed January 2012.

111. Phil Brown, *In the Catskills: A Century of the Jewish Experience in the Mountains* (New York: Columbia University Press, 2003), p. 2; researcher's copy.

112. "Jewish Agricultural Society (Baron de Hirsch Fund)," Guide to the Yivo Archives, *Yivo Archives* (http://www.yivoarchives.org), accessed March 2022.

113. Lavender and Steinberg: p. 28.

114. United States, Department of Justice, Immigration and Naturalization Service, Passenger and Crew Lists of Vessels Arriving at New York, New York, 1897-1957, SS *Rotterdam*, arrived 4 December 1920, p. 22, Lines 26-27, Chaja and Feige Grass; digital image, "New York, U.S., Arriving Passenger and Crew Lists (including Castle Garden and Ellis Island), 1820-1957," *Ancestry* (http://www.ancestry.com), accessed March 2019.

115. United States, Department of Justice, Immigration and Naturalization Service, Passenger and Crew Lists of Vessels Arriving at New York, New York, 1897-1957, SS *Deutschland*, arrived 23 August 1908, p. 60, Line 24, Peter Zwirn; digital image, "New York, Passenger and Crew Lists (including Castle Garden and Ellis Island), 1820-1957," *Ancestry* (http://www.ancestry.com), accessed March 2019.

116. United States, Department of Justice, Immigration and Naturalization Service, Passenger and Crew Lists of Vessels Arriving at New York, New York, 1897-1957, SS *Amerika*, arrived 1 February 1910, p. 3, Lines 18-19, Peter and Rosa Zwirn; digital image, "New York, Passenger and Crew Lists (including Castle Garden and Ellis Island), 1820-1957," *Ancestry* (http://www.ancestry.com), accessed March 2019.

117. 1930 U.S. Federal Census (Population Schedule), Brooklyn, Kings County, New York, ED 24-1357, Sheet 29a, Dwelling 366, Family 684, Peter Zwirn household; digital image, "1930 United States Federal Census," *Ancestry* (http://www.ancestry.com), accessed March 2019.

118. "Trailkill-Zwerin Relations," Family Trees, *rootsweb* (ttps://wc.rootsweb.com), accessed October 2018.

119. Mikołaj Gliński, "A Foreigner's Guide to the Polish Alphabet," Language, *Culture.pl* (https://culture.pl), accessed May 2022.

120. Lucas Kern, "German Alphabet ABC," *Learn German Easily* (https://learn-german-easily.com), accessed May 2022.

121. Harold Rhode, "Jewish Culture, History and Religion: Keys to Understanding Our Ancestors' Lives and to Asking the Right Questions," *Avotaynu: The International Review of Jewish Genealogy* XIV (Spring 1998): pp 4-8; researcher's copy.

122. Gary Mokotoff is an author, lecturer, and acknowledged leader in Jewish genealogy. He is the co-author of the Daitch-Mokotoff soundex system.

123. This was part of a response to a discussion thread on the Gesher Galicia Discussion Group on 20 November 2010 called "Children assuming the surname of the mother."

124. Mark Halpern was the long-time coordinator of the indexing of records from the AGAD Archive (Galician records) and the Bialystok Archive (records from the Russian/Congress Poland and the Pale of Settlement).

125. The original question was posed by Zev Scarson, and this response by Mark Halpern appeared on 6 October 2010 in the JRI-PL Discussion Group Digest.

126. This was part of a response to a discussion thread on the Gesher Galicia Discussion Group on 22 November 2010, called "Children assuming the surname of the mother."

127. Wynne: p. 56.

128. "Marriage," Browse, *The YIVO Encyclopedia of Jews in Eastern Europe* (https://yivoencyclopedia.org), accessed August 2022.

129. Wynne: p. 57.

130. Homberg was the government-appointed supervisor of Jewish schools in Galicia from 1787 to 1806. In 1812, he wrote *Bne-Zion*, celebrating the universal traits shared between Judaism and Christianity.

131. Wrobel: p. 102.

132. Wynne: p. 59.

133. Taken from a message posted by Mark Halperin on 21 August 2011 and in the Gesher Galicia SIG discussion group.

134. Warren Blatt, "Polish-Jewish Genealogy—Questions and Answers," InfoFiles, *JewishGen* (https://www.jewishgen.org), accessed April 2019.

135. Ivano-Frankivsk Regional State Archives (Ivano-Frankivsk, Ukraine), Index Card for Lea Kreisler, died 9 March 1938; Ivano-Frankivsk Regional State Archives, Ivano-Frankivsk, Ukraine.

136. Yad Vashem (Jerusalem, Israel), Page of Testimony, ID 1037689, Hana Jita Gras, submitted by Bentzion Schaffer; digital image, "The Central Database of Shoah Victims' Names," Digital Collections, *Yad Vashem* (https://www.yadvashem.org), accessed November 2021.

137. Fig. 31.

138. 1939 Poland Resident List, Stanisławów, Stanisławów County, 24 Sapizhinska Street, Chane Jeta Grass household; Fond 27, Inventory 1, File 742, Ivano-Frankivsk Regional State Archives, Ivano-Frankivsk, Ukraine.

139. Stanisławów (Poland) Town Council, Correspondence Regarding Statute Approval, Jewish Community Registration, Committees for Church Construction and Other Religious Unions and Societies, 1925-1939; Fond 2, Inventory 3, File 1227, Ivano-Frankivsk Regional State Archives, Ivano-Frankivsk, Ukraine.

140. "Virtual Jewish World: Warsaw, Poland," *Jewish Virtual Library* (https://www.jewishvirtuallibrary.org), accessed May 2019.

141. Станиславівські Синагоги.

142. Johnathan Shea, "Austrian Census Returns 1869-1890 with Emphasis on Galicia," Regions,

143. The Federation of East European Family History Societies (https://feefhs.org), accessed March 2022.

144. 1941 Ukrainian SSR Census, Stanislav, p. 8, Khana Ita Grass household; Ivano-Frankivsk Regional State Archives, Ivano-Frankivsk, Ukraine.

145. "Pages of Testimony?," Hall of Names, Yad Vashem (https://www.yadvashem.org), accessed May 2019.

146. It isn't clear from the story whether the "later" was days or hours after the murder of the Stanisławów Jews.

147. The Chase National Bank (New York City, New York), Money Order Receipt, H. Silberman to Benzion Schaffer, dated 5 April 1948; researcher's copy.

148. "Sarah Schaffer," photograph, circa 1945; researcher's copy.

149. "Bentzion and Hencia Schaffer," photograph, undated; researcher's copy.

150. Schlissel.

151. Kreisler.

152. My father's first cousin once removed (their father was my grandmother's first cousin).

153. Chana's youngest sibling, who was 25 years her junior.

154. I have found corroboration that this industry was one in which many Jewish families were involved in Stanisławów. In fact, the Jews dominated this industry for many years, but I have not found this family on the list of manufacturers.

155. Or maybe 1909.

156. This story also remains uncorroborated.

157. Literally, the in-laws of a family, but often used, as it is here, to refer to the extended family.

158. "Kreisler Family Portrait," photograph, undated; researcher's copy.

159. "Stanislawów (now Ivano-Frankivsk)," Holocaust Encyclopedia, *United States Holocaust Memorial Museum* (http://www.ushmm.org), accessed March 2022.

160. United States, Department of Labor, Naturalization Service, Declaration of Intention 168314, Blima Rose Grass, dated 16 February 1924, in the Supreme Court of Kings County, New York; digital image, "New York, County Naturalization Records, 1791-1980," *FamilySearch* (http://www.familysearch.org), accessed March 2020.

161. Blima Grass, Citizenship Class Notebook; researcher's copy.

162. Stanisławów (Stanisławów District, Galicia Province, Austrian Empire) Civil Registration Office, Jewish Marriages 1909, Number 61, Selig Grass and Chana Itte Zweifler vel Kreisler, married 21 March 1909; digital image, "Księgi metrykalne gmin wyznania mojżeszowego z terenów tzw. "zabużańskich"," *Archiwum Główne Akt Dawnych* (https://agad.gov.pl), accessed August 2018.

Afterword
In the Footsteps of
My Ancestors

Path to Ivano-Frankivsk Cemetery (Ukraine)

In the Footsteps of My Ancestors

It was in the hope of finding out the answers to the questions I had about my grandmother Blima and her family that I prepared for my 2009 journey to her birthplace, Stanisławów (now Ivano-Frankivsk). Ella, the granddaughter of Blima's brother Samuel and his wife, Diana, sent me a book in the 1990s with photographs of the city. I could make out some of the words in the narrative of the book but had no understanding of what I was decoding. The book is written in Ukrainian, which, like Russian, uses the Cyrillic alphabet. It is as different from Russian as Spanish is from French. That is, these similar languages share some common words, but most of the vocabulary and grammar are very different. By the time I left for Ukraine in 2009, I knew what had transpired in Stanisławów for my family and the rest of the Jewish population during the Holocaust but could not imagine what living there today would be like.

In preparation for the trip, I reviewed the local history. Despite conventional wisdom to the contrary, I decided not to hire a professional guide to take me around, show me the sights, and assist me with archival research. Part of my decision was based on comments written by Neville Lamdan in an *Avotaynu* article that appeared in 2006. He wrote that while:

> ...[i]t is true that we can hire someone on the spot to do the work for us, [] typically this does not produce convincing results. No matter how intelligent the hired researcher may be or how precise his instructions are, only you have the necessary information and background in your head to do effective archival research, spot the hidden clues, make the obscure connections and exploit them to the fullest by teasing out a missing sibling, pouncing on a distorted place name, judging whether information is relevant or valid, and fitting it into the larger jigsaw puzzle on which you have been working for years. The well-known genealogical maxim that "only you can do your own research" is absolutely true.

As a professional genealogist, I know that it is not always feasible to do the research yourself. In 2009, I had never been in archives outside the United States and thought the best way to learn about it was total immersion.

Planning

Ella and I began talking about my 2009 trip and planning for it about 18 months in advance. I eagerly pored over maps, trying to understand not only the geography of the places I wanted to visit but attempting to gain an understanding of their relationship to each other. Initially, I thought I would be able to fly to Romania and then work my way by train north from Suceava to Ivano-Frankivsk. That proved to be impossible—trains do not travel that route any longer, although they did more than 100 years earlier when my Silberman-Buchbinder ancestors moved from Husiatyn to Suceava. The Tisza River, a tributary of the Danube, flows through the Carpathian Mountains in Ukraine and Romania and links the ancestral homes of my father's ancestors in Ivano-Frankivsk and Suceava.

Most of my time in Ukraine in 2009 was spent in Ivano-Frankivsk, but my plan included stops in other cities to which I had ancestral ties: Zhytomyr, Husiatyn, and Skalat. In advance of my trip, I found that the Zhytomyr records I had an interest in finding should be located at the archive in Zhytomyr and that the records from Husiatyn and Skalat were in the archives in Tarnopol. There are many history books about the condition of the Jews in Czarist Russia and Eastern Europe, but I wanted to go beyond someone else's research and synthesis of data. I really wanted to make a physical connection with this part of Europe, and besides visiting there and trying to see beneath a hundred years or more of war and upheaval, I knew no other way to pursue this line of research. This was another reason I decided to eschew a professional guide. I wanted the liberty to wander at will and to change directions in both my research and plan as needed, or, as the mood took me. In retrospect, it may have taken more time to locate places and to cut through red tape, but the experience of having to search for buildings, deal with bureaucrats, and decide to stay longer or look for a place not originally part of the itinerary helped me gain a more complete perspective of the country and its past. I may have missed a lot, but on the other hand, I experienced the wonder of searching and then finding things and places. At the same time, I think I gained an understanding of life in Ukraine without having it filtered by someone whose business was tourism or research.

My reasons for avoiding a professional might seem naïve, but I wanted a pair of fresh eyes with me. I definitely needed a guide of some sort who was fluent in Ukrainian. I also needed that person to be someone who could look at

Fig. 1: 2009 market

documentation and cemeteries without preconceived notions of what we could
or should find. Horror stories abound regarding travelers paying guides and
researchers who were engaged based on advertisements and not through personal
recommendations, and who took payment and were never heard from again. It was
great to be able to rely on Ella and her wide network. After my time there, I knew
that another trip would be necessary. Although at this writing, more than 14 years
after that initial visit, I have been back to Ukraine, I still haven't spent sufficient time
there. I want to understand the myriad layers of its history and of the history of my
family. Planning the trip with Ella, spending time with her in Ukraine and in the United
States two years later when she came to visit, and visiting Ukraine again several
years later were amazing experiences. They were also bittersweet. I took my initial
trip too late to meet Eugene, Ella's father, who had died two years earlier. When
Eugene was born, my great-grandmother Chana Yetta wrote to my grandmother
that my dad and Eugene were like brothers. Neither my dad nor I ever met him. That
first trip in 2009, during which Ella and I spent amazing hours combing the records
in the archives and finding out more about our family and the fate of the Jews in

Ivano-Frankivsk, provided me with insight into the lives of the Jewish community there and intensified my emotional connection with my family and the rest of the Jews who were murdered not only there but all over Europe during the Shoah. That trip didn't set in motion my study of the Holocaust—that had happened years earlier. What it did was to make the work I do researching victims and survivors of the atrocities very personal. I connect not only to my own family but to the families of all the people whose families I research.

Endnotes

Cover image: Path to Ivano-Frankivsk Cemetery (Ukraine)

Fig. 1: 2009 market: provided by researcher

Acknowledgments

Park in Kyyiv

I have now spent several months, over a number of years, in archives in Ukraine, Poland, and Lithuania, and time in archives elsewhere in Europe, particularly in England, France, Romania, Moldova, and Hungary. On each of my trips since that initial one in 2009, I have been accompanied by other researchers with whom I work closely and who speak the languages and understand the process of research. That first trip was an incredible learning experience and one for which I am grateful. Recent trips have been postponed for various reasons. Beginning in 2020, the spread of COVID-19 worldwide made travel unsafe for quite a while. In addition to the regular precautions when traveling off the beaten track, we had to be aware of the restrictions that might be imposed if the virus spread to an area we were visiting. Then, in 2022, just as it seemed safe to plan travel for research and to take clients on ancestral home visits once again, the Russia attacked Ukraine. Fear spread throughout Eastern Europe. Millions of refugees fled Ukraine across borders to Poland, Moldova, and Romania and took flights on whatever airline could get them to more-distant points. In Poland, Romania, Moldova, and Hungary, which share borders with Ukraine, and in Lithuania, Estonia, and Latvia, precautions were put in place against possible military incursions from Russia. Travel to these areas was definitely no longer safe. How can a person expect to do something as frivolous as traveling somewhere under siege to do research? Digital repositories worldwide helped archivists in Ukraine gather digitized records for safe storage and fortified archives and their holdings against potential destruction.

The number of people who supported me in my research and writing is vast. So many people have encouraged me over the years. First, two people whose deaths affected me deeply—Rabbi Dr. Byron Sherwin, my mentor and advisor during my doctoral program and while I was writing my dissertation, and Ruth Ebner, who tirelessly read and reread my dissertation and told me when I needed to use more, not fewer, words to describe events. Ruth's questions about her own family's history led me to explore what happened to survivors after the war, and it is due to her that I learned so much about Displaced Persons Camps and survivors.

My life partner, Robert Clinton, has, for over 20 years, been my biggest fan (well, at least on par with my parents), supporting me in all my endeavors, including my travels into places he didn't think were safe for me to visit. Robert read all my drafts, not only of my dissertation, but also of all the articles I've written. He's been the person who heard me rehearse, time after time, almost all the presentations I've given and who, for many years, traveled with me whenever I went out of town to give a presentation. He rejoices and delights in all my successes. Robert taught me the value of using active voice. If any passive voice remains in these pages, it is due to my errors. He certainly tried to catch them all and show me the value of finding other words.

My grandparents, Blima Rosa Grass and Harry Silberman, and Sylvia Miller and Barnett Moldofsky, set my path in motion partly by refusing to answer my questions about the families' history. They insisted, by not answering questions, that I learn to do it myself and that I never stop searching for the answers.

My parents, Rhoda and Milton Silverman, and my sisters, Shari Levy (1955–2022) and Randi Smith, encouraged me in so many ways. Even when I thought I was at an insurmountable brick wall, they helped me climb it and suggested other approaches. Randi, especially in recent years, has posed questions and offered comments that set me on a path of more in-depth research. My father was my first teacher, helping me to learn to read English, French, and Hebrew. His education as a journalism major meant that he always coached me in identifying the who, what, where, when, why, and how. From my first paper in elementary school through college and graduate school, he read and critiqued almost every paper I wrote. He was my first and constant genealogical research partner. Without his help and unending guidance, I could not have accomplished as much as I have so far.

My cousin Susan Lipsky Raban brought puzzles to me—questions posed by her dad, Erwin Lipsky, that were unresolved at the time of his death. My aunts Iris Reisberg and Phyllis Lipsky and my uncles Mel Reisberg and Erwin Lipsky all shared stories, and many were the times we laughed over mangled names, places, and facts, attempting to figure out which parts of the memories were real and which were embroidered. Ella, my cousin in Ivano-Frankivsk, helps me understand a different culture and perspective, and without her, I would never have been able to navigate and understand the complexities of Ukrainian archives.

Terri Braun Pinchevsky taught me so much about the Holocaust and, through collaboration in writing curricula about it, made me push further to learn more. I owe much to the dedication and research skills of my amazing team at AncestryProGenealogists®—Marek Koblanski, Lindsay Levine, Lina Kuzminskaite, Ola Heska, Brian Podoll, Jackie Black, Gary Horlacher, Shalyn Schmelter, Stephanie Milner and Josh Perlman. I am especially grateful for Marek's willingness to help with translations. He never said no, and always provided context for the records. Lina was amazing, and her eagle eye checked all the footnotes, making sure that style and content were close to perfect. Any errors in them were purely my doing. Angie Bush taught me so much about DNA and tirelessly answers the same questions I ask over and over. I've learned a lot about travel and planning from Kyle Betit.

I am grateful to those from AncestryProGenealogists® who supported my vision, encouraging and assisting me in bringing this work to publication: Jon Lambert, Greg Kratz, Traci Vaughn-Grutta, Erika Edberg Manternach, and Sandy McDougle. Rudy Ramos Design Studio added the final touches and pulled everything together to help me realize the book I have dreamed about for so long.

I'm not ignoring two people who have had an incredible influence on me since their births, even though I've left mention of them until nearly the end. These are my children, Arielle Silver and Efrem Weiss, from whom I've learned incalculable wisdom. Their influence has directed and redirected me often over the years to look at and understand the changing world. It is for them and their children and grandchildren that the research is done. They will carry forth the stories and the memories.

My nieces Jenna, Dana, and Allison; nephews Jonathan and Alex; and their spouses Aaron, Reese, Michael, Sara, and Erin; my son-in-law, Darby; my daughter-in-law, Dacy, and my brothers-in-law Harold and Scott, have all posed questions leading to research and more research. In case you hadn't guessed by reading all these pages, the research is never-ending, and there is always something new waiting around the corner.

The lands my ancestors inhabited, the stories they must have known, and the places they traveled are preserved in memories, pictures, and books somewhere. Finding them and understanding more of the travails, celebrations, and experiences of their daily lives remain questions. I hope I've set the stage for my family and that, when I'm gone, they, in turn, will remember to tell these stories and more so that future generations remember.

Bibliography

A letter from Norbert Silberman to Blima Grass Silberman, 11 November 1926

Abelow, Samuel Philip. *History of Brooklyn Jewry*. Brooklyn, New York: Scheba Publishing Company, 1937.

The American Jewish Yearbook Volume 21. Philadelphia: Jewish Publication.

Society of America, (http://books.google.com), accessed March 2022.

Angel, Marc D. *La America: The Sephardic Experience in the United States*. Philadelphia: Jewish Publication Society, 1982.

"Antique Railroad Lanterns and Lamps," *Collectors Weekly* (https://www.collectorsweekly.com), accessed March 2022.

Aronson, George. "A Brief History of the Jewish Community in Gusyatin, Ukraine," *JewishGen* (https://kehilalinks.jewishgen.org/), accessed March 2022.

Bachrach, Susan D. *Tell Them We Remember: The Story of the Holocaust*. Boston: Little, Brown, 1994.

Bacon, Josephine, and Martin Gilbert. *The Illustrated Atlas of Jewish Civilization*. London: Quantum Books, 2006.

Bar-Zev, Asher. "The Mysteries of Yiddish Given Names," in *Avotaynu: The International Review of Jewish Genealogy: Vol. XIII, Summer, 1997* (CD Version).

Baron, Salo. *History and Jewish Historians*. Philadelphia: Jewish Publication Society, 1964.

Bart al, Yiśra'el. *The Jews of Eastern Europe, 1772-1881*. Philadelphia: University of Pennsylvania Press, 2005.

Bartov, Omer. *Erased: Vanishing Traces of Jewish Galicia in Present-day Ukraine*. Princeton: Princeton University Press, 2007. Print.

Beider, Alexander. *A Dictionary of Jewish Surnames from Galicia*. Bergenfield, New Jersey: Avotaynu, 2004.

______ "Discontinuity of Jewish Naming Traditions," in *Avotaynu: The International Review of Jewish Genealogy: Volume XXVIII, Number 2, Summer 2012*.

______ "Jewish Metronymic Surnames in Russia," in *Avotaynu: The International Review of Jewish Genealogy: Vol. VII, Winter 1991* (CD Version).

______ "Jewish Migrations to Eastern Europe," in *Avotaynu: The International Review of Jewish Genealogy: Vol. XIII, Summer 1997* (CD Version).

______ "Jewish Patronymic and Metronymic Surnames in Russia," in *Avotaynu: The International Review of Jewish Genealogy: Vol. VII, Winter 1991* (CD Version).

______ "Jewish Surnames in Russia, Poland, Galicia and Prussia," in *Avotaynu: The International Review of Jewish Genealogy: Vol. XIX, Fall 2003* CD Version).

______ "Jewish Surnames in the Russian Empire," in *Avotaynu: The International Review of Jewish Genealogy: Vol. VIII, Fall 1992* (CD Version).

______ "Names and Naming: Personal Names," in *The YIVO Encyclopedia of Jews of Eastern Europe*.

Found at http://www.forum.j-roots.info/viewtopic.php?f=133&t=24&start, last visited September 2012.

______ "A Scientific Approach to the Etymologies of Jewish Surnames," in *Avotaynu: The International Review of Jewish Genealogy*: Vol. XXI, Spring 2005 (CD Version).

Belousova, Lilia. "Jewish History as Reflected in the Documents of the State Archives of Odessa Region," in *Avotaynu: The International Review of Jewish Genealogy*: Vol. XXIII, Fall 2007 (CD Version).

Bendavid-Val, Avrom. The Heavens Are Empty: Discovering the Lost Town of Trochenbrod. New York: Pegasus Books, 2010.

Berkowitz, Joel. *Yiddish Theatre: New Approaches*. Oxford, Great Britain: Littman Library of Jewish Civilization, 2003.

Bingham, Emily. *Mordecai: An Early American Family*. New York: Hill and Wang, 2003.

Birmingham, Stephen. *The Rest of Us: The Rise of America's Eastern European Jews*. Boston: Little, Brown and Co., 1984.

Blatt, Warren. Faq: Frequently Asked Questions About Jewish Genealogy. Teaneck, New Jersey: Avotaynu, 1997.

______ "Jewish Given Names in Eastern Europe and the U.S.", in *Avotaynu: The International Review of Jewish Genealogy*, Volume XIV, Number 3: Fall 1998 (CD Version).

______ "Polish-Jewish Genealogy – Questions and Answers," *JewishGen* (http://www.jewishgen.org/), accessed March 2022.

Bloch, Susana Leistner. "Polish Patronymics and Surname Suffixes," *JewishGen* (http://www.jewishgen. org/), accessed March 2022.

Blumenthal, W M. The Invisible Wall: Germans and Jews: A Personal Exploration. Washington, D.C: Counterpoint, 1998.

Board for Certification of Genealogists (https://bcgcertification.org/), accessed March 2022.

Bogen, Elizabeth. *Immigration in New York*. New York: Prager Publishers, 1987.

Bonar, Andrew A. and Robert Murray M'Chane. *Narrative of a Mission of Inquiry to the Jews from the Church of Scotland in 1839*. Philadelphia: Presbyterian Board of Publication, 1845.

Boodin, Harry D. "Theories, Assumptions and Implications of Dictionary of Jewish Surnames from the Russian Empire," in Avotaynu: The International Review of Jewish Genealogy: Vol. IX, Fall 1993 (CD Version).

Bronstein, Chaim. "From the History of the Town," *Skalat: A Community Destroyed. JewishGen (https:// www.jewishgen.org)*, accessed March 2022.

Brown, Phil. *In the Catskills: A Century of the Jewish Experience in the Mountains*. New York, Columbia University Press, 2003.

Browning, Christopher R, and Jürgen Matthäus. *The Origins of the Final Solution: The Evolution of Nazi Jewish Policy, September 1939-March 1942*. Lincoln, Nebraska: University of Nebraska Press, 2004.

Brumberg, Stephan F. *Going to America, Going to School: The Jewish Immigrant Public School Encounter in Turn-of-the-Century New York City*. New York: Praeger Publishers, 1986.

Cannato, Vincent J. *American Passage: The History of Ellis Island*. New York: Harper Perennial, 2010.

Caplan, Sofie. "The Quest for the Topf Family," in *Avotaynu: The International Review of Jewish Genealogy: Vol. III*, Fall 1987 (CD Version).

C'étaient Des Enfants: Déportation et Sauvetage des Enfants Juifs à Paris. Paris, France: Skira Fammarion Les Expositions de l'Hotel de Ville de Paris, 2012.

Chernin, Kim. *In My Mother's House*. New Haven, Connecticut: Ticknor & Fields, 1983.

Christman, Henry M., Walt Whitman. *Walt Whitman's New York: From Manhattan to Montauk*. New York: New Amsterdam Press, 1989.

Coan, Peter Morton. *Ellis Island Interviews: Immigrants Tell Their Stories in Their Own Words*. New York: Fall River Press, 2004.

Cohen, Chester G. Shtetl Finder: Jewish Communities in the 19th and Early 20th Centuries in the Pale of Settlement of Russia and Poland, and in Lithuania, Latvia, Galicia, and Bukovina, and with Names of Residents. Los Angeles: Periday Co, 1980.

Coons, Lorraine and Alexander Varias. *Tourist Third Class: Steamship Travel in the Interwar Years*. New York: Palgrave MacMillan, 2003.

Cowan, Neil M. and Ruth Schwartz Cowan. *Our Parents' Lives: The Americanization of Eastern European Jews*. New York: Basic Books, Inc., Publishers: 1989.

Dalinger, Brigitte. "Yiddish Theater in Vienna," in *Jewish Women: A Comprehensive Historical Encyclopedia*, Jewish Women's Archive (*https://jwa.org/*), accessed March 2022.

Davis, Lauren B. Eisenberg. "Alternative Surnames in Russian Poland." Lecture Notes, 1996.

______ "Power of Extracts" in Kielce-Radon SIG Journal, Volume I, Number 1 Winter 1997, JewishGen. org (http://www.jewishgen.org), accessed March 2022.

Dawidowicz, Lucy S. *The Golden Tradition: Jewish Life and Thought in Eastern Europe*. 1st ed. Syracuse, New York: Syracuse University Press, 1996.

______ *The War against the Jews, 1933-1945*. New York: Holt, Rinehart and Winston, 1975.

de Certeau, Michel. *The Writing of History*. New York: Columbia University Press, 1988.

De Chervin, M. L. "Numéro de Mai: Section II Les Langues parlées en Autriche-Hongrie par les différentes nationalités—Galicie: Polonais, Ruthène, Roumaine." Journal de la Société de statistique de Paris Cinquante-Sixième (1915) année. Paris, Société de Statistique de Paris, 1915, *Internet Archive* (https://archive.org), accessed March 2022.

Desbois, Patrick. *Holocaust by Bullets: A Priest's Journey to Uncover the Truth Behind the Murder of 1.5 Million Jews*. New York: Palgrave MacMillan, 2008.

DeSilva, Cara. *In Memory's Kitchen: A Legacy from the Women of Terezin*. Northvale, New Jersey: J. Aronson, 1996.

Dillingham, Senator William P., Chairman of the Immigrant Commission. *Reports of the Immigration Commission: Steerage Conditions; Importation and Harboring of Women for Illegal Purposes; Immigrant Homes and Aid Societies; Immigrant Banks.* Washington, D.C.: Government Printing Office, 1911.

Diner, Hasia R. *Jews in America.* New York: Oxford University Press, 1999.

______*The Jews of the United States, 1654 to 2000.* Berkeley: University of California Press, 2004.

______, Jeffrey Shandler, and Beth S. Wenger. *Remembering the Lower East Side: American Jewish Reflections.* Bloomington, Indiana: Indiana University Press, 2000.

Dinnerstein, Leonard. *Antisemitism in America.* New York: Oxford University Press, 1995.

Doneson, Judith E. *The Holocaust in American Film.* Philadelphia: Jewish Publication Society, 1987.

Dora Teitelboim Center for Yiddish Culture (http://www.yiddishculture.org/), accessed March 2022.

D'un Monde Juif à l'autre: Un Seul Peuple. Paris, France: Association Culturelle du Plateau, 2011.

Dynner, Glenn. *Men of Silk: The Hasidic Conquest of Polish Jewish Society.* New York: Oxford University Press, 2006.

Einsiedler, David. "Fathers of Jewish Genealogy," in *Roots-Key the Journal of the Jewish Genealogy Society of Los Angeles.* Fall, 1994: Volume 14, No. 3.

Eisenberg, Azriel. *Witness to the Holocaust.* New York: The Pilgrim Press, 1981.

Elbogen, Ismar. *A Century of Jewish Life.* Trans. Moses Hadas. Philadelphia: Jewish Publication Society of America, 1946.

Eliach, Yaffa. *There Once Was a World: A Nine-Hundred-Year Chronicle of the Shtetl of Eishyshok.* Boston: Little, Brown, 1998.

"Ellis Island History," *The Statue of Liberty—Ellis Island Foundation, Inc.* (https://www.statueofliberty.org), accessed February 2022.

"Emergency Quota Act" *Wikipedia, The Free Encyclopedia* (https://en.wikipedia.org) accessed March 2022.

Esterson, Gerald L. *The Given Names Data Bases (GNDB)* (https://www.jewishgen.org), accessed March 2022.

______, and David Curwin. "Ashkenazic European Given Names: Databases for European and Foreign Countries," in *Avotaynu: The International Review of Jewish Genealogy:* Vol. XVII, Summer, 2001 (CD Version).

Falstein, Louis. *The Man Who Loved Laughter: The Story of Sholom Aleichem.* Philadelphia: Jewish Publication Society of America, 1968.

Federal Writers' Project (N.Y.) *New York City Guide: A Comprehensive Guide to the Five Boroughs of the Metropolis: Manhattan, Brooklyn, the Bronx, Queens, and Richmond.* New York: Random House, 1939.

Feldblyum, Boris. "Russian Revision Lists: A History," from a 1998 seminar at the International Association of Jewish Genealogy Societies in Los Angeles, California.

______ "Some Information About Jewish Zhitomir," in *Avotaynu: The International Review of Jewish Genealogy*: Vol. XII, Spring, 1996 (CD Version).

Fellner, Dan. "The Jewish Traveler: Lvov," *Hadassah Magazine*, 2008 (https://www.hadassahmagazine.org), accessed March 2022.

Filby, P. William, ed. *Passenger and Immigration Lists Bibliography 1538-1900*. Detroit: Gale Research Company, 1988.

Foer, Jonathan Safran. *Everything is Illuminated*. New York: Houghton-Mifflin, 2002.

Freeze, ChaeRan Y. "To Register or Not to Register: The Administrative Dimension of the Jewish Question in Czarist Russia," in *Avotaynu: The International Review of Jewish Genealogy*: Vol. XIII, Spring 1997 (CD Version).

Gaddis, John Lewis. *The Landscape of History: How Historians Map the Past*. New York: Oxford University Press, 2002.

Gidwitz, Betsy. "Jewish Life in Ukraine at the Dawn of the Twenty-First Century: Part Two." *Jerusalem Letter No. 452 22 Nisan 5761 / 15 April 2001. Jerusalem Center for Public Affairs* (https://www.jcpa.orgaccessed), March 2022.

Gitelman, Zvi. "The Jews of Ukraine and Moldova." in Miriam Weiner, ed. *Jewish Roots of Ukraine and Moldova*. New York: YIVO Institute, 1999.

Glazier, Ira A. ed. *Migration from the Russian Empire: Lists of Passengers Arriving at the Port of New York*. Baltimore: Genealogical Publishing Company, 1995.

Goldberg, Marvin A. *Zhid: A Russian Odyssey*. U.S.A., 2007.

Goldhagen, Daniel J. *Hitler's Willing Executioners: Ordinary Germans and the Holocaust*. New York: Knopf, 1996.

Gordon, Noah. *The Last Jew*. New York: St. Martin's Press, 2000.

Graham, David. "European Jewish Identity at the Dawn of the 21st Century: A Working Paper." A Report for the American Jewish Joint Distribution Committee and Hanadiv Charitable Foundation Presented to the European General Assembly of the European Council of Jewish Communities Budapest, 20-23 May 2004.

Green, Gerald. *Holocaust*. New York: Bantam Books, 1978.

Greenfeld, Howard. *The Hidden Children*. New York: Ticknor & Fields, 1993.

Greenwood, Val D. "Census Returns," in *Researcher's Guide to American Genealogy*. Genealogical Publishing Co., Inc., 1990.

Gross, Jan T. Neighbors: *The Destruction of the Jewish Community in Jedwabne, Poland*. Princeton: Princeton University Press, 2001.

Gross, Leonard. *The Last Jews in Berlin*. New York: Simon and Schuster, 1982.

"Guide to the Records of the Baron de Hirsch Fund, undated, 1819-1983," *The Baron Hirsch Jewish Farmers Community* (https://thebaronhirschcommunity.org/), accessed March 2022.

Guzik, Estelle M., ed. *Genealogical Resources in the New York Metropolitan Area*. New York: Jewish Genealogical Society, 2003.

Hamerow, Theodore S. *Remembering a Vanished World: A Jewish Childhood in Interwar Poland*. New York: Berghahn Books, 2001.

Handler, Davida Noyek, Vitalija Gircyte, Carol Coplin Baker, Alexander Karnovsky and Judith Langer Caplan. "Revision / Census / Family Lists Table," *JewishGen* (https://www.jewishgen.org), accessed January 2022.

"Helfman, Hessia Meyerovna." *Encyclopaedia Judaica*. Ed. Michael Berenbaum and Fred Skolnik. 2nd ed. Vol. 8. Detroit: Macmillan Reference USA, 2007. 783. Gale Virtual Reference Library. Web. 10 Aug. 2012.

Herzog, Elizabeth and Mark Zborowski. *Life is with People: The Jewish Little-Town of Eastern Europe*. New York: International Universities Press, 1952.

Hindus, Milton, ed. *The Jewish East Side 1881-1924*. New Brunswick, New Jersey: Transaction Publishers, 1996.

Horwitz, Gordon J. *In the Shadow of Death: Living Outside the Gates of Mauthausen*. Free Press, 1990.

Howe, Irving. "Sholom Aleichem: Voice of our Past." In *Jewish American Literature: A Norton Anthology, Volume 2000*, edited by Jules Chametzky. New York: W. W. Norton & Company, 2001.

_______, and Kenneth Libo. How We Lived, 1880-1930: A Documentary History of Immigrant Jews in America. New York: Richard Marek, 1979.

_______, and Kenneth Libo. *World of Our Fathers*. New York: Harcourt Brace Jovanovich, 1976.

Hundert, Gershon David. *Jews in Poland-Lithuania in the Eighteenth Century: A Genealogy of Modernity*. Berkeley, California: University of California Press, 2004.

Iggers, Wilma Abeles. *The Jews of Bohemia and Moravia: A Historical Reader*. Detroit, Michigan: Wayne State University Press, 1992.

"Immigration Legal History Legislation 1901-1940," *ILW.com* (http://www.ilw.com), accessed March 2022.

"Jarmulowsky's Bank," *EldridgeStreet.org* (http://www.eldridgestreet.org, accessed March 2022.

"Jewish Cemeteries, Synagogues, And Mass Grave Sites in Ukraine," a report by the United States Commission for the Preservation of America's Heritage Abroad, 2005.

Jewish Records Indexing-Poland (http://www.jri-poland.org/), accessed March 2022.

Job, Françoise. *Les Juifs de Nancy du XIIᵉ au XXᵉ Siècle*. Nancy, France: Presses de Universitaire de Nancy, 1991.

"Johnson-Reed Act: The Immigration Act of 1924," Office of the Historian (https://history.state.gov/), accessed February 2022.

«Journal de la Société de Statistique de Paris Cinquante-Sixième (1915) Année." *Paris, Société de Statistique de Paris, 1915: Section II – Galicie*; digital image, *Google Books* (http://books.google.com), accessed March 2022.

"Julian to Gregorian Calendar," *Ancestor Search* (http://www.searchforancestors.com), accessed March 2022.

Juni, Susannah R. "Ukrainian Research and Ancestral Travels," in *Avotaynu: The International Review of Jewish Genealogy: Vol. XIII, Winter 1997* (CD Version).

Kadison, Luba, Joseph Buloff, and Irving Genn. *On Stage, Off Stage: Memories of a Lifetime in the Yiddish Theatre*. Cambridge, Massachusetts: Harvard University Library, 1992.

Kaganoff, Benzion C. *A Dictionary of Jewish Names and Their History*. New York: Schocken Books, 1977.

Kaminska, Ida. *Ida Kaminska: My Life, My Theater*. New York: Macmillan Pub. Co, 1973.

Katz, Steven T. *The Shtetl: New Evaluations*. New York: New York University Press, 2007.

Kaufman, Jonathan. *A Hole in the Heart of the World: Being Jewish in Eastern Europe*. New York: Viking, 1997.

Kendall, Thena. "Memories of an Orthodox Youth." In Susannah Heschel, ed. *On Being a Jewish Feminist*. New York: Schocken Books, 1983.

"Kishinev," *The YIVO Encyclopedia of Jews in Eastern Europe* (http://www.yivoencyclopedia.org), accessed March 2022.

Klarsfeld, S., Cohen, S., & Epstein, H. M. *French children of the Holocaust: A memorial*. New York: New York University Press: 1996.

Klüger, Ruth. *Still Alive: A Holocaust Girlhood Remembered*. New York: Feminist Press at the City University of New York, 2001.

Kobrin, Rebecca. *Jewish Bialystok and its Diaspora*. Bloomington, Indiana: Indiana University Press, 2010.

Koenig, James B. "Calques, Kinnuim and Couplets: The use of Alternative Names by Jewish Families," in *ZichronNote*, vol. XXII, number 2, May 2002.

Komar, Żanna. Trzecie Miasto Galicji: Stanisławów I Jego Architektura W Okresie Autonomii Galicyjkiej. Krakow: Międzynarodowe Centrum Kultury, 2008.

Kotik, Yekhezkel, and David Assaf. *Journey to a Nineteenth-Century Shtetl: The Memoirs of Yekhezkel Kotik*. Detroit: Wayne State University Press in cooperation with the Diaspora Research Institute, Tel Aviv University, 2002.

Kriwaczek, Paul. *Yiddish Civilization: The Rise and Fall of a Forgotten Nation*. New York: Borzoi Books Division of Alfred A. Knopf, 2005.

Kurzweil, Arthur. *From Generation to Generation: How to Trace Your Jewish Genealogy and Personal History*. San Francisco: Jossey-Bass, 2004.

______. *My Generations: A Course in Jewish Family History*. New York, NY: Behrman House, 1983.

______, and Miriam Weiner, eds. *The Encyclopedia of Jewish Genealogy, Volume I:* Sources in the United States and Canada. Northvale, New Jersey: Jason Aronson, Inc., 1991.

LaCapra, Dominick. *History and Memory after Auschwitz.* Ithaca, New York: Cornell University Press, 1998.

Lamdan, Neville. "Onsite Archival Research in Minsk and Other Eastern European Archives," in *Avotaynu: The International Review of Jewish Genealogy:* Vol. XXII, Winter 2006 (CD Version).

Landau, Jerrold. "Stanislawow," in *Pinkas Hakehilot: Encyclopaedia of Jewish Communities, Poland Vol. II Eastern Galicia.* Jerusalem: Yad Vashem Martyr's and Heroes' Remembrance Authority, 1980.

Lavender, Abraham D. and Clarence B. Steinberg. *Jewish Farmers of the Catskills: A Century of Survival.* Gainesville, Florida: University Press of Florida, 1995.

Leeson, Dan. "A Jewish Genealogical Fable," *JewishGen* (https://www.jewishgen.org), accessed January 2022.

LeFoll, Claire. "The Jews of Belorussia in Western and Russian Historiography." *Bulletin du Centre de Recherche Français de Jérusalem.* Vol 11: Autumn 2002.

Leonardo, Vanessa. "Five Cents a Ride: The Cost of College in 1910," in Pace Press, the Weekly Student Newspaper of Pace University's NYC Campus. Wednesday, October 4, 2006.

Levin, Nora. *The Holocaust: The Destruction of European Jewry, 1933-1945.* New York: T.Y. Crowell Co, 1968.

Levin, Shmarya. *Forward from Exile: The Autobiography of Shmarya Levin.* Trans. Maurice Samuel. 1st ed. Philadelphia: Jewish Publication Society, 1967.

Lewin, Daniel. *A Jewish Genealogy: The Lewin-Steinberger Saga.* Great Neck, New York: Creative Type, 1993.

"The Lipshutz/Peoples Bank Passage Order Book Records Database for the Port of Philadelphia and Other US East Coast Ports," *JewishGen* (https://www.jewishgen.org/), accessed January 2022.

Lloyd, Martin. *The Passport.* Stroud: Sutton, 2003.

The Lost Wooden Synagogues of Eastern Europe (film) 2000.

Lower, Wendy. *The Diary of Samuel Golfard and the Holocaust in Galicia.* Lanham: Altamira Press in association with the U.S. Holocaust Memorial Museum, 2011.

Maltz, Joe. *My Story: Family History, Early Life, My Life at ABC.* Self-published 2011.

Marcus, Jacob Rader. *United States Jewry, 1776-1985.* Michigan: Wayne State University Press, 1990.

Margoshes, Joseph. *A World Apart: A Memoir of Jewish Life in Nineteenth Century Galicia.* Rebecca Margolis and Ira Robinson, translators. Boston, Academic Studies Press: 2010.

Mascia, Jennifer. "Few Laughs Left in a Catskill Town Struggling to Revive," in *The New York Times,* N.Y./ Region Section: December 18, 2009.

"Mauthausen (Austria)," *United States Holocaust Memorial Museum* (http://www.ushmm.org), accessed February 2022.

Mehr, Kahlile. "Russian Archival and Historical Terminology," in *Avotaynu: The International Review of Jewish Genealogy:* Vol. XII, Fall 1996 (CD Version).

Melamed, Efim. "Information for Jewish Genealogists in the State Archive of Zhitomir Oblast," in *Avotaynu: The International Review of Jewish Genealogy:* Vol. XII, Spring, 1996: 14 (CD Version).

"Metropolitan Cantor Institute of the Byzantine Catholic Archeparchy of Pittsburgh," *Metropolitan Cantor Institute* (http://www.metropolitancantorinstitute.org/), accessed April 2022.

Meyer, Michael A. "German-Jewish Identity in Nineteenth-Century America." In Sarna, Jonathan D. *American Judaism: A History. New Haven: Yale University Press, 2004.*

Mokotoff, Gary. *How to Document Victims and Locate Survivors of the Holocaust.* Bergenfeld, New Jersey: Avotaynu, 1995.

______ "Sallyann Amdur Sack," in *Jewish Women: A Comprehensive Historical Encyclopedia, Jewish Women's Archive* (https://jwa.org/encyclopedia), accessed April 2022.

______, and Warren Blatt. *Getting Started in Jewish Genealogy.* Bergenfield, New Jersey: Avotaynu, 1999.

______, and Sallyann Amdur Sack. "Rabbi Malcolm H. Stern (1916-1994), Dean of American-Jewish Genealogy," in *Avotaynu: The International Review of Jewish Genealogy:* Vol. IX, Winter 1993 (CD Version).

______, and Sallyann Amdur Sack, with Alexander Sharon. *Where Once We Walked: A Guide to the Jewish Communities Destroyed in the Holocaust.* Bergenfield, New Jersey: Avotaynu, 2002.

One-Step Webpages by Stephen P. Morse (https://stevemorse.org/) accessed April 2022.

Ogden, Maurice. "The Hangman," 1951, *edHelper.com* (https://www.edhelper.com), accessed March 2022.

Jewish Fiction. Carbondale, Illinois: Southern Illinois University Press, 1991.

Polish Citizenship Legal Guide (http://polish-citizenship.eu/), accessed March 2022.

Porath, Jonathan D. *Jews in Russia: The Last Four Centuries.* New York: United Synagogue Commission on Jewish Education, 1973.

Raisin, Jacob S. *The Haskalah Movement in Russia.* Philadelphia: The Jewish Publication Society of America, 1913.

Ramon, Einat. "Tradition and Innovation in the Marriage Ceremony." In Harvey E. Goldberg, ed. *The Life of Judaism.* Berkeley, California: University of California Press, 2001.

Revolt Amid the Darkness. U.S. Holocaust Memorial Museum, 1993.

Rhode, Harold. "Jewish Culture, History and Religion: Keys to Understanding Our Ancestors' Lives and to Asking the Right Questions," in *Avotaynu: The International Review of Jewish Genealogy:* Vol. XIV, Spring 1998 (CD Version).

Richman, Irwin. *Borscht Belt Bungalows: Memories of Catskill Summers.* Philadelphia: Temple University Press, 1998.

Rockaway, Robert A. *Words of the Uprooted: Jewish Immigrants in Early Twentieth-Century America.* Ithaca, New York: Cornell University Press, 1998.

Rosenberg, David. *Testimony: Contemporary Writers Make the Holocaust Personal.* New York: Times Books, 1989.

Rosenfeld, Alvin H, and Irving Greenberg. *Confronting the Holocaust: The Impact of Elie Wiesel.* Bloomington: Indiana University Press, 1978.

Rosenstein, Neil, *The Unbroken Chain: Biographical Sketches and Genealogy of Illustrious Jewish Families from the 15ᵗʰ–20ᵗʰ Centuries.* New York: CIS Publishers, 1990.

Rottenberg, Dan. *Finding our Fathers: A Guidebook to Jewish Genealogy.* Maryland: Genealogical Publishing Co., Inc.: 1995. March 2012.

Sack, Joel. *Dawn After Dachau.* New York: Shengold Publishers, 1990.

Sack, Sallyann Amdur and Gary Mokotof, eds. *Avotaynu Guide to Jewish Genealogy.* Bergenfield, New Jersey: Avotaynu, 2004.

______, and Gary Mokotoff. *Avotaynu Encyclopedia of Jewish Genealogy.* Bergenfield, New Jersey: Avotaynu, 2003.

______, and the Israel Genealogical Society. *A Guide to Jewish Genealogical Research in Israel.* Teaneck, New Jersey: Avotaynu, Inc., 1995.

Sanders, Ronald. *The Downtown Jews: Portraits of an Immigrant Generation.* New York, New York: Barnes & Noble, 2009.

______. *Shores of Refuge: A Hundred Years of Jewish Emigration.* New York: Henry Holt and Company, 1988.

Sandrow, Nahma. *Vagabond Stars: A World History of Yiddish Theater.* New York: Harper & Row, 1977.

Schneider, Gertrude. *Exile and Destruction: The Fate of Austrian Jews, 1938- 1945.* Westport, Connecticut: Praeger Publishers, 1995.

______, ed. *The Unfinished Road: Jewish Survivors of Latvia Look Back.* New York: Praeger Publishers, 1991.

Seller, Maxine Schwartz, ed. *Ethnic Theatre in the United States.* Westport, Connecticut: Greenwood Press, 1983.

Sherwin, Byron L. *Sparks Amidst the Ashes: The Spiritual Legacy of Polish Jewry.* New York: Oxford University Press, 1997.

______, and Susan G. Ament. *Encountering the Holocaust: An Interdisciplinary Survey.* Chicago: Impact Press, 1979.

Shtrait, Leo. *Stanislaw's Synagogues*. (Станиславівські Синагоги, Edited by Ivan Monolatiy. Ukraine: Лілея-НВ, 2010 (first publication 1934).

Smith, Marian L. "American Names: Declaring Independence," in *Immigration Daily*, August 8, 2005. Found at http://www.ilw.com/articles/2005,0808-smith.htm, last visited September 2012.

______"Certificates of Arrival and the Accuracy of Arrival Information Found in U.S. Naturalization Records," in *Avotaynu: The International Review of Jewish Genealogy*: Vol. XIV, Summer, 1998 (CD Version).

Soshnikov, Vladislav. "Jewish Genealogical Research in the Imperial Russian Empire," in *Avotaynu: The International Review of Jewish Genealogy*: Vol. XVI, Summer 2000 (CD version).

Spector, Seymour, editor. *The Encyclopedia of Jewish Life Before and During the Holocaust*. New York: New York University Press, 2001.

Spiegelman, Art. *Maus: A Survivor's Tale*. New York: Pantheon Books, 1986.

______ *Maus II: A Survivor's Tale: and Here My Troubles Began*. New York: Pantheon Books, 1991.

"Stanislawów (now Ivano-Frankivsk)" from *Holocaust Encyclopedia,United States Holocaust Memorial Museum*, (http://www.ushmm.org), accessed March 2022.

Stanislawski, Michael. "Russian Empire." In *Yivo Encyclopedia of Jews in Eastern Europe*, YIVO Institute for Jewish Research, Inc. and Yale University Press: 2005.

Stern, Malcolm H. *Americans of Jewish Descent: A Compendium of Genealogy*. New York: Ktav Pub. House, 1971.

______. *Jewish Genealogy: An Annotated Bibliography*. Nashville, Tennessee: American Association for State and Local History, 1981.

"Storahtelling," *Lab/Shul* (https://labshul.org/storahtelling/) accessed March 2022.

Strom, Yale, and Brian Blue. *The Last Jews of Eastern Europe*. New York: Philosophical Library, 1986.

"Suczawa," in *Geschichte der Juden in der Bukowina*. Edited by: Hugo Gold using information provided by Dr. N. M. Gelber, Martin Hass, and Dr. Chaim Kupferberg, translated by Jerome Silverbush. Tel Aviv: Olamenu Publishers, 1962.

Thorndale, William and William Dollarhide. *Map Guide to the U. S. Federal Censuses, 1790-1920*. Baltimore, Maryland.: Genealogical Publishing Co., 1987.

"Transports from France," *Aktion Reinhard Camps* (http://www.deathcamps.org), accessed February 2022.

"An Understanding of the Terms 'Ruthenia' and 'Ruthenians,'" from *Genealogy of Halychyna/Eastern Galicia* found at http://www.halgal.com/ruthenian.html, last visited January 2012.

United States Holocaust Memorial Museum, (http://www.ushmm.org/), accessed April 2022.

Vincenot, Alain. Vél' d'Hiv: 16 juillet 1942, des Survivants de la Rafle Témoignent. Montréal, Canada: L'Archipel, 2012.

Vital, David. *A People Apart: A Political History of the Jews in Europe 1789-1939*. New York: Oxford University Press, 2001.

Warnke, Nina. "Going East: The Impact of American Yiddish Plays and Players on the Yiddish Stage in Czarist Russia, 1890-1914." *American Jewish History* 92:1 2004.

Weiner, Miriam. *Jewish Roots in Ukraine and Moldova: Pages from the Past and Archival Inventories.* Secaucus, New Jersey: Miriam Weiner Routes to Roots Foundation, 1999.

Weyrauch, Martin Henry. *The Pictorial History of Brooklyn: Issued by the Brooklyn Daily Eagle on its Seventy-fifth Anniversary, October 26, 1916.* New York: Brooklyn Daily Eagle, 1916.

Wigoder, Geoffrey. *The Holocaust.* Danbury, Connecticut: Grolier Educational, 1997.

Winstone, Martin. *The Holocaust Sites of Europe: An Historical Guide.* London: I.B. Tauris, 2010.

Wishnitzer, Rachel. *The Architecture of the European Synagogue.* University of Michigan Press, 1964.

Wolff, Larry. *The Idea of Galicia: History and Fantasy in Habsburg Political Culture.* Stanford, California: Stanford University Press, 2010.

Wrobel, Piotr. "The Jews of Galicia under Austrian-Polish Rule, 1867-1918." Found at http://www.jewishgen.org/galicia/html/JewsOfGalicia.html last visited December 2011.

Wynne, Suzan. *The Galitzianers: The Jews of Galicia 1772-1918.* Tucson, Arizona: Wheatmark, 2006.

Yivo Encyclopedia of Jews in Eastern Europe (http://www.yivoencyclopedia.org), accessed March 2022.

Yodaiken, Len. "A Synopsis of 18th-Century Lithuanian-Jewish History," in *Avotaynu: The International Review of Jewish Genealogy:* Vol. XVIII, Spring 2002 (CD Version).

Zborowski, Mark and Elizabeth Herzog. *Life Is with People: The Jewish Little-Town of Eastern Europe.* New York: International Universities Press, 1952.

Zukerman, Baruch. "Our withered town, Kurenitz, Villeyka County, Vilnus District.," Translated by Carmel Levitan, *JewishGen* (https://www.jewishgen.org) accessed March 2022.

Zusak, Markus. *The Book Thief.* New York: Alfred A. Knopf, 2006.

Zylbercweig, Zalmen, "Leksikon fun Yidishn Teater (Lexicon of the Yiddish Theatre)" *Museum of Family History* (http://www.museumoffamilyhistory.com), accessed March 2022.

Glossary

L to R: Rhoda Moldofsky Silverman, Janette Silverman, and Milton Silverman, 2005

Although some of the terms included in this glossary are not commonly understood in genealogical terms, the definitions here are given as they pertain to genealogical research. Many of these words have multiple meanings, but only the definition that pertains to its use in this paper is given.

Aliyah—the honor of being called to the *Torah* to say a blessing during a *Shabbat* or holiday service or another day when the *Torah* is being read

An **Ancestry chart** records the ancestors from whom a person directly descends.

Aramaic, like Hebrew and Arabic, is part of the Semitic Language family and was widely spoken by Jews beginning with the period of the Babylonian exile in 586 BCE. Aramaic was a common language spoken in Babylonia, and the Jewish exiles adopted it, bringing it back to Palestine when they returned from exile.

An **archive** (pl **archives**) is a collection of historical documents or the place where they are located.

Auschwitz was a concentration and extermination camp in upper Silesia, Poland, 37 miles west of Krakow. It was established in 1940 as a concentration camp and then, in early 1942, became an extermination camp. It ultimately consisted of three sections: Auschwitz I, the main camp; Auschwitz II, or **Birkenau,** an extermination camp; and Auschwitz III (Monowitz), which was the I.G. Farben labor camp also known as Buna. In addition, Auschwitz had numerous sub-camps.

Baal Shem Tov is the "nickname" of Israel ben Eliezer, also known as the "Besht," which is an acronym of the Hebrew "Baal Shem Tov." Baal Shem Tov means "master of the good name." The title "Baal Shem," or "master of the name," was given to holy men who were said to work miracles through the power of God's name. He was a charismatic, mystical leader who lived in the early eighteenth century. He was born on the Polish-Russian border.

Blog is a shorthand term for "web log." These are generally informational sites that provide discrete entries or posts by an individual or members of a group. Often, comments can be made by the readers of "blog posts" and the owner of the blog can decide whether or not to share the comment. The bibliography of this paper contains a section called "Family Genealogy Websites & Blogs."

Blood libel is a false accusation that Jews murder Christians—especially Christian children—to use their blood for ritual purposes. These allegations first arose in the early Middle Ages in Europe.

Cadastral maps provide detailed information about property. The information on the map may include property ownership or occupants, type of buildings on the land, size of the land, and, if they are for tax purposes, valuation of the property.

Census—a population count; A census is a population count taken in many, if not all, countries; the United States census is taken every ten years on the decade. Censuses in England, Ireland, Canada, and elsewhere are taken every ten years in the year following the decade. New York State conducted a census in 1892, 1905, 1915, and 1925. In the United States, the census is now mailed to most households, but originally, the information was obtained by census takers going door to door and recording the information on a schedule specifically prepared for that decade's population count. The information gathered differed from decade to decade.

Chupah (also ***Ḥupah***)—marriage canopy under which Jewish wedding ceremonies are conducted. The ***chupah*** represents a temporary residence for the bride and groom and symbolizes the home they will build together. It has a top supported by four poles but no sides.

City directories, much like telephone directories, are lists created by publishing companies for marketing purposes. They were common in an era when few households had private telephones. City directories, while less common in the twenty-first century, still exist in some areas. Paid clerks took the information included in these directories by a door-to-door canvas. Information generally contains the names of the adults in the household and their address. This differs from a telephone directory, which is generated by a telephone service provider.

Death record—an official record documenting the deceased's name and the time, date, and place of death; often, the cause of death is included

Decode—to sound out letters in an alphabet, creating words, sounds, or syllables, not necessarily with comprehension of the results

Descendant chart—lists all the descendants of an individual

Drancy was a transit camp during World War II. Located right outside Paris, it was established by Pétain's Vichy government. Those transported from Drancy generally went to the death camps of Auschwitz-Birkenau.

Einsatzgruppen were mobile killing units, composed primarily of German SS and police personnel. These followed the German armies into the Soviet Union in June 1941. Uniformed German Order Police and auxiliaries of volunteers (made up of Estonians, Latvians, Lithuanians, and Ukrainians) supported them. They executed their victims, who were primarily Jews, by shooting. They buried their victims in mass graves, from which they were later exhumed and burned. At least a million Jews were killed in this manner.

Extermination camps were Nazi camps for the mass killing of Jews and others (such as Gypsies, Russian prisoners-of-war, ill prisoners, and homosexuals). Known as "death camps," they included: Auschwitz-Birkenau, Belzec, Chelmno, Majdanek, Sobibor, and Treblinka. All were located in occupied Poland.

FamilySearch Library—The the main library operated by FamilySearch, located in Salt Lake City. Other local or regional libraries are termed Family Centers.

False—Incorrect, often abbreviated as "f" in records. This meant that the surname was not the legally correct surname.

Genealogy report—report that presents family history in the form of a narrative rather than a chart.

Genocide is defined by Article 2 of the 1948 United Nations Convention on the Prevention and Punishment of the Crime of Genocide (CPPCG) as "any of the following acts committed with intent to destroy, in whole or in part, a national, ethnical, racial, or religious group, as such: killing members of the group; causing serious bodily or mental harm to members of the group; deliberately inflicting on the group conditions of life calculated to bring about its physical destruction in whole or in part; imposing measures intended to prevent births within the group; forcibly transferring children of the group to another group."

Gesher Galicia is the special interest group for those with Jewish roots in the former Austrian province of Galicia.

Goldeneh Medinah—Literally "the golden country," this expression, in Yiddish, referred to the freedom and riches to be found in the New World.

Genocide is defined by Article 2 of the 1948 United Nations Convention on the Prevention and Punishment of the Crime of Genocide (CPPCG) as "any of the following acts committed with intent to destroy, in whole or in part, a national, ethnical, racial, or religious group, as such: killing members of the group; causing serious bodily or mental harm to members of the group; deliberately inflicting on the group conditions of life calculated to bring about its physical destruction in whole or in part; imposing measures intended to prevent births within the group; forcibly transferring children of the group to another group."

Gesher Galicia is the special interest group for those with Jewish roots in the former Austrian province of Galicia.

Goldeneh Medinah—Literally "the golden country," this expression, in Yiddish, referred to the freedom and riches to be found in the New World.

Ḥanukkah is a Jewish holiday that falls in November or December. It lasts for eight days and celebrates the success of the Maccabeans' revolt against their Syrian-Greek rulers in the 2nd century BCE and the rededication of the Second Temple in Jerusalem. It is celebrated by kindling lights in a special nine-branched candelabra called a **Ḥanukkiah**. Each night, beginning with the first night, an additional candle is lit, progressing to the eighth night, with an extra light used to kindle the others. On the first night, two candles are lit, and on the eighth night, there are nine lights.

Ḥasidism is a movement started in Eastern Europe in the 1700s by Rabbi Israel ben Eliezer. This movement emphasized the ability to grow closer to God through everything we say, do, and think rather than through intellectual pursuits.

Hillel is the Foundation for Jewish Campus Life and provides religious, cultural, and social opportunities for Jewish students on more than 500 college campuses.

Holocaust—Between 1933 and 1945, Adolph Hitler and the Nazi Party held political power in Germany. By the time Hitler's regime had ended, more than six million Jews and almost another six million Hitler-termed "undesirables" were among the 30 million killed during World War II. The term "undesirables" included homosexuals, political dissidents, Blacks, Romani, Jehovah's Witnesses, and people suffering from a wide range of disabilities. These 12 million were systematically and consciously executed in what is now known as the Holocaust. The Jews and others who had committed no criminal acts were termed racially inferior and unworthy of life by the Nazis.

Hryvnia is the Ukrainian monetary unit also referred to as UAH. There are 100 kopiyok in a **hryvnia**. In November 2012, one United States dollar was equal to 8.16 **hryvnia**.

Husiatyn (Ukrainian: Гусятин Alternate spellings include Gusyatin, Husyatin, and Hsiatyn) is a town in the Ternopil province of western Ukraine, located at 49°4'0"N, 26°13'0"E.

Hutsl are members of an ethnic Ukrainian group who live in the mountains.

Ivano-Frankivsk (Ukrainian: Івано-Франківськ) is the modern name for Stanisławów, a city in western Ukraine. It is the administrative center of the Ivano-Frankivsk province and is located at 48°55'0"N, 24°43'0"E.

Jewish Agency for Israel (JAFI) was instrumental in establishing the State of Israel and in building the country's human and physical infrastructure.

The **Joint Distribution Committee** (JDC) is the world's leading Jewish humanitarian assistance organization.

Kabbalah is the primary corpus of Jewish mystical teachings. Its practitioners and followers are known as Kabbalists.

Kaddish is a prayer recited at Jewish funerals and by Jewish mourners. It is written in Aramaic, not Hebrew. There are no words of mourning or grief in the prayer, which praises God's attributes. The word "**kaddish**" means "to sanctify."

A ketubah is a marriage contract used in Jewish religious ceremonies. Traditional **ketubot** (plural) are written in Aramaic, not Hebrew.

Kiev (Ukrainian: Київ, Russian: Киев)—the capital city of Ukraine, located at 50°27'0"N, 30°31'24"E in the north-central part of the country on the Dneiper River.

Kolomyya (Ukrainian: Коломия, Polish: Kołomyja, Russian: Коломыя, German: Kolomea, Romanian: Colomeea) is a city located on the Prut River in the Ivano-Frankivsk Province in western Ukraine. It is at 48°31'50"N, 25°2'25"E and is the largest population center in the country.

Korban Olah (קרבן עולה)—a completely burnt sacrifice

Listserv—an electronic forum or discussion group which broadcasts to its subscribers email messages people submit. Listservs such as the *JewishGen* Discussion Group may be moderated—that is, every message is read by an individual who checks for suitability before the message is sent out to the list.

Lviv (Ukrainian: Львів; Polish: Lwów; German: Lemberg; Yiddish: לעמבערג; Russian: Львов) is a city in western Ukraine. It is the capital of the historical region of Galicia and is one of the main cultural centers in Ukraine today. It is located at 49°51'0"N, 24°1'0"E.

Manifest— A manifest is an immigration passenger arrival manifest that was created when an individual boarded a boat at a non-U.S. port. This passenger list often included vital information about an immigrant and was used by U.S. immigration authorities when determining who would or would not be admitted into the United States. Manifests separated U.S. citizens from non-citizens and steerage passengers from first- and second-class passengers. Separate pages were maintained for each port of embarkation. Pages at the end of the complete manifest indicated which passengers were detained and the reason for and result of that detention.

Mauthausen—Mauthausen is a camp for men that opened in August 1938 near Linz in northern Austria. Mauthausen was classified by the SS as a camp of the utmost severity. Conditions there were brutal, even by concentration camp standards. Nearly 100,000 prisoners of various nationalities were either worked or tortured to death at the camp before liberating American troops arrived in May 1945.

Matzevah—a gravestone.

Midrash—anecdotes told from generation to generation in a family that often intertwine factual occurrences with fiction

Mitnagdim (מתנגדים) is Hebrew for "opponents" and refers to the opponents of Hasidism.

Pale of Settlement—Empress Catherine II ("The Great") established the Pale of Settlement in 1791 as a territory in which Russian Jews could live. It housed more than 90% of the Jews in an area encompassing what is today Poland, Latvia, Lithuania, Ukraine, and Poland, Latvia, Lithuania, Ukraine, Moldova, Belarus, and parts of Russia.

Perestroika was the economic, political, and social restructuring of the Soviet Union.

Petition for Naturalization—A petition for naturalization, or final papers, could be filed by an immigrant who had lived continuously in the United States for at least five years after filing a Declaration of Intention. The petitioner was not required to provide documentation for any information about his origins or immigration. The only data that can be considered reliable is the date the petition was filed and the court at which it was recorded. Beginning in September 1906, the naturalization process was standardized and regulated by U.S. federal authorities. Prior to filing the "final papers," a petitioner would have filed a Declaration of Intention, often referred to as "first papers." These "first papers" could be filed immediately upon arrival. The requirement to file a Declaration of Intention ended in 1952.

Probate is a step in the legal process of administering the estate of a decedent.

Purim is a festive Jewish holiday commemorating a time when the Jews living in Persia were saved from annihilation.

Purim shpiel is the retelling of the Purim story, often acted out in costume.

Rabbinic dynasty is the succession of chief rabbis (**Av Beit Din**) of a town with a major yeshiva and their families.

Rebbe—A Yiddish word from the Hebrew "Rabbi," "rebbe" is often used to refer to the leader of a **Ḥasidic** sect.

Recte—correct; often abbreviated as "r" in records, it meant that the surname was being corrected to the legal name.

Revision Lists—"reviski skaski," or Eastern European censuses

Screenshot—also called a "screen capture" or "print screen," this refers to the capturing of an image on the computer screen that can be incorporated into a document or saved for later use.

Shehecheyanu is a prayer that is recited when doing or experiencing something for the first time or something that happens infrequently. In the prayer, thanks is given to God for "allowing us to reach this occasion."

Shiva is the weeklong mourning period in Judaism for first-degree relatives.

Shoah is the Hebrew word for the events termed "the Holocaust" in English.

Siddur—a prayer book

SS is an abbreviation, usually written with two lightning symbols. It stands for Schutzstaffel (Defense Protective Units). Originally Hitler's personal bodyguard, the SS was transformed into a giant organization. Although various SS units were assigned to the battlefield, the organization is best known for carrying out the destruction of European Jewry.

Skalat is a city in the Ternopil Province of western Ukraine. It is located at 49°26'0"N, 25°59'0"E.

Skvira (Ukrainian: Сквира; Russian: Сквира, Yiddish: Skvere, סקווירא) is a city in the Kiev Province in central Ukraine. It is located at 49°43'0"N, 29°40'0"E.

Stalin, Joseph served as premier of the Soviet Union from 1941 until his death in 1953. He also held the position of General Secretary of the Communist Party from 1922 to 1953.

Stanisławów (German: Stanislau, Yiddish: סטאַניסלע) see Ivano-Frankivsk.

Suceava (Polish: Suczawa, Ukrainian: Сучава, German: Suczawa, Yiddish: שאַץ) is the county seat in the Bukovina region in northeastern Romania. It is located at 47°39′05″N, 26°15′20″E.

Tarnopol (also **Ternopil** and **Ternopol)** is a city in western Ukraine on the banks of the Seret River. It is located at 49°34′0″N, 25°36′0″E.

T'fillin—phylacteries worn by observant Jewish men on their foreheads and arms during morning prayers every day except the Sabbath and certain Jewish holidays

Torah –the first five books of the Bible, commonly called Genesis, Exodus, Leviticus, Numbers, and Deuteronomy; in Hebrew, these same books are called *Bereishit, Shemot, VaYikra, BaMidbar,* and *D'varim.*

Vel—In addition to "recte" and "false," vel is also used between two names. It means "or" and is used to indicate an alternate surname.

Vilejka is located at 54°30″N, 26°55″E which is 100 kilometers, or 63 miles, from Minsk.

Vital records are birth, marriage, divorce, and death records.

Yeshiva (pl yeshivot) (Hebrew: ישיבה lit. "sitting"; pl. ישיבות, yeshivot) is a Jewish educational institution that focuses on the study of traditional religious texts.

"Z" or **"Z d" ("z domu")** is literally "from the house of," and the name which follows is the woman's maiden name. The letter "z" by itself could be a short form of **"z domu"** and means "from."

Zhytomyr (Ukrainian and Russian: Житóмир, Polish: Żytomierz, Yiddish: זשיטאמיר) is a city in the north of the western half of Ukraine. It is the administrative center of the Zhytomyr Province and is located at 50°15′0″N, 28°40′0″E.